From BELLOC *to* CHURCHILL

FROM *Belloc*

The
University
of North
Carolina
Press
Chapel Hill
and
London

Victor Feske

TO *Churchill*

PRIVATE SCHOLARS,

PUBLIC CULTURE,

AND THE CRISIS OF

BRITISH LIBERALISM,

1900–1939

Set in Garamond and Copperplate Gothic
by Keystone Typesetters Inc.

Designed by Richard Hendel

Manufactured in the United States of America
by Thomson Shore

The paper in this book meets the guidelines for
permanence and durability of the Committee on
Production Guidelines for Book Longevity of
the Council on Library Resources.

Library of Congress
Cataloging-in-Publication Data

Feske, Victor.

From Belloc to Churchill: private scholars,
public culture, and the crisis of British liberalism,
1900–1939 / Victor Feske.

p.   cm.

Includes bibliographical references and index.

ISBN 0-8078-2295-7 (cloth: alk. paper).

ISBN 0-8078-4601-5 (pbk.: alk. paper)

1. Great Britain—Historiography—History—
20th century. 2. Historiography—Great Britain—
History—20th century. 3. Great Britain—Politics
and government—1901–1936. 4. Liberalism—Great
Britain—History— 20th century. 5. Great Britain—
Intellectual life—20th century. 6. Churchill, Winston,
Sir, 1874–1965. 7. Belloc, Hilaire, 1870–1953. I. Title.

DA1.F45   1996

941'.0072041—dc20   96-10260

CIP

oo   99   98   97   96   5   4   3   2   1

For FRANCIS LOEWENHEIM

Contents

ILLUSTRATIONS

ACKNOWLEDGMENTS

The revision of this manuscript for publication was a particularly arduous, on-again, off-again affair, complicated by the successive interruptions that accompany the itinerant existence of any untenured academic. Throughout, Lewis Bateman, my editor at the University of North Carolina Press, has exhibited admirable patience as well as generous interest and support. Librarians and archivists across Britain and America were uniformly helpful in speeding the completion of my task, but special thanks are reserved for the staffs of Sterling Memorial Library, Yale University; the John L. Burns Library, Boston College; the Bodleian Library, Oxford; the British Library of Political and Economic Science, London; the Robinson Library, University of Newcastle-upon-Tyne; Trinity College Library, Cambridge; and the Churchill Archives Centre, Churchill College, Cambridge. I wish to thank the following individuals and institutions for permission to quote extracts of unpublished material for which they are the holders of copyright: Professor N. G. L. Hammond (J. L. and Barbara Hammond); Mary Bennett

(H. A. L. Fisher); University of Sussex Library (Leonard Woolf); Alexander Murray (Gilbert Murray); Lawrence Toynbee (Arnold J. Toynbee); George Trevelyan (G. M. Trevelyan, G. O. Trevelyan, C. P. Trevelyan, and R. C. Trevelyan); Archives Division, British Library of Political and Economic Science (Sidney and Beatrice Webb); Major General C. G. C. Vyvyan CBE (R. H. Tawney); Nuffield College Library, Oxford (G. D. H. Cole); the Principal and Fellows of Newnham College, Cambridge (Graham Wallas); Sir Winston Churchill Archives Trust (Winston S. Churchill); along with Mr. Louis Jebb and Peters, Fraser, and Dunlop Writers' Agents (the Estate of Hilaire Belloc, copyright 1995).

All or portions of the manuscript were read by Robin Winks, David Underdown, Martin Wiener, and Paul Kennedy. Each of their suggestions, comments, and criticisms received careful consideration. Special thanks to the last mentioned for offering me a teaching job when one was sorely wanting. A day spent just outside of Chicago discussing my work with Stephen Kern proved as useful as it was enjoyable. I cannot thank Frank Turner enough for his friendship and support over the years. With far more serious matters constantly weighing upon him, he waded through successive versions of the manuscript with great care and editorial skill. His attention to detail regarding form and content alike are an example to us all. Another who read the manuscript more than once is Francis Loewenheim, to whom this volume is dedicated. A true friend and longtime advocate, he knows only too well the wide variety of his eclectic contributions to the final product, up to and including the fortuitous offer of an intervening project that fully occupied my attention, allowing this manuscript to lie fallow for a year prior to revision.

My brother Steven, possessor of the surest intellect I have ever encountered, aided indirectly over the years by engaging me in animated conversations about a host of unrelated topics ranging from "pattern completion" to LSU football to the novels of Patrick O'Brian. To Anne I am indebted most deeply of all. She consented to put up with, not only the evolution of this book, but also the unsettled lifestyle that accompanied the process, all this despite the fact that she had expected a very different trajectory for our future when once upon a time she married a physician, apparently under false pretenses. To her, who once proofread an entire chapter backward, I announce that, mercifully, these proceedings are closed.

From BELLOC *to* CHURCHILL

INTRODUCTION
Liberalism and Historiography

The question of the decline of Whig historiography resembles that of the decline of the British aristocracy. It is a simple enough matter to detect degradation in self-confidence, ubiquity, and potency when comparing 1850 with 1970, but the devil is in the details. More difficult is obtaining agreement on the causes, chronology, completeness, and meaning of the recessional. J. W. Burrow distinguishes a decline in the brief span separating Thomas Babington Macaulay from E. A. Freeman and J. A. Froude, a depreciation that seems to originate from the internal dynamic of the practice of Whig history-writing itself.[1] Rosemary Jann and T. W. Heyck locate the transformation in the last third of the nineteenth century, with the adoption of Rankean scientific standards and the professionalization of the discipline providing the impetus.[2] Using a Kuhnian model,

P. B. M. Blaas discovered the demise of Whig historiography in the 1890s as political and economic change in late Victorian society sapped the explanatory power of traditional Whig paradigms. Blaas saw the process as dragging on into the early 1930s, when an anti-Whig reaction headquartered in the universities eventually triumphed.[3] Jeffrey Paul von Arx has demonstrated, however, that the erosion of mid-Victorian political sureties by the late nineteenth century might as likely elicit revamped versions of old Whig paradigms as their abandonment.[4] And both Christopher Parker and David Cannadine have called attention to the enduring strength of Whig characteristics in British historiography, both in and outside of academia, through the 1930s and well into the postwar era.[5]

This normal academic discordance is exacerbated by confusion over the term "Whig historiography." There is too much readiness to accept a priori the "classic" definition provided by Herbert Butterfield's 1931 essay *The Whig Interpretation of History*. Butterfield's work took scattershot aim at historians who organize their knowledge upon unconscious assumptions, who write on the side of Whigs and Protestants, who praise all successful change, and who emphasize certain principles of progress in the past, producing at the end a story that is both a ratification and glorification of the present.[6] Burrow exploits the elasticity of these categories to bring together under the same heading Macaulay, a Whig centrist; William Stubbs, a high Tory; Freeman, a populist and Romantic nationalist; and Froude, a Tory Radical and disciple of Thomas Carlyle. Blaas restates the Butterfield formula in even broader terms as finalism, extreme anachronism, and an exaggerated sense of continuity.[7] Clearly this collection of attributes is so nonspecific as to encompass too much and too many.

Yet there remains something less protean deserving of the designation *Whig history*. At its core the inherited nineteenth-century Whiggish historical tradition was concerned almost exclusively with the story of the gradual accumulation of liberty and freedom via the instruments of parliament and the English constitution. Inevitably, this emphasis meant that the narrative would exhibit a strong Protestant bias. Whig history attended to the unfolding of ideas, not the mechanics of institutions; it focused not simply upon development of the constitution but rather upon constitutional and parliamentary refinement as central agents in the moral progress of the English nation. Butterfield was correct in stressing the importance of moral judgments and a lexicon of morality to the practitioners of Whig historiography.

Butterfield claimed to treat the subject of the Whig interpretation of history as a problem of the psychology of certain historians rather than as a problem in the philosophy of history. But in this his analysis failed most noticeably. He mentioned no Whig historians by name other than Lord Acton, nor did he cite or examine any specific works. In his hands the concept of Whig historiography was disembodied and denuded of context. That approach is as ahistorical as supposedly is the Whig tradition which Butterfield excoriates. He ignores the fact that Victorian Whig historiography was not simply present-minded but invariably politically engaged, joined at the hip to Liberal politics. Its story of sustained moral progress resonated with the reading public because of a shared normative language of nineteenth-century English politics and culture. For Liberalism, more than for any of its rival political doctrines, the interpretation of history mattered desperately. The entire rationale for nineteenth-century Liberal politics stemmed from a particular understanding of, and reciprocal relationship with, Britain's past. As Michael Bentley has observed:

> Liberalism was never an effective statement of the intellectual, spiritual or economic requirements of a single epoch. . . . Liberalism always involved, and sometimes amounted to, an implicit language about the past and how the present had grown out of it. To the early Victorians it was the language of Revolution and Connexion; to the later ones it was the language of 1832 and 1867, of the secret ballot, free trade, religious toleration and the Grand Old Man; to the Edwardians it was all these things. . . . Liberalism was a myth: a story with a veiled meaning. . . . It was conscious of the need to impregnate politics with a morality derived not so much from a dogma as from an atmosphere breathed by the past. Liberalism existed because it was believed to exist as the guiding force of political progress, writ large between the lines of constitutional lexicons since the coming of William of Orange.[8]

Traditional Whig historiography provided legitimacy to the social and political realities of Victorian England by chronicling, in a direct line of descent, the evolution of liberty, justice, enlightenment, and prosperity from the Magna Carta and the Reformation, through the civil wars, the Glorious Revolution, and opposition to George III, to the reform acts of the nineteenth century. The language of history served as the primary Victorian medium of public discourse, and that fact was a great boon to Liberal politics. Whig history functioned as an instrument of transmission. Its aim was civic instruction, mediating the translation of an eighteenth-century aristocratic idiom into the vernacular of an expanding mass electorate.

The vitality of this sustained public interchange was essential to the health of Liberalism and the Liberal party, drawing strength as they did from the general acceptance of the contemporary relevance of a particular version of the national past. Aesthetically appealing Whig syntheses composed for the educated general reader reinforced the link between history and present politics. The substantial Victorian overlap between intellectual and political circles facilitated this intermingling. In the age of the amateur, men slipped frequently and effortlessly between the worlds of politics, letters, scholarship, the professions, and journalism. Looking back from 1928, H. A. L. Fisher cited as archetypal Whig historians Macaulay and G. O. Trevelyan, well-connected private scholars with a record of service as governors of British society.[9] George Grote was a civil servant and H. T. Buckle a lawyer. John Morley edited *Fortnightly Review* for years. He, James Bryce, and W. E. H. Lecky served as M.P.'s; Freeman stood several times unsuccessfully for parliament; and J. R. Seeley was approached as a possible candidate.

Because the Victorian intellectual elite formed a wing of an extended ruling class, they wielded enormous cultural authority. Besides erasing boundaries between the intelligentsia and members of the political class, a uniform educational pattern combined with occupational overlap among the upper and middle classes to instill a common set of assumptions. The result was supreme confidence among Victorian amateur historians in the intimacy of their relationship with their audience, an assurance that their writings invoked a shared set of values.[10] These men were self-consciously "public historians," convinced of the indispensability of their role and comfortable with their power and influence. In both respects they mirrored the traditional landed ruling class.

By the end of the nineteenth century, however, the open border between Britain's intellectual and political worlds began to close. The gradual importation of the critical methods of German scientific history with its emphasis upon original archival research rendered historiography as an avocation problematic. Professionalization of the discipline provided the sure means for satisfaction of the scientific impulse toward specialization and division of labor. Professional historians naturally gravitated toward the university setting, in the process weakening the link between present politics and the study of the past. The generation of historians that came of age at the turn of the century was the first for which an exclusively academic career might be considered the norm. Rarer thereafter, though not extinct, was the man who could function alternatively in both the scholastic and political arenas. This movement toward heterogeneity was part of the gradual fracturing of integrated late Victorian culture, the severance and, in some instances, alienation of the intellectual elite from the political class.

The early demise of a common forum of public discourse registered this trend toward a balkanization of English culture. The heyday of the great Victorian literary periodicals addressing a general readership was over by the 1890s, their decline confirmed in the rise of academic and professional journals employing esoteric language and catering to a narrow, specialized audience.[11] For example, when the *English Historical Review* (*EHR*) was launched in 1886 its organizers expressed an interest in tailoring their product to the tastes of the general public as well as that of "professional students of history." But by 1890 such ambitions were all but abandoned to the "scientific and special" character of the *Review*.[12]

Given the reciprocal nature and intimacy of the relationship between Victorian intellectual and political circles, it is hardly surprising to find the fin-de-siècle decline of the traditional territorial ruling class associated with a growing challenge to the syntheses and generalizations of the amateur public historian. Both experienced a similar crisis of confidence; the weakening of the hereditary political class's will to power and belief in its unique competence to rule recapitulated the public historian's diffidence in the face of exacting scientific standards. The aristocracy and gentry had to adapt to the claims of the cult of the expert much as their fellow amateurs, the literary historians, had to answer the criticisms of academic professionals. Efficiency was the new measuring rod, and, to paraphrase

Seeley, "volunteers" could not "resist regular troops."[13] The inexorable triumph of specialization heralded the end of the age of the gifted amateur in every field of endeavor.

The rhetoric in the conflict between academics and private historians sometimes sounded rather shrill. Freeman drew sharp distinctions between the old and the new historiography and denounced the latter in most violent and exaggerated terms. Seeley dismissed Carlyle and Macaulay as "charlatans" and literary history in general as "foppish."[14] The most celebrated episode of this long-running adversarial relationship was the young G. M. Trevelyan's impassioned rebuttal to "The Science of History," J. B. Bury's 1903 Inaugural Lecture as Cambridge Regius Professor of Modern History. Further muddying the waters was a protracted intramural contest inside the ancient universities, with professors advocating the adoption of the research ideal versus college tutors such as A. L. Smith of Balliol, who refused to surrender older notions of history as the centerpiece of a liberal education aimed at character formation and moral instruction.[15]

But this contest between private scholar and academic remained a very low-intensity affair. In Britain, continuities abounded among the amateur and professional traditions. The extent of overlap made it difficult ever to locate a pure "fact-grubber" or unadulterated "literary" generalizer. Reaction formation was the order of the day for those who failed to practice what they preached. For all his bluster about history as a science and the need for archival work, Freeman, the country squire and justice of the peace, remained a transitional figure, refusing to undertake original research himself and writing in a decidedly romantic style for the public ear. His successor as Regius Professor at Oxford, J. A. Froude, never claimed to write anything other than narrative histories for a general audience. Academic history grew steadily but only slowly from the 1880s: before 1900 there were fewer than thirty university-based professional practitioners, only two hundred by 1914, and fewer than four hundred at the outbreak of the Second World War. During that entire period most historiography in Britain still came from the pens of amateurs for the enjoyment and instruction of a broad laity.[16] Additionally, John Osborne has documented the endurance into the twentieth century of the "genteel tradition" of literary history inside the university.[17] Sir Charles Oman and J. A. R. Marriott, both of whom served as Conservative M.P.'s, appropriately enough continued to work and write in the fashion of their Victorian predecessors. As late as 1938 Christopher Hill could accuse Oxford don and former Liberal M.P. and minister in the Lloyd George coalition H. A. L. Fisher of still writing "bankrupt" old-fashioned history with a pronounced bias for the "narrow standards of the English ruling class" and for "Liberal politics."[18]

It should be noted that even the most vocal champions of "scientific" historiography never intended to abandon the wider audience that patronized literary productions. The "Prefatory Note" to the first issue of the *English Historical Review* advised that submissions should be such that "an educated man, not specially conversant with history, may read with pleasure and profit."[19] Neither Bury nor Seeley advocated abandoning historiography's traditional cultural duties. On the contrary, both anticipated that the adoption of scientific standards and techniques would augment its prestige and social and political influence. They, like many of their fellows, assumed their more rigorous judgments would command a special respect in an age that paid homage to scientific expertise.

But despite such optimism, inevitably, if glacially, the adoption of scientific methodology, the search for a neutral point of reference, and the increasing seclusion of historiography in a university setting exacted a stiff price: forfeiture of the cultural authority which Victorian amateurs had taken for granted. According to its editors, the *EHR*'s boast of professional status hinged upon its avoidance of "partisanship" and "burning questions."[20] Claims to disinterestedness and objectivity necessitated the use of value-neutral language and led to doubts about the propriety of academic historians intruding into partisan political debate. The result was a shrinking public visibility of the historian, a new aura of self-imposed detachment. Traditional cultural influence was sacrificed without general enthusiasm, but sacrificed nonetheless to the demands of scientific scholarship. Scholarly prestige rushed in to fill the void. More and more academics addressed only one another in a technical language inaccessible to the uninitiated; priests transformed themselves into monks. In place of didactic public history's provision of broad influence over a mass of educated laymen, the modern scientific incarnation of the discipline countered with a narrow academic authority, more imperious but less catholic.

In his obituary of Leslie Stephen, F. W. Maitland had to agree with his friend's candid self-appraisal, that he had "scattered himself too widely," that Stephen was "not a scholar, not a philosopher, not an historian, only an amateur." Maitland's attempt to soften the verdict by venturing that "such an amateur, if that be the right term . . . is worth more to the world than many professionals" could not hide academic condescension for the Victorian intellectual jack-of-all-trades.[21] This boded ill for expectations of an assumption by the academician of the latter's mediating role in British culture. Maitland himself rejected the Cambridge Regius Professorship precisely because he had nothing to say to the wider public of the "world at large."[22] The consequence, unintended or otherwise, of professionalization of the historical discipline was a trend toward political quietism and public disengagement.[23]

In 1878 John Morley had voiced concern lest the influence of science transform British historiography into something "narrow, pedantic, and trivial," capable of conveying only "sterile knowledge."[24] The succeeding decades did not bring quite the dramatic break prophesied by Morley or since described by T. W. Heyck, but neither did they witness simply Stefan Collini's innocuous "modulation of the forms of public debate."[25] A sense of history as knowledge without direct practical application or contemporary political relevance gained currency under the influence of professionals publishing technical monographs in specialized journals for an expert clientele. By deliberate choice, history slowly came to resemble an autonomous enterprise, in the words of T. F. Tout "a definite branch of knowledge to be studied by itself for its own sake," an end rather than a means to an end.[26]

A necessary accompaniment to the establishment of the dominion of the expert was a wastage of territory available for general public discourse. The triumph of the professional ideal threatened to confine a major segment of all serious public discussion to esoteric exchanges between trained experts, transforming the layman into an interested but essentially uncomprehending and impotent spectator. In the name of scientific detachment, value-neutral administrative or technical questions would replace the moral concerns that formed the organizing principle of liberal Victorian intellectual and political culture. This process was potentially fatal to political Liberalism, relying as it did so heavily upon history as a primary medium of public conversation and upon the dissemination of a paradigm of the past that was expected to retain contemporary relevance. Blinkered history that confined itself to mere technical competence rather than addressing great issues and deciphering large patterns was unsuitable to this purpose. Some observers recognized that professionalization was uncongenial to both the Whig interpretation of history and its political reflection. Overseeing the composition of a parliamentary history in the 1920s, the independent radical Josiah Wedgwood, M.P., warned that "the new history blackens England's past in an endeavour to belittle liberalism."[27] The growth of academic historiography promised little enough comfort for the Liberal party.

Alone, internal changes in the structure and practice of the discipline cannot explain Whig history's decline, nor do they exhaust the list of problems it faced as it entered the new century. With its fixation upon incremental constitutional development, the Whig interpretation of England's past had worked well enough in an age of successive reform acts. The dramas of 1832 and 1867 seemed to flow naturally from the ancient sequence: *witenagemot*, Magna Carta, Glorious Revolution. But by the 1890s the traditional scheme had begun to forfeit its explanatory resilience. Appropriating Kuhnian terminology, Piet Blaas has described in detail how Whig paradigms sacrificed their "scientific usefulness" as a mass of facts accumulated which could not be accommodated within the received pattern of national development.[28] A waning of the Victorian idealization of the embryogenesis of the constitution was hardly surprising in the face of an extension of the franchise to something approximating manhood suffrage, urbanization, industrialization, the surge in trade unionism, the appearance of mass politics and party machines, a renewed interest in empire, and a broadened awareness of Britain as a Great Power on the international stage.

This is the same catalog that bedeviled the late Victorian and Edwardian Liberal party, producing internal tensions and external pressures that precipitated the Unionist secession, adoption of Lib-Lab candidates, the rise of ginger groups like the New Liberals and the Liberal Imperialists, and the creation of alternative foci of power such as the National Liberal Federation. Similarly, external political, demographic, and economic realities contributed at least as much as the internal challenge of professional standards to stretching the boundaries of Whig historiography beyond the traditional limits of legal and constitutional questions. Whig historians now had to devise formulas to accommodate the Industrial Revolution. Narratives of economic change—even of sustained expansion—could not as readily conform to the Whig template of incremental moral progress as could the pattern of constitutional development. Somehow work such as that of Balliol's Arnold Toynbee, who proselytized for the unification of ethics and economics, had to be absorbed and assimilated.[29] Toynbee's catastrophic interpretation of the Industrial Revolution influenced, in the words of G. N. Clark, "the young paladin of liberal social reform" along with an entire generation of public historians: Sidney and Beatrice Webb and J. L. and Barbara Hammond directly via his published lectures and G. M. Trevelyan and Winston Churchill indirectly through their Harrow schoolmaster and Toynbee disciple G. Townsend Warner.[30]

The expansion of the apparatus of the state by the close of the nineteenth century also necessitated other accretions to the Whiggish historical canon. In 1912 A. F. Pollard, University of London professor and sympathetic expert on the Tudor effort at state consolidation, identified the dilemma of Whig historians.

> All power is distrusted by old-fashioned Liberals . . . but the forces of evil cannot be overcome by *laissez-faire*, and power is an indispensable weapon of progress. A powerless state means a helpless community. . . . Political liberty and religious freedom depend upon the power of the State, inspired, controlled and guided by the mind of the community. . . . It is not an engine of tyranny, but the lever of social morality; and the function of the English government is not merely to embody the organised might and executive brain of England, but also to enforce its collective and co-ordinating conscience.[31]

Like it or not, the Whig interpretation of English history, so long centered on legal and constitutional ontogeny, increasingly had to take into account the decisive role of the central government in the process of nation building. Yet, Pollard's claims notwithstanding, an expansion of interest in institutions and administration correspondingly weakened the traditional absorption with questions of moral progress. Despite this fundamental divergence from the fulcrum of its traditional narrative, Whig historians had to reach a modus vivendi with the academic administrative history of Maitland and Tout. In an era when the rhetoric of efficiency rivaled Victorian moral preoccupations as the ultimate standard of judgment, professional administrative history, unraveling the mechanisms for the accumulation, organization, and projection of executive power, exercised a strong appeal. Closely related were the calls, led by Froude and Seeley in particular, for a realignment of historiographic priorities that would place an analysis of power at the pivot of any national narrative. The insularity of the Whiggish constitutional myth was inadequate to answer the requirements of a Great Power with vast imperial holdings and immense global responsibilities.[32]

The Whig interpretation of history was to prove itself more durable than the Liberal party. The former offered nothing so sudden or dramatic as the loss of cohesion and electoral collapse of political Liberalism between 1906 and 1929. In his study of the decline and fall of the British aristocracy David Cannadine notes that its protracted eclipse was characterized by "much vigour and resolution, much resourceful resistance, much outright defiance, much adroit adaptation."[33] The same might be said for resilient Whig history. It survived in a variety of forms. Ironically, the demise of Liberalism as an electoral force enhanced the adaptability and, therefore, survivability of Whig historiography. Disarticulated from the ballast of the Liberal party, the Whig interpretation could give free rein to its protean potential. In the hands of a collection of self-consciously public historians thrown clear of the vortex of Edwardian Liberalism, Whig history donned an assortment of guises more suitable to the less forgiving climate of the twentieth century while resisting, with varying degrees of success, those who would dismantle or hijack it for alternative purposes.

Disillusioned after serving as a Liberal M.P. between 1906 and 1910, Hilaire Belloc attempted to uncouple the amateur, literary style of history-writing from its Whiggish associations. Perversely, he identified the universities as the refuge of Whig orthodoxy. Thus, as an accompaniment to his verbal assault upon the excesses of the Liberal, bureaucratic "Servile State," Belloc's writings represented an extended tirade against the "official history" of a monopolistic, professional, academic clerisy. From his perspective as a Catholic outsider, the dons appeared to function as the most vital *apparatchiks* of a pernicious Liberal establishment. Shedding his early Liberal sympathies and affiliations, Belloc provided his audience with a repudiation of the central Whig events of the Reformation and the Glorious Revolution that deviated only slightly from the Tory Radical tradition of Cobbett, Disraeli, and Ruskin, while sharing an affinity with the socialism of William Morris.

Less openly confrontational than Belloc, but no less single-minded in their aversions or ambitious in their aims, Sidney and Beatrice Webb hoped to recruit Liberalism to oversee its own execution. In this quest, historiography was to complement political activism. As Fabians and advocates of National Efficiency they looked to the institution of the state as the primary vehicle of progress. Their histories retained a Whiggish preoccupation with evolutionary forms but relegated constitutional development to the backseat. The Webbs introduced a new wrinkle into the practice of public historiography, hoping to create a new type altogether, civic history aimed primarily at an exclusive audience of experts. Pandering to the scientific agenda of the academic professoriate, the Fabian couple fashioned their works to resemble scholarly monographs. But the goal was never sterile academic authority. Camouflaged beneath austere packaging resided a partisan message that, for all its obsession with descriptions of administrative and institutional efficiency, laid greatest stress on what the Webbs saw as the moral disaster of post-1688 England. In this tale of woe they offered their select readers—including any New Liberals who might be listening—a historically validated indictment of the legacy of Victorian Liberalism.

J. L. and Barbara Hammond attempted to incorporate economic history into the traditional matrix of moral progress via constitutional development. As New Liberal reformists rather than revolutionaries, the Hammonds harbored no desire to dismantle completely a still serviceable Whig historiographic orthodoxy. They aimed instead to round off its sharp edges and replace its jarring primary colors with delicate pastels. In their hands the grievous errors and dead ends of the Industrial Revolution would share the foreground with Whig history's more familiar glorious episodes. In lieu of the traditional triumphal narrative of uninterrupted advancement, they offered a more complex and problematic, though still essentially progressive, mosaic of sin and redemption. The Hammonds were attracted to the modern techniques of the supposedly value-neutral social sciences and made a great show of adopting rigorous standards in their own work. But they were unwilling to abandon the moral imperative as the overt theme of all their histories, and Barbara, at least, rejoiced at her husband's failure to secure a university position that certainly would have diluted the power of their message while diminishing the breadth of its reception.

For reasons explained below, none of these projects achieved complete success: not Belloc's attempt to refute the Whig interpretation; not the Webbs' effort to co-opt it for their own devices; nor even the Hammonds' modest undertaking to rescue it with harsh words of affection. G. M. Trevelyan and Winston Churchill adopted a different approach. In their writings these two men drew together many of the ingredients so long ignored as alien by Victorian Whig historians, yet, while doing so, Churchill and Trevelyan still managed to retain the concept of moral progress facilitated via constitutional development as the organizing principle around which the themes of state formation, empire, economic growth, and the concentration and utilization of power revolved. Their method of preserving and transmitting the Whig historical tradition involved extraction of the overt partisan flavor, thereby transforming it into a national history of consensus. The acceptance of Whig history as the "national interpretation" occurred between the wars, not by the end of the nineteenth century as Butterfield, Burrow, and Collini have alleged.[34] After 1918 Trevelyan, in particular, tinkered with the orthodox Whig narrative so as to broaden its attractiveness with the expectation that Labour and Conservatism would mistake this altered image for their own reflection. In this fashion, Liberalism would at least survive by proxy, embedded in a revised history of consensus that itself constituted the moderate basis of a new politics of consensus.

Both Trevelyan and Churchill understood the threat to their aims posed by narrow academic professionalism. The young Trevelyan exiled himself from the personally suffocating atmosphere of Cambridge specifically to compose history for a general audience. His works attempted to embody his understanding of the familial link between literary historical forms, liberal governance, and contemporary public debate couched in a language about the past. By contrast, Churchill successfully manipulated the professional historical community in order to propagate a dramatic and synoptic brand of history designed to function exclusively in the public realm as a veiled celebration of ancient Whig paradigms.

Trevelyan and Churchill, along with the Hammonds, Belloc, and the Webbs, were united in their acceptance of a very Victorian commonplace, a conviction that even in the twentieth century, the reading of history could and should make a difference in the national consciousness, providing a forum for political discourse, impinging directly upon contemporary social mores, intellectual life, and policy decisions. The ambitious scope of their works dictated that each author expected his or her authority and influence to extend far beyond the boundaries of the professional historical community. As private scholars engaged in the composition of civic histories, they all, except for the special case of the Webbs, operated under the assumption that, since the writing of history was a didactic exercise, knowledge of the past was for the widest possible consumption. As seen below, the various connections of each author with political Liberalism—supportive, antagonistic, or otherwise—as well as their relationship with increasingly detached and autarkic academic scholarship were inseparable from their self-conscious adoption of the role of public historian.

1   HILAIRE BELLOC
The Path Not Taken?

Hilaire Belloc is best remembered today as the author of *Cautionary Tales for Children* and other nonsense verse. Secondarily he is recalled as political controversialist, maverick critic of capitalism, Catholic apologist and author of *A Path to Rome* (1901) and *Europe and the Faith* (1920), humorous novelist, skilled seaman, platform debater of H. G. Wells and G. B. Shaw, and the older but lesser half of "Chesterbelloc." But in his lifetime it was his writing of a militant Catholic history that monopolized the largest fraction of his attentions, serious and otherwise. And it was with these wide-ranging efforts at interpreting the past that Belloc best exposed the underlying connections between all of his other endeavors. Bellocian historiography offered the most

Hilaire Belloc in 1916, a few years after his departure from parliament and simultaneous break with the Liberal party. (UPI / Bettmann Archive)

radical, if not always the most subtle or effective, early twentieth-century refutation of Liberalism and its Whiggish historiographical support. Linking Britain to its ancient Roman, continental, and Catholic origins while positing a possible present other than the Protestant, capitalist, liberal status quo, he condemned in his writings the four centuries of national history since the Reformation as a tragic deviation from the natural state.

Included among his historiographical output of more than two score volumes between 1899 and 1939 were biographies of Danton (1899), Robespierre (1901), Marie Antoinette (1909), James II (1928), Wolsey (1930), Cranmer (1931), Charles I (1933), Cromwell (1934), Milton (1935), and Charles II (1939). These books, hastily written for money and therefore often brief and sloppily executed, provided their author with an unenviable reputation as a hack. "But then I am not a historian," Belloc declared by way of defense, "I am a publicist."[1] A 1933 *Times* review of Belloc's *William the Conqueror* was very kind, much kinder than he felt it deserved, for, he informed Maurice Baring, "I think it a rotten book. But nothing like as bad as my 'Charles I.' "[2] To friends he described his quick studies of Napoleon (1932) and Milton as only so much "hack work."[3] When in low spirits he mused on the futility of his efforts. "The only book I enjoyed writing, and which also sold well, was the 'Path to Rome,' and the books I have been [writing] (this historical sort) especially the biographies, are a hack work and very tiresome."[4] At such moments his solitary persistence seemed pointless. The difficulty was that, in spite of his own self-deprecatory asides, he did indeed consider himself a deadly serious historian, however much in private he admitted the justice of the case of his many detractors.

In conjunction with this sort of self-effacing insouciance, there was also a more confident, crusading side to Belloc the historian. He compensated for the obvious defects of his abbreviated biographies with a philanthropic devotion to his large-scale histories, works he approached in a more serious vein. This was particularly true of his *History of England* (4 vols., 1925–31). Within its pages Belloc constructed a full-blown refutation of the "official" Whig historiographical orthodoxy that he believed still imprisoned the mind of the twentieth-century Englishman. In his view, the sacrifices involved warranted his consideration as a serious reinterpreter of the nation's past. He explained his sense of mission to Hoffman Nickerson while completing the fourth volume in 1931. "If I did not feel it to be my task, to be completed before death, I would have given it up long ago for no one reads it and there is no money in it."[5] Conscious of the fact that the work would not sell and therefore promised no monetary rewards, he persisted in this "self-imposed task" principally because "it will do the right work in the right place which is all I care about."[6]

The missionary zeal on display here was a direct outgrowth of Belloc's position as an outsider in twentieth-century British society. His Catholic faith represented the central organizing principle in his life, dominating his views on politics, economics, psychology, sociology, and, most important for this study, history. The economic and moral critique of capitalism elaborated in his seminal and influential book *The Servile State* (1912) drew its theme of de facto working-class slavery, enshrined and historically validated in the property arrangements and political institutions of contemporary liberal society, directly from his understanding of the history of European Catholic civilization. According to Bellocian political economy, Europe's pre-Reformation culture, governed by the spirit of the church, formed the last example of a free society established upon the basis of cooperative crafts and guilds and village societies of economically independent small proprietors.

Belloc's identification with the plight of the modern industrial wage laborer originated in a nostalgic desire for a return to the halcyon days of Roman Catholic hegemony, rather than, as was true of most of his New Liberal associates, as an offshoot of liberal humanitarianism. The young radical based his Edwardian membership in the Liberal party upon an erroneous belief that the twentieth-century incarnation of what had once been Gladstone's fiefdom could and would champion both the dismantling of the old liberal sociopolitical order and its replacement with the Distributist state, the modern distillation of the best attributes of the High Middle Ages. Though entering politics at the same time as many enthusiastic New Liberal acquaintances, Belloc was unwilling to accept their sympathetic reevaluation of the role of the competent, efficient bureaucratic state in employing administrative reform to advance individual freedom. His subsequent disillusionment with, and estrangement from, the party of Asquith and Lloyd George stemmed from its incompatibility with his idiosyncratic Catholic radicalism, a discordance underlined by the Liberal party leadership's failure to exploit the revolutionary potential of the House of Lords crisis of 1909–11.

As the leading exponent of "Catholic history," that is, "true history," Belloc aimed at a *political* conversion of his audience rather than a moral or theological one.[7] Whether this made the job any easier was questionable, for it was a "fact that the whole of modern England was built up on breaking away from and opposing the Catholic Church. The result is the inheritance of strong and permanent opposition which sometimes becomes quite violent, especially in the case of individuals, but is *not* theological nor even ethical but almost wholly political."[8] Since the opposition to Roman Catholicism in all its forms was purely political in nature and since the intellectual foundations of the contemporary English liberal political system lay in a perverse interpretation of the nation's past, Belloc identified a revisionist historiography as the correct first remedy. His ambitious works as well as his more modest biographies were all of a piece in his lifelong campaign to reconcile two of his greatest loves, "the soil of England and the Catholic Faith."[9] And the inevitable target of his polemic was the Whig rendering of English history, which he identified as the primary supplier of a vindication of the growth of an increasingly intrusive state.

Fundamental in shaping Belloc's revisionist outlook were two episodes of friction with the status quo that engendered profound personal disappointment and disillusionment. The first was his failure to secure a position at Oxford in the 1890s, the second his frustrating experience as a Liberal M.P. between 1906 and 1910.

A Reliable Milch Cow versus the Dons

Seven years' instruction at John Henry Newman's Oratory School at Birmingham confirmed, if any confirmation was required, Belloc's self-conscious distinctiveness as a *Catholic* Englishman. His alien religious allegiance as an Oxford undergraduate laid the foundations for a life lived as a resentful outsider, while at the same time a cultivated eccentricity and flamboyance with the spoken word gained him a reputation that may not have been enviable in someone with academic pretensions. The experiences of a somewhat paranoid Roman Catholic reader of modern history at Balliol College seemed to confirm the suspicion that traditional English historiography was a skillfully employed tool of the Protestant social and political elite. Having been used to breed conformity and acquiescence and to dull inquiry for decades, it also surely possessed the latent potential to reverse the spell. The problem for Belloc personally was determining the best method to participate in this rehabilitation of national culture. The growing prestige of the university professorial guildsmen identified them in Belloc's mind as the future entrenched guardians of the official historiographical orthodoxy that he was slowly learning to detest. In the name of efficacy and economy of effort it would be preferable to counter his enemies' sallies at the source by enlisting in the guild rather than to oppose them from afar.

Belloc's great social and academic triumphs as an undergraduate convinced him that he could first gain acceptance and then survive as an insider at Oxford, or at least masquerading as such. He delighted in his chosen study of history, and, succeeding splendidly in the role of outsider-as-insider, he enjoyed even more the extracurricular activities that rounded out his Oxford experience. In 1894 he was elected president of the Oxford Union over stiff competition, including the equally brilliant J. L. Hammond, and then topped off a sparkling undergraduate career in 1895 by securing a First Class Honours. With three exciting and satisfying years at Oxford behind him, Belloc was in no hurry to leave, deciding instead, with the encouragement of his Balliol tutor A. L. Smith, to sit for an All Souls' Fellowship, a post that would secure him seven years of residential leisure to pursue historiographic projects without the complications of teaching duties. Flushed with his record of achievement, it never occurred to Belloc that the prize might be denied him. This misplaced optimism made All Souls' subsequent rejection all the more painful. He still hoped that Balliol or some other college might offer him a fellowship to remedy the oversight, but nothing was forthcoming. So desperate was Belloc for an Oxford career that, after marrying in 1896, he returned to apply for the lowly position of college lecturer at New College.[10] In the end even this was denied him, and his humiliation was complete.

In later years Belloc was to qualify expressions of regard for Balliol by saying, "I love my college though I know it to be thoroughly Protestant."[11] With that in mind, it is hardly surprising that he rationalized his rejection by Oxford as a consequence of religious bigotry,[12] but that explanation is unlikely, as a Catholic was awarded a fellowship the year following Belloc's failed candidacy. A more reasonable assumption is that the loud and opinionated Anglo-Frenchman was more personally unpopular than he realized and not generally regarded as sound academic raw material. Sir Charles Oman, perhaps with Belloc in mind, described in his memoirs such inappropriately sanguine candidates.

> Far the most interesting kind of examination in which I have ever taken part was the annual competition for the All Souls' Fellow-ships in October. The number of candidates was never very great, and all (with few exceptions) were picked men—there were only a few whose judgement of their own capacity was hopelessly optimistic, and rested on "Union" oratory, or popularity among their own particular literary or political clique, won by persistent self-assertion. These candidates gave little trouble when pinned down to the rather searching questions set before them—though I have known one or two who did give the fellows some little an-noyance in the smoking-room, where they tried to sparkle, or to demonstrate that they were men of the world or epigrammists.[13]

Whatever the actual reason, an embittered Belloc neither forgot nor forgave this denial of entry into the sanctum sanctorum of the university historical community. Their refusal to welcome him into their company transformed an outsider's latent antagonism toward "official" academic historians into a lifelong active hatred.

This injustice condemned Belloc to a life of "difficulty and anx-iety" writing for money, a "reliable milch cow" for publishers more concerned with quantity than quality, expected to produce prose "strictly by measure, like Cambridge butter, so much the inch."[14] After completing the manuscript of his biography of Marie An-toinette in 1909, he admitted that the book should be extensively rewritten, but where was he to find the time? "Ever since the idiotic Dons turned me out of doors," he complained, "not only leisure but even regularity of employment has been denied me."[15] Since aca-demic historians "cannot write clearly, let alone vividly" and "have never in their lives been able to resurrect the past," government subsidies of their research were a criminal waste of public funds.[16] Belloc had definite ideas where such money might be better spent. "The few—very few—who can do historical presentation ought to be free to do it. It would be an advantage to the State. Endowments are there for that, but they would never give me one."[17]

Forty years after his rejection by All Souls' Belloc still recalled the incident with resentment mingled with nostalgia and regret about what might have been. "Oxford is for me a shrine, a memory, a tomb and a poignant possessing grief. All could have been well if they would have received me in my young days of love & poverty: but they would not. Hence this complaint. There are places in Oxford I will not pass, lest the memories be too violent."[18] However, Belloc was not always so poetically delicate about this decisive episode of his youth. More often bitterness clouded his recollection.

> I determined on a Fellowship, which Dr. Jowett had told me when I first went up to Balliol I was pretty well bound to get. Everybody took it for granted I should have one. I based my life on that calculation. When the time came the religious prejudice was too strong. No one minds a man practising the Catholic religion, or any other; but what they do object to is the effect of religion upon character and especially upon views of public life, and I think they could not bear the idea of an historical Fellow who would have written and taught history in a fashion clashing with their own. Anyhow, I found that at first one college and then another turned me down, though in each one my friends among the Fellows told me I was certain. In this way I wasted the first critical years of my life. . . . I went to London, and have had to earn my living since then as best I could.[19]

This belated account of the affair, penned in 1933, illustrates how a personal and pecuniary grievance was translated into a religious one, which, to Belloc's way of thinking, merely provided a convenient cover for a fundamental political-intellectual prejudice against him on the part of the Whiggish dons.

It is easy to imagine how he later spliced his repudiation by Oxford onto his 1910 break with the Liberal party to produce in the Bellocian consciousness the notion of a seamless conspiratorial web spun by the anti-Catholic, academic-political power structure. The early twentieth-century vogue of administrative history led by T. F. Tout, with its focus upon the state as the principal agent of change (and, by extension, of progress), seemed ready-made to shore up the status quo. Belloc's hatred of dons as intellectual mercenaries for the sociopolitical establishment became a recurrent theme of his correspondence after his 1910 disillusionment with Liberalism. Some few, such as H. A. L. Fisher, whom Belloc recalled in 1940 as "the only don who was really my friend," were exempted from his generalized displeasure.[20] More generally Belloc's opinion of academics was decidedly less equivocal. They were alternatively cads, vermin, or ingenues, useful only to provide recreation for a weary, but still playful, Catholic purveyor of truth. For Belloc, saddled with the thankless task of refuting single-handedly, or so it seemed to him, two centuries of historiographical prejudice, the sport of "hunting Dons" was "almost as much fun as establishing Roman roads." He knew "all the didges [sic] for making them break cover and just where to stand to shoot them in the thorax when they get out of the wood into the stubble. I never wing them, I always kill." He recommended "get[ting] them on the footnotes" as the most effective means to make them "dance." But a still better and more playful line of approach was to "blaguard" academics for not being men of the world and for their unfamiliarity with women. Surely, if such a conflicted creature as a worldly don could conceivably exist, he would renounce his profession and "go to prison, or make money, or both."[21] This never-consumed rage at the official guardians of orthodox history eventually even adulterated Belloc's recollection of his pre-Oxford days. He distilled his adolescent dislike for Cardinal Newman down to the simple fact that, as he grumbled late in life, "Newman was a don."[22]

A Matter of Flair Rather Than of Facts

The mature Belloc's utter contempt for donnishness assumed concrete expression in his approach to his work. The restrictive methods of research and the desiccated prose style of the academician were just as suspect as the Whiggish message they enveloped, and Belloc consciously designed his histories to counter all of these interdependent failings. The writing of history for Belloc was a business with immediate and serious consequences for any society, hardly an enterprise to be entrusted to timid scholars with their feet of clay. "The history of what we were explains what we are," and "the accumulation of experience which history affords," he declared, provided our only "guide" to the avoidance of a cataclysmic future.[23]

The accumulation of facts—"scholarship" to Belloc—certainly had its place in this momentous search for historical truth. Those two great champions of the new academic exactitude Tait and Tout "may have been dull dogs, but," conceded Belloc, "at least they had their dates right."[24] Yet he was emphatic that the sanctity of facts should never be allowed to hinder an author's didactic purpose.[25] Self-described as "the most inaccurate of men," Belloc was confident that if the "how" and "why" of history were answered, the "what" would look after itself. "It is not bad history to make Waterloo fall on a Monday, but it is bad history to say it was won on the playing fields of Eton."[26] Whatever evidence was employed by the historian, alone it could not generate truth. Judgment, itself a product of common sense and a subtle understanding of unchanging human nature and the workings of the world, was the indispensable instrument wielded by the historian as sculptor as he released from a formless mass of detail a preexisting, and now recognizable, narrative pregnant with meaning.[27] The metaphor is appropriate, for Belloc was excessively fond of repeating Jules Michelet's description of the historian's task as one of the "resurrection of the flesh."[28]

The form this resurrection took was "essentially the telling of a story," a story illustrative of an eternal verity.[29] Attaining historical understanding in order to construct this story primarily involved an intuitive and irrational, although by no means arbitrary, process. Belloc's antipositivism reversed the standard academic itinerary; *Verstehen* preceded any form of research. "History is to *know* on one's first vision," announced Belloc, and then "to confirm and build by an immense deal of coincident *work* of research & judgement one's original knowledge."[30]

H. A. L. Fisher recalled a young Belloc's manner of conducting research at the National Library in Paris. Before a table piled high by perspiring assistants with books and pamphlets Belloc stood "with a smug satisfied expression as if to say, 'These damned dons accuse me of neglecting research. Well, look at this tableful of books.'" Over lunch, lubricated by a bottle of burgundy and with Fisher and the library's director as his audience, he proceeded to wax eloquent upon his own ideas about the writing of history. "'History,' said Belloc, 'is a matter of flair rather than of facts. You saw all those books which your staff were collecting for me this morning?' 'I did indeed,' said the Librarian who had himself spent an hour hunting for them. 'I have a flair,' said Belloc, 'that not one of them contains a single fact which is of the least use to me. I shall not return to the library.' "[31]

Confident in the clarity of his own historical vision, Belloc "gallop[ed]" through the dictation of the second section of his *Monarchy: A Study of Louis XIV* (1938) with the full recognition of how "incredibl[y] . . . ignorant I am about all that period."[32] More than three decades earlier, in 1904, when he undertook his biography of Marie Antoinette, Belloc seemed almost proud of his unfamiliarity with the historical technicalities involved, for he looked upon these lacunae as conferring an unusual advantage.[33] The absence of a burdensome clutter of minutiae, however accurate, allowed his imagination the freedom to reconstruct the events of the 1750s and 1760s in an unorthodox manner which, though guilty of distorting minor facts, managed to convey a greater truth in an entertaining fashion.[34] Belloc's poetic turn of mind, which by his own testimony devoured all that he read and "turn[ed] it into something different," was ideally suited to recognize the dramatic possibilities within any historical scenario.[35] Belloc readily admitted that his earliest books contained violent judgments and contrasts perhaps too strong for reality, but he defended these excesses with the claim that they could "never be too strong for arresting the reader of a great historic story."[36] Truth alone could never be enough; great history was synonymous with readable history, adorned with all the seductive attractions of "melodrama."[37] History was dull and ineffective only if its presentation, like its inspiration, was inartistic.[38] It had been the highly skilled but unsavory nineteenth-century Whig historians like Macaulay who, according to Belloc, first appreciated this secret of style, and he now hoped to exploit it in the service of a much needed revisionism. Belloc relished the irony that the formerly exclusive weapon of Whig amateurs, loaded with a new variety of powder and shot, would now be turned against their donnish successors.

Such satisfactions notwithstanding, Belloc, perhaps still nursing a secret desire to inhabit the world of learned argument and counterargument denied him by Oxford, sometimes assumed the visage of a don. Rather than arguing past his adversaries, he tackled them head-on, going to great lengths to overturn the smallest detail written by the mandarinate.[39] Belloc expended enormous sums of energy in particular attacking G. M. Trevelyan, "a typical product of the highly anti-Catholic English Universities and governing class."[40] As young Liberal firebrands at the turn of the century, the two men had worked side by side on the Radical weekly the *Speaker*, but there remained no trace of former friendship or political affinity in Belloc's subsequent assessment of Macaulay's grandnephew. In 1910 he took issue with the opinions expressed in the Liberal *Edinburgh Review* which "has a shit (si j'ose m'exprimer ainsi) writing on it whom I strongly suspect to be *George Macaulay Trevelyan*."[41] Belloc regarded Trevelyan as the most respected and visible of Britain's "official" historians. Therefore, although it represented "of course nothing more than the weak echo of his greatuncle Macaulay," Trevelyan's work remained the primary target of Belloc's historical rebuttals for over a quarter of a century, for prominence as a Cambridge don provided Trevelyan with what Belloc regarded as an artificially inflated and dangerous sort of automatic authority that demanded tireless refutation.[42] "Unfortunately the Universities are the home of fossil errors, especially in history, and if for no other reason than that they give us examples of this kind [i.e., Trevelyan's *England under Queen Anne*] by the analysis of which we can exactly expose the spirit of falsehood in history, we make use of them."[43] It was as essential occasionally to rout the dons by direct assault on terrain of their own choosing as it was to take them on the flank by envelopment.

Just how seriously Belloc sometimes took adherence to academic formalities in his long-running battle with institutionalized historical orthodoxy is captured in the following scene from 1912, when he wrote excitedly to George Wyndham of a "vast historical discovery" that Froissart had been mistaken in his assumption of the site of Edward III's passage of the River Somme prior to the battle of Crécy.[44] Belloc composed a long, detailed article in expectation of publishing his corrective in the *English Historical Review*.[45] But he hoped in vain. The *EHR* last acknowledged Belloc's work in a 1910 review of *Marie Antoinette* in which it warned that "Mr. Belloc is not to be taken too seriously" because "his prejudices and their source are alike undisguised."[46] To Belloc it appeared that his ostracism by the guardians of the Whiggish social, political, and intellectual status quo, begun with the 1895 rejection for an Oxford fellowship, was now complete and irrevocable.

Belloc was mindful that in flaunting his hasty methodology he risked appearing frivolous to his donnish opposite numbers. Forced to come to "definite conclusions in a hurry" while producing a short book on Waterloo in 1911, he admitted that it was "a bad way to write history," one that often "makes me look a fool later."[47] But the conscious adoption of this flamboyant literary style garnished with antiacademic bravado served Belloc's purposes well enough. His rejection by All Souls' convinced him that British historiography could be rerouted from its well-worn paths of error only by an appeal over the heads of the academic priesthood directly to the general reader by a historian who wrote "for the pleasure of his reader and not for his critic."[48] When faced with a choice between the unadorned statement of truth or history as "readable stuff fairly persuasive," the author should opt for the latter because to the modern audience the mere statement of truth would "fall flat and unheeded."[49]

To Belloc's way of thinking, the twentieth-century institutionalization within the nation's universities of the Whig interpretation of history paralleled the recent manipulation of the idea of the welfare state by the ruling elite to facilitate a bureaucratic institutionalization of the Liberal political and economic hegemony. This was particularly true of the symbiosis between Tout's new administrative history and the erection of the "Servile State," the former legitimizing the latter. It seemed that "carving in hard wood and against the grain [was] the only way to have any permanent effect" on these objectionable trends.[50] It was possible to break the academic, bureaucratic monopoly on historical truth only by endorsing a visibly provocative alternative. In conjunction with a critique of parliamentary politics in *The Party System* and of capitalism in *The Servile State*, this historical revisionism was to spearhead the intellectual transformation that would precede the eventual dismantling of England's malignant Liberal system.

By 1912 Belloc's opposition to the establishment in all its protean forms dominated his historiographic and political self-image. It is interesting to speculate on his attitudes had he been accepted for the All Souls' Fellowship in 1895. His claws might have been drawn as he settled in comfortably as an academic historian writing conventional articles, accompanied by a "plague of footnotes," for respectable scholarly journals. But such a complete co-optation by the university community was improbable, for Belloc's antipathy stemmed as much from deep-seated religious and political convictions as from memories of personal rejection. In all likelihood he would have remained a maverick historian, using his Oxford post as a staging area for attacks on the works of his colleagues. No one understood this better than Belloc himself.

> Maurice Baring always says that it was God's Providence the Dons would not let me become a Don. But I deny this! If they had taken me in I would have turned them inside out and given them such Hell that they would have had to invent a post to get rid of me. Also, once I had the Hall mark, I should have been able to expose their measly pretensions with authority. Writing, for instance, on the monstrous Elizabethan myth, leaving it a smouldering heap and signing the work Hilaire Belloc, MA sometime Fellow of All Souls', Senior Historical Scholar of Balliol Coll: Oxon.[51]

But denied the role of Trojan horse, Belloc was fated to spend five decades mounting formal siege operations against the citadel of historical orthodoxy.

An Opportunity for Stopping the "Big Rot"

The youthful Belloc's failure to infiltrate the Whiggish academic establishment did not discourage his political enthusiasms. The Liberal historiographic orthodoxy propagated at the university represented the intellectual arm of political Liberalism. Denied access to one avenue for political change, Belloc resorted to another. The post-Gladstonian Liberal party seemed to offer unlimited opportunities for a radical departure from the past, and therefore he hitched his fortunes to those of the traditional party of progress with the expectation that in its new expansive mood it could accommodate and foster his own peculiar brand of radicalism.

Personal relationships also made this decision a natural one.[52] Belloc's political associations at Oxford were almost exclusively left of center, rubbing shoulders as he did with young Liberals such as J. L. Hammond, F. W. Hirst, and John Simon. Likewise, his principal contacts among the faculty, A. L. Smith and H. A. L. Fisher, were of the Liberal persuasion. Half jokingly and half in earnest, the undergraduate Belloc formed a small group of four called the Oxford Republican Club.[53]

The immediate roots of Belloc's Edwardian Liberalism were, not surprisingly, to be found in his fervent support for Home Rule in Catholic Ireland, a belief in his own particular interpretation of the republican ideals of the French Revolution, and his concern for the deepening rifts in British society between rich and poor, inequalities that the natural progression of capitalism, insidiously encroaching upon the economic and political independence of the British laboring classes, seemed to have brought to crisis proportions. The politics of his critique of capitalism can be traced back to Thomas Carlyle, William Cobbett, John Ruskin, and William Morris, radicals who in differing ways admired the Middle Ages but who are seldom grouped together as seminal liberal theorists. However fin-de-siècle questioning of traditional laissez faire orthodoxy by such young turks of the New Liberalism as L. T. Hobhouse, J. L. Hammond, J. A. Hobson, and Graham Wallas funneled these older strains of thought masquerading as new into Liberalism's debate about its future.[54]

But any views Belloc might have shared with his New Liberal acquaintances were counterbalanced by fundamental disagreements that were to remain hidden, except for the occasional hint, until 1909–11. "The Liberal Tradition," his contribution to the 1897 medley *Essays in Liberalism* by Six Oxford Men, looked back to the ideal of a free state grounded upon the economic and political independence of the "individual possessor and producer of wealth." There was no hint of sympathy for the benevolent state envisioned by his New Liberal coauthors. Belloc repeated the litany of Charles James Fox, Richard Cobden, and John Bright but looked to William Cobbett as his true source of inspiration. Like Cobbett, Belloc's main concern was for the "community" of Old England—for Belloc a community linked to the remnants of pre-Reformation Catholic culture—nearly destroyed after two centuries of confiscation by capitalist landlords. He devoted most of the essay to the question of land reform in hopes of calling attention to the need for a substantial yeoman class that would provide the nation with "a strength and a kind of promised permanence which purely industrial aggregations could never afford."[55] Reading *Essays in Liberalism* today it is a simple matter to pick out the outlines of the fully developed "Distributism" of Chesterbelloc, but at the time there was little recognition of the potential ideological chasm separating Belloc from the volume's other youthful contributors.[56] There was only a faint whiff here of the antistatist, anticollectivist stridency of the mature Belloc and little evidence of his later fragile loyalty to the traditional parliamentary system.

However, his commitment to Irish Home Rule and free trade, along with his work on the Liberal *Daily News* and *Speaker*, certified Belloc as a "perfectly sound" and "acceptable" Liberal candidate for Parliament by 1906.[57] Elected by a majority of 852 to represent the Manchester South Salford constituency in the January Liberal landslide, he stressed to the voters that he was entering the Commons "on a whole-hearted and well-defined democratic programme."[58] Belloc hoped to assume the role of the ideologically pure and influential backbencher, a loyal member of "a strong Radical Party, who chiefly care for the results of their political creed and who do not expect office."[59]

Believing parliament to be an arena where important ideas were thrashed out in full public view between government and opposition culminating in decisions of national significance, Belloc worried that the magnitude of the Liberal party's victory in 1906 might prevent the "battle from appearing serious," for here at last was "an opportunity for stopping the big 'rot' which has eaten up English life for more than a generation," if only "the opportunity will be seized."[60] His notion of the "big rot" (later elaborated in *The Servile State*) involved the intensified modern complicity of the traditional political class, big business, and the omnicompetent bureaucratic state. This sort of preoccupation left the member from South Salford ill-suited to support the 1906 Liberal government from the backbenches. When the Lords' rejection of Lloyd George's "People's Budget" sparked a constitutional crisis leading to a new election in January 1910 in order to obtain a mandate from the voters, Belloc addressed his South Salford constituents, convinced that "England is at a turning-point." Now, he urged, was the time to create a new and better nation, beginning with the raising of enormous sums of money at the expense of society's privileged and wealthy. In the next few weeks, Belloc prophesied, either his listeners would push "the great weight of social reform and democracy" over the edge and send it down on the other side or they and their fellows would "allow it to slip back on yourselves and crush you."[61] Asquith, however, seemed unwilling or incapable of grasping the nettle. While the prime minister was obviously reluctant to assume the role of demagogue in a bold and ruthless offensive against privilege, Belloc favored linking the budget controversy and the question of the House of Lords' veto and carrying them both "by popular movement!" His studies of the French Revolution had persuaded him that

> a revolutionary change accompanied by an act of will need not hurt a nation, but the clinching and making final of a slip or lowering of efficiency does hurt a nation greatly. . . . If [the House of Lords'] powers had been taken away by a popular movement, England would only have suffered as one suffers from an operation, but the leaving of them with just those powers which suit the machine, and the taking from them of just those powers which are either traditional or valuable, and the doing of it quietly as a matter of form without popular support, will prove a fatal thing.[62]

Belloc was suitably disgusted when the episode ended without a radical reordering of the political structure. He felt he had taken parliamentary politics seriously and been duped in the process. What to Asquith and his cabinet seemed like a triumph of quiet, persistent diplomacy, to Belloc reeked of cynicism, connivance, and corruption.[63] He was never to recover from a disillusionment with the system engendered by his experiences of 1909–10. Public politics, which he had naively accepted as a genuine forum for debate on national questions, had proven instead to be a clever mechanism for dampening ideological conflict that might pose a threat to the traditional power structure. The labels *Liberal* and *Conservative* were mere window dressings so that the populace might take sides in a nonexistent contest with a predetermined outcome.

Belloc's newly inflamed opposition to the party system was hardly a unique phenomenon in the ever-shifting sands of post-1886 British political culture. But it differed in one important regard from the antiparliamentary critique of that motley but influential collection of Edwardian reformers, including the Webbs, usually grouped together as advocates of National Efficiency. Whereas the latter opposed partisan politics as usual in the new age of intense global economic and military competition on the grounds that it was taken far too seriously, monopolizing the legislator's time while it dissipated precious energy, Belloc saw instead a system in which staged contests of principle masked the ruthless and efficient acquisition and organization of power by a homogeneous governing class. The coarsely woven common thread knitting together these two variant analyses was their uncompromisingly antiliberal sentiments.

Under the circumstances, Belloc decided not to stand again in the general election of December 1910. He chose to remove himself from the sham theatrics of Westminster—"a deliberate and final decision"—but he had no intention of abandoning politics permanently, for in addition to its grave importance when taken seriously, Belloc the performer found it "very entertaining." But in future he was determined not to sink into the ineffectual position of a party member, since "my business and usefulness are in an independent position if it can be obtained."[64] As an accomplished writer Belloc slipped easily back into the independent niche available to all who choose to pursue politics by other means and carry on a *guerrilla* against the political establishment. As editor of *The Eye Witness*, a weekly dedicated to exposing the humbug of British politics, and as author of *Pongo and the Bull* (1910), a comic novel satirizing the party system, Belloc landed annoying pinpricks on the flanks of his adversaries. But with the subsequent publication of *The Party System* (1911) and *The Servile State* (1912), both ambitious combinations of analysis and polemic, he took more deliberate aim at the social and economic foundations of two centuries of liberal politics.

Christian Civilization and the Servile State

Belloc's essay into political analysis was one more manifestation of a pan-European phenomenon. Vilfredo Pareto's work on political elites (1916) and Robert Michels's examination of the nature of political parties (1911) simply represented more speculative contemporaneous expressions of disillusionment with the conventional political process. Challenging the notion that Great Britain was to any significant degree a democracy, Belloc argued instead in *The Party System* that the country was in fact governed by one party posing as two for appearances' sake only. Any disagreement of principle between the opposition and the government front benches was insignificant compared with the social, economic, and, most important, familial ties that blended them into a homogeneous ruling elite, incapable of fundamental internal disunity. Heightening the potency of his analysis was the wit and dexterity of Bellocian prose, amply demonstrated in an oft-quoted passage:

> We are not surprised at Romeo loving Juliet, though he is a Montague and she is a Capulet. But if we found in addition that Lady Capulet was by birth a Montague, that Lady Montague was the first cousin of old Capulet, that Mercutio was at once the nephew of a Capulet and the brother-in-law of a Montague, that Count Paris was related on his father's side to one house and on his mother's side to the other, that Tybalt was Romeo's uncle's stepson and that the Friar who married Romeo and Juliet was Juliet's and Romeo's first cousin once removed, we should probably conclude that the feud between the two houses was being kept up mainly for the dramatic entertainment of the people of Verona.[65]

Backbenchers of an independent turn of mind were powerless to influence the inertia of this covert transgangway alliance, arisen from mutual interests and sealed by marriage.

Belloc traced this deplorable state of affairs to its origins in the Revolution of 1689, which he maintained had been incorrectly portrayed as an early stage in the forward march of democracy. Echoing the refrains of eighteenth-century Country party ideology, Belloc declared that "what triumphed in 1689 and again in 1715 and 1745 was not the people but Parliament," an institution representing only a narrow class interest.[66] As long as parliamentary membership had been circumscribed by a restricted franchise, party organization remained rudimentary and party discipline virtually nonexistent. However, the Reform Acts of 1832 and 1867 animated this dormant moloch. Belloc argued that the party system, in its present form, was erected expressly to prevent the injection of true democracy into the fabric of English politics by transferring all effective power from the Commons as a body into the hands of the ministry, or, more accurately, the two front benches in league against the few remaining maverick M.P.'s.[67] In the past the primary evil of the system had been social and economic unfairness, but in the twentieth century iniquity was compounded by the mounting costs of incompetence. The complexities of national life rendered parliamentary politics inadequate to meet the challenges of the modern age. "On this thing all observant men are now settled: the House of Commons in its present inaptitude, producing as 'leaders' the type of men who play at the rotation of the party game, cannot deal with the vast and rapidly changing necessities of the country at home, where men starve—or abroad, where (behind their backs) they are humbled."[68] Starting with identical anti-Liberal sentiments but a fundamentally different rationale, clearly the antibureaucratic Belloc sometimes found himself in agreement with the statist-oriented National Efficiency movement.

The Servile State, published a year after *The Party System* from articles originally written for A. R. Orage's eclectic socialist newspaper the *New Age*, took Belloc's critique one step further by focusing upon the economic and legal arrangements underpinning the modern British political system.[69] Described by its author as "a book on Economics of a practical sort," it marked the first formal appearance of the Chesterbellocian doctrine of Distributism, a conglomeration of individual land distribution, the corporate organization of society, workers' control of the means of production, antistatist decentralization of power, and a true Jeffersonian-style democracy of a property-owning electorate.[70] Belloc and his friend and fellow Catholic G. K. Chesterton proposed this mixed bag as a remedy for the prison Britain seemed to be busily erecting for itself, a prison the senior member of the partnership dubbed the Servile State.

But in using the term Servile State, Belloc did not wish to be misunderstood to mean a collectivist-socialist state so subject to regulation and order as to be unduly oppressive. He claimed that his book did not discuss the socialist state at all, but rather the effect of socialist doctrine upon capitalist society "to produce a third thing different from either of its two begetters—to wit, the Servile State."[71] The latter he defined as "that arrangement of society in which so considerable a number of the families and individuals are constrained by positive law to labour for the advantage of other families and individuals as to stamp the whole community with the mark of such labour." The difference between the Servile State and the capitalist state was that under capitalism the majority of the population, although constrained de facto by economic vulnerability, remained de jure "politically free."[72]

Capitalism could not remain static, for it was only an inherently unstable transitional phase. "Because its social realities were in conflict with all existing or possible systems of law, and because its effects in denying *sufficiency* and *security* were intolerable to men," capitalism required a permanent solution to make it compatible with human nature's desire for stability, sufficiency, and security. Belloc recognized only three possible answers to capitalism's predicament: collectivism, Distributism, and the Servile State. Because the first two demanded revolutionary thinking in a country addicted to the cosmetic changes of reformism—a paralytic condition highlighted in the failure of 1910—the Servile State appeared inevitable.

The Servile State offered to the propertyless worker perpetual security enshrined in statute in exchange for the surrender of the political freedom that accompanied equality of legal status. Social welfare legislation would accomplish both sides of the equation since, according to Belloc, it would make official the inferior status of the proletariat as the recipient of financial aid, while it simultaneously conferred a superior status upon those taxed to fulfill that obligation. Legally the idea of commonality of citizenship requisite in a true democracy would be displaced by a division between laborer and employer, serf and lord, slave and citizen.[73]

The nature of Belloc's radical Liberalism had always outstripped the social reformist aims of the New Liberals. His support for Lloyd George's 1909 budget had been a combination of a sincere desire to help the poor and a hope that it represented the thin end of the wedge that would revolutionize the British economic and political system, recreating the conditions for the rise of the independent small producer Belloc associated with old Catholic England. Reforms that stopped short of radical change, even if they redistributed income to the lower classes, would only tighten the vise-grip of the ruling class on the reins of power through statutory reaffirmation of the superiority of a paternalistic elite. This conviction explains Belloc's strenuous opposition to so much of the ameliorative social legislation introduced by Asquith's prewar Liberal government.[74] To his way of thinking, the Insurance Bill of 1911 was "a vile enslaving measure," and he likewise denounced the Parliament Bill to reform the House of Lords as a scheme "to give more power than ever to a small group of perfectly irresponsible people. . . . If we had a Democracy, of course I should prefer the Parliament Bill to pass."[75] But the hollowness of twentieth-century British democracy made a mockery of all measured attempts at reform.

Max Weber located the origins of a distinctly capitalist mentality in the Reformation. The pessimistic German sociologist also identified a stultifying increase in bureaucratization as the dominant tendency in modern civil society. Although there is no evidence that he was familiar with Weber's analysis, Belloc accepted both of these propositions as preconditions of the Servile State and attempted to link them historically. For reasons of intellectual neatness and didactic efficacy, the resultant historical analysis was an indispensable element in his attack upon the status quo. It was possible, in Belloc's estimation, to prove the tendency toward the erection of the Servile State in modern Britain, even to one unaware of Europe's past. Yet it seemed clear that such an ignoble trajectory would appear more probable, more reasonable, "far more a matter of experience and less a matter of mere deduction" when the hearer fully comprehended "what our society once was, and how it changed into what we know to-day."[76] It was imperative that Belloc's audience understand that the modern version of the Servile State was in many ways a regression to the "old Pagan Servile State" based upon legalized slavery that had preceded the spread of Christianity in the early Middle Ages. Under the benign influence of the Catholic church, civilization had displaced this ancient system throughout western Europe in the form of a Distributist state grounded upon cooperative crafts and guilds and village societies of economically independent small proprietors. The few medieval restrictions upon economic freedom operated to prevent the growth of an economic oligarchy that could exploit the rest of the community. In this idyllic world the "restraints upon liberty were restraints designed for the preservation of liberty."[77]

Unfortunately for the modern Briton, the Protestant Reformation had dismantled "Christian civilization" in England. The redistribution of land among the middle classes after the confiscation of the monasteries in the mid-sixteenth century left a diminished and impoverished Crown unable to resist their encroachments upon the king's prerogative and upon the populace's economic rights. The majority of the population was dispossessed of land and capital, and the means of production were concentrated in the hands of a tiny sociopolitical elite. The civil wars and the Settlement of 1689 confirmed the new realities of power. Thus, Belloc determined, a system of economic exploitation of the working classes for the aggrandizement of a wealthy landed oligarchy was in place long before the onset of the Industrial Revolution. The industrialization of England took the pernicious form it did only because capitalism already dominated society by 1700. If, instead, England had been economically free, "industrial development . . . would have taken a cooperative form."[78]

For two centuries capitalism and capitalists had battled the instability inherent in the system with mixed results. But in the 1800s, the rise of rationalist bureaucratic organization on an unprecedented scale offered a temptingly simple yet permanent solution to their chronic predicament. Social reforms, providing financial security to placate a potentially revolutionary proletariat, could now be administered from a centrally directed civil service. The transition from a capitalist to a Servile State would allow the property-owning classes to continue to reap only slightly reduced dividends without a diminution in political control. The twentieth-century welfare state represented the final stage in the socioeconomic revolution begun inadvertently by Henry VIII in 1534.

According to Belloc, socialist dogma abetted capitalism in its transformation into the Servile State, for all reformers, especially socialist ones, recognized that the easiest way to remedy "insufficiency and insecurity" was to abrogate political freedom and impose order from above. Belloc allowed for subtle distinctions between a humanitarian socialist reformer, a practical socialist reformer—"a fool"—and the bureaucratically inclined socialist reformer, but he insisted they all, wittingly or unwittingly, aided in the establishment of the Servile State. The last type however shouldered a disproportionate share of the guilt. No one should imagine that the "so-called 'Socialist'" of this bureaucratic type had fallen into the Servile State by a miscalculation. Rather he had "fathered" it, welcoming its birth, because "he foresees his power over its future."[79] Belloc noted contemptuously of the Webbs that "'running' the poor is their hobby,"[80] and while his friend Chesterton might be willing "to let Mr. Sidney Webb look after the poor, if nobody else would look after them,"[81] he decidedly was not. The satisfaction of the aims of one Fabian would lead to the misery of millions, for a man like Mr. Webb "is disturbed by multitudinous things; and the prospect of a vast bureaucracy wherein the whole of life shall be scheduled and appointed to certain simple schemes deriving from the co-ordinate work of public clerks and marshalled by powerful heads of departments gives his small stomach a final satisfaction."[82]

The intellectual influence of *The Party System* and *The Servile State* is difficult to measure.[83] Belloc's dual critique sowed the seeds of doubt in so-called Radical Liberals intent on harnessing the power of the modern state to their reformist policies. Guild Socialist Maurice Reckitt recorded in his autobiography the devastating effects of the argument of *The Servile State*:

> I cannot overstate the impact of this book upon my mind, and in this I was but symptomatic of thousands of others who had passed through the same phases as I had. Belloc argued, with a rigorous cogency and with forceful illustration, that the whole allegedly socialist trend, which the Fabians were so fond of boasting that they had grafted upon Liberalism, was leading not to a community of free and equal citizens, not even to any true collectivism, but to the imposition upon the masses, as the price of the reforms by which their social condition was to be ameliorated, of a servile state, sundering them from the condition of those more prosperous members of the community not requiring to be subjected to such legislation. . . . That [Belloc's thesis] contained enough truth to blow the New Liberalism sky-high I was convinced.[84]

If the arguments of *The Servile State* were correct, all of New Liberalism's assumptions were turned inside out: legislation intended to lighten the burden of the disadvantaged, mitigate the worst excesses of capitalism, broaden political participation, and reform Parliament would have a paradoxical effect instead by institutionalizing a modern form of slavery and extending the power of a vulgar plutocracy.

A Vicious Circle of Mutual Advantage

Thus by 1912 Belloc had already stated in a clear and succinct fashion his assessment of Britain's modern predicament. But to convey to his readers the depth of these ills, their roots and the false assumptions and smug inertia to be overcome if they were to be cured, he relied upon a campaign of historical revisionism led by himself. The overthrow of orthodox British historiography was vital, for its story of Liberalism's uninterrupted progress provided a screen of legitimacy for the unjust twentieth-century social order and preempted all suggestions for dramatic metamorphosis.

In 1907 Belloc had read a history text for young boys that adhered to the Whig line by stressing that the modern English aristocracy was "old and rooted in the soil" and not a creation of the mid-sixteenth-century dissolution of the monasteries. At the time he was willing to overlook the omission, for as he noted, "I suppose these conventions must pass if history is to be a united thing."[85] After 1911 he was much less magnanimous. By that point he believed the scales had fallen from his eyes, and all had suddenly become clear. Whig history, or "official history" as he called it, was an integral part of the "system" that four years in Parliament had taught him to despise.[86] The capitalist organization of the economy, the social hierarchy, the bureaucratic state, and the contemporary political order were all reciprocally reinforcing. They, in turn, all depended upon the universal acceptance of a particular version of Britain's past as an unanswerable sanction of the status quo. This version was created and nourished by a small collection of university dons who received as a reward the seal of approval from the ruling oligarchy, stamping the national myth of Whig history as orthodoxy. In this cozy relationship all parties, and historical truth as well, were confined, in the words of Robert Speaight, "within a vicious circle of mutual advantage."[87]

Belloc believed he faced a daunting task. The tentacles of official history were intricately intertwined in the daily experience of every educated Englishman. "The historians whose works he had been given as textbooks, those who inform the fiction he knows, the classics of his tongue, the body of the literature with which he is familiar, are the historians in opposition to ourselves. Write down half a dozen names: Macaulay, Carlyle, Gibbon, Mommsen, Old Freeman, Motley, and the modern writer [G. M.] Trevelyan."[88] In England, with its stifling atmosphere of intellectual conformity that characterized "the modern phase of willful distortion," no trustworthy account of the sixteenth and seventeenth centuries vied for public acceptance for the simple reason that "no official historian over here will give the least countenance to Catholic, that is true history."[89] It was "weary work," Belloc lamented, "fighting this enormous mountain of ignorant wickedness" that constituted "tom-fool Protestant history."[90]

The immediate difficulty was twofold: both telling people what really happened *and* getting a skeptical audience to believe. Belloc likened the enormity of the challenge to "having to describe a journey round the world to people who believe in the flat earth theory, and while you are telling the ordinary facts you have at the same time to correct their absurd theory, otherwise the mere truth appears ridiculous to them."[91] It seemed clear enough to Belloc that the task of reeducation needed to begin on the ground floor with a "persistent re-writing of history," for the inherited tradition was "coloured." An identical "anti-Catholic bias" informed all official history. By this assertion, Belloc did not mean to suggest that orthodox narratives contained isolated inaccuracies or particular detailed falsehoods. The difficulty was more global. Official history conceived of all English development as "a process necessarily anti-Catholic." As such, the church was always cast as an institution "alien and hostile." Purveyors of this orthodoxy welcomed whatever seemed to lead to the modern state of affairs, especially the break with Rome and the withering away of the power of the Crown. Successive generations of official Whig historians had created a "whole social atmosphere around agreeable to false history, and instinctively rejecting truth."[92]

Catholicism was absolutely central to Belloc's entire project because it alone represented a true path to freedom away from the suffocating embrace of the modern state. Bureaucratic centralization and administrative efficiency were overtly Protestant phenomena. The rise of the English state in its present form began with the Tudors and their break with Rome. What historians passed off as the evolutionary expansion of freedom and prosperity since the 1530s was more accurately described as the forging of successive links in the shackles that now enslaved the common man. By offering a clear paradigmatic alternative to the Whig tradition, Catholic historiography promised to reorder the fundamental assumptions of English society and create in its wake a new cultural, political, and economic order. All that was required to ensure success was patience and unflagging diligence.

> Not only must we increase the volume of true history, but we must be perpetually challenging and correcting false. We cannot prevent any of the effects of a hostile atmosphere around us, whether it takes the form of neglect or abuse . . . or in general the untruth of the public balance; but we can, by widespread and diligent industry, undermine the position opposed to us. But we

need far more hands at work, and I think also a more robust antagonism to the official stuff presented to us.[93]

Until such time as new recruits stepped forward, Belloc continued to plow the furrow alone, sustained by a conviction that history was "a business of capital importance."[94]

The Role of Violence in the Reversion to the Normal: Belloc and the French Revolution

It is tempting to divide Belloc's histories into two discontinuous halves separated by the disillusionment with English politics of 1909–11 that ratified and deepened his earlier disillusionment with the Oxford establishment. He himself encouraged such bipartite categorization in the prefaces he appended to new editions of his older works, such as the 1928 reprint of *Robespierre*, a volume originally published in 1901. Twenty-six years after the fact, he apologized for some of his youthful and impetuous judgments.

> When I wrote this book, I had not, as I have now, a considerable and detailed acquaintance with what are called "representative institutions." I was at the time under the common illusion that it was not only possible but natural to combine these with democracy. I now know what a younger generation has thoroughly learned and experienced, that Parliaments are the negation of democracy, and save in a senatorial and aristocratic fashion can never work well in an ancient, complex and highly civilized society.[95]

By 1931 his political alienation was such that he rejoiced that the "grotesque election" in October of that year had dealt "another heavy blow at Parliamentarianism."[96]

Although his enthusiasm for modern representative institutions had cooled by degrees over the years since the Oxford fiasco, his allegiance to his reading of the principles of the French Revolution remained unshaken.[97] *Danton* (1899), *Robespierre* (1901), *Marie Antoinette* (1909), and *The French Revolution* (1911) were united by a consistent political philosophy that was carried over, in a slightly altered form, into his post-1914 writings on British history. Belloc's sympathy with the spirit of the French Revolution stemmed from his acceptance of Rousseau's description of popular sovereignty in *The Social Contract*, where the only source of all authority within a community was the "Common Will," not "the organic character of a native oligarchy" or "the mechanical arrangement of election by majorities."[98]

Thus Belloc found it unfortunate that in large communities the expression of the popular will became increasingly difficult as the central government gradually assumed a life of its own, with interests often antagonistic to the desires of its citizens. In such circumstances, the attachment of the community to the "rights of the Common Will" must be satisfied by "submitting the central government . . . to occasional insurrection and to violent corporate expressions of opinion which shall readjust the relations between governor and the governed."[99] As Belloc saw it, the French Revolution was the prototypical example of just such a periodic readjustment.

In his estimation, the events of 1789–94 were a reversion to the "normal." They constituted a "sudden and violent return to those conditions which are the necessary bases of health in any political community." The last period of good health in Europe had ended with the High Middle Ages, when Catholic civilization was infected with the spirochete of the Reformation and the virus of the Renaissance. The Revolution of 1789, with its ideal of true democracy in an equal and just society, attempted to remold Western culture into its former image. Those who sought to resist these forces for change "thought the Middle Ages were dead, when suddenly the spirit of the Middle Ages, the spirit of enthusiasm and of faith, the Crusade, came out of the tomb and routed them."[100]

Belloc allowed that the Jacobins had pushed the changes too far, for they failed to comprehend that it was possible to remake society while leaving certain fundamentals untouched. The Revolution "did more and possibly worse: it rebuilt from the foundation," and, as a consequence, "how many unquestioned dogmas were suddenly brought out into broad daylight!" As a devout Catholic, Belloc was disturbed by the religious doubt and anticlericalism that accompanied Jacobin ideology, but he still judged the French Revolution to have been the "noblest" experiment in modern political history.[101] This verdict was made easier by the paradoxical effect the upheaval appeared to have had upon Gallic Roman Catholicism. Belloc believed the Jacobins' vocal opposition to the church rekindled a nearly extinguished flame of French religious enthusiasm.[102] He may have thought it inevitable that any attempt, no matter how avowedly secularist, to reinvent medieval democracy should also reawaken the religion that had provided the entire framework for society in the Middle Ages. That this should occur was in no way anomalous, for Belloc insisted that, just as English anti-Catholic sentiment was fundamentally political rather than religious, the Jacobin hostility to Rome was institutional rather than philosophical. "No quarrel can be found between the theory of the revolution and that of the church," he declared, but only "between the revolution in action and the authorities of Catholicism."[103]

Belloc was quite mild in his criticism of the violent excesses of the Revolution, while attempting to distance his heroes from them. Thanks to Danton the pragmatist, the Terror had performed much useful work.[104] Robespierre, who for a few months was the guiding force of the "Renaissance of European democracy," Belloc defended by claiming that the reader of his biography would discover that this noble Jacobin protested nearly all of the most famous of the prosecutions of the Committee of Public Safety. In fact, that sanguinary body regarded Belloc's Robespierre as a "danger," one who "attempted to put a curb on the Revolution." It followed logically that those who finally overthrew and guillotined him were "men determined to push the Terror to a further extreme."[105] But Belloc's apparent equanimity in the face of extremism and gratuitous violence in Revolutionary France did not extend to a recipe for modern Britain, at least not in 1899. He warned his readers that they might find it difficult to sympathize with the methods of the Jacobins because no contemporary Englishman could understand how far "deadening conservatism" had been pushed on the Continent in the late 1780s. During the period of the great French upheaval,

> the constitution of England and the habits of her lawyers and politicians were still, for all their vices, the most flexible in Europe. Even Pitt could tinker at the representative system, and an abominable penal code could be softened without upsetting the whole scheme of English criminal law. To this day we notice in England the most fundamental changes introduced, so to speak, into an unresisting medium: witness those miniature revolutions, the Income Tax and Employers' Liability, which are so silent, and which yet produce results so immeasurable.[106]

It is clear that a decade before his break with the Liberal party Belloc still invested hope in wayward England's ability to right herself by small, incremental changes. But his Edwardian studies of Revolutionary France signaled to anyone paying close attention Belloc's minuscule stake in the Liberal investment in parliamentary procedures and institutions as well as a certain fascination with violence and violent change.

The experiences of 1909–11 shattered the remnants of a youthful faith in Parliament's competence, or even desire, to initiate substantive social, political, and economic reform. It now seemed clear that government had evolved into the representative of a single-class interest group at odds with the Common Will. Belloc had anticipated that Asquith and Lloyd George would place themselves at the head of a popular movement sparking the "occasional insurrection" necessary to "readjust the relations between the governor and the governed." But the twin crises of the "Peoples's Budget" and the Lords' veto, while emitting large quanta of light, had given off very little heat. So in a certain sense 1909–11 was a crossroads for Bellocian historiography. Thereafter, although his political convictions remained constant, he dispensed with whatever allegiance he had ever felt for the aim of reform via traditional parliamentary avenues. His subsequent writings emphasized the need for a complete break with the past, a complete overhaul of British society in contrast to the relatively minor repairs he had formerly advocated.

However, as was the case in the development of Belloc's sudden antagonism toward academic historians in 1895, the speed of conversion was more apparent than real. As in the earlier instance, his disillusionment sprang from fertile ground. Belloc's eventual estrangement from political Liberalism was almost certainly inevitable from the outset. He could not have long tolerated what he saw as its timid insistence on traditional forms and emphasis of theory over practice, both of which seemed to paralyze all suggestions of genuine reform, its finely colored distinctions that promoted indecision and compromise by obscuring the differences between good and evil, and its preference for continuity and order at the expense of the dangerous fluidity necessary to initiate any fundamental change.

In 1899 Belloc foreshadowed his later break with the Liberal party and its methods in his appraisal of the Girondins of Revolutionary France. It seemed their great fault was that "the pure theory which they justly maintained to be the one right government, could not meet Europe in arms." In the end they were shoved aside to make room for men of action, whose sometimes brutal methods the circumstances justified.

> Danton had forced on a dictatorship, and gave it the method of the Terror. But the Girondins, though they had been compelled to give up so much, yet refused to follow the necessary path. They refused the conscription; a volunteer army was the only one tolerable to free men. They refused diplomacy; it involved a secret method, and was of its nature based on compromise. They refused the requisitions to the armies, the forced taxes, the hegemony of Paris, the preponderance of talent or genius in the committees—in a word, they refused to sanction anything, however necessary, in that crisis, which they would not have sanctioned in a time of order and of a pure republic.[107]

Blinded by the same prejudices, the modern Girondins, led by Asquith, were similarly ineffectual and fated for extinction. Belloc was later to translate his pre-1910 image of a Liberalism passively immobilized by theoretical scruples into one of deliberate foot-dragging in the service of self-interest, this substitution of one incarnation for another serving simply to further underscore the incompatibility of the Liberal party and a radical Catholic agenda.

Made manifest in his writings on the French Revolution, Belloc's toleration of, even fascination with, violence was of a piece with his blanket rejections of Whig historiography, incremental reformism via parliament, and the augmentation of the state. Certainly the issue of violence and its role in effecting change had always presented difficulties for Whig historians, thus their preference for the "Bloodless" Revolution of 1688 over the sanguinary affair of 1642–49 and their concentration upon constitutional development at the expense of the imperial record with its unsightly succession of battles and conquests. The early twentieth-century shift of academic attention to administrative history as a reaction against the traditional Whig panorama was hardly more appealing to Belloc. True, it downplayed representative institutions as the center of action, but it paid even less heed to the role of violence in British history by pushing the evolution of centralized, bureaucratized government to the foreground. One continuity replaced another. Belloc wanted to emphasize discontinuity, the contributions of violence to the break with Britain's Catholic heritage, and the potential for violence to repair the breach.

Belloc's alternative histories reflected the tensions within late Victorian and Edwardian Liberalism, where the antistatism of the Manchester School and Herbert Spencer mingled with the anti-parliamentary, bureaucratic sentiments of the advocates of National Efficiency. Like other young radicals, Belloc was dissatisfied with the Gladstonian legacy but could never quite reconcile himself to the New Liberal attempt to balance the old emphasis on individuality and personal freedom with an enhanced role for the state as the agent for the collective promotion of personal character building via social reconstruction. A preoccupation with the "Catholic community" of pre-Tudor England ruled out a complete acceptance of atomistic notions of liberty, yet he feared the encroachments of the Servile State most of all. Half measures, like the New Liberal compromise, promised the worst of both worlds. Only the violent tendencies that seemed to threaten in 1909 could topple the old order. After the anticlimax of 1911, Belloc realized that ideas must necessarily precede action; he would begin by preparing the public consciousness to view violence as acceptable. Recognition of the catalytic nature of violence in history would interrupt the complacency with which modern Britain accepted the evolutionary Protestant version of its past.

But while recasting violence's pedigree, Belloc either failed to comprehend or refused to acknowledge that the ouster of the Girondins by the Jacobins—much like Lloyd George's toppling of Asquith in 1916—ushered in a state more powerful and intrusive than its predecessor. Violence was clearly a double-edged sword.

Undoing the Transformation of England

It was natural that after the publication of *The Party System* and *The Servile State* Belloc should turn his attentions to British history. His early work on the French Revolution contained a critique in embryo of the "official" version of Britain's past, and now he was ready to undertake the more direct approach. A concise and readable history of England from the Catholic point of view was something Belloc had always wanted to do, but he had hesitated because "such simple condensed history brings one up against one million disputed little points of fact, which involve immense labour in settling."[108] Four years in the Commons had alerted him to the insignificance of such reservations. The crisis conditions of contemporary British society could be understood only in relation to what he labeled the "transformation of England" between 1525 and 1689. Desperate times called for reckless measures, and, his antiacademic bias intact, the more mature Belloc was willing to risk the expert critic's "endless modifications" of his own sweeping historical outline because he knew that his general statements retained "the main truth."[109]

The lesson Belloc intended to drive home was the direct link between the events of those 160 years and the political corruption and economic misery of the twentieth century, with the specter of the modern Servile State lurking menacingly just over the horizon. Traditionally the Reformation, the civil wars, and the Glorious Revolution were grouped together in standard works of history as the three great summits in a heroic age. But, claimed Belloc, since the "transformation of England was essentially the act of a few men in power, working with difficulty against a confused popular reluctance," to identify these pivotal events with the national will constituted the most egregious of falsehoods.[110] "The old official Whig caricature of the past, wherein any revolt of wealthy men against the Crown is praised," stood the facts upon their head when it described, as a stage in the progress of freedom, the exchange of the village democracy of the Middle Ages for the rule of a closed caste of landed oligarchs assembled in Parliament to pursue their own private interests.[111]

Belloc actually began his reinterpretation of the nation's past in reverse order. In 1915 he produced for the Catholic Publication Society an eleventh volume to supplement John Lingard's ten-volume *History of England*, which had taken the story up to 1689 before the author's death in 1851. Lingard, a Catholic priest described by none other than G. P. Gooch as a "serious historian," had originally undertaken the *History* "to make the Catholic cause appear respectable in the eyes of the British public." He was "studiously reserved in his judgments of people and events . . . how different was his cool Catholicism from the Ultramontane rigour that came in with Pius IX."[112] Ultramontane rigor rather than cool Catholicism more nearly characterized Belloc's beliefs, and his completion of the series deviated considerably from his predecessor's moderation.

As required by the analysis of *The Servile State*, Belloc was determined to present the years 1689 to 1910 as a period of decay for the aristocratic victors of the Glorious Revolution, two centuries of illusory short-term gain at the expense of the long-term health and prosperity of the British polity. He was prepared to admit that an aristocratic oligarchy, "while still in its prime," was equal to the challenge of governing a state effectively and efficiently. It was clearly superior to a democracy or monarchy in coordinating its interests and in mobilizing its resources against a foreign menace. "Its curves of change are deliberate, and it remains cool in judgment in those periods of fever which deliver its foreign rivals, despotic [Louis XIV] or democratic [Revolutionary France], into its hands."[113] In addition, aristocratic rule grounded in capitalist ideology was a boon, at least initially, to economic strength, for, as Belloc observed, while the century-and-a-half period of development lasted, "England as a whole increased her wealth out of all past measure and beyond any possible rivalry." The nation was able to put that wealth to good use, funding a further extension of production and commerce while also providing for the defense of the "mercantile organism she had created."[114]

But inevitable failure was inherent in the aristocratic ethos, for it was "incapable of reformation from within, for the mass of its citizens are trained to no initiative. Its final and lethal change, which is a sinking of the Oligarchy into a mere Plutocracy, comes upon it almost unobserved and always uncorrected." Having enshrined capitalism as the source of its power and authority, England's ruling elite was helpless to prevent its eventual transformation into a vulgar plutocracy. By 1900 this slow bleeding of the "aristocratic spirit" had left the ruling classes "within grave peril of complete decay," for the only method remaining at their disposal for the retention of undiluted political control in the mature stage of capitalism was the introduction of the Servile State.[115]

Accommodating specific events to this rigid outline of British history—an outline he was to employ again in *A Shorter History of England* (1934)—made for some rather unusual and provocative interpretations. Echoing the ancient arguments of Bolingbroke and the Country party, Belloc asserted that the great evil of the wars of Marlborough was the creation of the national debt and the Bank of England to finance these sanguinary ventures, thus solidifying the link between Whig oligarchy and state.[116] Extending in both directions the chronological boundaries of what came to be identified during the interwar period as the Namierite view of mid-eighteenth-century British politics, Belloc equated the party strife of the Age of Queen Anne with that of his own day, a charade he had already exposed in *The Party System*. Then as now it was merely stage-managed politics within a group arbitrarily divided between Whig and Tory. Nominal opponents were so "closely allied by marriage, friendship and patronage" that "no social lines of cleavage distinguished one party from another." This dearth of practical and ideological friction within the eighteenth-century ruling classes was bequeathed across two hundred years to reappear as the Edwardian "party system" that Belloc loathed.[117]

He explained away the Seven Years' War as a Protestant coalition (England and Prussia) versus a Catholic one (France and Austria)[118] and portrayed George III as an unsuccessful savior of the embryonic nineteenth-century proletariat with his attempt to reverse the work of the Glorious Revolution and "transform the oligarchic character of the English polity into a more popular thing."[119] The long struggle with Revolutionary France clearly represented "a test whether a society formed on upper-class government and direction by the wealthy should survive, or perish at the hands of an all-embracing movement for human freedom."[120] England's final triumph in 1815 stamped her as a reactionary model for all of continental Europe in the nineteenth century.

Nineteenth-century Britain had witnessed an explosion of wealth that brought in its train an accelerating rate of aristocratic decay.[121] Industrial capitalism created a rich and influential class with no connections to land as the source of their power. The abortive absorption of this vulgar, unassimilable plutocracy into the ruling class sapped the vitality of the aristocratic ethos, endangering the future of two hundred years of landed, oligarchical legitimacy. Taxing to the limit his penchant for drawing provocative conclusions based upon little evidence, Belloc maintained that the initial response to the accompanying aristocratic sense of unease over their dwindling authority was "the capturing of the masses by a network of official administration and of police control, the like of which [was] quite unknown elsewhere in Europe."[122] This stopgap measure was ultimately succeeded by a more permanent solution to "stave off a crisis which threatens from the insecurity and insufficiency of the mass of Englishmen and from the discontent which is almost coextensive with the huge proletarian majority."[123] This temporary response, that is, the piecemeal introduction of social welfare programs, foreshadowed the coming of the Servile State, the final answer to the Bellocian version of the "crisis of the aristocracy."

Having analyzed effect in his history of the eighteenth and nineteenth centuries, by 1916 Belloc resolved to turn his attentions to cause.[124] As *The Servile State* had shown, his real interests lay in the period 1525–1689, where he located the seeds of modern decadence. Therefore, he undertook for Methuen publishers a multivolume *History of England* from its origins, choosing as his theme the rise, apotheosis, and eventual destruction of Catholic civilization in England. Belloc always considered this arduous, thankless task as his most significant and lasting contribution to historiography. He complained privately that no one would read it and that its many volumes promised few royalties, and yet the comprehensive and systematic refutation of the Whig interpretation of English history in his magnum opus would demonstrate beyond all doubt that official history would no longer go unchallenged. With four volumes appearing between 1925 and 1931, the *History* amounted to a greatly expanded and more detailed version of the interpretation originally sketched out in *The Servile State*.[125]

From the outset he stressed the roots of English laws and institutions in Roman civilization and the growth of a Catholic civilization upon that durable but imperfect template. Under the influence of the church, English culture had realized its supreme moment, the High Middle Ages. The full credit for this remarkable and unprecedented achievement of freedom and happiness went to Catholic philosophy alone. "There was no economic reason for the decay of the old servitude and the increase of personal position and freedom in what had become the mass of the unfree. It is Mind which determines the change of Society, and it was because the mind at work was a Catholic mind that the slave became a serf and was on his way to becoming a peasant and a fully free man—a man free economically as well as politically."[126] The moral and spiritual unity of society forged in the thirteenth century by the Catholic church compared favorably with the flimsy political and economic cohesiveness of modern Britain. Belloc argued that Catholic civilization weathered the trauma of the Black Death better than Edwardian society tolerated the Great War of 1914–18 because the earlier disaster "fell upon an active, hopeful, and vigorous culture, animated by one triumphant religion."[127]

Belloc generally affirmed, in the idealist tradition, that all great upheavals must begin as a change of heart and mind. "First comes in every great revolution of European affairs, a spiritual change; next, bred by this, a change in social philosophy and therefore in political arrangement; lastly, the economic change which political rearrangement has rendered possible."[128] However, in the pivotal event that forever altered England's future for the worse, it was incumbent upon Belloc to reverse the sequence. The Protestant Reformation, which overturned the splendor of the Middle Ages, he explained away as essentially a revolution imposed from above by a small group motivated by the naked desire for booty.[129] In this one historical instance, economic change (the transfer of monastery holdings into the hands of a wealthy oligarchy) catalyzed political change (the shrinkage of the power and influence of the Crown), with parallel shifts in the intellectual, moral, and spiritual spheres lagging far behind. It was unacceptable to Belloc that there could have arisen genuine popular enthusiasm for the overthrow of Catholic hegemony in early modern England. Instead he insisted that the "English people" as a whole sided with the ancient religion, for they possessed "a general instinctive feeling that the religious revolution would—as, in fact, it did—depress the masses to the advantage of the rich."[130]

Careful always to exonerate the "popular" monarchy, Belloc depicted Henry VIII as the dupe of Wolsey and Anne Boleyn and Elizabeth as the innocent tool of that nouveau riche upstart William Cecil, who ruled solely in the interests of the gentry. Because the Tudors reigned but did not rule, government policies in the second half of the sixteenth century abetted the dispossession of the English yeoman and peasant and the aggrandizement of the wealthiest classes. The lamentable result was the ebbing of the power of the Crown, the last sincere champion of the mass of the nation against these indiscriminate depredations.

Belloc had originally planned to take his *History of England* up to 1900 in seven or eight volumes.[131] But he never got past the fourth, which ended in 1612, still in the midst of the great "transformation of England." He eventually repaired the seventy-seven-year gap in his work (his addition to the Lingard series began with 1689) by the publication of a succession of biographies of the last three Stuart kings: *Charles the First* (1933), *The Last Rally* (1940, published in the

United States in 1939 as *Charles II*), and *James the Second* (1928). In *A Shorter History of England* (1934) he spliced all the parts together in a continuous narrative from prehistory to the Great War.

As interpreted by Belloc, the struggle between the Stuarts and the wealthy oligarchs of parliament bore a striking resemblance to his portrayal of the French Revolution, but with the roles each side traditionally occupied in the Whig historical canon turned upside down. The landed classes became the villains, posing as the sole representatives of the nation. By contrast, Charles I ruled "for the advantage, not of a class but of all."[132] In the circumstances of the seventeenth century the monarchy embodied the closest possible approximation to an expression of the "rights of the Common Will." The Crown, not parliament, represented the nation, and the Stuarts' intentions in the period 1625–88, like those of the Jacobins of 1789–94, were a reversion to the "normal," which, of course, was Bellocian shorthand for the harmonious Catholic society of the High Middle Ages. The seventeenth-century monarchy represented the last and best hope for a benign alternative to the rapacious rule of the gentry in the age of the aristocracy.

Belloc maintained that the same narrow window of opportunity existed in Britain of his own day. The one "real alternative" to the modern conduct of the affairs of the British state by organized wealth was nothing less than a substantive increase in the personal authority of the Crown. A resurgence of monarchical constitutional powers represented the surest remedy for the ailment "plutocracy" or, "in another aspect, servitude."[133] Belloc had little fear of a tyrannical abuse of monarchical power. A modern reassertion of the traditional prerogatives of the Crown would simply mimic the benevolent intentions of the later Stuarts. Charles II and James II had entertained no desire to impose an absolutist despotism on the model of Louis XIV. Rather, they had aimed at reintroducing the medieval "popular monarchy" with its attendant economic and political freedoms. But by 1660 that was a virtual impossibility, for four generations of anti-Catholic propaganda had secured the position of the Anglican church, the natural ally of the wealthy gentry in their opposition to the Crown.

Belloc sculpted his historical arguments to demonstrate that English anti-Catholicism arose and persisted solely upon the grounds of political and economic expedience rather than because of any genuine philosophical rupture. The ruling oligarchy of the late seventeenth century, indifferent to religious doctrine or creed, "had, for the most part, no conclusion on things unseen. . . . Yet their motives were not indifferent to Catholicism though they were indifferent to doctrines. The main body of the gentry, the lawyers, the wealthier merchants, felt instinctively that the spirit of Catholicism was a popular spirit making for popular monarchy: that it would combat the idolatry of rules (upon which legal and Parliamentary encroachment depended); and that it made against oligarchy . . . [which] was the very essence of the Revolution."[134] Arising from this unwholesome atmosphere, the Glorious Revolution was merely the final chapter in a story that had acquired the momentum of inevitability fifty years before. And in the hands of Belloc, British history was transformed into nothing more than a prolonged postscript to the Reformation, the tragic sequelae of a chronic, debilitating disease.

Lecturing in an Empty Hall?

There is no avoiding the fact that Hilaire Belloc was awash in contradictions. Particularly in his youth he posed as the advocate of objectivity in history, the supremacy of facts, and painstaking archival research as the sole route to truth. Later he would author an antipositivist essay entitled "Science as an Enemy of the Truth" and cast himself in the role of the champion of irrational historical understanding through artistic intuition, supplied with adequate source material by faith and legend.[135] He despised "orthodox" Whig historiography for its biased web of deceit, yet he admired Gibbon and Macaulay as much for methodology as for style. He openly vilified academic historians but spent two years of his life trying to become one and five decades mourning his failure. Denouncing within the pages of *The Servile State* the malignant consequences of the enshrinement of 1689 by Liberal historiography, Belloc could at times succumb to an almost Whiggish sort of nationalism, as in 1939, when (perhaps with the threat of Nazi Germany in mind) he wrote that patriots should not complain of English aristocratic government, since it had made the country "immensely stronger and wealthier and more important in every way."[136] A modern student of Bellocian politics points to the "consistent strain linking the surface contradictions in Belloc's personal perspective" yet still describes his subject as an unstable mixture of Jacobitism and Jacobinism.[137]

But the consistencies far outweigh the contradictions. No procrustean manipulations are necessary to demonstrate that Belloc's brand of radicalism, a derivative of his religion, emerged basically intact from his years as an active politician and lived, along with their author, to a ripe old age. For a time, mesmerized by Liberalism's amorphous post-Gladstonian state of flux that seemed to promise accommodation of any eccentricity of the left, he mistakenly believed that his volatile combination of English radicalism, French revolutionary ideology, and Catholic dogma could find expression through the Radical wing of the Liberal party. Membership in Parliament left him bitterly disillusioned, but only with traditional institutions as the potential vehicle for reordering contemporary British politics and culture.

Belloc was convinced that the seriousness of modern Britain's "grievous peril" was compounded by an unconscious resistance to any just and reasonable solution.[138] The unchallenged anti-Catholic, pro-capitalist stranglehold of official British historiography blocked any thoughtful consideration of a Distributist answer to the menace of the Servile State.[139] The public's ignorance about the past dampened their enthusiasm for reform and confirmed the monopoly of political power and economic benefits by a tiny ruling elite. Under the circumstances, a revision of history must precede any substantive sociopolitical change. The subject of *The Servile State* might indeed be, according to Belloc's own reckoning, "the chief political matter of our time," but unless he grounded that book of analysis and polemic in a detailed and thorough reinterpretation of British history, its influence would remain restricted, for a historiographic campaign that questioned accepted first principles constituted the most potent form of appeal to the common man.[140]

For this reason (along with expectations of increased monetary compensation), Belloc switched to writing English histories after 1912. He saw himself as a pioneer and a prophet. His task of historical revisionism would inspire others to follow his example, and the results would constitute a quiet intellectual revolution to prepare the way for the violent political upheaval to follow. "The work to be undertaken is laborious, but it still lies almost untouched, though the beginnings of a reform in this are almost apparent. . . . Remember that the effect of such [revisionist] writing taken up by an increasing number of men and continuously is incalculable."[141]

His feud with academic history, fueled by his All Souls' rebuff, fed directly into his interest in maximizing the political efficacy of historical revisionism. The disturbing conclusions of his books would possess no attractions for the closed club of university historians with their vested interest in the stability of the present system. He appealed to a broader audience and championed the literary style appropriate to such readers. Adoption of academic forms combined with a rejection of Whiggish content would consign him to a purgatory where neither the professors nor the general public would read his works. Conversely, the artistic presentation of provocatively unorthodox history provided the means to bypass the Latin of the priesthood and speak the gospel directly to the congregation in the vernacular.

His interest in reaching the largest possible audience, originating in his unpleasant Oxford experience, long antedated his political disillusionment and withdrawal from the Liberal party. In a 1908 Commons debate, a proposed education bill drew Hilaire Belloc M.P.'s fire when he declared that "there is not machinery for teaching history properly in the Universities, and still less in the great public schools of this country." The facts of history had been distorted to reinforce the Protestant Whig bias of the nation. Such a situation at the universities was at least tolerable "because the effect of University is vastly different from the effect of school teaching. The former is critical and falls upon a mature mind; the latter is formative and moulds a mind yet plastic."[142] In 1934 he attempted to remedy this deplorable state of affairs with a Catholic corrective, his *Shorter History of England*, intended as a secondary school textbook "to be read at the time of life when we receive our strongest and most lasting impressions."[143]

Belloc relied upon some approximation of youthful openness in his adult audience as well. Receptiveness was essential, for, in his view, he was combating generations of Whig indoctrination with its false equation of freedom, prosperity, progress, and Liberalism. But he swam with the current as well as against it, for the Chesterbelloc political doctrine with its attack on the Servile State represented a potent modern form of traditional Liberal anticollectivism.[144] Hence Belloc's politics acquired a certain amount of mainstream legitimacy through their direct link with the legacies of Cobden and Herbert Spencer.[145] And while his anticollectivist dogma may have alienated many of the self-proclaimed young saviors of Liberalism with their agendas for centrally orchestrated social reform, these same New Liberals were undeniably attracted to the anticapitalist, republican strains of his message.[146]

The key to sustained influence upon sympathetic minds was public visibility. Toward that goal Belloc flaunted his unorthodox dogmatisms in order to flush out his real enemies, the academic historians, to do battle in full view of the gallery. On completing the second volume of his *History of England* he evinced the hope that it "would excite as much controversy as the first."[147] Belloc maintained that the dons had had "everything their own way for so long that repeated challenge is beginning to tell on their nerves. And yet how easy it is to do the trick! One only has to change the emphasis, and bring out things which they had either suppressed or never heard of. With these two simple instruments in hand one can torture Dons to the limit of human endurance."[148] Nevertheless, all of his tactics of annoyance could not cajole the most prestigious scholarly journals into refuting his works.

There were other avenues open, however. Because the *English Historical Review* consistently refrained from taking notice of any of his mature books on English history, the "official" historians resorted to unofficial routes to answer Belloc's root-and-branch revisionism. But articles like T. F. Tout's unsigned 1925 *Times Literary Supplement* review of the first volume of *A History of England* only added to the author's indignation. After making the standard obeisance to Belloc's "great literary gifts," Tout attacked the general theses of the book as little more than poorly substantiated advocacy. Belloc's "old fashioned view of the functions of an historian" led to "eloquent and attractive preaching" rather than a "scientific point of view. . . . The plain truth is that Mr. Belloc in dealing with remote ages shows that he is without any real historical feeling. His atmosphere is a modern atmosphere, the personal atmosphere of a gifted man of letters, who would be well advised to adopt any other vehicle than history for expounding his point of view."[149] In the face of such blanket dismissals, Belloc endured a continual sense of frustration at his inability to come to close grips with his foe. He suspected that the anonymous Tout review was written by a university don, but it simply drowned him with syrupy praise of his style, then, after warning him off their exclusive preserve, contradicted his book's main points without offering specific negative proofs.[150]

Belloc once stated that rewriting English history came under the heading of a challenge that "risks violent opposition" but that had the weight of truth on its side.[151] In the end, the opposition became more of a necessity than a "risk," for Bellocian "truth" was too little visible without it. He courted controversies to draw attention to himself, his books, and his ideas, since otherwise, "no one ever reads things which are fundamentally Catholic in tone in this country," for the "Catholic standpoint in general history, or economics, or sociology strikes them only as a boring eccentricity."[152] He was indeed, as he claimed, a "publicist" for his personal understanding of the truth. When on the rare occasion his histories were attacked openly and in detail, as in 1937 by the Cambridge medievalist G. G. Coulton, Belloc clearly enjoyed the publicity and appreciated the entire cause célèbre, milking it for all it was worth.[153]

This link in his mind between notoriety and effectiveness partially explains the origins of Belloc's famous, aggressively self-advertising and prolonged refutation of H. G. Wells's *Outline of History* (1920). The two men were old friends, but that did little to dampen the apparent ferocity of this six-year combat of words. The prime targets of Belloc's displeasure were Wells's unsympathetic handling of the Roman Catholic church and his uncritical acceptance of the Darwinian theory of natural selection, and to demolish the latter, Belloc marshaled an entire compendium of nonscientific opinion.[154] Somehow, despite the deadly seriousness of this very public disagreement over first principles, the whole affair retained throughout the light air of a media circus sideshow. The playful side of the encounter and the ad hominem character of many of the arguments were in keeping with Belloc's fixation on publicity, and both are captured in his private 1926 postmortem.

> Wells . . . published a popular outline of history by way of attack upon the Christian religion. I skinned him carefully and slowly as did Apollo Marsyas showing that he had read little, knew nothing and could not think. I published my criticism serially in a number of syndicated small papistical papers which nobody ever sees. Nevertheless Wells went mad and published a very violent pamphlet against me calling me all manner of names, and saying particularly that I had invented the attack on Darwinism and that there were no European World authorities opposed to Natural Selection. I took up the challenge and printed a list of such au-

thorities, enough to convince a blind man that Natural Selection was dead. He has now retired bandaged, is telling everybody that he refuses to read my pamphlet, also that he is sick of the whole affair, which I can well believe. But he will yet take his revenge perhaps by the aid of bravos or perhaps by tripping me up on a dark night.[155]

Wells, with his antiliberal sympathies, was not the main enemy, but his book did offer a tempting target and an opportunity for a wider dissemination of Bellocian arguments.

The great fear that his work would be ignored haunted Belloc. *The Servile State* had sold extremely well, but in the 1920s and 1930s he worried constantly that each of his new histories would languish on the shelves.[156] The importance of rewriting English history was to tell people the truth, but if his audience dried up, "it is like giving a clear and loud lecture in an empty hall—an experience I have often had, and not an inspiriting one."[157] He always mourned the fact that what he considered his most important work, his four volume *History of England*, failed to attract a large following.[158] But his biographies, though narrower in scope and sloppier in execution, carried essentially the same arguments in piecemeal and, despite his consistently gloomy prognostications, continued to sell in respectable numbers.[159]

At least one academic experienced uncase about the potential influence of Belloc's historical interpretations among the less well-informed. T. F. Tout advised caution instead of complacency when he noted that "it is perhaps being over-serious to take Mr. Belloc so seriously. But there is a grave danger lest the unlearned reader, attracted by his style and assured by his dogmatism will take him at his word and simply accept his theories as a serious contribution to historical learning." Responsible historians had to maintain a constant vigil so that they could "assure such [naive and susceptible] readers that the very contrary is the case."[160]

By the late 1930s Belloc thought he detected within academia a deepening sense of the unease and defensiveness that had colored Tout's earlier admonition. Desperate for the least intimation of his influence, in 1940 he chuckled with the satisfaction of the self-deluded over the story of Auberon Herbert, the son of one of his oldest friends, who on going up to Balliol was asked by the dons what history he had read. "He said he had read sundry people including myself. When they heard my name they burst into roars of laughter. They still feel secure though rattled. They will not feel secure for long for my history has done the trick."[161] The dons were caught up in the general interwar reaction against Liberalism sweeping Britain along with the rest of Europe. It comforted Belloc to believe that the university guardians of the Whig intellectual tradition were "beginning to understand that the tide ha[d] turned and that their old confidence [was] misplaced."[162]

Belloc's own confidence in the survivability of his unorthodox message waxed and waned with his mood. His historiography of opposition had begun "by seeming nearly eccentric," and by 1941, after decades of hammering away, he was "afraid [it] has not got very far along the road to recognition." But he steadfastly held that "when any truth is told in history some proportion of it gradually seeps through."[163] A judgment such as that of the mainstream *Spectator*, suggesting that the second volume of Belloc's *History of England* "open[ed] up a new view, and one which can not be neglected, of the Middle Ages," indicated that there was indeed room for this sort of cautious optimism. Belloc clung to the belief that "if you peg away long enough something happens and often, surprisingly more than you intended." The effect sometimes appeared "at second or third hand" removed from the cause. On the eve of the Second World War, Belloc remembered how before the First he had tried to connect in the mind of the public "the two ideas of the Reformation and our present horrible industrial chaos." Then the futility of it all resembled "telling them that all physical disease came from riding bicycles." But now, after more than forty years of historical revisionism, he was convinced that the familial connections between the present capitalist system and the Protestant Reformation had "now become a commonplace," though regrettably, in the interim "everybody has forgotten the distinguished author!"[164]

Belloc's modern obscurity as a historian provides prima facie evidence that he represents a road not taken. Certainly modern academics regard his work with derision—a fact that would not have failed to satisfy Belloc.[165] Yet, on reflection, he remains not quite such an eccentric dead end after all. Strands of his arguments reappear in the work of Arthur Bryant, arguably the most widely read of post-1945 British historians. Although starting from Catholic rather than socialist premises, Belloc's blanket condemnation of all

British history after 1600 dovetailed in some particulars with parallel pronouncements from the Webbs, G. D. H. Cole, or R. H. Tawney. Belloc's precocious discovery of the inherent potential of literary historiographical form as a cudgel with which to beat his Whig adversaries about the head antedated Lytton Strachey's own. Undoubtedly neither the Webbs, nor Cole, nor Tawney, nor even Strachey would have admitted to any relation between their own work and that of Belloc, yet the broader parallels in intention and in negative impact upon Liberal orthodoxy appear virtually indistinguishable.

H. G. Wells believed that interest in Belloc's interpretation of history extended far beyond Catholic circles.[166] In 1908 Hilaire Belloc M.P. had discounted the idea that socialist by-election successes might undercut his political support because, as he phrased it, "my Liberalism is so advanced."[167] As if to ratify this self-appraisal, A. L. Rowse credited Belloc with influencing an entire generation of like-minded historians, journalists, and novelists and also with anticipating the leftist economic and political critiques of our own day.[168] Early evidence of the latter is George Orwell's flattering reference to *The Servile State* in a 1940 article in *Time and Tide*.[169] But certainly the more immediate impact of his work was its contribution to the sapping of the foundations of Edwardian Liberalism. His analysis of the social and political structure of modern Britain along with the historical interpretation that gave the analysis depth exposed, to his own satisfaction and that of many others, the Gladstonian variant of Liberalism as founded upon a fraudulent recollection of the sixteenth and seventeenth centuries. Guild Socialism and Syndicalism both drew inspiration and nourishment from this historically grounded critique.[170] Belloc also partially disarmed the New Liberalism by proclaiming that all of its hopes for a resurrection of the party through a reordering of the Gladstonian ethos would lead instead to a further, possibly irreversible, ossification of Britain's unequal system for the distribution of power and rewards.

Liberal historiography, much like Liberalism itself, faced a crossroads at the end of the nineteenth century. It could continue to reproduce the inherited version of British history as a triumphal march of liberty overseen by an enlightened Whig oligarchy assembled in parliament. But the desertion of the Whigs in the 1880s over Ireland, the palpable erosion of the wealth, power, and status of the traditional territorial elite, the broadening of the electorate in 1867 and 1884, and the emergence of Labour as a political force rendered this option unattractive. One alternative was retention of the general outline of the story of progress while adjusting the chronology, re-shuffling the dramatis personae, and placing the state at the center of the action. This was the choice of the Webbs. The couple's emphasis upon the state rather than the masses as the principal agent of social progress revealed the meager influence of Marxism upon British socialist thought. Others, influenced by New Liberalism—the Hammonds, Trevelyan, and Churchill—produced historiographic compromises that mingled elements of old and new. Belloc generated nothing so substantial or enduring. By temperament he was more demolisher than builder. His Catholic idiosyncrasies allowed him to sire a violent critique of the Edwardian Liberal party yet hindered the generation of a coherent alternative. In a similar vein, he failed to create a viable surrogate paradigm for the Whig interpretation of British history, to the destruction of which he devoted his life.

The potency of the Bellocian message for young Liberals, difficult to gauge under any circumstances, was surely enhanced by his egalitarian republicanism and consistent distrust of capitalism. Here he appealed to some of the deepest moral and intellectual urges of the New Liberalism. But subtle, almost imperceptible psychological impact was not what Belloc was after as an end point. However slow it might be in coming, he desired radical change, and his works were meant to shock, inform, and incite. He wanted to put his reader "into the position of the man in the waxworks who, on hearing the showman recite the story of the Passion, broke up the effigy of Judas Iscariot and excused his excitement by saying that the whole thing was news to him."[171] Belloc's own metaphor was an apt one, for he was indeed a showman. But by his own standards, he failed in his task, for, although he made his contribution to the demise of Liberalism, he could not arouse the vast majority of his audience to even the consideration of revolution. The former accomplishment was inconsequential without the latter, for Labour and Conservatism, feasting on Liberal carrion, seemed just as capable as their late predecessor of erecting modern Britain's agreeable prison, the Servile State.

2 SIDNEY & BEATRICE WEBB
A New Form of Public History

Prior to her marriage, Beatrice Potter fretted over the likelihood that both she and her prospective husband, Sidney
Webb, possessed "second-rate minds."[1] A decade later she
remained troubled by her perception of their intellectual
shortcomings, fearful lest they be remembered as "simply
compilers and chroniclers" rather than original theorists.[2]
Such a blanket dismissal by posterity would obscure the
ambitious scope of their writings, while perhaps threatening its sustained social and political influence.

Paradoxically, the danger of neglect was greatest in the
area where the couple lavished the most time and attention,
historiography. Today the Webbs enjoy a reputation as Fabian Socialists, political activists, propagandists, social sci-

*Sidney Webb and Beatrice Webb in the early 1900s, working on another one of
their "babies." (UPI / Bettmann Archive)*

entists, fellow travelers, and even as earthbound prophets,[3] but, after the polymathic fashion of Hilaire Belloc, only secondarily are they recalled as historians. In his standard 1962 study of Fabian Socialism A. M. McBriar asserted that "it is in the realm of historiography and the descriptive analysis of political institutions that we discover the true greatness of the leading Fabians; in the works of the Webbs, of Graham Wallas, R. H. Tawney, R. C. K. Ensor, and G. D. H. Cole is to be found some of the finest history written since 1890."[4] But as if to gainsay his own declaration of the preeminent significance of Fabian historiography, McBriar virtually ignored the subject in favor of an examination of overt Fabian political machinations. Equally distressing is the most recent dual biography of the Webbs, which treats their histories as an unproblematic adjunct to their other activities.[5]

Yet the Webbs simply cannot be understood without taking account of their historical scholarship. The sheer scale of the couple's historiographical output testifies to their own ordering of priorities and therefore demands careful attention. The 1920 edition of *The History of Trade Unionism* (first published in 1894) approaches eight hundred pages in length, and *English Local Government from the Revolution to the Municipal Corporations Act* (1904–29), the product of nearly three decades of intense labor, comprises eleven very thick and forbidding volumes. Few have recognized that the Webbs invested so much time and effort in producing this mass of paper because of their belief in the centrality of history to contemporary political questions.[6] Much like Belloc, they comprehended the inextricably intimate connection between history and theory, between the power of the past and the present to shape the future.

The roots of all of the couple's joint work on politics and sociology lay in their own prior historical investigations and the conclusions they had drawn about Britain's past. The Webbs constructed their 900-page theoretical study *Industrial Democracy* (2 vols., 1897) upon the foundations laid by the earlier *History of Trade Unionism*. Indeed, the authors looked upon the two books as consecutive volumes in a single study of British working-class industrial institutions.[7] The famous Minority Report of the Royal Commission on the Poor Law (1909) was in large measure the result of a decade of minute investigations into the history of parish, county, manor, and borough administration, undertaken for the first four volumes of the Webbs' *English Local Government*. Later works of political and economic theory such as *A Constitution for a Socialist Commonwealth of Great Britain* (1920) and *The Decay of Capitalist Civilisation* (1923) offered diagnoses of the present and prescriptions for the future that emerged from an exploration of Britain's past that had begun in their youth.

In the mid-1880s, long before meeting his future spouse, Sidney was already busy fashioning a coherent and comprehensive interpretation of history in a series of talks before London debating clubs such as the Zetetical Society and the Sunday Lecture Society.[8] During the same period Beatrice was working under the direction of the great social investigator Charles Booth.[9] Following the Webbs' physical and intellectual union, Sidney's historical sense, an offshoot of his youthful Comtean sympathies, fleshed out the static, two-dimensional snapshots of the Boothian analytic method to produce what the couple later described as their "own specialty," that is, "the analytical history of the evolution of particular forms of social organization."[10] The key ingredient was a dynamic approach to the social investigation of institutions, the marriage of history and sociology. Sidney had pointed the way in his contribution to *Fabian Essays in Socialism* in 1889. "Owing mainly to the efforts of Comte, Darwin, and Herbert Spencer, we can no longer think of the ideal society as an unchanging State. The social ideal from being static has become dynamic. The necessity of the constant growth and development of the social organism has become axiomatic. No philosopher now looks for anything but the gradual evolution of the new order from the old."[11] History, constituting in their estimation simply "the Sociology of the past," interested the Webbs only in an instrumental sense.[12] The survival of sociology as a distinct branch of study and, likewise, of their own historical sociology, depended, so they maintained, "on the world's experience of the practical utility of such a parcelling out of knowledge at the particular stage of the world's history that we may have attained."[13] Certainly for the foreseeable future a mastery of versions of the past was an indispensable tool in the crusade for contemporary political and economic reform.

Ironically, in their insistence on relating history and current concerns, the Fabian Webbs were carrying on a very Whig tradition. They could look back on a dozen major Victorian public figures who had also written history. Like such predecessors, the Webbs recognized the complementary value of public life and historiography. Yet, unlike many of these Victorian figures, they much preferred the life of an author to a career in politics, filled with "inconvenience, separation and turmoil."[14] It was "so much pleasanter to investigate and write rather than organize and speak."[15] Their partnership in historical inquiry filled them with an assurance of "worthwhileness" that politics alone could not provide.[16] In the end history seemed not only more satisfying but also more efficacious in furthering their aims. By 1927, with Sidney approaching seventy years of age and serving as a Labour Member of Parliament, day-to-day politics had become a positive intrusion into the time needed for what they deemed their genuinely important work. Her husband, Beatrice noted with irritation, was "merely walking through the part of M.P. and he could be writing books that would count far more than any speeches he is likely to make in or out of Parliament."[17] If nothing else, the circumscribed powers of a single M.P. could not satisfy what had once been the more grandiose political ambitions of the couple's earlier years, an ache to choreograph the dance of the high and mighty. Now only the ripple effect of revisionist history could hope to duplicate that sort of influence. A firm conviction in the significance of their writings also helped to rationalize their childless marriage. In a moment of self-doubt in 1901, Beatrice wanted to believe that the books she and Sidney had coauthored were "worth (to the community) the babies we might have had."[18] Thirty-four years later, on the completion of their latest book, husband and wife laughed over it and congratulated "one another on the birth of our last and biggest baby."[19]

A Fabian obsession with processes gradual and peaceful, along with an avowed distaste for abrupt change and breach of continuity, should not disguise the revolutionary nature of the Webbs' goals for their literary offspring. They looked forward to the complete reconstruction of Britain along socialist lines such that a more equitable and efficient institutional structure would be erected in conjunction with a new moral order based upon the selfless motives of service and obligation. Reeducation was the indispensable first step on the road to moral and structural regeneration. The social revolution was to be mainly a revolution in opinion.[20] All of the Webbs' conclusions about the organization of British society were to be thrown "at the head of the public in the form of massive historical analysis." Books of revisionist history constituted the "big artillery" of the siege train of socialism, pounding a breach in the enemy's defenses that would expose the weakness of the entire edifice and finally bring it crashing down.[21] Although progress was inevitable, the means of its realization could be evolutionary or violent. The "Zeitgeist" was "potent," but it still rested "with the individual to resist or promote social evolution, consciously or unconsciously, according to his character and information."[22] The role of the individual (employing the tactics of permeation) was to act as a midwife to change, minimizing the pain and disruption of its coming. Believing that socialism must be "prepared for in the minds of all," the task of the Webbs as historians-cum-propagandists was to lubricate the path to social reorganization through the instruction of public opinion. Sidney and Beatrice complained that the patterns of thought and action of the citizens of a modern state were "stiffened in intensity," but that did not mean "that it was impossible to change the habits and customs of a whole nation." Public opinion was a "supremely powerful factor" in effecting just such changes, and among the major influences that helped to create or mold public opinion was "the spread of new knowledge."[23] Education was better than agitation, and the cornerstone of public education was a reinterpretation of history.

As Gertrude Himmelfarb has noted, Sidney and Beatrice Webb were intellectuals in politics, and as such, they aspired to bring "the whole of politics into conformity with a large intellectual or rational scheme of things."[24] For them, politics was not an ad hoc, pragmatic pursuit of limited goals by limited means. Instead, it represented an ambitious attempt to mediate the chasm between ethics and reality, to reawaken and stimulate the dormant rational and moral side of man. The transformation of public opinion from an acceptance of individualist-capitalist values to an embrace of a new (and old) definition of civic virtue based upon "the general recognition of fraternity, the universal obligation of personal service, and the subordination of personal ambition to the common good" would proceed in lockstep with the erection of new institutions of social organization, government, and industry that incorporated, reflected, and promoted these new values of benevolence and altruism.[25] The perpetual antagonism of history and ethics, so pronounced during the period 1689–1835 when the Webbs believed liberalism had reigned unopposed, would at last be reconciled as the many paths receding into the distant past would finally be seen to converge in the new moral order of the socialist commonwealth of the future. History would emerge as a teleological record tracing the progression of culture to the "end of history." This was the present-mindedness of Herbert Butterfield's Whiggish historians with a socialist vengeance.

Authority and Scientific History

Beatrice once wrote that the "Fabians at any rate write history if they do not make it!"[26] But, of course, for the Webbs the distinction between the two activities was blurred and, in the end, extinguished. In the atmosphere of pragmatic utilitarianism which they cultivated in their circle, to write a good book in the conventional sense was not enough. Sidney might admire Graham Wallas's *Human Nature in Politics* and *The Great Society* for their "originality, insight, excellence of form, and even wisdom," but such uncommon virtues could hardly disguise their "essential futility."[27] In order to be truly good, in the lexicon of the Webbs, a book had to demonstrate effectiveness, that is, to influence contemporary culture and politics. Their aim as historians was "to be able to *make* history as well as to write it," or perhaps more accurately, to make history by writing it.[28]

To be effective as historians, people had to read their books. Unfortunately, by their own admission, the Webbs' works of history were "solid but unreadable."[29] Macmillan & Co., in declining to undertake the publication of *The History of Trade Unionism*, expressed the opinion that, though the subject was undoubtedly interesting, "the scale of your book seems to us too large to give much prospect of very extensive sale."[30] The proposed American publisher, G. N. Putnam, likewise was distressed "to learn that the work must be of so considerable a compass." He cautioned that the reforming author, in his zeal, often inadvertently damaged his own cause by overestimating the interest and attention span of the general reading public.[31]

There is little doubt that the Webbs wanted a large readership for their histories.[32] Ironically (in view of the pessimism of its potential publishers), their hopes for a broad appeal were fulfilled only with *The History of Trade Unionism*, and then only because of a ready-made audience of all union members, who purchased the books by the thousands. Unfortunately, there was no natural constituency to provide a similar preexisting demand for their magnum opus, *English*

Local Government (ELG). It was clear to the authors that "few will buy these ponderous volumes."[33] That was regrettable but not disastrous, for the Webbs were less concerned with quantity than quality. It was less important that their books acquire a mass audience than that the "right people" read them.[34] That their *Poor Law History* (Vols. 7, 8, and 9 of *ELG*, 1927–29) might be read by only a few specialists was acceptable, since that handful of experts would be the molders of opinion.[35] As they told Graham Wallas in 1908, "Before you can get to [the undergraduate], you must put your Pol[itical] Science Professor on the right line."[36] Consistent with their Fabian elitism, the Webbs believed it was only important for the intelligentsia and the decision makers to gain insight into the relationship between the past and contemporary reform. Unable to grasp the complexity of the issues and ideas involved, mass public opinion would follow its political and intellectual leaders in an instinctual, herdlike manner reminiscent of the processes of democratic politics. Perhaps the second part of their *Poor Law History* was too long and "meticulous," and perhaps the Webbs were a little depressed that it sold only 438 copies the first year.[37] But that paled to insignificance beside the fact that their history was read by the social scientists, bureaucrats, and M.P.'s working on a reform of the Poor Law that culminated in the Local Government Act of 1929.[38]

The Webbs' unusual wedding of an austere scholarly, "scientific" style with a proselytizing mission placed Sidney and Beatrice in an ambiguous position in the long-running feud between academic and amateur history. Their novel blending of method and assumptions appeared to leave them firmly in neither camp. But the couple took pains to make public their close identification with their scholarly and scientific colleagues. After studying proposed alternatives in the Cambridge Historical Tripos in 1897, Sidney wrote to King's College don Oscar Browning to lend him support "in stopping any retrograde step. I gather that the proposed changes not only exclude any treatment of History as Political Science, but they also ignore the technical training of the historian—if history is neither politics nor research, it seems nothing more than 'polite literature,' a study of the works which no gentleman's library should be without."[39] Like its subject matter, historiography was dynamic and progressive. Any turning away from modern academics' embrace of scientific techniques to a literary amateurishness represented a "retrograde step."

It was not that the Webbs failed to realize the power and influence of literary history or to appreciate the talent and conviction of some of its more distinguished practitioners. The young G. M. Trevelyan might be "a consummate prig," but "in intellectual parts" he was "brilliant, with a wonderful memory, keen analytic power and a vivid style." Although they believed Trevelyan wasted his energies upon the reiteration of conventional interpretations of banal political events, he approached his work with "enthusiasm and industry, and that is better than paradoxical originality without these qualities."[40] But no amount of talent or brilliance could compensate for the built-in handicaps of "literary" rather than "scientific" training of the historian. Only strict adherence to scientific techniques could guarantee the proper critical scrutiny of available evidence, producing, at the end of the methodical process, conclusions free from premeditated political bias and unconscious personal predilections.[41]

Perhaps more important, scientific technique as applied to the historical discipline represented a symbolic break with the past, a rupture of both form and content with the old intellectual order. The prosaically dynamic, methodically energetic, machinelike argumentation of the historian as scientist would supersede the literary product of the complacent, old-fashioned Whig rhetorician. Neither Liberal politics as usual nor its handmaiden Liberal historiography could withstand the force of science wielded simultaneously as a tool of cultural destruction and regeneration. The Webbs hoped to further in the mind of the public an identification of science and Liberalism as mortal antagonists. As both demolitionists and architects they intended that their own work should be synonymous with the systematic and objective critique of orthodox interpretations of the past as well as with a new, nonpartisan, scientific reordering of society's collective memory.

The Webbs were fond of using natural science analogies to describe the actual mechanism of their research.[42] Their technique had a direct correspondence with "experimentation," being "not at all unlike testing in a laboratory, or manipulating figures in the working out of a mathematical problem."[43] In this setting, data acquired a special sanctity. As a point of departure, the pure fact, in isolation and free from interpretation, guaranteed the objective and impartial nature of their "experimentation." In the spirit of scientific objectivity, even the method of recording assumed an essential significance. The investigator came upon facts in "conglomerates," and "in sociology, as in mineralogy, 'conglomerates,' have always to be broken up, and the ingredients separately dealt with." It was "vitally important, in the subsequent consideration of the notes" upon which the facts were entered, "to be set free from the particular category in which the note-taker has found any particular fact, whether of time or place, sequence or coexistence."[44] The appendix to Beatrice's *My Apprenticeship* (1926), entitled "The Art of Note-taking," is only the most notable of many examples of the Webbs' preoccupation with the proper techniques for the acquisition and arrangement of facts.[45] One fact, and one fact only, was to occupy each separate sheet of paper of identical size and shape, accompanied in the margin by the date and source. The strict use of "detached sheets" was a must, for it allowed the researcher the luxury of shuffling and reshuffling these separate bits of data indefinitely.[46] This fixation on the minutiae of the art of historical research has usually been ignored by commentators on the Webbs, although one acute observer has noted its centrality to their grand design. "For the Webbs the recording of each fact on a separate piece of paper of uniform size and in uniform fashion was nothing less than a warrant of objectivity, since it permitted the facts to be arranged and rearranged at will—the implication being that the facts thereby acquired a life, independence, and integrity of their own apart from the historian."[47] This self-contained solidity of the simple fact, solitary and value-free, guaranteed the impartial scientific credentials of their work. They believed that in the proper hands, it was, "indeed, not too much to say that this merely mechanical perfection of note-taking may become an instrument of actual discovery."[48] The fact that data gathered and recorded in the proper scientific fashion seemed to generate conclusions virtually spontaneously reassured the Webbs that they could aspire to a role beyond that of mere "compilers and chroniclers."[49]

Although their rigorous advocacy of scientific standards of historical research and documentation denied them mass appeal, it certainly made the Webbs and their work attractive to the reform-minded academics engaged in professionalizing history within the British universities. The Webbs' thoroughness of treatment, breadth of outlook, and prolific use of footnotes (the latter furnishing "invaluable bibliographical information") uniformly delighted their reviewers in the academic historical journals. The *Economic History Review* determined that though their three volumes on the history of the English Poor Law contained more than fifteen hundred pages, "not a page [was] redundant."[50] The renowned economic historian J. H. Clapham declared their *English Local Government* to be "one of the great monuments of learning of our day."[51] In an otherwise enthusiastic 1910 piece for the *English Historical Review* that maintained that it would "certainly be difficult to praise [the first two volumes of *ELG*] too much" appeared a solitary academic reservation. The "obvious criticism" of the merits of these otherwise outstanding tomes was of "literary form or lack of it." The "great work" was "copious and complete," but its indigestible bulk required "a lucid and even literary form."[52] Not too surprisingly, the author of this renegade review was the Balliol tutor and former mentor of Hilaire Belloc A. L. Smith, a don out of sympathy with professional designs for reform of the teaching of history at university and for the new emphasis on specialized research. The official imprimatur of academic recognition and sanction of the Webbs' works of history came in 1910, when Sidney was asked to write the chapter on "Social Movements" for the twelfth volume of *The Cambridge Modern History*.[53] The two Fabian historians appeared to have been successfully co-opted by the academic historical community as the name "Sidney Webb, L.L.B., Barrister-at-Law" turned up as coauthor among an impressive list of Ph.D.'s.

Academic enthusiasm for the Webbs was not fully reciprocated, however. In 1926 Beatrice noted in her diary, without any accompanying denial, R. B. Haldane's conviction of the Webbs' prejudice against "university education."[54] There was never any open confrontation between the Webbs and academia. Indeed, with its apparent otherworldly absorption in intellectual pursuits—"the open and avowed cultivation of your intellect without fear of ridicule or abuse for selfishness"—the college life exercised an undeniable fascination and charm for the Fabian couple. But it was the illusory charm of the monastery, isolated and irrelevant.[55] Gatherings of Oxbridge dons "gave a lifeless and derelict impression" mirroring the narrow confines of their self-imposed monkish existence, with its conscious "divorce of thought from action."[56] Sounding a bit like a subdued forerunner of Hilaire Belloc, Sidney summed up his impressions in 1890. "Oxford, I admit, is a grievous spectacle, and the more so because one does not see how it can get amended. The outsider has no power, and the insider no will or capacity, to change things for the better. Some one must stay on at Oxford and become a don; yet one would not desire one's worst enemy to run that danger."[57] For Webb as well as for Belloc, the problem with the academic environment was not so much its lingering didactic predisposition but rather its slavish conformity and complicity in the preservation of the prevailing cultural and political orthodoxy.

Just as universities were not islands of knowledge possessing their own unique logic as complements to their own grammar, the products of research were not ends in themselves but merely means to an end. History, as "the Sociology of the past," was part of a much larger science of social organization, and, therefore, it had no separate, inviolable existence apart from the present and the future. Like all the sciences, it attracted interest and study for its practical applications. History could make no prior claims as a detached and disinterested repository of truth. Instead it was a utensil, pure and simple. It functioned in conjunction with political science, providing concrete prescriptive examples for its theoretical counterpart.[58] Exhibiting an attitude exasperatingly Liberal and Victorian, the Webbs viewed history as a unique fusion of past, present, and future, offering irreplaceable instruction to the modern reformer.[59] Beatrice was convinced that "this intimate knowledge of what past generations of one's own race have actually done—of the motives upon which they acted—of the potential machinery they invented, or cast on one side, gives larger scope to one's imagination as a reformer of the present state of things."[60] In *Fabian Essays in Socialism* (1889) Sidney had emphasized that ignorance of the past and of its meaning for the present erected political barriers to progress. Graham Wallas understood that the Webbs' works of history were written specifically to provide "the politician with the material of his thoughts and the suggestion of his inventions."[61]

As both social researchers and publicists the Webbs inhabited the houses of both public science and public history.[62] Their endorsement of scientific method came with ideological strings attached. Science, correctly applied, held the key to progress, and scientific principles applied to the study of history would supply the requisite blueprint.[63] Perhaps most appealing to the Fabian couple was the deceptive malleability of this blueprint. History, practiced as a science, provided not only a versatile tool but one that could be molded to fit the hand of its user. Its composition of millions of verifiable facts frozen in time and space gave it the appearance of rigidity and authority. But in reality, history retained a flexibility that even pure theory could not match. As Beatrice noted, the "sequence involved in history writing" was "artificial"; arrangement remained "purely a subjective process."[64]

This inherent plasticity of history dovetailed neatly with the view of truth which the Webbs had adopted by the interwar years. In "What I Believe" (1931) Beatrice presented her interpretation of Hans Vaihinger's *Philosophy of "As If"* and William James's *Will to Believe*. She agreed with the authors that "whenever no hypothesis can be scientifically proved or disproved, and yet some hypothesis must be accepted as a starting-point for thought or as a basis for conduct, the individual is justified in selecting the hypothesis which yields the richest result in the discovery of truth, or in the leading of a good life."[65] Extrapolating from this proposition, all reality became a function of usefulness, itself a very subjective concept. This instrumental understanding of truth allowed the Webbs great latitude in manipulating the results of scientific inquiry in order to make it conform to their predetermined judgments regarding social utility.[66] Science dealt only with processes; it had nothing to say of the purposes of individual life, of society, or of the universe. The generation of values took place outside the closed system of science in a manner irrational and intuitive.[67] History provided an effective tool for such self-appointed creators of value as the Webbs, since the instrumentality of truth allowed the events of the past to be organized and presented so as to corroborate their preconceived notions of the purpose of the social organism. In their hands, history would portray the progressive convergence over time of the "is" and the "ought."[68]

Providing the perfect medium for linking process and purpose, wonderfully malleable historiography allowed the dexterous worker-researcher to drape the niceties of scientific method and objectivity over a Fabian version of the old discredited Victorian didacticism. In this new garb, the prescriptive offering of the Webbs' histories was barely recognizable. Just as they designed the London School of Economics neither as an old nineteenth-century factory for good citizenship nor as the modern ideal of disinterested scholastic endeavor, the Webbs carved out a unique territory for their works of history. They produced books that appeared to conform to the most rigorous demands of scientific scholarship without ever sacrificing their utilitarian fixation on social function. Particularly in the eleven volumes of *English Local Government*, this potent mixture was remarkably well suited to its anti-Liberal agenda. On one plane its conclusions directly refuted the claims of traditional Whig historiography, while on another its self-conscious adoption of scientific form challenged the literary style that seemed the only proper and effective means of presenting Liberalism's three-hundred-year tale of triumph. In addition, the Webbs' use of the scientific methodology of the reforming university professoriate gained for the Fabian couple the commendation and support of the academic community, a closed elitist preserve of knowledge and power which the Webbs looked upon as Liberalism's natural antagonist. It seemed that the Webbs had fashioned the perfect weapon to strike at Liberalism's heart, nurtured as the latter was upon a specific and vulnerable version of the nation's past.

Laden with their Fabian preoccupation with bureaucracy and the state, the Webbs happened along at the correct moment. They had no use for the ancient Whig public historiographical tradition. But they harbored a patent affinity for the emergent discipline of administrative history, itself a clear by-product of the late nineteenth-century bureaucratization of European society so admired by the Webbs. The work of academics like Tout, Maitland, and Pollard pushed into the spotlight the art of governance and the evolution of the state as a nearly autonomous entity. Though in part fueled by a reaction against the Victorian orthodoxy of constitutional history with its anachronisms and fetishistic fixation upon the interplay of ideas, administrative history retained elements of the Whiggish skeleton. Progress measured via the augmentation of liberty contributed a narrative subplot, but this time with the organs of the state providing the main thrust. Focus shifted away from constitutional debates and allied attempts to limit executive power, onto the workings of orderly government with its propensity for incremental advances in centralization and division of labor. As Tout said, "Even under modern conditions, administration is more important than legislation."[69]

The *how* of the organization and function of the machinery of government now took precedence over the *why*. The principal standard of historical evaluation of any era was less its contribution to abstract liberty than the new, apparently more value-free yardstick of "efficiency." This burgeoning interest in the state redirected the energies of historians. Periods judged to have witnessed leaps forward in administrative efficiency elbowed aside the routine Whig tableau. While not quite reduced to epiphenomena, the once epic constitutional struggles of the 1640s, 1680s, 1770s, and 1830s shrank in stature.

This general trend was a godsend to the Webbs. As members of that amorphous collection of Edwardian jeremiahs reacting against "Gladstonianism" with calls for "National Efficiency," Sidney and Beatrice depicted themselves and their enthusiasms as nonpartisan and apolitical. Their primary concern was the *how* of British governance not the *why*, form not content. Thus the apparent ease with which they omnivorously flitted from party to party, always canvassing for listeners and converts. This nonpartisan pose was likewise central to the Webbs' historiography. They researched the evolution of the mechanisms of local government, not the divisive constitutional disputes over the extension of political participation. By their historical reckoning, the Elizabethan Poor Laws of the 1590s, the Municipal Corporations Act of 1835, and the Local Government Act of 1888 clearly overshadowed the Reform Acts of 1832, 1867, and 1884. Despite their public affiliation with Fabian Socialism, the character of the couple's historiography provided the Webbs with a substantial claim to impartial detachment. Methodology replicated subject matter; science equaled objectivity. Tout himself conceded the inescapable dullness of detailed administrative history with its "patient and plodding working out of apparently unimportant detail." Because this drudgery afforded the best method for the historian to "advance his science," it was "irrelevant to say that the process by which it has been reached is technical and dreary."[70] Far from immaterial to the Webbs, this admission meshed perfectly with their own cultivated image as disinterested scientific plodders. The contemporaneous outpouring of administrative history from the universities provided an apparent academic reflection of the Webbs' historiography, further validating its conclusions.

To Make History as Well as to Write It:
The Intellectual as Eminence Grise

The Webbs fashioned their historiographic output to complement their own more direct political involvement. They wished to function as stage manager as well as playwright and critic, to fill the role of intellectual as eminence grise. Despite their protestations of sincere belief in gradualism and inevitability, political quietism held little attraction for these two Fabians, lacking, as they did, a simple Marxist faith in the dialectic of history.[71] Permeation necessitated active advancement of their agenda, and from 1890 to 1910, a Liberal party in flux appeared to provide the sufficient means.

Presuming that they would wield "a kind of indescribable influence which cannot be measured" after the 1892 election of Gladstone's fourth government, the Webbs luxuriated in the knowledge "that we shall be able to drive the official Liberals into the sea of Socialism before they know where they are."[72] But failure on this broad front soon rerouted their attentions to the Liberal imperialist wing of the party. With their joint interest in National Efficiency, the Webbs and Lord Rosebery appeared perfectly matched, particularly since, in Bernard Shaw's estimation, the "Limp" leader was little more than a "political tool ... screaming for somebody to come and handle him."[73] But the relationship quickly soured under the weight of Rosebery's vacillations. Undiscouraged, Sidney and Beatrice actively courted the receptive young radicals of the New Liberal persuasion, most assiduously those with reasonable prospects for office and the power that accompanies it. It seemed to Beatrice in 1908 that "every politician one meets wants to be 'coached.' "[74] The recent convert to New Liberalism Winston Churchill just happened to be more receptive than most. In conversation the young man seemed to Sidney "most obsequious—eager to assure me that he was willing to absorb all the plans we could give him."[75] The Webbs could never resist a politician who informed them directly, as did Churchill: "I hope you will feed me generously from your store of information and ideas."[76] In the face of such agreeable plasticity the possibilities for permeation appeared limitless.

But inevitably, inflated expectations foundered once again. The young minister, who had posed as their most vacuous and therefore potentially most obedient pupil, soon displayed an infuriating independence of judgment.[77] Indeed, Churchill's relationship with the

Webbs was a microcosm of his voracious yet habitually cautious employment of expert advice. As we shall see, this was to prove particularly true in Churchill's composition of history, when, never hesitating to milk academics and technicians for every bit of available effort and suggestion, he then invariably made up his mind based upon his own stubborn, often prejudicial, reading of the facts. In both politics and historiography, Churchill did not mind allowing his advisers to overestimate their influence, for that only redoubled their ardor on his behalf. He retained a confidence in his own intellectual faculties as well as in his ability to take ultimate control of any situation, a confidence that allowed him the freedom to use the expert without being cowed or co-opted by him.

By 1910–11 the Webbs' multiphasic dalliance with official Liberalism was all but over. Hilaire Belloc had broken with the Liberal party at approximately the same moment, when it likewise refused to conform to his falsely conceived expectations. Although he despised the Webbs and all they stood for, like them he was ultimately interested in revolutionary social and political change. Both Belloc and the Webbs had mistakenly believed that Liberalism in its early twentieth-century incarnation was a vehicle for the initiation of truly radical reform. In the heady atmosphere after the 1906 electoral victory many things seemed possible. But there came at last a common realization that the vestiges of Old Liberalism remained deep and powerful beneath what they now believed was merely the superficial veneer of New Liberal radicalism. Belloc was convinced that Old Liberalism (abetted willingly but unwittingly by the ideology of the New Liberalism) was engaged in the construction of a bureaucratic Servile State in order to institutionalize the capitalist-oligarchic system upon which rested the superstructure of traditional Liberalism. Conversely, the Webbs credited Old Liberalism's stubborn adherence to laissez-faire individualistic principles in government and economics with successfully retarding the administrative reforms that would usher in the new socialist commonwealth, a bureaucratically efficient yet benevolent welfare state.

Edwardian Liberalism's confusion about the proper attitude to take toward the institution of the state and its role in society lay at the heart of this paradox. Pulled in different directions by the interests of Nonconformists, Free Traders, Liberal Imperialists, Home Rulers, Gladstonians, New Liberals, and exponents of National Efficiency, post-1900 Liberalism could never quite make up its mind about centralized, bureaucratic authority; was it progressive and beneficent or malignant and tyrannical? The Fabian Socialists identified the persistence of laissez-faire individualism as the author of their political frustrations, while the Catholic Distributists emphasized the friability of that ancient Liberal vestige. The remarkable thing was that Liberal doctrine remained fluid enough to be able to appear headed in diametrically opposite directions to Belloc and the Webbs—a clue, perhaps, that neither understood the nature of the beast they each had tried to transform into their own stalking-horse.

Much like Belloc, for a brief moment the Webbs imagined that the crisis over the "People's Budget" and the House of Lords' veto would transform the whole of the Liberal party into "extremists." "Political radicalism would be finally merged into economic collectivism. The Fabian Society would be, in fact, triumphant."[78] But parliamentary compromise and the resiliency of traditional Liberal principles left Beatrice and Sidney shunned as intriguing "Socialists."[79] After 1912 the Webbs, noticeably deficient in enthusiasm, threw in their lot with the Labour party. "A poor thing, but our own," noted a resigned Beatrice.[80] The direct campaign to co-opt and reroute Liberalism had led to a succession of failures. In lieu of other options, the Webbs now turned their principal efforts to an indirect approach. They hoped that conclusions drawn from their elaborate and scientifically unassailable revisionist histories would undermine the traditional assumptions that formed the bedrock of contemporary political Liberalism and its economic, social, and cultural counterparts. Having experienced a frustration akin to Belloc's own, the Webbs now resorted to a similar shift in strategy.

Old Wine in New Bottles:
The Collective Idea from Feudalism to Trade Unionism

The Webbs' concurrent historiographic production represented the harmonic counterpoint to twenty years of attempting to redefine and capture contemporary British political discourse. In their examination of the past the Webbs aimed to demonstrate that Liberal doctrine, with its hostility to the state and stubborn refusal to surrender Victorian shibboleths regarding the virtues of laissez-faire and individualism, was antiquated and ineffectual in the changed circumstances of the twentieth century. The radical nature of the argument flowed from its indictment of the traditional Whig version of history as fatally flawed. The Victorians had misidentified the vehicle of progress. Rather than proclaiming it a spontaneous elaboration from the clash of competing ideas and interests enshrined in the development of the English constitution, the Webbs baptized the promethean state, in all its incarnations—local, regional, and central—as the bringer of order, prosperity, liberty, and efficiency.

As Sidney matured as a historian, his choice of subject matter moved from the general to the specific. His 1883 lecture "The Rise and Fall of Feudalism," first given when he was only twenty-four, presented, heavily spiced with a large dose of Victorian present-mindedness, an early version of his preoccupation with history as the waxing and waning of institutions. This potent combination (one that was to recur again and again in the work of the Webb partnership) allowed Sidney to rummage among the organizational carcasses of the past for the precursors of the machinery of the present and future socialist society. Unlike his future pointillistic technique, at twenty-four he employed only a few broad and daring brushstrokes to compose an uncluttered landscape.

The young Sidney's portrayal of the feudal landlord was that of a benign local authority performing essential community tasks as policeman, soldier, judge, and administrator. Webb argued that the bulk of the landlord's income was "devoted to social purposes." As a group these civic-minded receivers of rent functioned in much the same fashion and with a similar ethos as did the modern civil servant. The central government gradually assumed the feudal landlord's duties, this merger of responsibilities sowing the seeds of modern state bureaucracy. "In short, the whole of the functions now performed by the central government were at one time or another, so far as they were needed or thought of at all, performed out of the rents and payments created by feudalisation. This progressive State Socialism which forms our whole history and which is so very distressing to the mind of the Liberty and Property Defence man, is therefore no new thing."[81]

According to Sidney's version of the Middle Ages, the prevailing notion that the rise of feudalism had destroyed the original freedom of the democratic village community, reducing it to sullen dependency on the will of the manor lord, betrayed a misunderstanding of the institution itself and of its historic role. Feudalism had, of course, introduced certain restraints upon individual liberty, but this "human subjection [was] accompanied by a real gain in personal freedom." Feudalism's occupation of a transitional position between the "wild freedom of individualism" of England's Teutonic forefathers and the "supremacy of society incidental to a more civilised and populous community" suggests the phrase "the higher freedom of collective life," which Sidney was to use three decades later to characterize the fledgling Social Democratic state of early twentieth-century Britain.[82] "The rude order and union of Feudalism was a clear advance on the wild and barbarian individualism which preceded it, but was itself very inferior to the specialized administration of trained officials." In his teleology Sidney hoped to rebut the notion that feudalism was "productive of nothing but evil."[83] His depiction of it as the direct ancestor of the efficient and disinterested bureaucracy of the modern socialist state linked feudalism to the reformist zeitgeist, allowing its blemishes to be overlooked in the broader perspective of its contribution to progress.

In other lectures he outlined factors that had inflicted temporary reverses upon the beneficial trends originating in feudalism. The Reformation, by overthrowing the institutions of the Catholic church, had replaced the medieval emphasis on social duties with a Protestant reaction toward individualism. Sidney admitted of no purely doctrinal reasons to account for the Reformation; nor would he accept that it was a popular movement, for in his estimation, the typical sixteenth-century English peasant was not a Christian in any real sense, but rather more of a superstitious believer in a patchwork quilt religion of astrology, magic, and pagan rituals.[84] Rejecting the idea of the Reformation as a theological dispute or a proto-democratic revolt, he explained it as a reaction against institutional and bureaucratic malfunctions within the hierarchical structure of the Roman Catholic church. "The tendency of organizations is to rigidity: and where there are officials there is always the danger of abuse." The Reformation had performed a necessary historical service by clearing away a petrified institution that blocked "the way for the new organization of humanity to which we are gradually tending." But this was no cause for unqualified celebration, since "the Catholic Church, imperfect as it was, nevertheless points . . . the way to the golden age we seek and the Protestant reaction towards individualism must, I think, be reckoned as a check—though an inevitable one—in the history of social progress."[85] The similarity here between the Bellocian and Webbian versions of the Middle Ages is uncanny. Both connected the Catholic church to a Golden Age, in the former case to an extinct one, in the latter to only a potential one. But Catholicism and the culture it generated were associated by both historians with a philosophy of society superior and antithetical to the Protestant individualism that succeeded it.

According to Sidney, the Reformation and the rise of capitalism in the sixteenth and seventeenth centuries had firmly entrenched institutions based upon the philosophy of pure individualism, itself "an attribute of barbarism, and particularly . . . one main cause of the poverty and privation which accompany barbarism." Industrialization under capitalist direction had precipitated an age of misery and exploitation. But the internal dynamic of industrial organization, through its attenuation of the individual Darwinian instinct among the masses, ensured the resurgence of the collective ideal. "The progress of industrialism has bound everyone of us into one great army of workers, in which each no longer fights for himself but for the whole, and receives no longer what he individually produces, but a share of the whole. We fight the battle for life shoulder to shoulder throughout the whole universe." Sidney Webb's history of nineteenth-century England was a series of small victories of cooperation over individualism. Gradual administrative adjustments embodied in reform bills, sanitation measures, and factory acts provided the vehicles for progress against selfishness.

The wide-selling and influential *Fabian Essays in Socialism* contained Sidney's essay on the historic basis of socialism, outlining in general terms the "gradual transformation, both of opinion and of institutions, from an essentially Individualist to an essentially Collectivist basis."[86] The essay was substantially a continuation of the major themes of the lectures of the early 1880s, but it focused much more upon the last one hundred years. Sidney altered the chronology somewhat to accommodate this new emphasis. The collapse of the medieval system and the origins of the unrestrained license of individualism were elongated, now extending from the Reformation all the way to the onset of the Industrial Revolution in the late 1700s. This approach permitted the triumph of socialism, represented by the political, administrative, and economic reforms from 1832 onward, to appear as an institutional reaction to the "period of anarchy" ushered in by the apotheosis of laissez-faire.

Having outlined the broad movement of the zeitgeist as a bachelor, Sidney, with the aid of his new bride, turned his attention to tracing the evolution of particular institutions within this general interpretive framework. The Webbs began work on *The History of Trade Unionism* during the period when the Newcastle Programme still offered hope that the Gladstonian form of Radicalism would accept Fabian tutelage without resistance. The wholesale adoption of a collectivist goal as orthodoxy by the ideological core of the Liberal party would greatly simplify matters for the revisionist socialist historian. Instead of completely overhauling Whig historiography, it would be necessary to make only cosmetic adjustments linking the growth of the benevolent bureaucratic state to a once regrettably essential, but now superseded, Liberal ancestry.

The first half of the book was researched and written in this optimistic vein. With Sidney and Beatrice lacking a Marxist faith in the proletariat, their history concentrated on organizational development as the key to understanding. There was no attempt by the authors to present a morality play of bad employers versus good laborers, nor was there any emphasis placed upon the ideological origins of the working-class movement. The Webbs presented the trade union movement as a significant part of the political history of England—in their words, the "history of a State within a State."[87] Just as the social and economic circumstances of the late eighteenth and early nineteenth centuries spawned the rudiments of efficient, bureaucratic central government, they had also given birth to the same structure within the trade union movement. The Webbs traced the movement's progress to the rise of a labor union "civil service" paralleling the growth in numbers and status of the state civil service.[88] The trade unions' need to centralize finance and harmonize local autonomy as well as to obtain "exact knowledge" and "facts" regarding their industrial and social conditions prompted the switch by the mid-nineteenth century to permanent salaried officials.[89]

Headquartered in London, this Junta—"the cabinet of the Trade Union Movement"—successfully adopted legal, parliamentary tactics in pursuit of its interests—tactics that suspiciously resembled those later advocated by the Fabian Society.[90] Like the Fabians, the Junta was "powerless to coerce or even intimidate the governing classes, they could only win by persuasion." Yet they were instrumental in catalyzing what the Webbs called the "revolutionary" change in the British constitution that was the slow and almost imperceptible incorporation of the trade union movement into the governmental structure of the nation.[91]

The Webbs' book is now remembered, perhaps most notably, for its interpretation of English trade union history as discontinuous, that discontinuity being the substitution in the 1880s of a radical "New Unionism" for the conservative, craft-based "New Model Unions" represented by the mid-Victorian Junta.[92] Sidney and Beatrice reckoned the new permeation of socialist ideas into the movement via the New Unionism as "the chief event of Trade Union history at the close of the nineteenth century," symbolizing above all "the spiritual rebirth of organisations which were showing signs of decrepitude."[93] It is interesting to speculate just how much this picture of discontinuity was a product of their evidence and how much it owed to their disappointment with political events of the 1890s.

The Webbs' composition of the post-1870 section of the book coincided exactly with their growing disillusionment in 1893 with Gladstone's timid ministry. The first four chapters, all completed by the summer of that year, chronicled an essentially stepladder development in a trade union institutional structure that had matured far beyond "the Revolutionary Period" of 1829–42.[94] But while working on the book the Webbs confessed to "watching eagerly the course of politics."[95] By the early fall their patience with the government's inactivity was exhausted. Just before their frustrations boiled over in the 1 November publication of an anti-Gladstonian manifesto entitled "To Your Tents, Oh Israel!," the Webbs completed Chapter 5 of *The History of Trade Unionism*.[96] This chapter, entitled "The Junta and Their Allies," described the long, skillful, and ultimately successful struggle of the unions, led by the Junta, for political reform and formal legal recognition. However, the chapter's very end (written in early September) suddenly takes the reader by surprise as the narrative pauses to allow the coauthors to launch pointed criticisms at the Junta and its methods.[97] This censure seems to echo the Webbs' disappointment on finding that Gladstonian Liberalism was an unsuitable conduit for Fabian reformist ideas. The Webbs' depiction of the Junta reenacted the contemporary incompatibility of collectivism with the individualist dogma of Liberal orthodoxy.[98] Their final verdict was that the trade union leadership's political triumphs of the 1860s and 1870s in the name of the working classes were purchased at too steep a price, for the men of the Junta "gained their point at the cost of adopting the intellectual position of their opponents."[99] Blinded by the successes of its lobbying efforts, "the Junta had begun to be unconsciously converted from the traditional position of Trade Unionism to the principle of Administrative Nihilism, then dominant in the middle class."[100] Inevitably, according to the Webbian version of events, the Junta's adoption of the middle-class individualist ethos led to its forfeiture of rank-and-file trade union allegiance, thus the need for the "New Unionism," the reassertion of socialist ideals, and the "spiritual rebirth" of the 1880s.

In "To Your Tents, Oh Israel!" the Webbs had attempted to unmask traditional political Liberalism as a dead end for genuine reform. They declared that there could be no direct progression from Liberalism's individualist, laissez-faire philosophy to the higher organization of the socialist commonwealth. The Liberal party could align itself with the forces of progress only by severing all connections with its past, and the Webbs' story of the rise of trade unionism contained exactly the same moral. A dramatic discontinuity was absolutely essential to detach the modern, forward-looking, collectivist-inspired trade unionism of the 1890s from its retrogressive progenitor. Historiography recapitulated the Webbs' understanding of contemporary political realities.

A Big Indictment of Liberal Orthodoxy: The Webbs' *English Local Government* and Civic Virtue

From their study of trade unionism the Webbs developed "a new view of democracy," a new theoretical framework that would eventually steer them toward a thirty-year investigation into the history of local government.[101] After their prolonged research on the institutions of the working-class movement, they "now realised that Democratic organisation involves the acceptance, not of a single basis—that of the undifferentiated human being—but of various separate and distinct bases: man as producer; man as consumer; man as citizen concerned with the continued existence and independence of his race or community."[102] The Webbs determined that in their *History of Trade Unionism*, because of an oversimplified understanding of man as a social being, they had treated man's relationship with his government as one dimensional. Their failure to distinguish between what they dubbed voluntary associations of producers and compulsory associations of consumers and of citizens made it impossible for them to assign local authorities their appropriate place and function in the "Social Organism."

In the 1931 reissue of *Fabian Essays in Socialism* Sidney admitted that in the original 1889 edition, he had thought of local authorities as little more than shadowy reflections of capitalist enterprise, organizing production for the sake of the unemployed in the form of alternative cooperative factories and shops that would, under the management of town and city councils, "beat the profit-maker with his own weapons, at his own game." It had never occurred to him then "that the Parish Vestry, the Municipality, and the County Council were, like the Co-operative Societies, essentially Associations of Consumers, not Associations of Producers; Associations in which membership was obligatory on all local residents, instead of being voluntary, but the function of which was equally the collective provision for the citizens, as consumers, of whatever services they, as consumers, required."[103] Because man was more than simply a producer, government, properly understood and organized, functioned as an entirely different species when compared with capitalist business institutions.

The Webbs classed trade unions among the voluntary associations of producers. Despite all of their admirable qualities, despite their reaffirmation of allegiance to the collectivist ideal after 1880, trade unions, like other wholly voluntary producer organizations, had built-in limitations as the sole organizing institution of civil society. Their vision and interests were narrow and exclusive. A society arranged only on the basis of man's inclination as a producer to group himself voluntarily into associations for the pursuit of selfish interests would result in a corporate state. Each separate component of such a "producers Democracy"—to use the Webbs' designation—"tend[ed] always to become, within the community, a privileged body. . . . When Democracies of Producers own the instruments of production; or even secure a monopoly of the service to be rendered, they have always tended in the past to close their ranks, to stereotype their processes and faculties, to exclude outsiders and to ban heterodoxy."[104] By its very nature, a "producers Democracy" was incapable of pursuing the best interests of the community as a whole. Government organized along these lines alone could not promote the health of the Social Organism.

The Webbs believed that in view of the obvious inadequacies of a producers democracy, a just, harmonious, and progressive civil society could result only from government by compulsory associations of consumers and citizens. Since all members of a community were consumers of public services, individual selfish impulses could be counted upon to maintain such services efficiently if local government participation was mandatory for everyone. But much more important were the obligatory associations of citizens. The Webbs were convinced "not merely that compulsory association in government had necessarily to be added to voluntary association . . . as producers . . . but also that this inevitable compulsory association of man as citizen was demanded for much more than national defence and the maintenance of internal order. [They] saw that to the Government alone could be entrusted the provision for future generations, to which neither producers nor consumers could attend as such."[105] Associations of producers and consumers operated on the principle of individualism and selfishness. Provision according to need was foreign to their characteristic activities or desires. Civic needs could be met only by a civic consciousness, and the latter was a product of personal identification with the community itself, that is, of man in his role as citizen.

These revelations provided Sidney and Beatrice with "a new vision of social development," one grounded on the principle of public service, conducted by salaried officials who limited their personal ambitions to public honors and special promotions.[106] The progress of the Social Organism, past and future, was contingent upon the selfless pursuit of communal interests by complex individuals whose multiple roles as producer, consumer, and citizen fully integrated them into a pluralistic society. Rejected, by extension, was the traditional liberal scenario of the realization of freedom, prosperity, and progress via the unhampered pursuit of selfish personal interests by atomistic individuals.

It was only a short step from a theoretical critique of the philosophical foundations of political and economic liberalism to detailed historiographic corroboration. The Webbs intended the overly long, deadly dull volumes of *English Local Government* as the objective counterparts to their anti-Liberal theoretical insights.

The books described a historical discontinuity caused by the temporary and anomalous ascendancy of liberal principles similar in many respects to the discontinuity outlined in *The History of Trade Unionism*. In the Webbs' version of history, the theory of mutual obligation upon which feudal institutions had been founded was gradually superseded in the 1600s by an alien liberal-individualist ethos. For almost 150 years after 1688, self-perpetuating, voluntary bodies of wealthy producers, who indiscriminately ignored community needs in the pursuit of their own selfish interests, had controlled local government. Only slowly had the vestigial notion of mutual obligation reawakened as voluntary associations of consumers formed to address specific community requirements such as policing, sewers, street lighting, and better relief of destitution. These bodies, born out of a reaction against the neglect of the regular authorities, were "subsequently transformed by local Acts into compulsory associations of citizens."[107]

This interpretation, in line with the lectures Sidney had delivered two decades earlier, stood traditional Whig historiography on its head. In the Webbs' version, the Glorious Revolution and the philosophy that fueled it had retarded the social and political progress of England. Two centuries of the dominance of liberal ideology represented a historical aberration, a regrettable hiatus in the advancement of the zeitgeist. The slow resurgence of collectivist principles in the late nineteenth century was simply a reassertion, in a more scientific and efficient form, of the medieval concern with the community instead of the individual.

The Webbs' recognition of the intimate connection between present policy and interpretations of the past altered the nature of their task from the start. They had originally planned to analyze and describe local government in England from 1834–35 (the years of the passage of the Poor Law Reform Act and the Municipal Corporations Act respectively) to the present for the "use of would-be reformers as well as students."[108] But when they actually began work on *English Local Government* in 1898, they discovered that the inclusion of a brief preliminary chapter about pre-1835 local government—"the antiquities"—was inadequate, since the current system of local government was so firmly rooted in the two centuries preceding the 1832–35 reforms. The period 1688 to 1832 formed a clearly defined, deviant segment in the normal evolutionary flow of

English history. "For the first time, and perhaps for the last time in English history, the national Government abstained from intervention in local affairs, practically leaving all the various kinds of locally governing bodies to carry out their several administrations as they chose, without central supervision or central control."[109] The Webbs believed liberalism's selfish, individualist ideology had first fostered and then thrived in that sort of chaotic atmosphere.

Utilitarian considerations rather than any rigorous scholastic desire for historical roundedness prompted the decision to take 1688 rather than 1835 as the starting point for their work. As they said in the introduction to Volume 1, they anticipated that their investigations into the "experiments in Poor Law and Municipal Enterprise" undertaken between 1688 and 1835 would prove "instructive to the reformers of today."[110] The volumes of *English Local Government* would provide negative examples of the application of liberal principles to local administration—"a big indictment . . . of the eighteenth century"—as well as praiseworthy examples of the first stirrings of an institutional reaction against the inadequacies and immoralities of government organized along business lines as a voluntary association of producers.[111]

The overall structure of *English Local Government*, published over two-and-a-half decades from 1904, was rather ad hoc. For example, the Webbs took time out after the publication of the third volume in 1908 to produce *English Poor Law Policy* (1910), their major contribution to the Campaign for the Break-Up of the Poor Law. The couple later incorporated this dual exercise in scholarship and propaganda into the tenth volume of *English Local Government*. Volume 11, *The History of Liquor Licensing in England* (1904), curiously enough was the first completed and was not originally intended as part of the series at all. It was only added years later as an afterthought. However the theoretical core of the massive work, consisting of the first four volumes, appeared in chronological order over a relatively brief span: Volume 1, *The Parish and the County* (1906); Volumes 2 and 3, *The Manor and the Borough* (1908); and Volume 4, *Statutory Authorities for Special Purposes* (it was not finally published until 1922, but most of its research and composition had been completed years earlier). Beatrice judged *Statutory Authorities* to be "the most original and, certainly, the most significant of our series on the constitution of English local government prior to 1834."[112] Whereas Volumes 1 through 3 were preoccupied with dying institutions, *Statutory Author-ities* described what the Webbs believed were the true ancestors of the reformed, proto-collectivist machinery of modern local government. Therein lay its importance for the Fabian coauthors.

The Parish and the County told the story of the demise of the last vestiges of the ancient feudal institutions of local government. The Webbs described the seventeenth-century administrative unit as "an organ of local obligation."[113] Traditionally, "judicial" rather than "executive" arrangement had governed both parish and county. Local government, exercising its duties in a judicial setting of "Open Court," had functioned primarily as an interpreter and enforcer of legal obligations. The chief magistrate's role was more that of judge than administrator, and the frequent use of juries had provided the community with a voice in important decisions.[114]

However, the final triumph of liberalism in 1689 set the evolution of local government upon a new course. Executive authority gradually replaced judicial governance. As a capitalist market economy developed, landholdings and manufactories consolidated. A tiny minority acquired monopolistic control of the means of production, reducing the majority of the population to propertyless wage labor. Closed oligarchies of producers assumed the direction of local affairs as the notion of obligation passed into abeyance. According to the Webbs, between 1689 and 1835 local government metamorphosed from a public forum for the airing and adjudication of community grievances into a mechanism for the pursuit of particularist, selfish interests by exclusive social, political, or economic groups (most often these three were indistinguishable). The creation of new "services" (usually benefiting only the ruling oligarchy) at the expense of the rates further enhanced the unprecedented emphasis on executive authority. Administering these services were an ever-increasing number of corrupt officials appointed by and responsible only to the ruling oligarchy.[115]

Though noting the frequent eighteenth-century retention of the trappings of the traditional judicial machinery, the Webbs felt they had discovered nothing less than an extralegal revolution in the constitution of English local government, and it was a revolution they believed to have been pernicious. The couple deplored "the extra-legal developments of county [and parish] government [that] fostered the spread of corruption."[116] Besides being corrupt, parish vestries, comprised almost exclusively of privileged groups of tradesmen and the middle classes, were incompetent, inefficient, disorganized, and rent by party turmoil.[117] On the surface, county government appeared to have offered an appealing contrast. Controlled by the nobility or landed gentry—"men of remarkable incorruptibility and public spirit"—it exhibited a greater resistance to the penetration of capitalist ideology and a firmer allegiance to the traditional belief in local government as an organ of obligation and duty.[118] However, despite their undoubted public-spiritedness, the climate of the times ensured that eventually even the rulers of the county would succumb to temptation and abuse their official positions to pursue a "selfish 'class-policy.'"[119] In time, they followed the parishes' example in adopting the substance of executive authority, creating an oligarchy of producers even more socially, politically, and religiously exclusive than their middle-class counterparts on the vestries.[120]

During the writing of *The Parish and the County* Beatrice confessed to becoming obsessed with her own pet scheme for transforming English local government. Wondering if such an unadorned and apparently impartial historical narrative as theirs conveyed transparently enough its contemporary utility, she now perceived that "it would be desirable to have a [part] to our book on Theory of Local Government, giving an 'analysis' of the assumptions upon which 18th and early 19th century Local Government was based—with [the] rise of new assumptions. With our mass of facts needful to have a brilliant and *dogmatic* theoretical part, quite apart from the concrete narrative and based on a *personal creed*."[121] Perhaps the Webbs' historiographical method was too clever by half. There was always the danger that the moral of the story would be lost among more than six hundred pages of data and narrative. The simple description of example after example of parish or county governmental evolution between 1689 and 1835 could not, unexplicated, be trusted to elucidate the truth alone, since in the final analysis, truth was instrumental rather than absolute. The theoretical organizing principle for the facts could originate only from value judgments about health, progress, and good and evil, all based upon a "personal creed."

The couple devoted more attention to "dogmatic" theoretical exposition in the two volumes of *The Manor and the Borough*. The story related here resembled the one presented in *The Parish and the County*—an "analogous evolution" from the transaction of all manor and borough civic business via the judicial process to administration by oligarchic committees employing a salaried staff of extralegal officers.[122] This time the Webbs were more explicit about what they saw as the deeper social and philosophical implications of this institutional arrangement. They suggested that the breakup of the traditional medieval Court Leet could be attributed

> to the abandonment by the English people of the root-principle on which the Court depended. This principle, to put it shortly, was that, however men might differ in faculties or desires, they were all under an equal obligation to serve the community, by undertaking, in turn, all the offices required for its healthy life. . . . It lies at the base of the [Court Leet's] usual absence of any permanent staff or Corporate revenue. . . . We may recognise a noble element in this idea of universal equality of civil and political rights . . . the twentieth-century student will perhaps regret that it was not the element of identical equality, but the very notion of social obligation itself, which was swept away by the rival panacea of universality of civil and political rights.[123]

The Webbs determined that liberalism's blind fixation upon civil and political rights alone had permitted the perversion of municipal government service. What citizens had once viewed as public duty was seen after 1689 as a legitimate opportunity for private advantage. The liberal substitute for a civic virtue of communal responsibility was a false Mandevillian civic virtue in which selfish individual interests were supposedly harmonized by an invisible calculus for the greater public good.

The Webbs mourned the passing of the old principle of social obligation and the sense of community it had fostered, but they did not class themselves among the utopian idealists who expected, or even hoped, for its resurrection. Beatrice and Sidney believed that "however virtuous or wise may be a principle of public or private action, its survival as the ostensible method of achieving a desired result, *after that principle has ceased to be applicable or adequate to the circumstances of the time*, undermines the very foundations of personal conduct and social organisation."[124] Irreversible social and economic changes had accompanied the century-long apotheosis of liberal doctrine. The judicial system of local government born of the communal sense of social obligation was indeed admirable, but primitively unsuitable to modern circumstances. What was needed were "new principles" that incorporated the best of the old ideas while accommodating themselves to the contemporary "physical and mental environment."[125]

Statutory Authorities for Special Purposes traced the origin of these new principles. The Industrial Revolution had created a profusion of pressing problems far beyond the meager capabilities of the corrupt and incompetent administrations of the Hanoverian parish, borough, or county.[126] The expedient of "contracting out" proved an unsuitable remedy, for it fostered a tension between personal and civic interest, usually to the detriment of the latter. The Webbs maintained that from mid-century onward, the community responded to local government passivity with the creation of a "new species of authority," voluntary associations of consumers, eventually converted by statute into permanent compulsory associations of citizens.[127]

But local government required one further evolutionary step to consummate the cultivation of competence. In the first decades of the nineteenth century there emerged, "in contradistinction to the notion that any man of honesty and zeal is equal to the duties of any office whatever, the modern conception of specialist qualifications, without which even the most virtuous candidate would not be deemed fit for appointment."[128] The Webbs linked the rise of a modern professional municipal bureaucracy to the prior establishment of statutory authorities for special purposes. Government by an association of producers which had been replaced by an improved government of "unpaid, compulsorily serving citizens" was now, in turn, superseded by an efficient, permanent civil service machinery.[129]

Liberalism had demonstrated to the Webbs' satisfaction that it was incapable of providing a just and workable philosophy of government. Good government required rulers possessed of civic consciousness, a concept the Webbs believed foreign to the very essence of liberalism.[130] But the changed social conditions created by a century and a half of political and economic liberalism made a simple return to the ancient communal virtue of mutual obligation impossible. Urbanized, industrialized Britain required a novel solution that would reintroduce civic virtue into government while simultaneously organizing a complex society along scientific, collectivist lines. For the Webbs the answer was well-paid, professional civil service administrators, for only they could combine scientific expertise with a disinterested approach to municipal problems. In his official capacity, the salaried bureaucrat had no "self interest" as such. Civic virtue was a natural outgrowth of his nonpartisan identification with the community that he served and that paid his salary.[131]

The idea of bureaucratic administrative superiority invalidated the whole foundation of the Gladstonian approach to self-government. Mid-Victorian Liberalism expected participatory government to provide an indispensable theater for the playing out in each individual citizen of a moral struggle between personal and public interest. Participation in the political process afforded each citizen an opportunity to contribute to the creation of a just and rational society as he overcame selfishness; good governance provided public evidence of the personal triumph of reason over irrationality.

The Webbs' version of history indicated that this process was incompatible with modern social conditions. Their chronicle of the dismal record of local government from 1689 to 1835 seemed to prove that the most basic assumptions of liberal politics were fatally flawed.[132] As early as 1897, in *Industrial Democracy*, Sidney and Beatrice had declared obsolete the ancient form of democracy that "meant an 'equal and identical' sharing of the duties of government, as well as of its advantages." Conditions now demanded trust and reliance "on a specially selected and specially trained class of professional experts."[133] Unfortunately, even with the benefit of education, each citizen of a collectivized, postcapitalist Britain could not be expected to be an authority on the selection of choices for leading the "good life," that is, the life that balanced personal fulfillment and communal duty. Direction by technocrats was the Fabian couple's answer to a society that was no longer capable of acting in its own best interests. The state and its agents could best preside over the moral as well as material advancement of society.

This infatuation with professional experts meshed nicely with the Webbs' two inconsistent views of truth. On the one hand, because the scientific amassing of all relevant facts could point to only one rational solution to each problem, there could be no quarrel with the decisions handed down by the technocracy. On the other hand, since truth was instrumental and therefore malleable—a fluid construct outside the realm of science—the expert could use his authority to impose a single normative concept of truth—one consistent with his own personal values—upon the uninitiated, avoiding the chaotic mess the public, in their ignorance, would otherwise provoke. The Webbs felt it was imperative to remove civic virtue and the public interest from the uncertain realm of ethics and institutionalize them.

This, then, was the primary message of *English Local Government*: a prolonged trial of liberal politics had failed, and it was time to face up to the facts and search for alternatives. Taking issue with Max Weber's view of bureaucratization as inherently alienating and ultimately destructive of any genuine sense of community, the Webbs expected that their own preference for central control via an elaborate professional bureaucracy, historically validated in *Statutory Authorities* as the natural reaction to inept Liberal governance, would strike a sympathetic chord in either the Liberal Imperialist or New Liberal camps. But Sidney and Beatrice misread the heavily qualified statism of these new brands of Liberalism and, in a fit of frustration, overplayed their hand in the campaign for Poor Law reform. In the end they found that the internal dynamic of their historiography as much as their politics left them isolated from the Edwardian corridors of power, able only to turn to that "poor thing" called the Labour party.

History as Applied Sociology

During their lifetimes the Webbs certainly believed that their historiography made a difference. Indeed, it was specifically designed to affect public policy and opinion directly and decisively. They were frantic in early 1928 lest the final two volumes of their *Poor Law History*, entitled *The Last Hundred Years* (*ELG* Vols. 8 and 9) would not be completed prior to the introduction of Neville Chamberlain's Local Government Bill, legislation widely expected to abolish the Poor Law Guardians.[134] Their reaction to an unexpected delay in the bill's progress through the Commons in 1929 was one of relief at the extra time afforded them to complete their labors.[135] The division and emphasis of the two volumes of *The Last Hundred Years* betrayed the Webbs' intentions. The first part of less than 500 pages sufficed to cover the entire period from 1834 to 1905, while the generous 554 pages of the second installment traced in much more painstaking detail the quarter-century since Balfour's appointment of the Royal Commission on the Poor Law. Recycling mounds of material from the Minority Report of 1909, the Webbs clearly aimed to influence contemporary public policy on the reform of poor relief in the 1920s.[136] Sidney said as much in 1928 when he advised Beatrice that the publication of this latest addition to their *Poor Law History* should be timed to coincide with the passage into law of Chamberlain's Local Government Bill. The *History* would suggest provocatively that this new piece of legislation *"leaves all the problems of policy unsolved"* and "that the new administration should take care not to repeat the mistakes of their predecessors, and hence should read our book."[137]

Although its specifics adhered more closely to the Majority Report of 1909 than to the Webbs' own recommendations, they were confident that the Chamberlain bill was the thin end of the wedge signaling the eventual adoption of the entire Minority Report. Their *Poor Law History* would prepare the ground for "younger and more scientifically trained minds to build on—like Chadwick did for public health."[138] Here was the dramatic conjuncture of historiography and politics for which they had labored. "To be able to *make* history as well as to write it—or, to be modest, to have foreseen, twenty years ago, the exact stream of tendencies which would bring your proposal to fruition, is a pleasurable thought! So the old Webbs are chuckling over their chickens!"[139] For Sidney and Beatrice their *Poor Law History* comprised the last chapter in the history of the Poor Law.[140] By creating a common memory of the institution among reformers, M.P.'s, and ordinary citizens, the Webbs believed their written record had directly entered into a segment of the historical process and brought it to a conclusion. As far as the couple was concerned, they were not only making history as well as writing it; they were actually making history *by* writing it. The two volumes of *The Last Hundred Years* were a perfect expression of historiography correctly functioning as applied sociology.

Sidney and Beatrice once wrote that "history, to be either interesting or significant, must be written from a point of view; and this is the less likely to be harmful the more plainly it is avowed."[141] Contemporary reviewers remarked on the particular point of view of the Webbs' historiography but also on the impartiality of its conclusions.[142] Intermittently, the Webbs had their own doubts about the latter, with Beatrice agonizing in her diary that

When it is scientific and applied to men organized in groups or committees, history like personal observation, statistics or the art of interviewing is one of the methods of the science of sociology. But unlike other sciences, sociology, whether historical or statistical or geographical, can seldom be *impartial* because it is necessarily affected by the historian's scale of values in respect of human conduct and the organisation of political, social and economic life. Whether your bias is based on the knowledge of facts as well as your emotional preference—your scale of values; and whether this knowledge has modified your social aims (as much prejudice is the result of man's ignorance of facts) will determine your power to foretell and perhaps alter events. There is also literary history, poetical, biographical history, romantic or wishful history. The history which the Webbs have written is assuredly not literary, nor poetical, still less dramatic. Whether it is *wishful* is another question. We have *wished* to make it scientific; have we succeeded?[143]

Whatever their own doubts about the objectivity of their historiographical work, the Webbs certainly intended to make it *appear* scientific and therefore permanently legitimate and influential. The couple hoped that their histories' unmistakable partisan flavoring would be lost among analogies with the natural sciences, a most un-Bellocian plague of footnotes, and carefully publicized attention given to the techniques of fact-gathering and note-taking. In essence, the Webbs strove to create a paradox, a new typology of public history appropriate to the mass politics of the twentieth century, a public history that by virtue of its opaque and recondite form avoided intense public scrutiny. The Victorian literary history accessible to everyman that catered to the ancient and chaotic liberal organization of society would give way to an abstruse scientific public history whose technical impenetrability would complement the benevolently authoritarian bureaucratic technocracy of the future.

Just as the Webbs looked forward to public acceptance of the disinterested decision making of a bureaucratic administrative hierarchy, they anticipated that their readership would readily accept at face value the authority of their scientific and scholastic credentials and, therefore, of their historiographic conclusions. But not quite everyone was prepared to extend to them a wholly unsecured line of credit. Leonard Woolf, for one, was dismayed by the Webbs' indiscriminate and ruthless mixing of history and politics.

> Their politics and political actions were directly determined by their political theory, but their politics had a reciprocal—and often unfortunate—effect upon their political thought. No one who knew and worked with them could fail to recognise and admire their complete personal disinterestedness. . . . But they were so certain of the rightness of the ends which they were pursuing that they did not worry very much about the means which they used to attain them. The first time I worked closely with Sidney I was puzzled and troubled by this extraordinary mixture of scrupulousness with regard to ends and an almost ingenuous unscrupulousness with regard to means.[144]

The Webbs demonstrated a very unscientific preoccupation with ensuring the general adoption of their preconceived ends and of an organizational structure for viewing the past which would guarantee that those ends remained a logical imperative. Once accepted as orthodoxy, their rigid Linnaeanesque system of classification promised to absorb and assimilate the findings of all future historical research.

The Webbs wished to establish the foundation upon which others would build according to predetermined specifications. A *Daily News* review grasped the magnitude of the Webbs' ambitions when it declared "without exaggeration" that *English Local Government* would "necessitate the rewriting of English history."[145] Their success in the field of history has been a remarkably durable phenomenon. Already by the late 1930s their *ELG* had achieved the status of a classic, one interwar expert noting with evident satisfaction that all that remained for others was to complete the Webbs' general picture "gradually by a series of local studies."[146] The Webbs' eleven-volume history, with its general theme of the slow emergence of bureaucratic order out of ad hoc and corrupt liberal administrative chaos, survived as the definitive study on the subject well into the post-1945 period. Admirably suited as it was to the welfare-state-erecting Labour-Conservative consensus of the 1950s and 1960s, the analytic framework of *English Local Government* shaped the approach of all subsequent works in the field for three decades after the death of the Webbs.

Much like Belloc, the Webbs aimed at nothing less than a revolution in the way Britain thought about its past. But the Fabian couple possessed clear advantages denied the author of *The Servile State*. The sustained chorus of reverence for the methods and conclusions of Webbian historical analysis attests to the couple's profound grasp of the prestige and authority attached to the trappings of science in the modern age. Having cast their lot with this new historical form, they reaped its not inconsiderable benefits, in particular the presupposition of objective impartiality. Association with the discipline of academic administrative history further buoyed the Webbs' legitimacy. Equally important was the fact that, while Belloc necessarily dismissed the inherited Whig interpretation in toto, the Webbs retained enough traditional elements for their audience to recognize and feel comfortable.

Sidney and Beatrice would likely have been willing to preserve even more Whiggish elements in their histories if their own political ambitions had met with greater success. If the Edwardian Liberal party had embraced Fabian policies, perhaps the Webbs would have credited the landed oligarchy that governed Britain until the last quarter of the nineteenth century with prudently nurturing the modern bureaucratic state. But, since no accommodation proved possible with contemporary political Liberalism, its sanctioned version of history received no quarter.

Civic-minded gentrymen and Whig aristocrats filled the pantheon of the Liberal narrative of the seventeenth and eighteenth centuries. By contrast, the Webbs indicted the territorial ruling elite—infected and co-opted by the bourgeois spirit of the boroughs—as the authors of the interruption of national progress lasting from 1688 to 1835. In the Fabian account, the Victorian era inaugurated a methodical reformism that restored the autonomous state previously hijacked by a corrupt and inefficient landed oligarchy. Belloc envisioned the traditional ruling classes as far more protean, adaptable, and persistent than did the Webbs. Also, he could not employ the same progressive framework, so familiar to the British historical consciousness, because he did not rejoice at the growth of centralized authority. This last was not the least of the advantages that potentiated the influence of the Webbs' historiography. Their books aided in the creation after 1900 of a citizenry more ready to entertain a positive view of the proficiency and beneficence of the state. Reordering the past created the conditions to shape the future.

3   J. L. & BARBARA HAMMOND
A Case of Mistaken Identity

The Webbs embraced the segmentation of British intellectual life which gathered momentum in the last quarter of the nineteenth century. The rise of specialization and a professional ethos severed the Victorian occupational overlap between politicians, men of letters, journalists, and the professoriate. The result by the early 1900s was at least the beginning of the end of the integration of British intellectuals into the fullness of society. Although they wore many hats, the Webbs felt most comfortable addressing bureaucratic and academic specialists, a preference reinforced by their failed approaches to Liberal politicians between 1890

John Lawrence Hammond and Lucy Barbara Hammond, ca. 1930, around the time of the publication of their Age of the Chartists. *(Courtesy of Nicholas G. Hammond and the Bodleian Library, Oxford, MS.Photogr.c.76, fols. 2, 4)* and 1910. By design, theirs was a new form of public history aimed expressly at a restricted but influential audience. The fragmentation of the common culture of Victorian elites meant a shrinking arena for public debates as each specialty shifted to its own venue and adopted its own jargon. The decline in the great Victorian periodicals by the 1890s and the concomitant appearance of abstruse technical journals addressing narrow readerships registered this change. The Webbs felt at home in this more claustrophobic milieu.

The fragmentation of the Victorian intellectual inheritance likewise led to the abandonment of a shared vocabulary of character and morality. This process was a disaster for Liberalism and for Liberal historiography in particular. Whig history, as traditionally conceived, concerned itself with such moral concepts as the growth of constitutional freedom as the collective representation of the maturation of character of the individual Englishman. But the use of such moral arguments as a unifying theme necessarily involved some appeal to values shared by both speaker and audience. The splintering that invariably accompanied professionalization shattered this bond of unspoken assumptions between Victorian author and reader. The Webbs understood intuitively the incompatibility of rampant specialization and Liberal historiography and, more generally, Liberalism itself. The devil was in the details. With their use of technical grammar, the new scholarly subfields of institutional, administrative, and economic history restricted public consumption while substituting for the unspoken moral assumptions of the grand old synthesis of constitutional progress a particularist focus upon managerial efficiency.

The Webbs were on dangerous ground here because there remained only a short step to historiography's complete surrender of practical purpose and cultural authority, an outcome that interested Sidney and Beatrice not in the least. J. L. and Barbara Hammond recognized the perils and proceeded with caution. They held no brief for the received Whig historical tradition and admired the strides made by pioneering "scientific" scholarship, especially in the realm of economic history. But as lifelong Liberals, they were loath to abandon the moral vocabulary which they deemed integral to public history. The Hammonds were never entirely comfortable in the intellectually frayed world of twentieth-century Britain. Lawrence eyed a university chair in the same way a condemned man

J. L. and Barbara Hammond 99

savors his last meal; the gastronomic delights could not hide the fact that the feast heralded the end. The academic setting was decidedly not for him, as his wife clearly understood from the start. The Hammonds wished to recast the Whig historiographical tradition without abandoning its literary style, its popular audience, its cultural authority, or its moral voice. It was an ambition fraught with difficulties.

Complicating their self-appointed task was a chronic inability to shake the Fabian shadow of the Webbs. While Lawrence was away in May 1924, Barbara Hammond wrote to her husband of a strange and comic visitation to their home. A former schoolmistress (Barbara couldn't even recall the name) had appeared on their doorstep requesting the loan of one of their books. The visitor was preparing to address a gathering of Berkshire women on the subject of temperance and needed details on the growth of public houses, information that she claimed could be found in some unnamed history by the Hammonds—presumably one of the Labourer trilogy (1911–19). Barbara, unable to remember authoring anything of the sort, was a bit rattled by the women's persistence. "I was sorry we c[ou]ldn't oblige her—but she was positive and convincing 'give me the book & I'll show you.' My head began to go round & I wondered if you had inserted something—then I brightly suggested the Webbs' History of Licensing Laws. That was scouted—she'd never read it. However a long search convinced her."[1] Barbara's suspicion that the teetotaling schoolteacher was really interested in Sidney and Beatrice Webb's *History of Liquor Licensing in England* was an instinctive response, conditioned by years of public reaction to the Hammonds' historiography.

As left-leaning historian couples offering an innovative revision of England's past from the "bottom up," the Webbs and Hammonds often appeared to lack separate and distinctive identities in the public consciousness. Superficial similarities led to what Gilbert Murray called "the inevitable comparison."[2] Reviewers always insisted on mentioning the Hammonds and the Webbs in the same breath.[3] Even Sidney and Beatrice encouraged this contemporary tendency to conflate the historiography of the Hammond and Webb husband-and-wife partnerships.[4] Posterity has not proven itself to be much more discriminating. E. P. Thompson lumped the Hammonds, the Webbs, and Graham Wallas together as "men and women of Fabian persuasion."[5] Peter Quennell's 1976 autobiography recalls Lawrence and Barbara Hammond as "old-fashioned Fabian Socialists, belonging to the same high-minded school as Beatrice and Sidney Webb."[6] Quennell was wrong on all counts. The Hammonds never belonged to the Fabian Society, nor could they have ever been considered socialists.

In the case of the Hammonds, the Webbs' attempt to orchestrate a reinterpretation of the traditional Whig version of English history achieved success in an unexpected fashion. Flattering the Hammonds as "colleagues who equal us in literary skill," Sidney and Beatrice assumed the role of patron, bombarding Lawrence and Barbara with advice on choosing appropriate historiographical subject matter while unsuccessfully recruiting the couple for Fabian Society membership.[7] This proselytizing failed completely to convert the Hammonds to Webbian conclusions. But the fruits of such efforts fell into the Fabian couple's lap all the same. The high visibility of books like *The History of Trade Unionism* and the public's too eager association of them with the writings of the Hammonds dictated the terms of the latter's critical reception. Thus in 1917 the Fabian Research Department referred to the Hammonds as "a storehouse of facts for those who wish to indict the system."[8] In the same vein, an anonymous reviewer of *The Village Labourer, 1760–1832* (1911) declared that "to the worker fighting for Socialism history is, of course studied for its utility" and that "serious purpose receives ample service from the Hammond histories."[9] One well-read manual laborer, an iron turner for some sixty-one of his seventy-five years, wrote to Lawrence criticizing *The Town Labourer* for its radical and inflammatory tone.

> It strikes me that your book has an animus, not only against the selfish & callous but against property owners, against the rich, against governments, and also the main mass of people not manual labourers, say the middle classes, are somewhat ignored. This will encourage the unreflecting to tolerate devastating revolution bringing misery on all. Your animus should be directed solely against callousness in property owners, in the rich, in small employers, workmen or others. That would include callousness in governments. Without governments the people perish. Without a rich class no country produces anything raising the people above a mere animal life. Progress can only come by raising

the moral tone of all classes. Not by setting one class against another.[10]

A casual remark by a trained historian like G. M. Trevelyan that if a cheap edition of *The Village Labourer* was ever made generally available to the poor, Britain would face revolution—even if made half-facetiously—indicates the pervasive nature of this extreme interpretation of the Hammonds' work.[11]

But, of course, the Hammonds were never satellites of the Webbs, nor is it accurate to label their histories as revolutionary. Examination of their carefully nuanced writings reveals a message unpalatable to the authors of *The History of Trade Unionism*. The lines of narrative often appeared identical in the foreground, but through the dexterous use of delicate shading, the Hammonds always ensured that theirs converged at a vanishing point different from their Fabian counterparts. In a review of the Hammonds' *Lord Shaftesbury* (1923), Elie Halévy, the great French historian of England, recognized in their work the direct antithesis to that of the Webbs and described the biography as "useful" in counteracting the "anti-Liberal bias of Mr. and Mrs. Sidney Webb in their *History of Trade Unionism*."[12] The consequences of the Hammonds' work were potentially radical, but unlike Hilaire Belloc and the Webbs, they lacked any interest in a root-and-branch dismantling of the status quo through a complete devaluation of the nation's liberal past. Primarily concerned with the moral effects of economic change, the Hammonds' understanding of good and evil encompassed many shades of gray that found no place in Belloc's *Servile State* or the Webbs' *English Local Government*.

This ambivalence about the past—and the present as well—made the Hammonds' work distinctive and interesting. It was this same problematic sensibility that vitiated the effectiveness of their histories as vehicles for the dissemination of a moderate twentieth-century Liberalism. Their determination to strike a balance between the traditional celebratory Whig version of English history and corrosive socialist revisionism captured the inherent tension within the New Liberalism. At their historiographic best, the Hammonds accepted the complexity of England's ancestry, recognizing the intimate intermingling of blemishes and beauty. Their politics ultimately derived from this same belief in the ambiguity of events, past and present. While embracing a socially conscious, reformist variant of Edwardian Liberalism, the Hammonds steadfastly refused to reject what they maintained was the traditional and essential moral core of all forms of Liberalism, that is, an allegiance to righteousness and justice that could be traced back to Gladstone, Charles James Fox, and beyond.

Pushing by the Back Wheel

From his father Lawrence received an infusion of the Gladstonian brand of Radical Liberalism.[13] At Oxford (where he made friends with a Hilaire Belloc two years his senior) Hammond soaked up the still potent influence of T. H. Green via St. John's College tutor Sidney Ball. Ball and the friendship of the young classical scholar Gilbert Murray cemented young Lawrence's tendency to view the problems of society in moral terms and to see the state as a benevolent actor in history.[14] New Liberal conviction that collectivism was really all about the advancement of individual character rather than simple institutional arrangements surfaced in his post-Oxford forays into journalism. Hammond joined Belloc in *Essays in Liberalism* in 1897, contributing an essay, "A Liberal View of Education," calling for an activist state to "promote" and "extend freedom in th[e] positive sense."[15]

Later, as editor of the Radical weekly the *Speaker* (where he was briefly reunited with Belloc) and in a volume coauthored with Gilbert Murray entitled *Liberalism and the Empire* (1900), Hammond explored the problematic relationship between Liberalism and power by analyzing colonial and foreign affairs. As a pro-Boer he opposed the war in South Africa, yet his outlook was cautiously optimistic. Liberalism appeared compatible with the exercise of power in the long term. Political reform could control capitalists and capitalism. The increasing democratization of the electorate would inevitably curb the worst excesses of British imperialism. A political democracy was "open to intellectual and, still more, to moral conviction." With its "capacity for grasping and acting on simple ethical principles," a well-informed, politically active citizenry would allow for the pursuit of virtue in the nation's external affairs.[16]

Hammond's critique of imperialism reproduced in miniature what was soon to become his general approach to historical judgment. It proceeded under the assumption that England's liberal rulers were indeed guilty of a long list of transgressions, past and present, which the scrupulous historian should not hesitate to detail. However, this catalog of sin, balanced as it clearly was by so many enduring virtues, in no sense invalidated the utility of the liberal system of government and economics. Liberalism's track record was a mixed one, but along with its many failings it possessed strong evidence of a built-in mechanism for self-repair and improvement, fueled and directed by its fundamentally moral nature. Capitalism's implication in the Boer War did not signal its incapacity for redemption. Similarly, liberal mistakes of omission and commission during the early Industrial Revolution did not argue for the jettisoning of liberal culture. Hammond's politics remained reformist, not revolutionary, and his historiography always retained a link to the old Whig tradition of continuity combined with progress. Unlike Belloc or the Webbs, neither his politics nor his interpretation of the past admitted of any great discontinuities.

As his personal political development distanced him from his comrades since undergraduate days, Hammond formed a new and more lasting partnership. His marriage in 1901 to Lucy Barbara Bradby provided him with an intelligent spouse who enthusiastically seconded the social and political sympathies of her journalist husband. More important, she proved an invaluable confederate in researching and writing the histories to which Hammond was shortly to turn his attention. Barbara's delicate health led her physician to recommend a change of residence from London to the country. First at Hampstead Heath and then later at Oatfield in Piccott's End, Hertfordshire, the couple developed a strange, ascetic lifestyle of horseback riding, gardening, and long walks, punctuated by eating and sleeping outdoors—all of which they considered therapeutic.[17]

Despite her infirmities—real or imagined—Barbara's description of Lawrence as the "brains" and of herself as the "muscles of Oatfield" was essentially accurate.[18] Ironically, she had been the superior student, topping Lawrence's own Second with a First in Greats at Oxford. Yet she once confessed to her husband, "I hate using my brains."[19] Her intellectual talents were more attuned to "putting great masses of fact & detail in order, seizing their significance & seeing how they should be set out."[20] She did most of the research and organization, while Lawrence assumed the bulk of the writing chores. It proved a congenial and fruitful collaboration. Sometimes accompanied by her husband, but more often alone, Barbara would journey into London from the country early in the morning to the British Museum or the Public Record Office, where she would work all day among the documents, always taking care to leave early enough, even in the winter, to reach home so that she could sleep in the camp beds of their open-air shelter. Arnold Toynbee's description of these research expeditions as "trials of endurance" and "diver's descents" was apt.[21]

Three decades earlier a man like Lawrence might have combined journalism and the writing of history with a career in politics. But like many New Liberals, Hammond did not possess the self-confidence of his Victorian predecessors. The division of public life into separate spheres called into question the complementarity of history and politics in the twentieth century. Lawrence actually toyed with the idea of running for parliament in 1903–4.[22] But instead he retired to the haven of a civil service sinecure at eight hundred pounds annually. He informed Gilbert Murray, "I was very averse from the idea [of accepting the post] because I disliked the prospect of going out of contentious politics."[23]

More likely he welcomed the self-imposed exile. It seemed that the ambiguities of Edwardian Liberalism rendered it impossible to inhabit the world of politics and scholarship and still retain intellectual consistency. The party of Campbell-Bannerman and Asquith was slow to embrace the New Liberal notion of the state as an agent of moral progress. The reaction of the Hammonds to formal Liberal politics between 1905 and 1914 oscillated between satisfaction and exasperation.[24] They suffered many of the same frustrations experienced by Hilaire Belloc and Sidney and Beatrice Webb. Belloc and the Webbs had hoped that the Liberal party might metamorphose into a true instrument of revolution, peaceful or otherwise. The comprehensiveness of their subsequent historiographical assaults upon Liberalism and its ancestry echoed the depths of their disappointment. By contrast, the Hammonds' expectations remained modestly reformist—they mourned the loss of "the *old* Radical feeling"—and thus their disenchantment was attenuated.[25]

Political frustrations convinced the Hammonds of the chasm between theoretical New Liberalism and the practice of Liberal politics as usual. Duplicating the initiative of the Webbs and Belloc, the Hammonds assumed the task of reshaping Liberalism by reinventing its past. In Gilbert Murray's opinion, Lawrence's "business" was "to preach advanced Liberalism," and it was with this exhortation in mind that Hammond approached the writing of history.[26]

His first book, *Charles James Fox* (1903), contained an obvious contemporary homily—one reviewer called it "an inspiration in this age of political lassitude and indifference"—and Hammond offered no apologies for his partisanship and present-mindedness.[27] In *Essays in Liberalism* Hammond had solemnly linked the "sacred" cause of education and Liberalism, education being the only sure guarantee for making government "more democratic, citizenship more real, and national life more self-conscious."[28] Hammond never questioned history's didactic role in the service of Liberalism. In 1908 he advised G. M. Trevelyan to postpone writing a biography of John Bright because it was the wrong moment for such a book "from a Liberal point of view."[29] Three decades hence Hammond was still preaching the primacy of history's educative function, though, on the eve of world war, on a more bipartisan basis. "If in teaching history by lesson or pen, I have to think of the making of good citizens, I must begin by asking what I mean by good citizen . . . the qualities I should look for . . . are a sense of duty to the community, an understanding of the value of personal and political freedom, a spirit of toleration, and the power of seeing national politics in the larger medium of the atmosphere of a universal society."[30] This assurance of the indispensability to society of historiography's cultural and moral function accounts in the main for the Hammonds' reluctance over years to reconcile fully their own eclectic style to the scientific dictates of the university academy.

Gilbert Murray judged the Hammonds' *Village Labourer* (1911) a book that would make a "permanent difference," while A. M. D. Hughes imagined that its considerable influence went "a good way towards compensating you for having had to give up active politics, for it is a pushing at the cart which has to be got forward, albeit by the back wheel, but then again that is the most effective place to push at."[31] The Hammonds' faith in the efficacy of pressure applied to the back wheel permitted them to retire to a life of writing in the country with a measure of equanimity. Like many intellectuals who have recoiled from political involvement, the Hammonds rationalized away the guilt that settles over a life of relative inactivity and potential impotence. In their unobtrusive way they hoped to create a more profound and lasting impression than did the evanescent discussions conducted via the medium of popular politics, to give fundamental truths "a hold over the imagination, thus gaining for them the support not merely of intellectual assent, but also of moral feeling."[32] The writing of history provided a means of contributing to the contemporary debate through the back door. The Hammonds' historiographic style, a deft combination of intellectual persuasion and moral appeal, seemed to guarantee longevity of influence without sacrificing immediate impact.

Lawrence's first venture into historiography preceded either his decision to refrain from politics or his discomfiture with hesitant post-1906 Liberal ministries. Thus *Charles James Fox: A Political Study* openly exhibited the author's instinctive identification with Liberalism's historic roots. As he readily admitted in the preface, the book was neither a standard biography nor a conventional interpretation, since his conviction that his subject was both a "great man & a heroic liberal" was an enthusiasm not shared by most of his acquaintances.[33] His depiction of Fox as "one of the few Whigs who anticipated the great Liberal doctrine of national rights" established his protagonist as modern Liberalism's direct link with the past, and therefore he projected onto Fox his understanding of Edwardian Liberalism's present virtues and hopes for its future development. Hammond particularly admired Fox because he believed they shared a common love of "justice and freedom" and that that love "never made freedom second-best." To the National Efficiency–style argument of Pitt the Younger that "the life of a nation [was] a mere symmetry of administrative excellence and precision," Fox responded that "self-government is better than good government." Hammond defended this view by emphasizing the connection between broad political participation and the growth of civic virtue and the nurturing of community spirit.[34] By 1903 New Liberal statism and the claims of institutional history had made little headway against Lawrence's acceptance of the main thrust of the traditional Whig narrative equating constitutional development with the growth of freedom.

Hammond faced a problem, however, for he recognized that his hero was a member of an exclusive ruling oligarchy that had monopolized power at local, regional, and national levels. It was essential to portray Fox as a man who accepted the system and yet was passionately committed to its eventual reform. Hammond could not too closely identify him with the revolutionary rhetoric of the Painite Radicals, yet Fox must still be made to appear sympathetic to the same democratic ends. If his Fox stood somewhat apart from "the visions of the democrats, he had a great conception of the state as based on wide citizenship, the attribute of personal independence, and he transformed the Whig principles of Locke into a system compatible with a genuine democracy." Through such graceful devices Hammond strove to lessen the gap between the liberal Whiggism of an eighteenth-century parliamentarian and the reformist New Liberalism of his own day.[35]

Hammond had little use for the great Whig ruling houses of the eighteenth century. Years before Lewis Namier would detail their multiple failings, Hammond recorded that they "were not remembered for the protection of the poor, or the disarming of corruption, or the championship of public integrity. Office had been their object, not because they saw in it an opportunity of serving their country, or of achieving some great and necessary reform, but mainly because they wished to see their own friends rather than the friends of others quartered on the public funds." Amidst this Namierite wasteland Fox set to work to inject, or as he saw it, to reinject, principle into a Whiggism grown decadent. According to Hammond, Fox "lived to plead great causes, which the Whigs of tradition had never dreamt of," yet he fancied himself in a strict line of succession whose ancestry could be traced back to the Revolution of 1688. In this fashion Fox placed history at the service of politics; Burkean arguments were harnessed to the wagon of reform. Hammond believed that the Painite Radicals and Fox started at opposite ends of the debate and yet managed to emerge at essentially identical points. "The difference between Fox and such radicals as Paine was that Fox started from the Whig Revolution and Locke's interpretation of it, whereas they started from an abstract individual right, which they regarded as positively outraged, and not merely imperfectly recognised, in the British constitution." Fox maintained that Britain's already existing institutions were sufficient potential instruments of freedom, that her constitution expressly recognized the doctrine of the sovereignty of the people and the Rights of Man, and that real control of the government could be handed over to the common citizenry under the aegis of constitutional precedent. While acknowledging the justice of many of the claims of "visionary demo-crats," he cautioned that a reliance upon their extreme remedies would only lead to a period of anarchy and revolution.[36]

Resembling nothing so much as Gladstone, this impressionistic sketch of Fox as champion of parliamentary and electoral reform, advocate for Irish home rule, defender of religious toleration, and exponent of morality in foreign and colonial affairs came as close as Hammond dared to a statement of his own turn-of-the-century views. In essence, *Charles James Fox* constituted an eloquent defense of Liberal reformism versus revolution, a statement of confidence in the ability of Britain's social and political institutions to restructure themselves along more progressive lines. The ticklish part was that Fox used what Hammond judged to be a false interpretation of his-tory to legitimate his choice of the correct path to progress. Fox's re-pudiation of dangerously radical democratic methods was grounded upon his direct familial linkage of late-eighteenth-century liberal reformism with the Whig settlement of 1688. This was a connection that Hammond could not quite accept in 1903. Unlike Fox, he judged the Rockingham Whigs a new party with new principles, not merely "a return to the normal and the recovery of an old simplicity from the misgrowths and perversions with which it was overlaid."[37] Whereas Fox felt he was only adjusting the Lockean principles that sustained the settlement of 1688, Hammond believed Fox's transfor-mation of them represented an unrecognized or at least an un-acknowledged rejection of these same tenets. This crucial inconsis-tency in the book's argument was never adequately resolved. For now Hammond ignored the problem, as did his appreciative review-ers, but the difficulty was to resurface in a form less easily overlooked or explained away in his later books on the Industrial Revolution.[38]

The Village Labourer: A Lower Plane of Truth?

Research began on the first two volumes of the Hammonds' famous Labourer trilogy, *The Village Labourer* and *The Town Labourer*, in 1908 in step with the couple's heightening frustration at the ap-parent timidity of the Asquith government, and the actual writing commenced just as the constitutional crisis over the "People's Bud-get" and the House of Lords reached a fever pitch in mid-1910. Completed by the end of January 1911, the manuscript was submit-ted to Longmans, which deemed it "sound historically though written from the Radical point of view."[39] A vexing problem of excessive length was overcome at Barbara's suggestion by dividing the manuscript into two complementary books to be published separately. *The Village Labourer* appeared in mid-1911, and its sequel, *The Town Labourer*, delayed by the war, followed in 1917.

The complete title of the first book was actually *The Village Labourer, 1760–1832: A Study in the Government of England before the Reform Bill*. Available to the interested reader were any number of histories detailing the development of England's parliamentary system, the evolution of her legal system, the nation's acquisition of colonies, and its conduct of diplomacy and war. Missing was anything more than a thumbnail sketch of the relationship between governors and governed. The Hammonds set out to remedy this oversight by describing "the life of the poor" during the period of the Industrial Revolution. It was their object "to show what was in fact happening to the working classes under a government in which they had no share."[40] The book opened with a discussion of the survival of the ancient village system into the mid-eighteenth century. The Hammonds allowed that no one familiar with the novels of Henry Fielding and Samuel Richardson could be so blind as to idealize this old society as "an age of gold." But its virtues were undeniable. "The most important social fact about this system is that it provided opportunities for the humblest and poorest labourer to rise in the village . . . whatever the pressure outside and whatever the bickerings within, it remains true that the common-field system formed a world in which the villagers lived their own lives and cultivated the soil on a basis of independence."[41] Drawing upon the Webbs' work in the recently published first three volumes of *English Local Government*, the Hammonds identified the rise of a landed aristocratic oligarchy after 1689 as the chief culprit in the dismantling of the village system.[42] As the authority of the ancient manorial courts declined amidst the concentration of power and influence in the hands of the county justices of the peace and the local squirearchy, so too was a rough form of democracy replaced by what amounted to arbitrary government. The basis of the oligarchy's hegemony was land ownership, and the incentive to acquire more land was overwhelming. Enclosure was expedited through Parliament where petitions of protest from small proprietors stood little chance when read before a tribunal of wealthy landowners. The Hammonds' recounted the effects of decades of legalized expropriation: the breakup of the village community, the degradation of the laborer and his family, the introduction of the disastrous Speenhamland system of wage supplementation, the rise in distress and crime, and, in the final two dramatic chapters, the agonal spasm of a dying world, the laborers' revolt of 1830.

This focus upon the indecent origins and dire consequences of the modern English agricultural system underscored the historical legitimacy of Edwardian Liberalism's advocacy of land reform as well as the specific land tax provisions of Lloyd George's 1909 budget, while dealing a heavy blow to the justice of the Lords' resistance in the eyes of the public. But the Hammonds, unlike the Webbs, were not about to consign to the dustbin the century and a half of English history after 1689. Their evaluation of the governing class between 1760 and 1832 was a heavily nuanced refusal to write off the rulers of the counties as destructively insensitive instruments of ruthless capitalism. Avarice alone had not killed the old village communities. Greed was perhaps a sufficient motive, but "greed was in this case clothed and almost enveloped in public spirit."

> In addition to the desire for social power, there was behind the enclosure movement a zeal for economic progress seconding and almost concealing the direct inspiration of self interest. Many an enclosing landlord thought only of the satisfaction of doubling or trebling his rent: that is unquestionable. . . . But there were many whose eyes glistened as they thought of the prosperity they were to bring to English agriculture, applying to a wider and wider domain the lessons that were to be learnt from the processes of scientific farming.

Landlords defended enclosure in good conscience as necessary for the spread of the undeniable public benefits of economic progress. Identification of the small farmer, the cottager, and the squatter with the "old-fashioned routine" resulted in "a state of mind [that] passed rapidly and naturally to the conclusion that the wider the sphere brought into the absolute possession of the enlightened class, the greater would be the public gain."[43]

In their conclusion, the Hammonds revealed the extent of their admiration for England's historic ruling class. They noted that, unlike in France, the small group that monopolized social and political power in eighteenth-century England remained a "race of country gentlemen," embracing the rural life in lieu of the leisure and profligacy of life at court. To this peculiarity the Hammonds attributed the resistance of the aristocracy, corrupt and selfish though it remained, to the "supreme vice of moral decadence." Abandoning somewhat the mild cynicism of Lawrence's earlier *Charles James Fox*, the Hammonds credited the fundamentally ethical nature of the English governing class with preventing a degeneration of eighteenth-century politics into an unvarnished scramble for place and power. "An age which produced the two Pitts could not be called an age of mere avarice. An age which produced Burke and Fox and Grey could not be called an age of mere ambition. The politics of this little class are illuminated by the great and generous behaviour of individuals." In this fashion, the lineage of contemporary Liberalism dating back to the great Whig houses of the 1700s—left in doubt in 1903 in *Charles James Fox*—was at least partially reaffirmed in *The Village Labourer*.

> In glancing at the class whose treatment of the English poor has been the subject of our study, it is only just to record that in other regions of thought and conduct they bequeathed a great inheritance of moral and liberal ideas: a passion for justice between peoples, a sense for national freedom, a great body of principle by which to check, refine, and discipline the gross appetites of national ambition. Those ideas were the ideas of a minority, but they were expressed and defended with an eloquence and a power that have made them an important and a glorious part of English history. In all this development of liberal doctrine it is not fanciful to see the ennobling influence of the Greek writers on whom every eighteenth-century politician was bred and nourished.

Anxious not to toss out the baby with the bath water, the Hammonds carefully enumerated the sterling qualities of the English ruling elite which held the promise of future domestic reform.[44]

The obvious discrepancy between this sort of carefully worded praise and the blanket condemnations launched by Belloc and the Webbs against the liberal-capitalist ethos of the squirearchical offspring of the Glorious Revolution requires no reiteration. The Hammonds' dissatisfaction with Edwardian Liberalism was never more than partial at the worst of times. Like the great majority of

New Liberals, they retained their faith in the fundamental virtue of the older variant. Their history of parliamentary enclosure demonstrated the impatience of youth with its elders but softened by the sympathy and understanding that develop within families.

Many of the book's admirers on the political Left failed to make allowances for the qualifications the Hammonds introduced into their conclusions. C. P. Trevelyan confessed to having known "the bare outline of the story of the great land robbery," but it was the Hammonds' work that had finally opened his eyes to the "enormity of the wickedness and the evil."[45] Roused to anger by the book's "overmastering sense of dramatic force," Graham Wallas compared it to *Uncle Tom's Cabin*, hoping that "it, too, may start a national movement of humiliation and amendment which may ultimately reach the classes who are now profiting in hard cash by the events which it describes."[46] The Radical Josiah Wedgwood congratulated the Hammonds on constructing "the most crushing inditement [*sic*] of every previous English historian as well as the squirarcy [*sic*]."[47]

The hybrid form of the book may have accounted for some of this overreading of its message. The Hammonds had perfected a new kind of economic history that appealed directly to the emotions, a genre with numerous modern offspring. The book was self-consciously literary with its references to Tocqueville's *Ancien Regime*, Mirabeau's *Ami des Hommes*, Spenser's *Fairie Queene*, Milton's *Paradise Lost*, and Dryden's *Tales from Chaucer* and its unapologetic use of French and Latin quotations and obscure Greek historical metaphors. Lawrence crafted his beautiful prose to achieve just the right effect. Carried along by the stream of the story, A. E. Zimmern found the Hammonds' aptitude for extracting "emotion" from "plain facts . . . quite Thucydidian."[48]

The sheer novelty of the subject matter also contributed to the book's tremendous impact. *The Village Labourer* did have one major historiographical forebear; Arnold Toynbee's *Lectures on the Industrial Revolution of the Eighteenth Century in England* (1884) had pioneered the sociopolitical angle of approach to the history of industrialization. But while the Hammonds saw themselves modestly enough as Toynbee's heirs, their work was "breaking new ground."[49] It proved necessary to base *The Village Labourer* almost entirely upon original source material. As they explained in 1929, they had stumbled upon their subject quite by accident. Browsing through the *Political Register* while toying with the idea of writing a life of William Cobbett, Lawrence "was startled to come upon a series of events quite new to him: the rising in the southern counties in 1830. The two authors began to study first these events, then others on which few histories had much to say. The three Labourer books were the undesigned result."[50] This unusual topic led them to the relatively untilled fields of the Home Office Papers, the eventual source of so much of their documentation, particularly for the final two chapters of *The Village Labourer*.[51]

Initial sales figures registered the success of this groundbreaking attempt to incorporate economic history into a literary form.[52] But, anxious that their popularly conceived work should double as work of serious scholarship, the Hammonds were disappointed to find the academic community underwhelmed by their pioneering research. The *English Historical Review* completely ignored the book. The *Economic Journal*, the one academic publication paying any attention, was less than complimentary. There the renowned economic historian J. H. Clapham of Cambridge attempted to refute the Hammonds' arguments as well as their heretical approach to the field of economic history.[53] Clapham conceded that *The Village Labourer* was "a brilliantly written social tragedy, full of pity and terror," yet his judgment was a harsh one. The book's "bias against the governing classes" led to harsh and unfair conclusions drawn from atypical examples. But more important, it ignored the crucial question of productivity. That omission left the reader with "a picture that is out of drawing." Enclosure, viewed in isolation as the Hammonds had done, appeared more important and less inevitable than had actually been the case. Clapham worried lest the "unlearned reader" carry away the impression that "but for greed things could have gone on very well as they were." Reproaching the authors of *The Village Labourer* for neglecting the issue of "how common-field agriculture was to meet the needs of England," he maintained that the Parliament so roundly criticized by the Hammonds had had to focus upon what was "desirable from the national standpoint." The question of enclosure could not be disarticulated from the question of productivity. The Hammonds could answer that they " 'are not concerned.' But in judging a government they ought to be concerned," admonished Clapham.[54]

It might appear that Clapham's rebuttal missed the point entirely.

But though Clapham and the Hammonds may have been arguing past each other, it was certainly not because of any failure of comprehension on the part of the former. It was simply a question of Clapham's disapproval of this sort of economic history as partial and misleading. He maintained that economic history's "methodological distinctiveness hinges primarily upon its marked quantitative interests; for this reason it is or should be the most exact branch of history."[55] Barbara Hammond was later to confess that she wrote as "one whose ignorance of mathematics is profound."[56] Clapham believed that this sort of admission was fatal to the discipline, for any good economic historian knew that all nonquantitative sections of his work "will be on a lower plane of truth than that to which the fully equipped inductive economist may conceivably attain."[57] A disregard for statistics could never be countenanced. In *The Village Labourer* there was no suggestion in the text "or in the footnotes or in the bibliography that any serious study of prices has been so much as attempted." The unfortunate result of this glaring oversight was the "impression that inclosures were the cause, or the main cause, of the price rise in the [seventeen-]nineties." Clapham, with his social-imperialist conception of government, certainly had differences with the Hammonds over the contemporary political implications of their work, but his main concern was to prevent the unchallenged acceptance of their impressionistic, highly literary style of economic history within the sanctum sanctorum of quantitative scholarly treatment which he was attempting to construct. He charged the Hammonds with "complain[ing] somewhere of the 'simplifying philosophy of the eighteenth century,' while themselves simplifying its economic history." His self-appointed task was to limit the metastasis of this sort of simplification. Compared with the emotional narrative of *The Village Labourer*, an orthodox text of economic history appeared as "bloodless as a Board of Trade return" but still remained eminently preferable.[58]

Clapham, engaged as he was in the task of professionalizing economic history, reacted instinctively against the liberties taken in *The Village Labourer*. The book's indiscriminate mixing of moral and scientific vocabularies provided it with access to a direct public hearing. The sort of public history that evoked a visceral response among a broad lay readership subverted the narrowly focused influence of the restrained and considered opinions of the expert. Conversely, public economic history as practiced by the Webbs, political activists though they might be, seemed less threatening, more ally than rival really. Encoded in a strictly scientific format, the cryptic social and political agenda of *English Local Government* seemed to appeal on a purely intellectual plane to a restricted audience of elites, thereby buttressing the hard-won privileged position of the academic professional expert.

In a new preface composed for the 1913 edition, the Hammonds practiced damage control against the Claphamite critique. They readily conceded that enclosure "made the soil of England immediately more productive," but in a reprise of the original text, they insisted that they "had not set out to examine the general economic effect of enclosures, but the methods by which these enclosures were carried out and their social consequences."[59] It was a question of ends and means. Regardless of the impression a reading of their book might convey, they did not condemn the economic revolution wrought by the enclosure of the village lands. They took issue only with the callous argument "that the misery of the labourer was the price the nation had to pay for that advance." The implied message of *The Village Labourer* was that "the actual revolution that was accomplished was not the only alternative to the old unreformed common field system."[60]

Thus the Hammonds were politely underscoring their own refusal to accept efficiency as the sole, or even principal, measure of progress. Britain's eighteenth-century governing elite had fashioned a "new civilization," but at a needlessly high price. The Labourer trilogy argued that the moral element must always take precedence in historical assessment. Despite the valuable contributions of the scientific disciplines of economic, institutional, and administrative history, their narrow disregard of a broader ethical context meant that their conclusions remained partial. Liberalism, as Lawrence and Barbara understood it, would be poorly served relying upon such blinkered versions of the past. British history was indeed a story of material and organizational progress, but only as a subplot embedded in a greater narrative of moral development and backsliding. Though the Hammonds might quibble with nineteenth-century Whig historians about answers, they were all agreed about which were the important questions to ask. In that vital respect, Lawrence and Barbara were the progeny of traditional Victorian Liberal historiography.

From *The Town Labourer* to *Lord Shaftesbury*:
On the Trail of Liberalism's True Heritage

World war, intervening before the publication of the sequel to *The Village Labourer*, sorely tested the Hammonds' relationship with official Liberalism. The couple's unease stemmed from the now familiar Liberal dilemma regarding the concentration and uses of power. Between 1914 and 1916 it seemed to them that the government demonstrated its incompetence almost daily, and Asquith's feet of clay made any change unlikely. But the swap of Asquithian lethargy for the dynamism of Lloyd George was equivocal at best because, in Barbara's estimation, "the Asquith regime means certain & moderate disaster; the Ll[oyd] G[eorge] either absolute disaster or success."[61] A member of the government's Reconstruction Committee from 1916, Lawrence fretted that, in their single-minded focus upon victory, policy makers would ignore the lessons of 1793–1820. Repression and economic hardship followed triumph over Napoleon. He now called upon the Lloyd George coalition to use an analogous opportunity as a catalyst for the furtherance of domestic social and political liberation.[62]

To underscore this advice with a litany of historical parallels, the Hammonds brought out the second volume in their trilogy, *The Town Labourer*. When faced with seemingly insurmountable structural problems in 1915, the Hammonds had agreed with Longmans that its publication should be postponed until after the war.[63] By the end of the year, however, Graham Wallas was pleading that they "*must* get the book out so as to influence the social discussion that will follow the making of the peace."[64] *The Town Labourer*, essentially drafted by the end of 1911, required extensive revision prior to any serious consideration of publication. In the book's preface the Hammonds stated that it was almost ready for the printers in the summer of 1914, "when it was put on one side for the more pressing tasks of the war."[65] However their correspondence reveals that work progressed on the book all through the period 1914–17. During Lawrence's brief army service in 1915–16 Barbara continued the job alone, discussing the finer points with her husband through the post.

After dividing their manuscript in 1911 and publishing the first half separately as *The Village Labourer*, the Hammonds discovered that further work on its sequel had swollen the text to unmanageable proportions. The result was an uncomfortable mixture of topics, with analyses of the "New Town," the "New Discipline," and the psychology of the rich trailing off into minute descriptions of individual industrial occupations. Adding to the "chaos of material" was an extended section on Luddism and a chapter titled "The Adventures of Oliver the Spy."[66] In the end, instead of abridging the nearly 700 page text, the Hammonds adopted the solution of 1911 once again and divided it into two.[67]

Roused to action by assurances that their book would count heavily in the debate about postwar England, in June 1917 the Hammonds instructed Longmans to publish *The Town Labourer* as soon as possible.[68] In an eloquent preface the Hammonds spoke candidly about their intent. They had chosen exactly that moment to publish the book because "the subject it discusses has a direct bearing on problems that are beginning to engage the attention of the nation as the war draws, however slowly, to its end." The preface took its cue from Lawrence's memoranda for the Reconstruction Committee. The social system of Disraeli's "two nations" had been the product of a "spirit of complacent pessimism." Taking the accumulation of economic power as its single aim, the age of industrial revolution had reduced the mass of Britons to the status of "the cannon-fodder of industry." In 1917, however, Englishmen were in revolt against "iron laws" and the predestinations of "economic necessity." The war had taught new lessons of cooperation and unity and had given birth to a new capacity and will to bring to the nation's problems "the ideals for which the noblest of its sons have given their lives."

Curiously enough, the Hammonds asserted that historiography's role in this whole process was to present normative criteria. "The more closely any period of history is studied, the more clearly does it appear that the mistakes and troubles of an age are due to a false spirit, an unhappy fashion in thought or emotion, a tendency in the human mind to be overwhelmed by the phenomena of the time." Historicists by no means, the Hammonds believed that absolute standards of good and evil could be applied to the past. Historiography that was not afraid to judge could demonstrate that the evils of the past were mainly the result of a transient, fashionable myopia. Highlighting the mistakes of the Industrial Revolution would prevent their repetition; it would convince men of the present that it was their business to control, rather than merely submit to and explain, "the forces of the hour."[69]

The Village Labourer chronicled the death of an old civilization, and *The Town Labourer* portrayed the painful birth of a new one. The two stories were complementary, and the Hammonds elected to tell the second one in much the same way as the first, drawing many of the same conclusions along the way. *The Town Labourer* analyzed the social and economic exploitation of the laboring classes during the early phase of rapid industrialization. Included were discussions of the severe and unfamiliar discipline of the factories, the use of the justice system to enforce this new industrial discipline, the crowded and filthy living conditions in hastily constructed new towns, the part played by the Napoleonic Wars in heightening the vulnerability of the workers to the harshness of the new system, and, in two eloquently impassioned chapters, the horrors of child employment.

The most interesting and important part of *The Town Labourer* was devoted to an analysis of ideology: six chapters on the mind of the rich, the conscience of the rich, the spirit of union, the spirit of religion, the mind of the poor, and the ambitions of the poor. The Hammonds hoped to demonstrate that the wrongs of the "new civilisation" were a product, not of conscious malevolence on the part of the governors, but of their unquestioning acceptance of the reigning philosophy of the "dismal science." There was no "conscious hypocrisy" that squared the prejudices of the ruling classes with the writings of Adam Smith and the teachings of the church. The manufacturers had simply adopted the ethos and language of the landlords. Telling themselves, "L'Etat, c'est moi," the factory owners had equated their own well-being with that of the nation.[70]

In *The Village Labourer* the Hammonds had looked to political democratization as the primary remedy for the appalling social sequelae of enclosure. But the experience of the Great War had raised their awareness of the need for cooperation and broadened participation on all levels, and they pointed to an industrial alliance between capital and labor as an indispensable supplement to any political solution for the ills of an industrializing—or industrialized—society. Genuine industrial cooperation could come only as a consequence of mutual appreciation of and respect for the values, traditions, and aspirations of each group participating in production. In their dissection of ideology in *The Town Labourer* the Hammonds demonstrated that this sort of understanding had been in short supply in the late 1700s. Decades of misery for workers and their families were the sad result. The mistakes of the past were presented as an immediately applicable lesson for Britain in the 1920s.

Some commentators placed *The Town Labourer* squarely within the moral reformist tradition of Liberalism, while Hilaire Belloc praised its graphic corroboration of his own radical, anti-Liberal interpretations of English history.[71] But as P. F. Clarke has noted, the book accommodated itself more easily to a socialist construction than did *The Village Labourer* The apparently protean nature of the Hammonds' message was, in part, simply a case of each segment of the Left distorting the image just enough to reveal its own reflection. But the ambiguity was also a by-product of the Hammonds' political uncertainties. They had harbored a distaste for the Labour party before 1914, complaining that a combination of lethargy, fear, and indifference within its ranks left the Liberals as the sole defenders of the rights of workingmen.[72] However the incompetence and timidity of Asquith's direction under the stress of war and the apparent carelessness with which successive coalition governments trampled Liberal principles underfoot shook the Hammonds' never firm allegiance to official Liberalism. In 1917 Lawrence moved closer to Labour's orbit, agreeing to serve on the party's Advisory Committee on International Questions. His membership in the Romney Street Group brought him into contact with the novel ideas for postwar reconstruction of such fertile young Labour theorists as G. D. H. Cole.[73] Lloyd George had stage-managed the war to a successful conclusion, but in all other respects he was a great disappointment to the Hammonds, especially by comparison with the pronouncements coming across the Atlantic from President Woodrow Wilson. After the armistice, Barbara summarized her feelings in a letter to Lawrence: "I always said I'd sooner win the war under a cad than lose it under a gentleman, but one does wish that the cad c[ou]ld become a gent[tleman] for a day or two at the end."[74]

The Asquithian rump offered a no more inspiring alternative. The Hammonds felt "sick at heart" over the Coupon Election and the former prime minister's reluctance to challenge Lloyd George's approach to the Versailles negotiations. "What a moral position Asquith & Co. c[ou]ld have secured," Barbara bemoaned, "if they'd taken the right line ab[ou]t indemnities instead to trying to go one more Jingo."[75] The Liberal party split left Radicals such as themselves with a paucity of options, and during the general election of November 1918 the couple split their votes between Labour and independent Liberal candidates. To Lawrence, the drubbing sustained at the polls by both Liberal factions in the 1922 general election spelled "the end of Liberalism."[76] Enveloped in this atmosphere of pessimism the Hammonds seemed ripe for recruitment into the Labour party. H. N. Brailsford certainly thought so, urging Lawrence to take up writing for the *Labour Leader* in 1922.[77] That Lloyd George should have been misinformed by C. P. Scott in 1925 that Hammond was a member of the Labour party appears unobjectionable in light of Hammond's contention in 1924 that, so far as he owed allegiance to any party, he was a "Labour man."[78]

But the Hammonds' ties to the Labour party were never official and certainly never very enthusiastic. In 1921 Lawrence lumped its members together with the vacillating and ineffectual Liberal rump, complaining to Murray that "neither Asquith nor [Lord Robert] Cecil nor the Labour people nor Grey give the country the impression that they mean business."[79] The couple's support of the 1924 Labour government rested largely upon a belief that recruits to the party from Liberalism were supplying the ideas behind policy initiatives. "As the constituencies don't seem to appreciate the Liberals," Barbara informed Mary Murray, "its [*sic*] a pity their brains can't fertilise the Labour fields, which badly need them."[80] Sidney Webb's 1923 invitation to join the Fabian Society was diplomatically ignored as the Hammonds searched for evidence of a vestigial dynamism among the ruins of organized Liberalism. By 1928 the Hammonds were generally acknowledged as unrepentant Liberals, only conditionally sympathetic to Labour.[81] That year Leonard Woolf urged Lawrence to assume one-half of a joint editorship of the new *Political Quarterly* as the representative of the "general outlook" of Liberalism, acting as a counterweight to coeditor Harold Laski's socialist bias.[82]

Political uncertainty in the inhospitable postwar atmosphere turned Lawrence's thoughts to the acquisition of a perch above the partisan fray. He had sat for a St. John's Fellowship in 1895 at the end of his Oxford undergraduate days. Perhaps his Second in Greats accounted for his rejection. Much like Belloc at Balliol, Hammond was discouraged by this apparent failure. Although, unlike his Anglo-French friend, he was able to avoid an all-consuming bitterness against the academic community, the residual effects of the rebuff surfaced in his successive attempts to compose public history that satisfied the university expert while it simultaneously captured the imagination of the general reader. His friend Graham Wallas had predicted in 1917 that when the "average don thinks of scores of W.E.A. classes reading your [*Town Labourer*] he won't find it possible to be perfectly self-complacent."[83] As prophesied, with the 1919 publication of *The Skilled Labourer*—the final and artistically least successful member of the Labourer trilogy—the Hammonds finally gained some favorable though belated notice by the academic community.[84] The time seemed ripe for relocation. Out of place in the polarized postwar political climate of Labour versus Conservative, coveting a measure of the special authority and prestige accorded his academic critics, and perhaps still smarting over his 1895 St. John's Fellowship rejection, Lawrence began an almost desperate search for a university teaching post in 1922. Academic friends like Ernest Barker, J. L. Stocks, and Arnold Toynbee were enlisted to help, but their efforts met with little success. Barker informed Hammond that King's College, London, had nothing available, suggesting that the London School of Economics might suit him better.[85] Inquiries addressed to Oxford's Magdalen, Queen's, St. John's, and New Colleges all received the same polite but negative reply.[86] The best that could be arranged was a part-time position lecturing and coaching Oxford's newly launched "Modern Greats" curriculum at several colleges simultaneously.[87] Toynbee thought it might be "rather interesting work," but Barbara strongly discouraged Lawrence's involvement in such a no-win situation. She warned that if he did it right, it would take up far too much time, and to do anything less would be "dangerous." "I doubt whether anyhow you w[ou]ld go down [well] in the carping critical atmosphere of Oxford. If you didn't, I mean if you weren't making a hit you w[ou]ld be horribly upset at the waste of time for nothing & at the nasty things they w[ou]ld say. All the history people w[ou]ld love to get a knife into you."[88] Lawrence was sorely tempted to accept an initial offer of eight lectures in the hope that something permanent would turn up, and Barbara admitted that if he passed up the chance he would "go on regretting it."[89]

In the end, Lawrence turned Oxford down on the pretext that the couple's latest project, a biography of Lord Shaftesbury, demanded all of his time and attention. Barbara did not hide her relief.

"Intellectual stimulus" was one thing, but she remained "sceptical as to whether the arid & cavilling atmosphere of Oxford w[ou]ld provide [even] that."[90] She seemed to understand more clearly than her husband that despite the scholarly integrity of their histories, theirs was the sort of work that would never gain complete acceptance within the university cloister. The reaction of Clapham to their books demonstrated as much. It was unlikely that anything resembling their Labourer trilogy could have been produced in such a stifling climate of conformity. The broad implications of its moral vocabulary would have clashed head-on with the narrow, objectively neutral image under intensive cultivation by modern economic historians at the academy.[91]

Despite their academic accoutrements, the Hammonds remained self-consciously public historians with their gaze fixed upon the contemporary political impact of their efforts. Lawrence's continuing part-time journalistic contributions to the *Manchester Guardian* preserved a direct connection with politics that formed the core of their Whiggish approach to historiography. Taking an academic post would entail severing that vital link. The time when one could address the general reading public from a university chair was fast becoming a memory. When Barbara comforted Lawrence over his decision against acceptance of the Oxford post by suggesting that "I don't think you'd like that kind of life or work," she evinced a profound comprehension of the source of their work's vitality. Barbara expressed the hope that a "hit" with *Lord Shaftesbury* (1923) might help Lawrence's "personal position" such that a more attractive university offer might soon be forthcoming.[92] But he must have realized that he had passed up his last genuine opportunity for an academic career, and he may have been thinking of the loss when he penned the concluding words of *Lord Shaftesbury*: "Shaftesbury always looked on himself afterwards as a man who had relinquished his career for a cause, and though he never regretted his choice, his reflection sometimes made him bitter and exacting."[93]

Besides providing a metaphor for Lawrence's disappointment, the minor work *Lord Shaftesbury* was in many respects a pivotal book in the evolution of the Hammonds' postwar relationship with Liberalism. They found its subject uncongenial; Barbara reminded Lawrence of "the many times you have said that none c[ou]ld be interested in Shafter himself & that the only way to write a readable book about him was not to mention him."[94] Out of sympathy with Shaftesbury's religious absorption, the two authors were accused of downplaying the Evangelical roots of his philanthropic crusades.[95] The book sold surprisingly well, but critical notices were mixed, possibly because the Hammonds' conclusions were so equivocal.[96] Amid this uncertain reception, Harold Laski, a socialist who found it impossible to identify with Shaftesbury, captured the personal importance of the book for the Hammonds when he noted, "What is so arresting is the way in which you have given generous sympathy and understanding to a man who is obviously not of your kith and kin."[97] But the point was that Barbara and Lawrence had discovered that Shaftesbury, despite his unappealing rigidness of character and narrowness of vision, was indeed, in some perverse fashion, their "kith and kin" after all.

The publication in 1919 of *The Skilled Labourer* had represented the high-water mark of the Hammonds' migration toward socialism. All along the way they had attempted to balance a defense of Britain's historic ruling class with a critique of the society erected and sustained by the ideology of that dominant group. This volatile mixture had worked reasonably well in *The Village Labourer*, but by 1919, with *The Skilled Labourer*'s descriptions of the Luddite "riots" and the "adventures" of Oliver the Spy, the emphasis had shifted noticeably to the left. *Lord Shaftesbury*, written at a time when the Hammonds were poised to join so many of their Liberal friends in jumping ship to the Labour party, seemed to reaffirm their allegiance to Liberalism in very hushed tones.[98] Here, in the unattractive form of Ashley Cooper, was the personification of an unyielding morality at the heart of nineteenth-century English culture. Even as it had nourished the Industrial Revolution, England's liberal conscience had begun the task of humanizing the callousness of industrial society. Driven by compassion and a tyrannical sense of justice, Shaftesbury had taken some of the first halting steps along that path. Unlike those who followed, he was willing only "to repudiate rather than to challenge the new materialism."[99] Shaftesbury had made the richer orders familiar with the idea of personal work in the slums. Later, the men of Toynbee Hall developed that initiative "along the lines of comradeship rather than along Shaftesbury's lines of benevolence. It was the aim of these reformers to bring together rich and poor in a common interest in the better government of the squalid and neglected districts of London, rather than to try merely to soften the worst inequalities of life by a Christian kindness that was apt to degenerate into patronage."[100] But these later cooperative accomplishments were possible only because of Shaftesbury's pioneering efforts. Lawrence was to write four years later, "It is sometimes said that no man is indispensable but if ever the epithet could be used of any man it could be used of Shaftesbury."[101] He had imparted a new tone to the English gentleman by demonstrating the invalidity of an economic law that forced reason and pity into conflict. Shaftesbury had succeeded in softening the manners and politics of his age and in taming the "savage logic of the Industrial Revolution."[102] Through him the Hammonds had rediscovered that the ethical core of the New Liberalism was derived directly from the heart of Victorian precursors. The villains of the Labourer trilogy appeared to possess the seed of their own redemption.[103]

Between Two Abusive Camps:
The Search for a Dissolving Center

Having relinquished academic ambitions, Hammond turned his attention to educating a wider public. He agreed to write the third volume of G. D. H. Cole's planned four-volume social and economic history of England, proposing to the publishers "a book popular in style but giving the results of modern research, and one that can be used as an authority for educational purposes."[104] Cole's series never materialized, but the Hammonds' book was published separately as *The Rise of Modern Industry* (1925). Consisting of a brief overview of the origins of early nineteenth-century industrial capitalism plus an assessment of its social consequences, this slim volume "brought the results of [the Labourer trilogy] together under a single focus."[105] All of the old themes were present: "The Destruction of the Peasant Village," "The Destruction of Custom in Industry," "The Curse of Midas," and "A World in Disorder." But while the moral failings of industrialization were cataloged as vividly as ever, in the spirit of *Lord Shaftesbury*, the ethical impulse toward self-reform of these inadequacies was the dominant theme of the concluding chapter, coloring the reader's judgment of all that came before.

In the final section the Hammonds posited a struggle running throughout the ages between an impulse to organize society according to "use" and another impulse "to make a society in which men co-operate." The former forged a world of ambition, fear, avarice, and exploitation. Its rival created a society of fellowship, sympathy, beauty, and truth. With the advent of the Industrial Revolution, "this conflict was resumed on a larger theatre, for the new inventions increased the power of both these instincts." After a period of chaos and national misery, the classical education of the English governing classes had provided them with the knowledge to overcome the predatory philosophy of industrial capitalism and to construct a new society with factory laws, a civil service, trade unions, and reform acts. The best representatives of the ruling classes were steeped in the humanism of the classics of ancient Greece and Rome, and "it was from the classics that men of liberal temper derived their public spirit, their sense for tolerance, their dread of arbitrary authority, the power to think of their nation in great emergencies as answering nobly or basely to some tremendous summons." Their own classical educations demanded that Lawrence and Barbara give pride of place to the influence of Greece and Rome on the erection of a more humane society by the governors of Victorian England. But they also credited Christianity with an incalculable contribution. Shaftesbury was simply the "greatest name" in a religious revival that included the Methodists, the Clapham Sect, and the Tractarians. Abetted by the spirit of the French Revolution, classical humanism and Christian compassion had combined in a "mystical force" slowly to reassert the principles of civilization in a world of injustice and cruelty.[106]

Having written *The Rise of Modern Industry* expressly "for the general reader and not for the specialist," the Hammonds now found themselves directly confronted by the concentrated hostility of the academic world, a hostility that had formerly masqueraded as indifference.[107] Despite Clapham's relatively benign reviews of *The Town Labourer* and *The Skilled Labourer*, his views had not softened, and in 1926 he took up the old cudgel of statistics to beat the Hammonds once again. In the preface to the first volume of his *Economic History of Modern Britain* (1926) he wrote, obviously with their work in mind, "The legend that everything was getting worse for the working man, down to some unspecified date between the drafting of the People's Charter and the Great Exhibition, dies hard." The great difficulty was that "the work of statisticians on wages and prices [was] being ignored by social historians."[108] The Hammonds were used to Clapham's solo denunciations, but his voice now swelled to a chorus. After the *English Historical Review* notice of 1920, the couple was judged fair game, exposing their work to the critical scrutiny of the entire academic historical community. A number of quantitative studies led by *Population Problems in the Age of Malthus* (1926) by the Cambridge historian G. Talbot Griffith challenged statements concerning demographic expansion in *The Town Labourer*, particularly the rash assertion that "it is well known that population increases with a decline in the standard of life."[109] Even more disturbing was a March 1926 *Economica* article by W. H. Hutt which openly questioned the Hammonds' use of sources.[110] The crowning blow came in a January 1929 *Quarterly Review* rebuttal of *The Town Labourer* by A. A. W. Ramsay in which the author posed as a defender of the "science of Economic History" against the Hammonds' manipulation of emotions and misrepresentation of data for partisan ends.[111]

This was all a case of be careful what you wish for because you just might get it. These sorts of scholarly attacks were the price exacted for decades of soliciting academic approval from outside the academy. They demonstrated the precarious nature of the Hammonds' position, capturing the tension between the demands of "scientific" scholarship and political ideology that pervaded all of their writings. Although they defended themselves against their academic assailants principally by addressing technical points, as public historians the Hammonds had always known—in fact they had relied upon the knowledge—that it was impossible to cordon off the question of political content in emotionally charged historiography such as theirs. While denying the "sin of wilful and scheming unfairness," they conceded that the "Labourer books must be judged for what they are: studies of a period inspired by a *particular outlook on the past*."[112] A self-consciously didactic approach to their work, however strictly governed by the constraints of scientific scholarship, equipped the couple to enter directly into an ongoing contemporary sociopolitical debate. Despite all of their ill-conceived dreams of scholarly seclusion, that was the way they liked it. Popular visibility was as essential to the Hammonds' purposes as it was to those of Hilaire Belloc.

Barbara and Lawrence always felt most comfortable on the margins between academic and popular history, admitting that they approached the historical discipline with only the most old-fashioned and even primitive equipment. "Armed with a little Latin and Greek, and with the habits of mind formed by study, however indifferent its success, of a complete and significant civilisation, we stepped into a world where men spoke the language and breathed the air of the strictest science."[113] As one of their correspondents noted, "the professionals mostly didn't like" the nonexpert "touching the ark of 'scientific study.' "[114] On more than one occasion the Hammonds were cautioned to distance themselves from mere popularizers, as when E. D. Bradley described their citation of H. G. Wells's *Outline of History* in *The Rise of Modern Industry* as an "insufficient authority" that "puts a reader off."[115] Perhaps not the reader but certainly the professor. After finding the doors of the universities closed to his petition for a teaching post in 1923, Lawrence had reacted by turning his attention to more popular books. But the challenges of the latter half of the decade had drawn him, along with Barbara, back to his old concern for addressing the academic historical community.[116]

Lawrence's insistence on writing books that would appeal to academics was rewarded by oases of scholarly support during A. A. W. Ramsay's 1929 denunciation of the entire corpus of the couple's work. Before the Hammonds' reply appeared in *Quarterly Review*, George Trevelyan judged that "no one at Cambridge is inclined to prejudge the controversy against you."[117] But cultivation of such sympathies was balanced by more pressing demands. "Scientific" economic history as practiced by Clapham and others at the universities was excessively narrow in its focus and therefore misleading in its conclusions. It seemed to Lawrence that Clapham's kind of history left you "with the feeling that nothing has ever happened."[118] Barbara believed that their own scholastically sound yet more broad-based approach had allowed the Hammonds to "overcome the paralysis that affects all economic historians sufficiently to generalise."[119] Conceding Clapham's "intimate learning . . . combined with a rare power of marshalling facts," Lawrence staked out a claim to an alternate portion of the subject matter of economic history. His own classical education predisposed him to look at an age not merely as a history of institutions or a struggle for power but as the interplay between events and the human imagination. This approach seemed to Lawrence as valid as any other.

The history of the world only becomes intelligible if it is studied and interpreted in different aspects by different minds. It is not the writer's contention that the way of looking at the Industrial Revolution which he has described is necessarily the best way, or that the impressions so received should not be checked by others based on other standards of value. But those impressions cannot be disregarded if we are to understand the discontent of the nineteenth century.[120]

T. H. Marshall warned that the Hammonds' novel methods threatened to split economic historians "into two abusive camps," a condition that neither Barbara nor Lawrence wished to foster.[121] Some academics, however, such as T. S. Ashton, though horrified at the thought of the fragmentation of their subspecialty, felt a greater sympathy with the Hammonds' blending of economics and ethics than with detached statistical analysis alone. He assured Lawrence that "if there is to be a change as to the way in which economic history ought to be written—if we have to divide ourselves into camps (which Heaven forbid)—I have no hesitation about my allegiance."[122]

But Ashton's pledge of support was an exception to the general rule. Hostility to the Hammonds' work emerged in part from the struggle of university-based scholars to professionalize their discipline and establish themselves as the sole arbiters of historical questions. Challenging the broad cultural authority of public history was simply one aspect of this protracted turf war. Additionally, the mood of the interwar years was uncongenial to the acceptance of Liberal interpretations of the past.[123] The flowering of scientific, value-neutral history suited the political climate of the 1930s. The narrow technical competence of academic economic and institutional history meshed well with domestic politics in the age of Baldwin. Scholarly concentration upon the mechanics of administration rather than ideologically charged great issues flourished amidst the split of the Labour party, the lowering of the temperature of partisan politics after 1931, and governance by a "National" coalition. The moral vocabulary of the Hammonds grated in a decade more attuned to consensus than had been the 1920s.

The year after the General Strike, L. T. Hobhouse, another former New Liberal familiar with the recent work of the Claphamite school, remarked to Lawrence upon "this sudden effort to rehabilitate the Industrial Revolution socially . . . extremely interesting—part of a general reaction."[124] Downplaying discontinuity, Clapham and his supporters emphasized the snail's pace and patchy nature of the first Industrial Revolution. He dismissed present-minded criticisms from the Hammonds of nineteenth-century administrations in a passage that would have warmed the hearts of hard-pressed cabinet ministers faced with apparently intractable economic difficulties between 1931 and 1939. "Judged as governments are perhaps entitled to be judged, not by what proved practicable in a later and more experienced day, not by what reformers and poets dreamed and were not called upon to accomplish, but by the achievement of other governments in their own day, that of Britain . . . makes a creditable showing."[125] The Webbs could hardly have been pleased to witness how "detached" economic and institutional history appeared ready-made to provide ballast for lethargic Baldwinian Conservatism, but the continued incompatibility of that austere historiographical style with Liberalism provided a measure of consolation. Although attempting to fashion a Liberal version of the nation's past serviceable in the changed circumstances of the twentieth century, the Hammonds invariably fell between two stools, finding their hybrid form of public history embraced too eagerly by the Left and dismissed as part of a "Socialist conspiracy" by the Right.[126]

The Hammonds never shied away from drawing parallels between their histories and the present. But they could not control the manner in which their works were interpreted and employed. They never intended that their books should be understood as an unqualified attack upon capitalism or upon its symbiotic aristocratic-parliamentary cousin. They had always aimed to strike a correct balance in keeping with the principles of the New Liberalism: an unblinking concern for social reform, democratization, and the aspirations of the working classes combined with the traditional Liberal faith in individual freedom, a free market economy, and parliamentary governance. Waiting upon the unlikely event of a resurrection of a moderate party of the Left, Lawrence and Barbara, two confirmed Edwardian Liberals, continued to scan the political horizon, unable to locate a dissolving center.[127] Ground between the upper and nether millstones of Labour and Conservatism, they believed the need for a Liberal alternative more acute than ever by 1931 and turned their pens to the task of attempting to create one from the outside.

The Age of the Chartists, 1832–1854 (1930) was a step in that direction. Despite its title, this was not a book about Chartism but rather about the conditions that led to the working-class discontent that finally sparked the Chartist movement. According to the Hammonds, the English rulers faced a nearly insurmountable problem in the 1830s. Industrial capitalism, corrosive of all but the cash nexus, had dissolved the "custom" that had formerly bound society into a stable network of relationships. It was necessary to discover some new means of knitting the various elements of society together in mutual sympathy and confidence. Alone, the solution of the materialists was obviously inadequate. Aspirations for wealth and individual accumulation might capture the imagination and provide a sense of personal independence, but they did little or nothing to foster a common sense of fellowship and purpose among citizens. The Hammonds insisted that man's communal instinct required nourishment as well. In the book's introduction the Hammonds made a final concession to Clapham and the "optimists" concerning the standard-of-living question, granting that though the "evidence is of course scanty, and its interpretation not too simple . . . this general view is probably more or less correct."[128] But this magnanimous admission only served to underline more forcefully the argument of *The Age of the Chartists* that discontent among the working classes after 1832 was a product of the starvation of the spirit, a point seized upon by G. M. Trevelyan, who congratulated Lawrence on "us[ing] the criticisms directed against your earlier work by Clapham . . . to lead you not back but *on* to the discovery of another and larger truth."[129]

Returning to the classical themes of *The Rise of Modern Industry*, the Hammonds described the great triumph of ancient Greek civilization with its union of freedom and fellowship. Nineteenth-century England suffered by comparison, the philosophy of the Manchester School providing for the former while ignoring the latter. The result was a sense of alienation among the lower orders. In stark contrast to the ancient Greek polis, the bleak character of the new industrial towns with their absence of art, beauty, grace, and social amenities captured the obliviousness of the unalloyed philosophy of capitalism. More than a tenth of *The Age of the Chartists* was devoted to a discussion of the loss of municipal playgrounds and parks.[130] That Parliament earnestly debated this single problem indicated to the

Hammonds that early Victorian England's failure to provide a solution was less a deliberate disregard of public interests than a temporary deficiency in imagination and foresight.

Despite this deficiency, however, the Hammonds recorded how a humanist protest against the simplistic materialism of the Manchester School made slow but steady progress throughout the middle third of the century. A more complex understanding of man's material and spiritual needs gradually supplanted Bentham's one-sided view of human nature that postulated the world as an unfriendly "collection of persons each pursuing his separate interest or pleasure, in which the law, religions, and public opinion, imposing their general sanctions, serve to prevent more jostling than is unavoidable." A long series of national reform measures and local initiatives registered Victorian society's acceptance of the indispensability of a true sense of community to national and individual well-being: the founding of lending libraries; the tremendous growth in popularity of public lectures and concerts, social clubs, music halls, and museums; the extension of Saturday half-holidays to clerks; parliamentary provision of funding for public walks and parks (the ruling classes also made private subscriptions—for example, Robert Peel donated a thousand pounds to the city of Manchester in 1846); the passage of public health legislation; and the "most striking and important manifestation of the new spirit," the Ten Hours Bill.[131]

Perhaps even more than in their previous books, the authors heavily qualified their critique of capitalism in *The Age of the Chartists*. Classical political economy entertained an overly restricted notion of the nature of man and society, but the Hammonds allowed that it had an important contribution to make nonetheless. The evils of the first half of the nineteenth century were not ascribable to capitalism but instead to uninhibited capitalism. The Hammonds believed the great virtue of England's liberal-parliamentary system was that it was able to overcome the myopia of its temporal prison and to measure its newly industrialized society by universal standards of classical origin. In a difficult but admirable evolution, England's rulers had progressed beyond their initial failure of imagination to provide capitalism with a human face. In contradistinction to the Webbs in their *English Local Government*, the Hammonds argued that the civic impulse could grow directly out of Liberalism—in fact, it had done just that between 1832 and 1854—for Liberalism was a much more heterogeneous phenomenon than the reductio ad absurdum of the Benthamite calculus of pleasure and pain. No revolution, not even the peaceful institutional revolution of the Webbs' imagination, was necessary to create a just and humane society. Every member of a community organized according to Liberal principles was capable of demonstrating a high degree of disinterested civic virtue. The ethical side of the Liberal tradition obviated the need for civil servants to adjudicate selfish individual disputes. When the Hammonds' complex and problematic image of Liberalism replaced the Webbian straw man, bureaucrats became the servants of civil society rather than its leaders.

This sort of defense of Liberalism was far too muted and opaque to garner much attention. The subtitle to *The Age of the Chartists* was *A Study of Discontent*, and it was that upon which the reviewers fastened.[132] T. H. Marshall in the *English Historical Review* noted that the revolt against a view of life and protest against a general system documented by the Hammonds had had little success over the years, for that same "view and . . . system . . . though much modified, are in essence still with us."[133] One reviewer thought "the picture a shade too sombre," while another described the book as "a masterly study of nineteenth-century barbarism."[134] As so often before, the Hammonds' defense of Liberalism remained conditional and difficult to dissect out from among descriptions of the misery of agricultural and industrial laborers. To make Liberalism's case in the 1930s required a more direct approach.

The Pitfalls of Fine Distinctions

Lawrence decided that the dark atmosphere of the late 1930s, "with the English mind thrown on the defensive by the rise and claims of the totalitarian states," called for a clearer voice and an uncluttered message.[135] Political history provided the appropriate vehicle for a direct statement of Liberalism's noble lineage and contemporary relevance, delivered to a British reading public made receptive again, by the fascist menace, to the traditional moral vocabulary of the public historian. In *Gladstone and the Irish Nation*, published in 1938 during the dismemberment of Czechoslovakia, Lawrence took up once more the arguments of 1903 and *Charles James Fox*. Hammond's Gladstone wished to capture the imagination of the Victorian electorate by placing the issue of home rule in a moral context, both cosmic and temporal.[136] The Grand Old Man was tapping the same moral reserves of Liberalism that had ended the slave trade, transformed the harsh face of the Industrial Revolution, and created a political system which, for all its faults, acknowledged the dignity of the individual and his right to choose as a moral being.

Britain's political culture and the ruling class that dominated it had received their share of praise in the Labourer trilogy and its sequels, but the Hammonds' concentration upon the ill effects of early industrial capitalism had often upstaged that subterranean theme. With the "barbarians at the gate" in the 1930s, liberal Britain's historic political accomplishments assumed a new and overriding importance in the eyes of Lawrence and Barbara. *Gladstone and the Irish Nation* was an attempt to redress the historiographic balance by showcasing the system that had generated a peaceful and just resolution to the misery of 1760–1832.

But the message of *Gladstone and the Irish Nation* could not overturn the public's view of the earlier work of the Hammonds. Beginning with *The Village Labourer* in 1911, their books had been read in most quarters as a stinging indictment of liberal capitalism. It seemed that the subtle complexities of the Hammonds' histories had been wasted. Those who should have known better consistently ignored or misinterpreted the presence in all of the couple's major volumes of a qualified defense of Britain's liberal social, political, and economic order.

Liberals in the 1920s believed that a significant segment of the country shared their *Weltanschauung*. But in order to turn that latent sympathy into votes and avoid political oblivion the party needed a statement of doctrine and policy that would establish its special niche in the political spectrum. The Hammonds offered nothing nearly so concrete or utilitarian. Their case for Liberalism rested upon an identification of its ethical spirit with the engine of moral progress throughout modern English history. Gladstone had managed to harness such intangibles to a political apparatus and win elections. But the language of politics had changed in the twentieth century, as had the methods of political mobilization. A delicate structure like the Hammonds' brief for Liberalism could hardly have survived on its own in the harsh polarized ideological climate of post-1918 Britain. It required a confident and stable parliamentary party to which it could attach itself. In the long run it might be true that the theorist was more influential, but, as the Hammonds well knew, "it is a good thing for him if he can get a practical man to take him up."[137] The absence of a viable Liberal alternative in the 1920s left the work of the Hammonds in the hands of the practical men of Labour by default.

Adoption of their histories by the far Left attracted fire from the political Right, which in turn triggered more rhetoric from the Left on the Hammonds' behalf. It is a curious fact that the Webbs' *History of Trade Unionism* and *English Local Government* never evoked a similar barrage of ideological refutation and counterrefutation. The difference in passion as conveyed through literary style was almost certainly the reason. The Webbs' work sapped the very foundations of the liberal-capitalist order, yet they presented their arguments in an almost indigestible form which camouflaged its true implications to any but the most patient and careful of readers. While bamboozling potential ideological opponents, they satisfied the most demanding of academics (e.g., J. H. Clapham) with their strictly clinical approach to historiography. Conversely, the Hammonds' blend of popular style and rigorous research techniques appeased no one. Their dissection of moral and spiritual issues left the academic economic historians dissatisfied, and their manipulation of the reader's emotions exaggerated the subversiveness of their critique of liberal capitalism in the eyes of conservatives.

The Hammonds had fashioned a new, hybrid form of public history which exercised undeniable influence. The verdicts of the Labourer trilogy remain the starting point for modern arguments between "optimists" and "pessimists." But by their own standards as Liberals, their success as public historians remains equivocal. Their subtly shaded attempt to forge a contemporary vindication of Liberalism's ancestry without hiding the warts came to an unexpected end. Just as they are so often incorrectly remembered as Fabian Socialists, their work is accepted unproblematically as a restrained but important evolutionary precursor of the New Left historiography of the 1960s and 1970s. Although expressing impatience with their reluctance to admit of any serious revolutionary sentiments among the Luddites, E. P. Thompson in *The Making of the English Working Class* (1963) clearly looked upon the Hammonds, with their "catastrophic view" of the period 1790–1830, as the forerunners of his own work.[138]

A willingness "to moralise history"—the phrase is Thompson's—such as that exhibited by the Hammonds had, once upon a time, served the Victorian Whig historians well. But twentieth-century Liberalism's crisis of confidence rendered it incapable of sustaining that sort of overtly judgmental approach to interpreting the nation's past. It fell to the historians of the post-1945 Left to claim as their own preserve this emotive style of historiography. And principally upon the basis of style rather than content, the Hammonds are linked in the modern imagination more closely with these illegitimate successors than with their Whig progenitors.

4 GEORGE MACAULAY TREVELYAN

The Insider as Outsider

Stefan Collini has argued that the complete integration of
Victorian intellectuals into politics and society precluded
their indulgence in cultural pessimism. Since mid-nine-
teenth-century historians lacked a distinctive group identity, little reason existed to cultivate detached social criticism, in contradistinction to Germany, where a more rigid
separation between a professionalized university community and the world of affairs led some academics, embittered
by *Kulturpessimismus*, to address posterity rather than their
contemporaries. Even in Britain of the twentieth century
the divide between the "merely literary" public historian
and the "fact-grubbing" academic remained partial. Yet the

*George Macaulay Trevelyan, ca. 1930, soon after his return to Cambridge follow-
ing a self-imposed exile of more than two decades. (Courtesy of The British
Academy)*

claims and standards of the research ideal inevitably—even among those like Belloc who ostentatiously rejected them—altered the character of historiography in a thousand subtle ways, in the process redefining the permissible limits of its practice. The *image* of professionalization, however incompletely carried through in practice, implanted new inhibitions regarding the propriety of academic intervention in partisan political controversy.[1] Though not by choice, university-centered professionalization meant the sacrifice of the historian's public visibility and cultural influence.

It seemed to many that more narrowly based academic authority, with its attendant relative isolation, hardly compensated for the greater loss. Yet it was increasingly difficult after 1900 to inhabit simultaneously the diverging worlds of scholarship and civic affairs. George Macaulay Trevelyan inherited what he saw as an artificially segregated order. As a member of an ancient Northumberland gentry family, he belonged to the traditional ruling class. Yet by the turn of the century, Trevelyan and his kind had lost their will to govern along with the necessary confidence in their right and ability to do so. Unlike his grandfather, great-uncle, father, and even elder brother, Trevelyan refrained from active participation in politics. He pursued a university professorship yet deplored technical, obscurantist academic historiography's severance from its natural audience, the general reader. So Trevelyan belonged to and withheld himself from the twentieth-century political and academic establishments. In these two arenas he functioned as both insider and outsider. Though born to rule, he never ran for public office; though he held the Regius Chair of Modern History at Cambridge, as an academic historian he was never quite pukka. Conscious of his anomalous position, Trevelyan mourned the Victorian age when men such as himself formed the intellectual wing of an extended governing class.

Unlike Belloc, who rejected the world of the dons with great fanfare, or the Hammonds, Churchill, and the Webbs, who actively courted the university mandarinate with varying degrees of assiduity and success, Trevelyan slipped back and forth between the role of professor and that of literary amateur without ever abandoning the Victorian ideal of the public historian. Starting out at Cambridge as an assistant lecturer, he denounced that form of monasticism and exiled himself from the university setting for nearly a quarter-century until his return in the mid-1920s. This nomadic wandering between poles captured the intellectual tension gripping an essentially nineteenth-century man forced to live in the twentieth. In 1941 he recalled Gladstone telling his father that the Victorians should be grateful for living in the great age of Liberalism. "Other generations, my dear Trevelyan, will be less fortunate."[2] Trevelyan believed that the total integration of intellectuals into civic life was a precondition for the survival of liberal society. A corollary of this general proposition was the necessity for provision by public historians of a directly meaningful and useful past for the general populace. Combined with his sense of contemporary Britain's political decay, Trevelyan's despair at the increasing self-imposed isolation of his own discipline made it impossible for his narratives to recapitulate the moral optimism of his Victorian predecessors.

Throughout his life Trevelyan remained a man in search of a stable and moderate center—in both art and politics—a center that he identified in both instances with the lost equipoise of the Victorian Liberal ethos. After some partisan posturing in his youth, he attempted with his writings to mediate the dispute between the particularist and exclusive scientific historiography of the academic and the generalizing, didactic, broadly aimed work of the literary amateur. He recapitulated this mediatory impulse in his politics, where after sampling every pre-1914 variant of Liberalism, he set about constructing a consensus history for twentieth-century Britain, one based upon the traditional Whig model yet elastic enough to accommodate the postwar extremes of Labour and Conservatism. The great-nephew of Macaulay, Trevelyan was the most self-conscious of public historians and, as such, readily accepted the notion that his discipline should function to arbitrate between apparent political incompatibles.

Without a doubt Trevelyan was the most popular and widely read English historian of the first half of the twentieth century. The first volume of his legendary Garibaldian trilogy (1907–11) went through three reprintings and a second edition in the first five months, the original three thousand copies having been sold in three.[3] The second volume duplicated this success, and the last, *Garibaldi and the Making of Italy*, did even better, with Longmans' first printing of three thousand all ordered within a few days of publication.[4] In the 1940s ownership of this set was so common that on one occasion escaped British P.O.W.'s used Trevelyan's maps of Garibaldi's campaigns to elude German pursuers in Italy during the Second World War.[5] His examination of the Victorian Age, *British History in the Nineteenth Century* (1922), sold more than ten thousand copies its first year and averaged over two thousand per annum for the next decade. His *England under Queen Anne* (3 vols., 1930–34) enjoyed comparable prosperity. Trevelyan's *England under the Stuarts* (1904) was the only commercially successful volume of an otherwise forgettable Methuen History of England series. Even his doctoral dissertation, published in 1899 as *England in the Age of Wycliffe*, continued to sell more than two hundred copies a year three decades after its appearance.[6]

More spectacular still were the sales figures of Trevelyan's massive *History of England* (1926). An enthusiastic general public purchased nearly 30,000 copies in the first year, more than 56,000 after four, and over 200,000 by 1949.[7] If size of readership is any guide to influence, then obviously Trevelyan's was enormous. Reinforced by his more narrowly focused works, his single-volume synthesis served to define the general context for understanding their nation's history for the vast majority of three generations of Englishmen. His refurbished Whig interpretation with its emphasis on continuity, and the via media created a sympathetic connection between England's Liberal past and present in the post-1945 era of Attlee, Bevan, and Macmillan. His popularity survived into the Thatcher years and beyond, with a revised and illustrated edition of the *History of England* still in print and selling briskly. Serving as Plato to Macaulay's Socrates, Trevelyan had overseen the survival of the basic literary framework of Liberal historiography for another century beyond the demise of formal Liberal politics. In publicly confronting and challenging his conclusions, contemporary revisionists of the Left or Right, academic or amateur, implicitly acknowledge the remarkably durable hold of his consensus history upon the popular mind. Because twentieth-century British historiography imagines itself locked in a debate with the Whig interpretation and because Trevelyan is usually remembered as the last unrepentant, unreconstructed champion of the Old Cause, all modern British historiography is, ironically, an extended footnote to Trevelyan.

Clio, a Muse: The Cause of Literary and Liberal History

As the son of the Gladstonian cabinet minister G. O. Trevelyan and great-nephew of Thomas Babington Macaulay, G. M. Trevelyan viewed his joint inheritance of Liberal politics and stylish Whig history as interdependent. Liberalism as a political creed depended upon continuous reaffirmation of the present as the beneficent outgrowth of a particular version of the past. The Liberal historian functioned to maintain an ongoing discourse with the general reading public, deploying time-honored arguments about constitutional progress that capitalized upon a shared moral vocabulary embedded in the deepest recesses of British civic culture. Only traditional literary narrative forms were appropriate to this end. Trevelyan understood, as did his contemporaries the Webbs and Hammonds, that the ethos of scientific history was potentially lethal to Liberalism's purpose. Its austerity, dispassion, and unapologetic self-absorption circumscribed scientific history's political utility as it limited the breadth of its appeal.

This is the correct context in which to examine Trevelyan's passionate sponsorship of "literary" history against the "scientific" variant of the discipline. As an undergraduate at Trinity College, Cambridge, in the mid-1890s, he fretted lest he "drift into the selfish but worthy egoism which we know as 'academical.'" George resolved, "I will *not* be academical, as I may have been tending to be lately. . . . Service to mankind, though it may be the same thing as service to truth, must be put first. . . . I must act as interpreter of history, in its truest sense, to all those who can understand it, to those in fact who read books."[8] Trevelyan's enthusiastic service from 1899 as a regular evening lecturer at the London Working Men's College provided him the opportunity to perform his civic obligation, to unite quite directly politics and the teaching of history.

The same preoccupation informed his affection for Lord Acton and antipathy toward Seeley while at Cambridge, as well as his celebrated confrontation with their successor as Regius Professor, J. B. Bury, over the latter's Inaugural Address, "History as Science." In "The Latest View of History" (1903), his published response to Bury, Trevelyan laid greatest stress upon the need for conscious crafting of historical writing so as to fulfill historiography's cultural duties. History's vital function was educative, to breed passion for noble ideals from the past and loyalty to their modern offspring. The ascendancy of scientific history threatened a calculated neglect of the needs of the general public. He grieved that already "the public is less interested in history, and by a habit of mind now inbred, thinks that a professional historian must be writing his best books not for the nation but for his fellow-students. And the worst of it is that this lamentable error was put about in the last generation by the historians themselves, when they denounced from the altar any of their profession, alive or dead, who had dealings with literature."[9]

Yet for all their talk of "scientific" history, both Seeley and Bury sympathized with Trevelyan's concern regarding the surrendering of cultural authority. Seeley, the positivist, believed in the possibility of history as an inductive science of politics, deriving general laws from the observation and classification of facts. He advocated a two-tiered division of labor with academic brahmins constructing an accurate canvas while a lower caste of historians served as intermediaries, responsible for diffusing scholarly discoveries to the community at large. Bury's notion of history as science had little in common with Seeley's. Bury made no facile analogies between historiography and the natural sciences. For him history was science only in the sense that it was disinterested scholarship, accumulating and presenting data about the past in an orderly and comprehensible fashion. His advocacy of the research ideal partook of many of Trevelyan's ambitions for the discipline. Bury envisioned a future in which historiography would become "a more powerful force . . . for shaping public opinion and advancing the cause of intellectual and political liberty."[10]

Despite their differences, neither Seeley nor Bury wanted or expected history to relinquish its traditional cultural influence. On the contrary, both anticipated that an appeal to *Wissenschaft* would bolster history's authoritative claims. But Trevelyan feared that the embrace of the methods of scientific history would spawn dire unintended consequences. Regardless of the aspirations of its advocates, the research ideal was inherently incompatible with involvement in contemporary civic discourse. Like the Webbs, Trevelyan grasped the symbiotic nature of literary form and Liberal content. A narrative of moral progress required an emotive vocabulary to make its case and evoke from the audience a response born of shared values.

Thus Trevelyan's decision to leave his academic post in 1902 followed logically from the installation of what he saw as an unsympathetic Bury regime at Cambridge. As he described it nearly half a century later, in order "to write literary history" he required "more spiritual freedom away from the critical atmosphere of Cambridge scholarship."[11]

Literary History as Problematic:
Resistance to the Ascendancy of the Ironic Mode

Leonard Woolf once described the Trinity undergraduate George Trevelyan as "a rather fiercely political young man." In 1903, soon after Trevelyan's departure from Cambridge, Woolf wrote a paper entitled "George or George or Both?" concerning the "life of action as opposed to the life of contemplation. . . . It asks the question whether we ought to follow the example of George Trevelyan and take part in practical politics, going down into the gloomy Platonic cave, where 'men sit bound prisoners guessing at the shadows of reality and boasting that they have found truth,' or whether we should imitate George Moore, who though 'he has no small knowledge of the cave dwellers, leaves alone their struggles and competitions.' "[12] But as scion of a territorial ruling class in slow decline as well as member of a generation conditioned to see politics and scholarship as separate spheres, young George's passion for the world of affairs was more apparent than real. Trevelyan, like J. L. Hammond, remained the most reluctant of politicians.

In his 1910 roman à clef *The New Machiavelli* H. G. Wells lumped his Trevelyan doppelgänger George Crampton together with "people . . . of the Parliamentary candidate class." As one of a select group of "prospective Liberal candidates," Crampton was supposed to be "tremendously keen upon social and political service," living an exemplary life that derived its satisfaction "in political achievements and distinctions."[13] But Wells could not have been more wrong. Despite a "keen" interest in Liberal politics, Trevelyan recalled in his autobiography that he was a poor speaker and "never dreamt of standing for Parliament." He was more self-deprecating regarding his reluctance in a 1907 letter to Bertrand Russell, a man of letters who had not shrunk from the rigors of the art of politics. "So now you [Russell] have 'fought a contested election,' which Teufelsdrockh puts with the state of being in love, as being the second greatest experience of human life. I am the greater coward that I have never done the same, and probably never shall."[14] Trevelyan's natural diffidence extended even beyond the hustings. Despite prewar membership with other Radicals on the Russian and Balkan Committees, he remained steadfastly cautious about lending his name to out-of-doors Radical pressure groups, a fastidiousness amply demonstrated when in 1903 he declined Graham Wallas's invitation to sign a petition calling for reform in India on the grounds that "one should get up a subject a little bit before taking a part in controversy or public action, and I have no time to get up India even a little."[15]

Trevelyan documented his own psychological incapacity for the dual role of politician and historian in a polite but firm refusal of Sidney Webb's 1908 offer of the directorship of the London School of Economics. Such a position required

> a complete devotion of all my faculties; I work up to [the] break-ing-point as it is . . . I am a "little person" and like other "little people" must husband my slender resources and must *specialize*. History to me is both a science and an art; science and art are severally the most exacting things in the world. Together, when one is really writing a history book, they demand every mental muscle—it is like mountain climbing when you are half-way up a chimney, when it would be distinctly unwise to begin doing ju-jitsu as well.[16]

Trevelyan never possessed the supreme confidence, either in his abilities or in his beliefs, that had enabled the Victorian man of letters to double as a man of action. Prone to vacillation on the edge of the fray, he confessed to his activist brother Charles that "I must be one of those who sit, and watch the battle fought out by such as you."[17] George determined at a tender age that if he would "ever do anything for democracy it must be through literature."[18] Like his great-uncle, his destiny was "to write *heavy books*, history and the like."[19] Here he conveniently ignored Macaulay's parliamentary service.

Gilbert Murray insisted in 1911 that Trevelyan's Garibaldian histories were indeed "books that made a permanent difference in one's outlook," while C. R. Buxton congratulated their author on choosing "a really usefuller life than the political."[20] But Trevelyan was never fully convinced. During the Boer War he wondered to his parents "whether under these conditions writing history is a particularly manly occupation."[21] Just prior to his 1902 departure from Cambridge he confided to his father a desire to move to London in order to enter the political fray more directly. "One can't write history all one[']s life," he added.[22] Such guilt-inspired sentiments kept Trevelyan hovering hesitantly on the fringes of active politics for nearly three decades.

But experiences outside the university environment extinguished Trevelyan's fragile confidence that in the twentieth century it was still possible to fuse public historiography and politics. By the close of the Great War Trevelyan's faith in Liberalism's contemporary resiliency had reached its lowest ebb. It was precisely at that moment that the publication of Lytton Strachey's *Eminent Victorians* (1918) ruptured what he had long proclaimed to be the necessary connection between Liberalism and public history rendered in literary form. Strachey had taken deliberate aim at evangelicalism, messianic imperialism, humanitarianism, and the cults of education and progress—in other words, at the entire moralistic structure of nineteenth-century Liberal society. The liberties of fact taken by the author with psychological portraits of Cardinal Manning, Florence Nightingale, Dr. Arnold, and General Gordon forced Trevelyan to reevaluate his earlier sweeping critique of suffocating and demanding scientific history. History that slipped all its moorings to critical standards of scholarship, no matter how poetically evocative or intuitively profound, remained ultimately unacceptable by any valid modern criteria. The conspicuous disregard for even the minimal constraints of fact and the absolute subservience to the demands of dramatic effect on display in *Eminent Victorians* ventured far beyond permissible boundaries, even taking into account the obligatory disclaimer of poetic license. Thus his relationship with Strachey forced Trevelyan to explore the limits of his approval of the uncompromisingly aesthetic treatment of history.

The two men had first become friends as Cambridge undergraduates, often breakfasting and walking together, but the bond between them was constrained by opposite temperaments. Strachey, with his sardonic wit and mocking intelligence, found Trevelyan "very—I think *too*—earnest; and paternally kind,"[23] and it was under the influence of the former that the Cambridge Conversazione Society—the famous "Apostles"—shed its priggish solemnity and single-minded concern with matters of religion, philosophy, and morality favored by elder members like Trevelyan. But Trevelyan was tolerant above all else, and he recognized talent when he saw it, writing to his mother that Strachey "will write history well some day if his health keeps, and I am leading him out of cynicism into the dry land of Carlylean defiance and pity."[24] For a time, at least from Trevelyan's vantage point, they seemed to be marching in step.

Trevelyan as a Fellow of Trinity College at the turn of the century. Lytton Strachey found the young Trevelyan "very—I think too*—earnest; and paternally kind," while Leonard Woolf described him as "a rather fiercely political young man." (Master and Fellows of Trinity College, Cambridge, ref.FA.I.114)*

Bury's 1902 Inaugural Address had evoked nearly identical responses from the two young friends. Like Trevelyan, Strachey wrote his own rebuttal, answering Bury's declaration that history is "a science, no less and no more" with the argument that the greatest historians were artists of necessity.

The first duty of a great historian is to be an artist. . . . Uninterpreted truth is as useless as buried gold; and art is the great interpreter. It alone can unify a vast multitude of facts into a significant whole, clarifying, accentuating, suppressing, and lighting up the dark places with the torch of the imagination. . . . Indeed, every history worthy of the name is, in its own way, as personal as poetry, and its value ultimately depends upon the force and quality of the character behind it.[25]

There was nothing here with which Trevelyan could not in theory agree. But when Strachey finally did turn his hand to historiography, Trevelyan's response fell far short of enthusiastic. *Eminent Victorians* (1918), *Queen Victoria* (1921), and *Elizabeth and Essex* (1928) all sold extraordinarily well, but their popularity hinged upon the author's selective use of sources, the superficial reduction of history to personality and accident, the complete neglect of context, and the bending of facts in the interest of constructing a seamless narrative with dramatic unity. Such was the result when the scientific claims of history were disregarded altogether.

Publicly Trevelyan expressed his admiration for *Eminent Victorians* and *Queen Victoria*.[26] But his private remarks in conversation were much less kindly toward his old friend.[27] He resented the unrestrained attacks upon the Victorians and particularly the satirical skewering of Thomas Arnold, the great-grandfather of his wife. Even worse was Strachey's ridiculing of Macaulay in *Portraits in Miniature* (1931).[28] Perhaps most outrageous and unforgivable of all was Strachey's irreverent parody of the scholarly feud between the Liberal historian E. A. Freeman and his arch-nemesis J. H. Round, a sketch that concluded by relating how, in a silent fury at his tormentor Round, Freeman "had gone pop in Spain."[29] According to Virginia Woolf, the trivialization of Freeman's death with the expression "gone pop" had left Trevelyan "foaming at the mouth with rage."[30]

There was no denying that Strachey made history "fascinating" to the reader, but by taking so many liberties with the facts he betrayed the central educative function of the discipline. Strachey treated historiography as a game, while to Trevelyan, the writing of history was "no child's play. The rounding of every sentence and of every paragraph had to be made consistent with a score of facts, some of them known only to the author, some of them perhaps discovered or remembered by him at the last moment to the entire destruction of some carefully erected artistic structure. In such cases there is an undoubted temptation to the artist to neglect such small, inconvenient pieces of truth."[31] Artistic imagination was properly the servant, not the tyrant, of historiography.

Equally disturbing was Strachey's attitude toward his subjects. Trevelyan believed that history acted as a school of political wisdom by molding the mind to a just understanding of the great affairs of the past and to a sympathy with other men.[32] In his early works, however, Strachey wrote not to create sympathy across the centuries but rather to disrupt it by employing the literary weapons of irony and caricature. Trevelyan genuinely approved of his old friend's last major book, *Elizabeth and Essex*, because, as he put it to Strachey, the Virgin Queen "is much subtler and a much greater subject than Victoria and one more completely suited to your genius." After the maliciously hostile *Eminent Victorians* and *Queen Victoria* Trevelyan believed that this latest production represented Strachey's "greatest work." Beyond that,

> its success bears out my theory as against your own—or what used to be your view. You used to tell me that your strength was satire and satire alone, so you must choose people whom you did not much like in order to satirize them. I thought the argument bad then, and now the time gives proof of it. Your best book has been written about people to whom you are spiritually akin—far more akin than to the Victorians. And it is not a piece of satire but a piece of life.[33]

According to Trevelyan, history could accomplish its cultural mission only when there existed a sympathy between author and subject, and by ignoring this charge Strachey had merely succeeded in the creation of historiographical grotesques.

Heretofore Trevelyan had identified literary history exclusively with the Whig tradition, but Strachey stood that notion on its head. Describing his own *Eminent Victorians*, Strachey informed G. Lowes Dickinson that he had hoped to "eradicate the weed" of that "damned Macaulayism!"[34] Such subversion of literary style was even more unacceptable to Trevelyan's purposes than the methods of the academic Dryasdust of the "scientific school," for, up to that point, his own attempts to contribute to the preservation and defense of

England's Liberal traditions in an increasingly hostile age were contingent upon an inextricable linkage between Liberal and literary history. Before 1914 he might refer to scientific history as "the enemy," but Trevelyan did not fear that its accumulations of data would overturn what he saw as the essential truths of Whig historiography.[35] Adoption of a dry, scholarly form of presentation lacking any trace of popular appeal simply offered no means for an author to exercise the culturopolitical authority requisite to public history. On the other hand, Strachey's corrosive iconoclasm dressed up in the artistic finery of literary history turned the most potent weapon in the arsenal of the Liberal historian against him. In the hands of what have been called the "suave practitioners of denigration," men like Belloc, Strachey, and Philip Guedella, there resided the potential for undoing all the good literary history had wrought in the past and was capable of in the future.[36] Once, on hearing a paper of Strachey's read, Trevelyan remarked, "This is the end of all that I care for."[37]

Postwar Liberalism, in a most vulnerable state, found its most powerful traditional ally transformed into a potentially lethal threat. It appeared problematic whether "liberal" historiography could survive now that the direct and exclusive link between "liberal and literary history" had been severed. Nursing a chronically shaky personal faith in traditional Liberalism further shattered by the experiences of 1914–18, Trevelyan attempted to pick up the pieces as best he could, busying himself catholicizing the old Whig version of English history so as to encompass both Labour and Conservative variants. He had resigned his Cambridge Fellowship in 1903 in public protest against the encroachment of scientific history upon the prerogatives of its literary cousin. By the 1920s, harboring doubts about the proselytizing capacity of any message as latitudinarian as his own, Trevelyan began seriously to consider a return to the university setting. There he hoped at least to benefit from the professional aura of authority as compensation for his own lack of partisan conviction. In light of the popular success of Strachey and others in using literary historiographical forms to assail Liberalism, it appeared that Whig history, just like Liberal politics, might no longer be capable of surviving a contest in the public forum. Refuge amidst its erstwhile enemies in the academy corresponded to the Liberal politician's strategic withdrawal to the moderate edges of the Conservative and Labour parties.

Trevelyan had actually begun repairing his bridges to Cambridge before the Great War as part of his leisurely paced recoil from active political involvement. In 1909 he agreed to deliver a course of lectures at Trinity on the later Stuart period, journeying up from London twice a week during the Michaelmas term.[38] But only six years since his leave-taking, he was clearly not prepared to return permanently to an institution inhabited by the same "fatuous dons" who, he complained, comprised the membership of the British Academy.[39] Urged by friends to consider nomination in 1911 as Reader in history at Cambridge, a sorely tempted Trevelyan hesitated and then declined. By way of explanation he observed that such a Readership was "anything or nothing"; to do the job right required total immersion in the Cambridge world, and Trevelyan was not yet ready to relinquish his public persona.[40] He had left Cambridge in the first place to ensure the maximum political impact for his writings. However, a necessary accompaniment to that sort of substantive influence was direct involvement in political controversy combined with high public visibility, and he found that dissipation of effort trying, if not downright distasteful. Clearheaded enough to realize the infirmity of his present position, Trevelyan longed to return to the academic refuge. But paralyzed as much by overblown expectations as by sensitivity to his own limitations, he was as yet unwilling to step backward just as he was unprepared to forge on ahead. He feared the squandering of influence which semiexile at Trinity might bring, but, as a "little person," he had no flair for dealing with the ephemera of day-to-day politics. The award of an O.M. to his father in 1911 bolstered Trevelyan's confidence that history, particularly the literary variety, rivaled "politics and realistic novels and journalism" in the contest for prestige and cultural authority "in the present age," but he was as yet unwilling to surrender as superfluous his public pulpit.[41] The republication of "The Latest View of History" in 1913 as "Clio, a Muse" provided a temporary answer to Trevelyan's dilemma by angering some people at Cambridge and thereby delaying any precipitous retreat into the university.[42] Pangs of conscience at his possible dereliction of duty were stilled for the moment, but the issue was not finally settled.

After 1918, Trevelyan began once more to reconsider his relationship with academic history and the university. Twentieth-century menaces to Liberal parliamentary democracy were greater and more imminent than anything imaginable before 1914. Then it had seemed appropriate to defend the "cause" of Liberal-literary history from an extraacademic redoubt, but in the altered circumstances of the 1920s, the professional historical community, with its carefully guarded prestige and authority, offered intriguing cooperative possibilities. The democratic leveling of politics and culture in postwar Britain raised the specter of historiographical demagogy within an unstable public domain. The tremendous sales of Trevelyan's own books proved that the public appetite for historical literature was greater than ever, but the relatively less well-educated reader had neither the time nor the inclination to tackle the undigested masses of facts produced by university scholasticism and interpret them for himself. Instead he usually resorted to impressionistic or even fraudulent historiographic productions like those of Belloc, Strachey, or H. G. Wells. Trevelyan fretted that for lack of any real alternative, the reading public turned "to books like Mr. Wells' History of the World [i.e., *The Outline of History* (1920)] and Mr. Strachey's essays. Mr. Strachey is not a man of deep historical learning, but he is a man of letters of the first order, and so there is a large public in England that 'wants' whatever he has to say about history." Trevelyan allowed that by connecting history with the literary art and by interesting the public in historical themes, Strachey was "doing history a great service."[43] But by the mid-1920s, Trevelyan had witnessed the damage potential of purely "literary" history unfettered by the claims of research or academic peer review, responsible only to the dictates of dramatic effect or authorial prejudice. He now looked to an academic clerisy as a moderating and steadying influence. It would offer interpretive guidelines to a reading public otherwise susceptible to all sorts of sophistry. "I should be sorry if those who know most about history, those who give their whole lives to the study of history, relinquished the interpretation and exposition of history entirely to novelists and to literary men who were not primarily historians."[44] In 1903 such scientifically inclined historians had appeared as impediments to the search for historical truth by limiting it to an unacceptably narrow range. Two decades later this same monopolistic clerisy seemed to hold the key to the only means available for the salvation of Liberal historiography.

Trevelyan intended his *History of England* (1926) to inculcate among the public a sense of citizenship in the Liberal tradition, and now he proposed that the mandarin elitism of Jowett's Balliol be updated and expanded to perform the same function.[45] Whereas the ancient universities had once assumed the duty of fostering the virtues of citizenship among an exclusive ruling class, they should now assume the more ambitious task of instructing and vertically integrating the entire national community. In their devaluation of England's past, historians of dubious credentials like Strachey and others carried on, by proxy, the divisive modern assault on reason and culture; logically, therefore, organized resistance should begin among the intellectual elite. "How and where are we to fight these dangers to our common heritage? Largely, it is clear, in the universities. They must play the leading part in the difficult battle to keep alive in our machine-driven society some standard, some sense of value."[46] Since the postwar publishing experience proved that Gresham's Law apparently held for historical literature as well as for money—bad books invariably drove out good ones—the isolated position of any serious amateur historian appeared untenable in the long-term.[47] It was essential to devise a new strategic defense of Liberalism and its historiography that utilized the universities.

Trevelyan's rapprochement with the academic community, driven by this intellectual imperative, progressed by stages. After the war he was appointed to the Royal Commission on Oxford and Cambridge whose 1922 report laid the foundations for modernizing revisions of curriculum and finance. Viewing his work on the commission as directed toward ensuring the survival of "culture" in the "conditions of the democratic postwar world," Trevelyan longed to resume his former place within that repository of culture.[48] In 1925, while congratulating H. A. L. Fisher on his new post as warden of New College, Oxford, Trevelyan declared his love "of things academic, historical and literary," an unlikely triumvirate from the man who had published "The Latest View of History" in 1903.[49] But two decades had passed, and Trevelyan now pursued his own diplomatic revolution with the dons. He worked hard at and fretted over his relations with academic historians. After T. F. Tout praised a 1926 lecture by Trevelyan before the Historical Association, he dared to "hope the medieval part of my book [*History of England*] will be 'accepted' by the profession."[50] His eventual reconciliation with the university community must have seemed a foregone conclusion to Virginia Woolf, who later coined the title "The complete Insider" to describe Trevelyan and those of his ilk who were the "perfect product" of the "University machine."[51]

But of course Trevelyan was never the "complete Insider" of Virginia Woolf's imaginings. Resentment still lingered in 1927 among some Cambridge dons over the changes inaugurated by the Royal Commission for which he was largely held responsible (which may account, in part, for the failure of the *English Historical Review* ever properly to review his *History of England*).[52] Regarding the practice of his discipline, an older, wiser, and more diplomatic Trevelyan conceded some formerly disputed points to his academic colleagues but still refused to compromise his beliefs regarding the preponderant importance of literary style and poetic imagination in the presentation of history. Professor Vinogradoff's *Growth of the Manor* (1905) was scholarly but "stiff"; L. B. Namier he pronounced "a great research worker but no historian"; and he argued that with his own literary skills and air of enthusiasm, he had preserved the integrity while adding a "freshness" to his *History of England* despite openly acknowledged deficiencies of expertise.[53] In his own mind Trevelyan still occupied a position of strength in comparison with his academic counterparts, for he exhibited the courage to venture beyond the numbing confines of his own area of specialization and assume the onerous task of mediation between cryptic scholarship and the educated citizen. Even the chastened Trevelyan of the 1920s still found much in the ascetic, self-denying ordinances of compartmentalized modern scholarship antithetical both to the spirit of Liberal historiography and to the public discourse it nurtured. But alliances of convenience involved bilateral compromises. Even as academic history absorbed into its ranks one of the most prominent critics of its claims to exclusivity, Trevelyan expected it to donate its prestige in shoring up an ailing Liberal historiographical tradition.

At the death of Bury in 1927, Stanley Baldwin named Trevelyan Regius Professor of Modern History at Cambridge. He was glad to be back where he had now decided that he could do the most good. Life seemed "very full" for him in his new capacity, "fuller than it ha[d] been for many years."[54] Reflecting this sense of satisfaction as well as a keen understanding of the potential support for Liberal history available from a kindly disposed academic community, Trevelyan's Inaugural Lecture, "The Present Position of History," was a skillful exercise in conciliation. Seeley and Bury both received belated praise. Perhaps with the excesses of Strachey in mind, Trevelyan applauded the virtues of historical research in a much less oblique and ambiguous fashion than he had in "Clio, a Muse," while his championing of the paramountcy of literary presentation sounded less of an obsession.[55] He had overstated the danger of scientific historiography's swamping of the discipline in 1903, and there were now other, more pressing issues. Trevelyan offered up the address as a blueprint for the adoption by the Cambridge historical community of his own didactic agenda. Characterizing himself as no "publicist" (in marked contrast to Belloc), he denied that history could ever properly be used as propaganda, even in the service of the best of causes. Nor was it a direct guide for dealing with contemporary affairs. But if taught or read with broad human sympathy, it could "give a noble education to the mind of the student, not only in politics, but in all kinds of civic and social responsibility, and even in the domain of personal, religious and ethical ideals." If taught correctly, history would "cultivate a more intelligent patriotism that respects the claims of others." History held the key to the survival of the English tradition of liberal toleration. Wrongly taught, it helped to create an atmosphere of animosity and alienation that led to warfare and civil strife.[56]

Although he did not mention it in his Inaugural Address, perhaps Trevelyan was thinking of F. W. Maitland's spurning of the Regius Professorship after Acton's death in 1902, a decision tied to a faulty belief that technically proficient scholarship should not presume to speak to the world at large. The subsequent popularity of the suspect work of dilettantes had proven the bankruptcy of that policy of solipsism. By denying the moral autonomy of their discipline Trevelyan hoped to induce the mandarinate of the Cambridge History School to accept an immense responsibility, one which he believed their cultivation of technical expertise and professional esprit de corps equipped and obliged them to shoulder. He felt certain that now "historians could not see with indifference the popular presentation of history pass mainly into the hands of others." The autarkic professoriate must be made to acknowledge the altered requirements of the modern sociopolitical equation. Having broken the monopoly of the amateur historian, the universities now stood "in a more important and direct relation to historical production than in former times." With the audience expanded to include clever persons of all classes the great task for contemporary historical writing was "to establish a satisfactory contact between the academically trained historians and those who *should* be their readers." In the semieducated democracy of twentieth-century Britain the immediate future was "full of possibility and hope for historians" in the public arena, if only they would rise "to the call and to the challenge of the age."[57]

It could hardly be said that Trevelyan had changed his mind regarding the fundamental incompatibility of scientific and public history. But lacking a suitable out-of-doors alternative, he now determined to attempt a conversion of detached critical scholarship to his own views. If he failed in his bid to convert the university community into willing allies, he at least intended to mobilize its prestige for his own devices. The University of London don A. F. Pollard— sympathetic to Trevelyan's aims—recognized the futility of this interloper's task of attempting to orchestrate an unconscious revolution from above. It was indeed true that instead of "parading the streets," Trevelyan now sat in the chair of the Regius Professor who had banned him "with bell, book and candle." But Pollard reminded his readers that "the rebel has succeeded . . . *not the rebellion*."[58] As the *Times Literary Supplement* noted in 1930, "Professor Trevelyan almost alone connects the world of learned history with the English history which the English public will read; a cleavage which is not healthy for any of the parties concerned, since the public tend to read no other history at all, while serious history has inclined to dwindle down into the cult of a few score Brahmins."[59]

The publication of Herbert Butterfield's *Whig Interpretation of History* in 1931 disclosed the depth of vestigial resentment quartered inside university walls against Trevelyan and his work, as well as the tenuousness of the latter's newly acquired position within the academic circle. Although Trevelyan's name was never mentioned in the essay, he was clearly the primary target.[60] A man like Hilaire Belloc would have garnered little encouragement for his own much maligned efforts from Butterfield's ridiculing of "manufacturers of commercial literature" engaged in "loose thinking" or in the latter's observation that the objectionable errors of historical present-mindedness and flabby logic were "not merely the property of whigs."[61] But Belloc could have taken a certain measure of comfort from Butterfield's blanket denunciation of the ingrained tendency of Trevelyan and other clones of Macaulay to write on the side of Protestants and Whigs, to praise revolutions provided they had been successful, and to emphasize certain principles of progress in the past, thereby producing a story that amounted to the ratification, if not actually the glorification, of the present. According to Bellocian dogma, the donnish defenders of "official" history should have welcomed Trevelyan into their company. That the opposite was true leads one to the conclusion that Trevelyan's wary and pessimistic assessment of the complex and potentially antagonistic relationship between academic historiography and Liberalism was more perceptive and closer to the mark than Belloc's own paranoic assertion of consanguinity.

The Russians Won't Produce a Man as Attractive as Garibaldi: The *Risorgimento*, Liberal Conscience, and the Edwardian Fascination with Violence

Trevelyan was unable to duplicate the relative ideological consistency over time of the Hammonds. In the shifting eddies and currents of post-1886 British politics, he sometimes appeared too eager to abandon his leaky but still seaworthy craft and grasp whatever driftwood came within reach. His pedigree was Whiggish Gladstonian, though his father had very briefly broken with the Master of Hawarden over the first Home Rule Bill. At Cambridge George earned a reputation as an ardent Radical, but by the early days of the Boer War, having "ceased to feel for the Newcastle programme Liberalism," he, along with his brother Charles, sampled the Liberal Imperialist wing of the party.[62] Within two years he had metamorphosed into a pro-Boer.[63] By the end of 1901, Trevelyan had enlisted under the banner of the New Liberalism, occasionally contributing to the *Speaker*, where he rubbed shoulders with Lawrence Hammond and Hilaire Belloc. He also authored a piece for *The Heart of the Empire*, a collection that coupled New Liberal social reformism with mild anti-imperialist sentiments. Trevelyan's essay "Past and Future" exhibited an incipient affinity for the statist bureaucratic arguments of the Edwardian National Efficiency movement.[64] It is hardly surprising to discover that he was a dues-paying member of the Fabian Society and frequent guest at the home of the Webbs, though never evincing any real passion for Fabianism.[65]

Trevelyan's nomadic wanderings suggest a lack of clarity regarding the true identity of modern Liberalism. He wished to serve Liberalism, but its protean nature in the early twentieth century handicapped his attempts to get a firm fix on his prospective client. He valued his Whig heritage as the record of moral progress through constitutional development. But he had learned from his Harrow history master G. Townsend Warner, whose *Landmarks in English Industrial History* (1899) echoed Arnold Toynbee's depiction of the Industrial Revolution as a social catastrophe, that the story was not an uncomplicated linear ascent.[66] New Liberalism was in large measure a reaction to the perceived costs of the Industrial Revolution, and Trevelyan's own attraction to New Liberal doctrine derived from his conclusions about the inadequacy of political reform in isolation. Thus his acceptance of the necessity for a powerful, active state and his Fabian affiliation. Like so many young Edwardian Liberals, Trevelyan experienced recurrent misgivings about the liberal parliamentary system. Was it an effective and sufficient instrument in the modern age? Such doubts intruded into Trevelyan's most famous early work, his Garibaldian epic, which, though received as an unproblematic account of a celebrated liberal triumph, displayed a sustained fascination with violence that should have given pause to any Whig constitutionalist.

In October 1905 Beatrice Webb recorded in her diary that Trevelyan planned to devote the next several years to the "somewhat conventional and banal task" of writing a history of England between 1790 and 1810 which was to glorify Fox and rehabilitate the French Revolution.[67] It is unclear how she came to such a conclusion, for he was set to embark upon an entirely different undertaking, a trilogy chronicling the exploits of Giuseppe Garibaldi set against the backdrop of Italian unification. Although in his autobiography Trevelyan recollected a 1904 wedding gift of Garibaldi's memoirs as the catalyst for his interest in the Risorgimento, it most likely arose much earlier from his frequent Italian walking holidays.[68]

Whatever the origin of this new enterprise, he approached it with "the most intense enthusiasm . . . more than I am ever likely to feel for anything else."[69] Several months searching through scattered Italian archives and interviewing surviving Garibaldian veterans in the spring of 1906 supplemented written sources readily available at the British Museum. While in Italy he also carefully retraced the steps of Garibaldi's heroic 1849 retreat from Rome to Cesenatico.

Returning to England, he fell to work "like one possessed . . . driven by a fierce imaginative excitement." The result of these frenetic labors, *Garibaldi's Defence of the Roman Republic* (1907), was completed in only twelve months and, according to Trevelyan, bore the marks of both inspiration and haste.[70] The next two volumes in the trilogy, *Garibaldi and the Thousand* (1909) and *Garibaldi and the Making of Italy* (1911), were researched and written in much the same manner although at a rather more leisurely pace.[71]

Although Trevelyan believed that he had approached stylistic "chastity" with the first volume, to the modern ear this study of Garibaldi—according to its author "the most romantic life that history records"—sounds the most overtly poetic of all of Trevelyan's histories.[72] The author paraded his aesthetic sympathies before the reader in the introduction.

> That there should ever have been a time when Mazzini ruled Rome and Garibaldi defended her walls, sounds like a poet's dream. In this book I wish to record the facts that gave shape to that dream, to tell the story of the Siege of Rome, than which there is no more moving incident in modern history; and, in the last chapters, to narrate the events that followed as an epilogue to the siege—the Retreat and Escape of Garibaldi, a story no less poetical and no less dear to Italy's heart, though more neglected by English writers, because of its smaller political importance.[73]

Trevelyan presented these words as a challenge to the practitioners of scientific history whose methods he judged inadequate for conveying the essence of the events he lovingly described. His brother Robert, a poet and literary critic, urged that the introduction be placed at the end of the book, but George resisted the suggestion, noting that "in the present state of history in England, a history book is treated as an historic monograph, and consigned to 'historical students' unless it violently proclaims that it regards itself also as literature and appeals to the general public."[74] By appealing to the lay reader over the heads of the professional historians, Trevelyan hoped to demonstrate that "history is something far more wonderful than a process of evolution which science can estimate or predict."[75]

Trevelyan anticipated a wide and diverse readership because, as he told his father, Garibaldi was "a universality."[76] Concerned, like most New Liberals, with the great Edwardian dilemma of reconciling Liberalism and Labour, he believed that he had found a subject who transcended class divisions. Garibaldi's exploits had captured the imaginations of both the mid-Victorian working class and their social superiors who formed the backbone of the Liberal party in the age of Gladstone.[77] Trevelyan's own researches had demonstrated that in contemporary Italy the story was "very dear to rich and poor, learned and ignorant, in a progressive and free country," and he expected a similar ecumenical interest in modern England as well.[78] Mid-Victorians had entertained a "passionate enthusiasm" for Garibaldi, "pure of all taint of materialism and self-interest." Trevelyan's description of the civil administration of Mazzini's short-lived Roman Republic reflected his hopes for an appeal that transcended class divisions. He argued forcefully that the republic was neither socialist nor communist but anticlerical and liberal in policy and philosophy and therefore sympathetic to, and popular with, all classes under its rule.[79]

Among the many reasons that, at the time, Trevelyan referred to the Garibaldi trilogy as the "most important work of my life" was his clear attempt to spell out within its pages the inextricable connection between Liberal politics and literary history.[80] Like poetry, the drama of well-constructed historical narrative nourished the imagination while creating a sense of idealism and self-sacrifice that corresponded to Trevelyan's conception of the roots of four centuries of liberal thought. Since thought was readily translated into action, social progress, the creation of new nations, and the adoption of more rational and just principles of government had been in the past and still remained the work of "appeals to the imagination." "Imagination is the force that propels, though state-craft may guide. . . . But in order that men may aspire, it is necessary that they should have something to remember."[81] Only if bolstered by continual glimpses of past examples of success could the progressive movement championed by Western liberalism maintain its forward momentum. This was the practical function of the poetry of Trevelyan's Garibaldian epic. As he wrote in the introduction to the second volume in 1909:

> How then . . . do the legendary exploits of Garibaldi appear? Does the surrounding atmosphere of poetry and high idealism, when considered curiously, evaporate like a mirage? Or does it

not rather take shape as a definite historical fact, an important part of the cause of things and a principal part of their value? To my mind the events of 1860 should serve as an encouragement to all high endeavour amongst us of a later age, who, with our eyes fixed on realism and the doctrine of evolution, are in some danger of losing faith in ideals.[82]

It was no coincidence that the Garibaldi trilogy, the most thoroughly artistic of all his books, marked the zenith of Trevelyan's Liberal exuberance; in this pre-1914 context the two seemed to complement each other handsomely. At the time, he approached this task as, in many ways, an ideological imperative, even postponing the "*political* duty" of writing the biography of John Bright in order to complete the last two volumes of Garibaldi.[83] The Garibaldian trilogy seemed to Trevelyan's mind to answer the needs of the Edwardian Liberal agenda as well, if not quite as directly, as a study of Bright.

But exactly what Liberal agenda did the intellectually peripatetic Trevelyan have in mind? Garibaldi, the trilogy's inspiring protagonist, was a professional revolutionary, practicing his trade of irregular warfare at each stop in his wanderings from Europe to South America and back again. His rudimentary political philosophy began with a belief in some ill-defined Saint-Simonian notions of universal brotherhood and the extinction of classes, developing very little as Garibaldi aged. In the 1830s he simply incorporated a fervent attachment to Italian nationalism without exploring potential contradictions with any older ideological allegiances. In 1864 during his triumphal tour of England, Florence Nightingale quickly deduced from conversation that the Italian hero did not seem to understand properly the causes for which he fought. In South America in the 1830s and 1840s, Garibaldi's unexamined loyalty to causes of questionable propriety often blurred further the already indistinct demarcation between revolutionary and brigand. While displaying an admirable degree of romantic idealism and personal integrity throughout his career, Garibaldi also demonstrated a persistent fondness for dictatorial powers that, by all rights, should have compromised his exalted status in the eyes of any Liberal. After the fall of the Roman Republic in 1849, Garibaldi censured Mazzini's weak-kneed reluctance to assume the power and title of dictator. Complementing this affection for dictatorship was an unremitting disdain for messy parliamentary democracy. Garibaldi held that representative government might work well enough in the special circumstances of England or Switzerland, but in Italy such a system resembled "a prostitution worse than the most open despotism." Exposing his Utopian Socialist roots, Garibaldi advocated, after the unification of his homeland, a "temporary" Italian dictatorship to replace parliamentary rule until society was rendered less corrupt and egotistical.[84]

Ignoring all this unpleasantness, Trevelyan's own characterization of Garibaldi combined elements of the stolid civic virtue of Cincinnatus with the sacrificial romanticism of Gordon of Khartoum.[85] Trevelyan described Garibaldi, his role in the achievement of Italian unification apparently completed, returning quietly to private life on the island of Caprera, the great patriot, devoid of ambition or bitterness, "left alone again with his mother . . . Earth . . . industriously putting seed into the scrapings of earth which he called his fields."[86] Here was also an implicit comparison with that other Cincinnatus-like liberal hero George Washington. Privately Trevelyan made the one-to-one correspondence more explicit, assuring his father that the story of Garibaldi was even better than that of Valley Forge.[87]

But only the sanitized Garibaldi of Trevelyan's trilogy could survive such an analogy intact. After 1860 there was for the red-shirted Italian nationalist nothing like a Mount Vernon retirement, interrupted only by statesmanlike duties. Washington had gone to war after long deliberation, pursued the conflict with restraint, and disbanded the Continental Army with relief. Contrast this record with Garibaldi's own. In 1861 the German socialist Ferdinand Lassalle visited the famous Italian in an attempt to enlist him in a project for a general European revolution. The following year Garibaldi raised a small army of volunteers under the slogan "Rome or Death!" in order to conquer the last papal possession for Italy. It took several volleys from troops of the Italian government to scatter the expedition at Aspromonte. In 1863 a restless Garibaldi considered traveling to the United States to fight for the North and to Poland to fight Russians, meanwhile dispatching his lieutenants to assess the chances of sparking rebellion in Galicia and Transylvania. More of the same followed: in 1865 he thought of sailing to Mexico to battle Maximilian; in 1866 he led troops against Austria and in 1867 against the French garrison of Rome; and in the wake of the French debacle of 1870–71 Garibaldi could even be found contemplating a campaign against Prussia.[88]

Trevelyan's poorly focused Edwardian Liberal passion revealed a very illiberal tolerance of, if not downright enthusiasm for, violence. While sincerely preaching the causes of peace, retrenchment, and reform, Gladstone had reluctantly employed coercion in Ireland and gobbled up Egypt. In his treatment of Garibaldi, quite unintentionally, Trevelyan captured the tension between reality and the ideal in Gladstonianism, a tension now made manifest in the extremist and overtly violent politics of the post-Gladstonian era.

As one of the members of the prewar Russian Committee Trevelyan worked to "disseminate facts about the internal condition of Russia" with the declared object of promoting "the development of constitutional and humane government."[89] The abortive Russian Revolution of 1905–6, coming as it did in the midst of Trevelyan's research for *Garibaldi's Defence of the Roman Republic*, invited the inevitable comparisons. Yet though a highly visible advocate of propaganda to drum up support in England for the Russian democrats just as feeling had been worked up for the Risorgimento fifty years before, Trevelyan was not quite so naive as to equate 1860 exactly with 1906.[90] The moderate liberalism that he believed had triumphed in Italy through the efforts of Garibaldi and Cavour seemed an improbable outcome given the unpromising political substrate available in modern autocratic Russia: "If one could be sure of the result, one would welcome the struggle however sanguinary. But it seems extremely doubtful, the more so because the Duma had not sat long enough [before being dissolved by the czar] to make itself an authority of great power, and one fears the revolution will have no centre, and will run to extremes and divisions if momently [*sic*] or locally successful. But however many generations it may take, Russia will be free some day." What was significant here was not so much Trevelyan's admission that political liberalism was an unlikely outcome of revolution in czarist Russia but instead his readiness to sanction large-scale violence if such a resolution appeared at all likely. Immersed in writing about the heroic defense of Rome in 1848 by Garibaldi's international contingent, he mused that if he were single he would journey to Russia and fight for liberty himself. Yet he sensed that he was temperamentally ill-suited to

engage in warfare of the elemental savagery that one might antici-
pate in primitive Russia. "The amount of blood that will be shed will
be frightful. The Italian and French Revolutions will be childsplay to
it." For the immediate future he fretted for the cause of liberalism,
telling his mother, "I am afraid the Russians won't produce a man as
attractive as Garibaldi,—at least not as attractive to us Westerns
[*sic*]."[91]

Despite such assurances of Garibaldi's sublimity to Western eyes,
the constant refrain of violence running through his career from
beginning to end clearly presented problems for a biographer committed to the "cause" of Liberal and literary history. As a remedy
Trevelyan chose to glorify it, drawing parallels between the struggle
for Italian unification and some of the highlights of the Whig version of English history. In that vein he compared the assassination
of Pellegrino Rossi with that of the Duke of Buckingham in 1628,
suggesting that the political situation in Rome of 1848 was analogous to that in England of the 1620s.[92] But analogies were restricted
to the early Stuart period and the Civil War. There was no mention
of 1688–89, the greatest event in the collective memory of English
Liberalism, nor could there have been. Even the most tortuous
manipulation could not force the events and characters of the Risorgimento to conform to the patterns of the Glorious and Bloodless
Revolution. It is important to note that in 1860 accusations circu-
lated that Garibaldi spoke in "the language of Cromwell."[93] What
was Trevelyan to do with a biographical subject who, superficially at
least, so nearly resembled the Puritan Lord Protector, a personality
Churchill was to describe in the 1930s as "a representative of dictatorship and military rule who, with all his qualities as a soldier
and statesman, is in lasting discord with the genius of the English
race."[94]

Trevelyan rounded off the narrative's hard edges with a poetic
rendering of the military campaigns for Italian unification that was
not balanced by a faithful representation of the cruelty, suffering,
and hardship involved. Even more effective in placating the potentially confused Liberal conscience of the twentieth-century reader
was Trevelyan's failure critically to examine the net results of all this
sacrifice and bloodshed. His story stopped abruptly in 1860, permit-
ting no analysis of postunification Italian history, particularly of the
fact that Piedmont had unified the peninsula in a manner not dis-

similar to that employed by Bismarck in Germany. Instead, the author seemed to take it for granted that the unexamined long-term consequences of Garibaldi's exploits were impeccably liberal and parliamentary, eminently satisfactory to the exacting tastes of the modern Briton.

The spectacular sales of all three volumes testified to the efficacy of Trevelyan's selective reticence. As one reviewer put it, these books and their enthusiastic public reception proved to modern Italy "that in England her hero is not forgotten and that the ideals for which he strove are still cherished."[95] Critical notices were almost uniformly favorable. The *Times Literary Supplement* was typical of the lay press in its extravagant praise, pronouncing Trevelyan a consummate storyteller whose obvious Liberal devotion, although it might betray him into an occasional indiscretion or injustice, supplied just the right note of enthusiasm required to create sympathy in the reader without indulging in the special pleading of rabid partisanship.[96] His good friend G. P. Gooch even found room for the young historian's name in his *History and Historians in the Nineteenth Century* (1913), citing the volumes on Garibaldi as some recent works of distinction that had "won an enthusiastic welcome by their brilliant style and patient research."[97]

Despite Gooch's judgment, however, the academic reception, though less tepid than after some of his earlier work, still fell short of enthusiastic. In the *English Historical Review* Trevelyan's artistic dexterity met with approval, but the reader was warned to accept his political judgments with caution. Although Trevelyan was without question an "excellent scholar," the reviewer criticized his decision to close his history in 1860 rather than continuing on to 1870–71 as an obvious concession to dramatic unity that should have been eschewed in a piece of historiography with pretensions to seriousness.[98] Satisfied with these mixed impressions, Trevelyan told his parents that "considering the English Historical Review is the enemy's organ—the organ of 'scientific' history—it might be worse."[99]

Despite technical second-guessing from academic circles, Trevelyan actually began to experience doubts of a more ideological nature about the soundness of his work. His decision to write about the Risorgimento as a political duty while postponing an important biography of John Bright exemplified his Edwardian confusion over the nature of modern Liberalism and his relationship to it. His fascination with Garibaldi betrayed his own infatuation with the image of the "man of action" and his chronic obsession with attempting to adapt himself to that ill-fitting role. His glorification of "good" violence without fully analyzing its long-term legacy was reminiscent of his attitude toward the Russian Revolution of 1905–6. His hagiographic treatment of Garibaldi was, in many respects, as unexamined and conflicting as Garibaldi's own political sympathies.

Then in 1911 the Italian invasion of Tripoli shattered even this rickety structure of intellectual inconsistency as the liberal myth constructed around the Garibaldian trilogy collapsed of its own weight. The "Tripoli horrors and the whole folly of war" left Trevelyan, engaged at the time in writing *English Songs of Italian Freedom* (1911), terribly discouraged. "I don't think I shall have the heart to go to Italy again for many years. I have got to bring out in a week or two 'English Songs of Italian Freedom' . . . but I have no heart for it now, or even for Garibaldi." Trevelyan refused to find a direct link between the hero of his narrative history and the crimes of the modern Italian nation-state. But he did allow that the scandalous actions of "the degenerate Italians of today" at the expense of European peace made a mockery of his previous work, briefly draining him of the desire to write.[100] He had held up the achievements of Garibaldi as a shining example of the permanent momentum of liberalism. Now, at least in Italy, it appeared that a harsh new world had been called into existence to redress the balance of his antiseptic version of the old. William Miller in the *EHR* observed that "when Mr. Trevelyan wrote [the final volume of the trilogy], it was true to say that Italian nationalism had not been directed to conquest abroad. But that was before Tripoli."[101]

Trevelyan's transient pacifism in July 1914 may have been, in part, residue from his initial disillusionment over the fruits of violence as displayed in Tripoli in 1911. His former sympathies quickly reasserted themselves, however, and he became a strong supporter of the war effort, choosing, significantly enough, to serve in Italy. Likewise, his support for Lloyd George's "Dictatorship" in a time of "greater danger" for England "than we have ever been in our history" recalled a general concern with ends over means patterned after the priorities of his earlier historiographical treatment of Garibaldi, Cavour, and their cause.

Trevelyan experienced a similar confusion about the Russian

Revolution of 1917. At first, he praised the Revolution as a "living weight rolled off our life . . . [the] first great triumph of the principles for which we are fighting." For a fleeting moment the great event stilled his "fear that progress and liberty had been stopped for a century" by the catastrophe of war. But Trevelyan soon realized that his father's equation of the Russian cataclysm with 1792 was more apt than his own comparison with 1688. "I wish the Russians were Whigs, but as they aren't one must hope for the best to happen in some other odd, new democratic way. The dangers are too obvious to remark on." But the violence in Russia did not necessarily force Trevelyan to rethink his fondness for Garibaldi. Lenin and the Bolsheviks simply gave credence to his warning from 1906 that "the Russians won't produce a man as attractive as Garibaldi." Trevelyan's final judgment was that the October Revolution betrayed every basic principle of liberalism, a bitter pill to swallow for a man who for two decades had championed the overthrow of the czarist autocracy. Charles Trevelyan ridiculed his brother's negative verdict, finding it strange that a man who had secured his reputation with a sympathetic portrayal of the Italian *Risorgimento* should possess no understanding whatever of the Bolshevik Revolution.[102]

After the armistice, Trevelyan continued to defend the general spirit of his prewar histories, resorting now to the tactic of highlighting the disparity between the laudable Garibaldian form of nationalism and thoroughly discredited Bismarckianism. In the trilogy he had depicted Garibaldi and his accomplice Cavour as representatives of a peculiarly English conception of nationalism: liberal in origin and temperament, internationally benign, and indistinguishable from that preached by Mazzini. "Cavour had trained himself—for no one was his teacher—in what was then the British school of politics. Passionate Italian as he was, his political and economic ideas were based on acute observations made in England, and on a close study of the work of Grey and Peel. . . . And if then the example of Cavour had been preferred to that of Bismarck as the model for the patriots and statesmen of modern Europe, the whole world would now be a better place than it is."[103] This sort of apologia was disingenuous—particularly after Tripoli and Versailles had demonstrated the extent of the Italian expansionist appetite—in its disregard of the historical congruences between Italian and German reunification. Before 1914 the idealism that shaped Trevelyan's portrait of

Italian nationalism still held undeniable nostalgic appeal for an Edwardian England confronted with what it believed to be the dangerous offspring of Bismarck's appropriation and perversion of what had once been liberalism's sole preserve. But following the Great War, Trevelyan hoped in vain to hold firm in the mind of the public a clear distinction between the pragmatic brutality and ethnic exclusiveness of Bismarckian and Kossuthian nationalism and what he professed to be the liberal and universal nationalism of Garibaldi and Mazzini: "After [Garibaldi's] death his disciples went in their red shirts to fight for Greece in 1897, because he had taught them to ask, 'What can I do for the world?'—and not merely 'What can I do for Italy?' In his mind, as in Mazzini's the two questions went together. If all the victors and all the vanquished in the late war had believed in the Nationalism of Garibaldi instead of the Nationalism of Kossuth, Europe would be in a very different plight to-day."[104] It was one thing to make this argument in 1920; it was quite another for it to gain acceptance.

Trevelyan informed his parents in 1920 that he expected a resumption of good sales of his decade-old Garibaldi trilogy.[105] But the mood of the public had changed, and it took some time for Trevelyan to catch up. The Great War served as the incubator, if not actually the procreator, of the ironic mode of twentieth-century literature.[106] The naïveté and unquestioning innocence of Trevelyan's treatment of Garibaldi lacked its prewar resonance after 1918. As Harold Laski explained to Oliver Wendell Holmes in December 1920, "I re-read Trevelyan on Italy and, to my astonishment, found a large part of it merely brilliant rhetoric where ten years ago I remember being swept off my feet by it."[107] Trevelyan's attempt to revisit his success with Garibaldi and the Risorgimento in a 1923 sequel, *Manin and the Venetian Revolution of 1848*, was a resounding failure. Much of the fault lay with the subject matter itself. Ensnared in the subterranean intricacies of Venetian politics, Manin was a poor substitute for Garibaldi. Trevelyan could hardly be expected to make bricks without straw. But the outdated method of presentation shared equal blame for the book's unpopularity. On the strength of Trevelyan's reputation *Manin* sold well (over 2400 copies) the first year, but, unlike the Garibaldi trilogy, sales trickled away to nothing by the second.[108] The tastes of the postwar reading public were no longer attuned to linear narratives of liberal heroics, with good and evil scrupulously delineated and paradox, contradiction, and irony expunged. The last, unspoken chapter—that is, the catastrophe of 1914–18—of any story of nineteenth-century European liberalism's triumphs demanded a rethinking of the entire structure of the narrative, for it seemed that the moral of the story had now received a final wicked twist.

Appropriately enough, what the author would not supply the modern age could. Irony was injected ex post facto into Trevelyan's Italian quartet from the outside by Mussolini's Black Shirts. A decade earlier reviewers had warned that the liberal promise of the efforts of Garibaldi had not been realized by his successors.[109] In a public lecture at Oxford in 1923, later published as *The Historical Causes of the Present State of Affairs in Italy*, Trevelyan reluctantly and belatedly agreed. He would allow that Signor Mussolini was a great man and "a very sincere patriot," but Trevelyan feared for the survival of free institutions in a fascist Italy. Despite (or more likely because of—something Trevelyan was not yet ready to consider), the legacy of Mazzini, Garibaldi, and Cavour, parliamentary governance had never gained a firm foothold in Italy, where the new rulers "regard the suppression of free speech not as one of Cromwell's 'cruel necessities,' but as a good thing in itself, an ideal realized." Extremism on the Right had answered extremism from the Left. "It was as natural for the Italian socialist to terrorize his fellow citizens as for the English socialist to walk to the polling booth."[110]

In the 1920s reality intruded brutally upon art. It seemed that history had revealed the essential deceptiveness of the tone and spirit, if not the actual facts, of Trevelyan's Garibaldian narrative. This wrenching discovery left Trevelyan more confused and pessimistic than ever about the modern fortunes of Liberalism. Betrayed by developments in Italy, he turned back to English history for solace, for it now seemed "that there is only one decent race on the earth—the Anglo-Saxon."[111]

Providing the backdrop to all this was the aforementioned general postwar disillusionment with nationalism in any form, which in turn sparked an effort in Britain to widen the horizons of Whig historiography beyond its monomaniacal parochialism. The expectation was that the national narrative could be extended to the global arena. Liberal-minded historians—professionals and amateurs alike—"left high-and-dry by the death of the Liberal party in the 1920s," proceeded to reconstruct the old Liberal framework on a much grander scale with moral progress measured by the international advance of the principles of Wilson and the League of Nations. The cosmopolitan result was a succession of interwar publications: C. K. Webster's major studies *The Congress of Vienna* (1919) and *The Foreign Policy of Castlereagh* (2 vols., 1925–31), Harold Temperley's *Foreign Policy of Canning* (1925), and G. P. Gooch's collaborative editorial efforts with A. W. Ward on *The Cambridge History of British Foreign Policy* (3 vols., 1922–23) and with Temperley on *British Documents on the Origin of the War* (11 vols., 1926–38).[112] But liberal internationalism proved a flimsy reed in the 1920s and 1930s for the historiographical resuscitation of the Whig narrative of moral progress.[113] As an Edwardian harbinger of this trend, the Mazzinian flavor of Trevelyan's Garibaldian epic succeeded brilliantly. But the failure of *Manin and the Venetian Revolution of 1848* following the experience of 1914–18 foreshadowed the interwar bankruptcy of liberal internationalism as the savior of Liberal historiography.

Trevelyan the Trimmer:
From Whig Orthodoxy to Ecumenism

Before 1914 Trevelyan had written several major works on English history, all of them dominated by the strong Liberal flavor that pervades this concluding passage from *England in the Age of Wycliffe* (1899):

> In England we have slowly but surely won the right of the individual to form and express a private judgment on speculative questions. During the last three centuries the battle of liberty has been fought against the State or against public opinion. But before the changes effected by Henry the Eighth, the struggle was against a power more impervious to reason and less subject to change—the power of the Medieval Church in all the prestige of a thousand years' prescriptive right over man's mind. The martyrs who bore the first brunt of that terrific combat may be lightly esteemed to-day by priestly censure. But those who still believe that liberty of thought has proved not a curse but a blessing to England and to the peoples that have sprung from her, will regard with thankfulness and pride the work which the speculations of Wycliffe set on foot and the valour of his devoted successors accomplished.[114]

This conclusion brimmed to overflowing with all the prejudices of orthodox English historiography condemned first by Belloc, then later by Butterfield. At the time one reviewer complained that in future works on the Middle Ages Trevelyan should "start with an open mind . . . distinguish[ing] between the barons of the fourteenth century and the Whigs of the seventeenth, or the Radicals of the nineteenth."[115] Such criticisms did nothing to soften his calculated Liberal point of view. In any subsequent rewrites of *England in the Age of Wycliffe*, Trevelyan boasted to his parents, he planned to "stick on the warpaint in the preface and elsewhere."[116]

The nineteenth-century historian W. E. H. Lecky had written, "We are Cavaliers or Roundheads before we are Conservatives or Liberals."[117] Having cut loose from the restrictions of Cambridge in 1903, Trevelyan might have been expected to throw his weight behind the cause of Liberalism, churning out unabashed Whiggish history bordering on political propaganda. Yet he managed to moderate, if not entirely curb, his partisan instincts. *England under the Stuarts* (1904), his first post-Cambridge production, exhibited an admirable restraint and balance in apportioning credit and blame that foreshadowed the author's subsequent interwar historiography of consensus. In Trevelyan's contribution to the Methuen History of England series, the same country squires whom the author identified as the saviors of England's local liberties and parliamentary institutions were also indicted as the administrators of a prejudicial and cruel justice system. There was no attempt to gloss over the distasteful fanaticism and intolerance of the Puritan victors of the 1640s. Trevelyan disappointed partisan Whig expectations most noticeably in his evenhanded distribution of the credit for the civil and constitutional gains of the seventeenth century. In his construction there was rarely a clear-cut hero. More often than not, he ascribed beneficial or benign outcomes to the interplay of opposing forces, fortuitous births resulting from the antagonisms of selfish or myopically fanatical factions on both sides. "The English could not be argued into toleration by their reason, but they could be forced into it by their feuds." Individual liberty, freedom of thought and expression, and religious toleration were the unintended by-products of unresolvable spiritual and political squabbling. "In an age of bigotry, [the Englishmen's] own divisions had forced them into religious Toleration against their real wish; while personal liberty and some measure of free speech and writing had been brought about by the balance of two great parties." The reader was left contemplating the paradoxical genesis of eighteenth-century England's virtues. The margin for praise is severely diminished when a happy ending is accidental. In this qualified cynicism about the victories of the 1600s, Trevelyan's innate pessimism peeked through.[118]

The regulated evenhandedness of the historical interpretation evinced in *England under the Stuarts* recapitulated the precarious Edwardian resolution of Trevelyan's inner ideological turmoil. Radical and Gladstonian influences each received their due. Soon thereafter, Belloc, the Webbs, R. H. Tawney, and, to a certain extent, even the Hammonds would begin to attack the record of the sixteenth, seventeenth, and eighteenth centuries as a gross perversion of English history. Not immune to the powerful attraction of this critique, Trevelyan did not attempt either to hide or excuse many of the most obvious blemishes.

But his Whiggish sympathies remained lodged athwart the path of this criticism, blunting its momentum.[119] Trevelyan's story was still the standard one of constitutional progress by means of revolutions, citing England's transference of sovereignty from the Crown to Parliament as her unique achievement. Although he might criticize the narrowness and parochialism of the members of the Commons of the early 1600s, he cited their "freshness of mind" as the surest protection of national liberties. Perhaps thinking of the recently concluded Boer War, he credited upper- and middle-class sixteenth-century Puritanism with the origination of "a sense of moral responsibility in foreign affairs, which was neither sentimental nor hypocritical." His cynicism had prescribed limits. Concerned as he was in his own day to resolve the "*ultimate* question" of the relationship between Liberalism and Labour, he refused to countenance an interpretation of the events of the 1630s and 1640s based solely or even primarily upon issues of class and economics, issues that formed the backbone of the Radical historiographical critique. "In England the revolutionary passions were stirred by no class in its own material interest. Our patriots were prosperous men, enamoured of liberty, or of religion, or of loyalty, each for her own sake, not as the handmaid of class greed." Trevelyan hoped that the "moral splendour" of the tale of the Great Rebellion might exercise a contemporary bipartisan appeal, for the modern Labourite as well as the Liberal—and even the right-thinking Tory—could readily identify with the disinterested aims of the Roundheads.[120]

Working on his Garibaldian trilogy for the next seven years, Trevelyan vented the revolutionary and sometimes violent sympathies that had figured so prominently in his public school fantasy life. But following the 1911 Italian seizure of Tripoli, a reaction toward Gladstonian principles took hold, and, in keeping with that mood swing, he gratefully assumed a commission for a biography of John Bright.[121] In *The Life of John Bright* (1913) Trevelyan presented his subject as "the introducer of democracy," and the peaceful means employed by Bright in obtaining this result offered an implicit rebuke to the violence of the *Risorgimento*.[122] Yet the *Times Literary Supplement* found "nothing incongruous" in the transition from Garibaldi to Bright. "In spite of all the real and superficial differences, there is a true kinship between the man of war and the man of peace. . . . The true genius of both, in fact, lay in their gift for attacking and carrying apparently impregnable fortresses . . . not even Garibaldi served the cause of freedom with a purer devotion than [Bright]."[123] For the time being it was satisfaction enough for Trevelyan that Tories did not like the book and Liberals certainly did. "That is all I ask," he wrote.[124]

Trevelyan underwent a personal transition in the opposite direction, from "man of peace" to "man of war" beginning in August 1914. When he served on the British Neutrality Committee before the outbreak of hostilities, he described himself as an advocate of "Norman Angellism."[125] Later, serving as commandant of a British Red Cross ambulance unit on the Italian front, he experienced the same agonies as did the Hammonds back home trying to reconcile a commitment to victory with an older allegiance to Liberal tenets.[126] Although, like Barbara Hammond, he thought Lloyd George "a bit of a cad," Trevelyan supported the creation of the December 1916 coalition because the new prime minister seemed the only man equipped to save the country. Sounding strangely like Hilaire Belloc in *Robespierre*, Trevelyan wrote to his parents: "I am glad of the change, just as if I had been a Frenchman in 1793 I should have acquiesced in the Jacobin supremacy, and replied to my Girondin friends—'My friends, I greatly prefer you to the Jacobins, with whom I should not care to associate, but you began this war and have failed,—are failing—to win it, and these other gentlemen, certainly of inferior virtue to you, appear to have more energy.' ”[127] Trevelyan had been unwilling to defend the tyranny of arbitrary Cromwellian military rule a decade earlier in *England under the Stuarts*, but now, in the midst of "greater danger than we have ever been in our history," he regretfully admitted that resort to a "Dictator" seemed the only conceivable answer. Here was a dangerous inconsistency from a man who in a few short months would be denouncing Lenin and his Bolshevik Revolution as too Jacobinical and insufficiently Whiggish.

However, the great difficulty for Trevelyan in adopting a consistent posture toward the Great War was not so much one of guilt over principles compromised as one of a chronic lack of philosophical clarity regarding the true nature of Liberalism in the twentieth century, a confusion merely rendered more acute by this watershed of horrors. Trevelyan's drifting from Liberal camp to Liberal camp prior to 1914 demonstrated an underlying uncertainty, an infirmity of belief and of purpose. On Trevelyan's watch it seemed that all traditional navigational buoys had quietly slipped their moorings, leaving each pilot, with a lee shore off the starboard bow, to improvise as best he could. "With a world going to ruin," Trevelyan had observed in 1901," it is impossible to act and work as one would act and work in a classical period of literature and politics."[128]

Trevelyan credited his experiences in the Great War with having helped to free him from "some party prejudices and from too easy an historical optimism."[129] But the Whiggish partisanship so evident in *The Life of John Bright* was not expunged from his first postwar history, *Lord Grey of the Reform Bill* (1920), a book begun in 1913. Three chapters of an eventual sixteen were completed by August 1914, when work was suspended. After the armistice, Trevelyan wrote of his joy and relief at returning to the interrupted task: "Having fun with the Grey papers ... slipping back luxuriously into an old world of thought and imagination that I love."[130] The problem was that he allowed himself to slip too far back and in the process lost his bearings. While still at work on the book in 1914 he had explained to his mother, "The difficulty is not to seem too partisan in telling the purely domestic history of the 1790s. Pitt was *really* such a mean cad, and the world doesn't know it and thinks it a 'Whig tradition.' But it will have to get accustomed to the truth about him again."[131] This attitude, reminiscent of the one on display in *The Life of John Bright*, was not easily adjusted when he resumed work in 1919.

His head bulging with analogies between 1914–19, the Napoleonic Wars, and their reactionary domestic aftermath, Trevelyan could not quite summon up that pragmatic impartiality which the political muddle of the 1920s was to prove indispensable. The passage at the end of Chapter 3 that bridged a four-year hiatus in composition clearly demonstrated that when he resumed work on *Lord Grey of the Reform Bill* in 1918, Trevelyan had not yet successfully modulated from his pre-1914 partisan Liberal key. "Since the above was written another great war has been fought and won. It has been fought on behalf of the principles of Fox and Grey . . . against the despotic principles represented by Prussia and Austria, the powers of darkness whom the posthumous victory of Burke and Pitt made master of the continent for a hundred years."[132] As he later testified in his autobiography, "The theme of glorious summer (in this case the summer of Reform) coming after a long winter of discontent and repression is... congenial to my artistic sense."[133] The symmetry of 1832 and 1918 made the subject all the more dramaturgically irresistible. Following on the heels of Strachey's *Eminent Victorians*, Trevelyan flirted with the Stracheyesque sin of allowing aesthetic considerations, abetted by political prejudices, to overwhelm sober historical judgment.

But the declining fortunes of the postwar Liberal party soon dampened residual partisanship. Trevelyan had great difficulty finding his niche in an unfamiliar political landscape. As he wrote in 1922, "In so far as I am anything I am still a Liberal." In a similar vein, he mourned the party's 1924 collapse as a "catastrophe."[134] Yet despite all this handwringing, the post-1916 demise of Liberalism greatly simplified things for Trevelyan. With all reasonable political options now gone, guilt at nonparticipation ceased to divert him from his preferred duties as a historian. More significant, the rapid demise of the Liberal party—all those "liberalisms" that could never quite be reduced to a "liberalism"—helped to clear away the intellectual confusion that had splintered all of his prewar efforts.[135] Although on a national scale it might represent a "catastrophe," on the personal plane Liberalism's postwar political impotence was perfectly suited to the narrow talents of a political manqué such as Trevelyan. Like it or not, the immediate future of contemporary politics belonged to the Conservative and Labour parties. Trevelyan, displaying a heretofore untapped vein of political pragmatism, looked forward to Ramsay MacDonald's assumption of office in 1924 as a means of domesticating the party of socialism, of drawing it toward the middle ground. "As an historian and an Englishman it delights me to see the flexible old machine of the constitution swallowing and assimilating yet another 'bloodless revolution'—we have had such dozens of them." The presence of Liberal blood in MacDonald's cabinet reaffirmed "the 'continuity' of English political life."[136] When Trevelyan assured his brother Charles in 1935 that "I am a strong party man," he was commenting on the permanent nature of his own vestigial Liberalism. He then continued, "But I look to see the two-party system reestablished on the basis of Conservative & Labour, and don't therefore much care when Labour next gets in."[137] Within the confines of such a stable two-party system, the creation of a moderate, centrist political consensus between Left and Right was the nearest Trevelyan could envision to an authentic Liberal rebirth.

The poor sales of *Lord Grey of the Reform Bill* and *Manin and the Venetian Revolution of 1848* merely confirmed what Trevelyan already suspected.[138] The market for traditional liberal histories had all but disappeared along with the electoral support for Liberal candidates. Trevelyan possessed no confidence in the revival of either. Instinctively assuming an ecumenical attitude, he sought to salvage and rehabilitate what he could of Liberal paradigms by producing a history of consensus. The moral of the story with its triumph of individual freedom, constitutionalism, and prosperity remained essentially unaltered, but, at a time when organized Liberalism appeared exhausted, the story's scope was broadened, its cast of heroes enlarged, and the revised product offered up for adoption. The creation of a consensus national history based primarily, but not exclusively, upon the ancient Whig model would serve to perpetuate Liberalism's still considerable cultural influence long after its parliamentary clout had shriveled away.

British History in the Nineteenth Century (1782–1901) (1922) was the initial installment in this self-appointed task of redeeming the present by recalling the past. The book flowed naturally from his recent work on John Bright and Lord Grey but, unlike either of these previous studies, incorporated an altered tone that accommodated itself to postwar political realities. For practical reasons Liberal prejudices were submerged. With one chapter left to complete, Trevelyan confided the extent of his self-censorship to his parents: "I have to observe a kind of neutrality for the sake of getting the rest of the book into acceptance. I cannot say freely all that I think and feel."[139] In a remarkable tour de force Trevelyan successfully reconciled all the conflicting groups, ideas, and passions of the previous one hundred years of British history into a handsome portrait of consensus. He took as his theme the absence of any nineteenth-century revision of the principles of the British constitution, "only a constant amendment and extension of its details, and an entire though gradual change of view." Some mild Webbisms qualified the usual Whig genuflection toward 1689: the Glorious Revolution had secured political liberty but regrettably at the expense of efficiency and reform in administration and of the popular element in local government. Even more than the Hammonds, however, Trevelyan balanced his criticism of rule by an aristocratic oligarchy with expressions of admiration for the group's many sterling qualities and the consequent benefits to the nation. "In the government of the country and the Empire there was much to blame as well as to praise, but no aristocracy has ever better fulfilled the functions for the performance of which an aristocracy specifically exists, but in which it too often fails." Trevelyan readily conceded the evils of the Industrial Revolution, going so far as to describe the period from 1782 to 1832 as, "in its social consequences, mainly destructive." He joined with Clapham in regarding enclosure on a grand scale as necessary to increase grain production and to keep pace with changes in industry. Somehow he still managed to agree with the Hammonds as well that the enclosure methods adopted were ill-conceived and socially disastrous.[140] But in recounting the tragedy of the agricultural laborer Trevelyan refused to cast the gentry in the role of villain. Just like the workers, the landlords were the victims of impersonal forces such as war with its fluctuations of taxes and rents. Their misguided remedies—the Speenhamland system and the 1815 Corn Laws—were bad policy, not sins, an all-important distinction. Trevelyan consistently resisted awarding any group or class sole occupancy of the moral high ground.[141]

He was equally ecumenical with the book's political judgments. Within the political philosophy of Burke—a philosophy once identified with the powers of darkness in Trevelyan's biography of Lord Grey—were "enshrined in a perfect form the conservative principles which constitute one-half of our political and social happiness." The spirit of liberalism, "never neglected without disaster," was the corresponding antithesis in the progressive dialectical process that was modern British history. Just two years after the publication of *Lord Grey of the Reform Bill* Trevelyan lumped Pitt the Younger and Fox together as well-meaning men of principle and courage standing above party interest. Their disinterested, bipartisan contributions to Britain's political achievement were repeated time and time again throughout the century. Trevelyan labeled Peel a "Liberal-Conservative" because he combined the best of both persuasions: hatred of corruption, respect for public opinion, reverence for traditional institutions, and an overriding regard for the general interest.[142]

There was something here to suit every palate. Trevelyan cited concern for the national welfare rather than party tactical considerations as the motivation underlying Disraeli's support for the Second Reform Bill. Gladstone was singled out as the man who had done more than any other to adapt Britain's parliamentary institutions to modern democratic conditions. Meanwhile, Randolph Churchill had led the Conservative party toward "broader views and more democratic methods." Nineteenth-century working-class and socialist movements were subsumed within this consensus as well. According to Trevelyan, Chartism had "pointed the working class back to political action and a belief in Parliament," while the modern Fabians, "eschewing revolution, and intent on the actualities of England at the end of the nineteenth century," had "exonerated Socialists from the heavy obligation of reading Karl Marx," allowing them instead, in the best British manner, to concentrate on "practical possibilities" through traditional legislative channels. Elaboration of the many contributions of the state as an instigator of moral and material progress complemented praise of Fabianism. The overall effect of this integrative analysis displayed British history since 1832 as nothing less than "the story of the building up of a new world, of a wholly new type of society. . . . It has been the work of all classes and of all parties, whether in co-operation or in conflict, over a space of eighty years of gradual but rapid and continuous reform." In all fairness, no group could call this a historiography of exclusion.[143]

In Trevelyan's hands the Whig historical tradition, once the sole property of the Liberal party, had been reshaped to encompass the two dominant political parties of the 1920s. In his study of fin-de-siècle Britain Trevelyan had detected signs of the erosion of the "balance maintained between tradition and democracy, which had been the essence of the Victorian age." One of the many causes of this premature deterioration, perhaps the most important, appeared to be the substitution of "doctrines of race war and class war" for the "ethical and liberal interpretation of history, which had held the field for many years."[144] *British History in the Nineteenth Century* was the first of Trevelyan's ambitious attempts to ensure the survival and eventual back-door triumph of Liberal historiography by broadening its appeal beyond the partisan confines of official Liberalism. With its creation of an updated "national" liberalism the book constituted a political as well as a literary event.

Reviews of the book from across the ideological spectrum testified, at the very least, to the success of his method. J. L. Hammond certified Trevelyan's survey of the Victorian Age as "brilliant," although he found the author's assessment of the evolution of reform a trifle Panglossian.[145] Trevelyan might occasionally irritate a conservative by his preferences, remarked the *English Historical Review*, but the wonderful thing was "that the general tone and temper of the book are so free from prejudice and partisanship. His fairness goes a long way to vindicate those who believe that recent English history and what is called 'civics' or 'civism' can be perfectly well taught without being coloured by party feeling."[146] The Fabian *New Statesman* pronounced Mr. Trevelyan's tone "fair-minded and sympathetic," only very infrequently deviating "from his attitude of impartial appreciation."[147] According to the calculations of the *Times Literary Supplement*, Trevelyan had judiciously apportioned credit for the alleviation of the horrors of the factory system in equal measure between Liberals and Conservatives.[148] Observing that the author wrote "like a judge and not like an advocate," giving "the jury of public opinion true premises for forming their conclusion," John St. Loe Strachey, Unionist Free Trader and editor of the *Spectator*, wanted to record in his notice "how fair [Trevelyan] is to all classes."[149] And the Tory *Saturday Review* applauded the great-nephew of Macaulay for his willingness to deviate from traditional Whig dogma regarding the Industrial Revolution.[150]

In the opinion of the *English Historical Review* Trevelyan had risen above party prejudices to produce "a national possession."[151] He was amused that he should receive praise for his impartiality from the Tory as well as the Liberal press, feeling he must be like the man who "was so upright that he fell over backwards."[152] But clearly he had struck just the right chord. More than 10,000 copies of *British History in the Nineteenth Century* were sold in 1923 alone, and sales hovered around 2000 per annum for the rest of the decade.[153] Having designed this volume expressly for "the student or general reader," Trevelyan was conducting a national "civics" lesson.[154] Like his great-uncle before him, it was his intention to educate an entire society to see itself and all of the apparently disparate pieces in its modern sociopolitical mosaic as legitimate offspring of hermaphroditic liberal—not Liberal—pedigree.

Trevelyan's *History of England* (1926) represented the climax of his postwar historiographical-political efforts to create a national consensus. All of his work that followed was simply an extended postscript. The idea for such a book had first come to him near the war's end when, with his mind newly "cleared . . . of some party prejudices," he had imagined writing a literary history of England "for the people." His aim was to fashion a successor in style and popularity to J. R. Green's celebrated *Short History of the English People* (1874).[155] From 1923 to 1926 Trevelyan labored to produce a book that would duplicate the impartiality of *British History in the Nineteenth Century* on a grander scale.

The result of all this self-conscious effort was the most balanced and inclusive history possible from Trevelyan's pen. As he wrote in describing medieval monasteries, "Good and evil are hard to disentangle." Judged by immediate social consequences, enclosure was cruel and harmful, but the balance was at least partially redressed by a consideration of its long-term agricultural and economic benefits. The centralized Tudor monarchy saved the nation from Spanish conquest but fettered religious and political freedom for several generations. Kudos were awarded, if not quite in equal measure, to both sides engaged in the quarrels of the seventeenth century. "It may be fairly doubted whether any set of men, since the victors of Marathon and Salamis, had done as much to establish human freedom on a practical basis as the Roundheads and the Cavaliers, the Whigs and the Tories of the Stuart Parliaments." Nothing escaped qualification. The Settlement of 1689 was criticized as having had "the defects of its qualities," while Trevelyan's self-styled "undogmatic" approach to the history of the Industrial Revolution followed naturally upon the heels of his equivocal assessment of the living conditions of preindustrial English society.[156]

The public response to this catholic approach to history was overwhelming. Almost 30,000 copies were sold in the first year.[157] In step with their readers, reviewers resumed the chorus of praise that had greeted *British History in the Nineteenth Century*, judging Trevelyan "careful almost to a fault not to obtrude his own point of view." Seemingly unburdened by any ax of his own to grind, he had given his audience a "wonderfully complete and fair-minded book." That the author remained a Liberal was obvious to one reviewer, but it was just as obvious that "his Liberalism does not blind him to recognitions which Liberals usually leave to Conservatives." He saw history "with the eyes of a Liberal in the European sense," and therefore his work avoided the pejorative label "Whiggish."[158] The nationalistic complacency and self-satisfaction of the book, criticized by American reviewers, garnered little attention in British notices.[159] Even in the year of the General Strike, or perhaps especially in that year, there seemed little enough reason to question Trevelyan's grand conclusion that modern English society and the parliamentary democracy it sustained were "the natural outcome, through long centuries, of the common sense and good nature of the English people, who have usually preferred committees to dictators, elections to street fighting, and 'talking-shops' to revolutionary tribunals."[160]

But a brief "Epilogue, 1901–1918" had been imposed upon Trevelyan against his will by the "Publisher's view of necessity."[161] In dealing with the immediate past, particularly 1914–18, personal ideological affinities and a pessimistic affect were camouflaged only with great difficulty. The grim litany of the last eleven pages—a "blot" according to its author—was relieved only by its juxtaposition against the Napoleonic era. One unexpectedly happy outcome might presuppose another. But at least one commentator fastened upon the final somber judgments as the key to Trevelyan's historical evenhandedness and understated style. In a trenchant piece for the *Edinburgh Review*, W. R. Inge speculated that Macaulay's robust and boisterous Liberal confidence would have been misplaced in a history of England written in 1926, for the nation had reached a "real *fin de siecle*" with no real notion of what was coming "except that it will probably be something unpleasant." Ultimately England's judgment on the past, and the nineteenth century in particular, would depend largely upon its twentieth-century legacy. It was plain to Inge that Trevelyan's sympathies lay with the Liberal movement of the latter half of the nineteenth century, but those sympathies were underplayed, perhaps unconsciously, because Liberalism had come to a sad end.

> Recent developments mean that the whole of the political and economic structure built up in the nineteenth century is crumbling. . . . The war, which was absurdly said to be waged in order to make the world safe for democracy, has revealed the fact that the basis of democracy is everywhere undermined. . . . All the new movements, such as Socialism, Syndicalism, Bolshevism, and Fascism, though they agree in nothing else, agree in repudiating democracy. Principles which in the last century were treated as self-evident and almost sacred are now openly derided. The twentieth century is not the inheritor of the ideas of the nineteenth: it has thrown those ideas aside. It is possible that so convinced a Liberal as Mr. Trevelyan may be too reluctant to acknowledge that the flowing tide is no longer with him and his friends.[162]

Of course, it was precisely Trevelyan's unblinking acknowledgment of Liberalism's recent setbacks and dire prospects which accounted for the absence of Macaulayesque braggadocio. The time for books like his Garibaldian trilogy was long past. But the restraint of his mature prose reflected not resignation but rather a conscious effort to transform necessity into a virtue. The recruiting of loyal adherents to a newly constituted latitudinarian orthodoxy from a wider gene pool encompassing both Labour and Conservatism would at least preserve many of the essentials of nineteenth-century Liberalism against the threats of all the modern variants of totalitarianism while sacrificing only minor doctrinal extravagances.

After his return to Cambridge in 1927 Trevelyan hoped to appropriate academic sanction for his history of consensus. *England under Queen Anne* (3 vols., 1930–34)—in many respects the best of all his books—*Grey of Fallodon* (1937), and *The English Revolution, 1688–1689* (1938) each in turn reiterated the overarching themes of *British History in the Nineteenth Century* and the *History of England*. While defending the measures of Sir Edward Grey's prewar diplomacy, Trevelyan reaffirmed the traditions of continuity and bipartisanship in British foreign policy. In his history of the Glorious Revolution, without overturning the broad conclusions of his great-uncle, he supplemented Macaulay's "personal bias" with Sir Charles Firth's more contemporary "balanced judgment."[163] Preoccupied with the examples of fascist Italy and Nazi Germany, in *The Peace and the Protestant Succession* (*England under Queen Anne*, vol. 3) he applauded the comparative restraint, "despite their nonsense and violence," of both factions engaged in the bitter and long-running political duel during the reign of Queen Anne. "It is only in States based on the less civilized principles that no party may exist save the party of government, that liberty of press and person can be totally destroyed, whether in the Eighteenth or the Twentieth Century. That is not the English tradition." Instead, "kindly old England" had always "in the long run revolted against 'fascist' experiments at the permanent suppression of 'the other side.' "[164] In short, Trevelyan's histories of the 1930s were simply footnotes to his major volumes of the 1920s with their stress on toleration and the benefits to society of civilized, principled disagreement in the political and intellectual spheres.

Trevelyan undertook his intensive study of the age of Marlborough with the intention of resuming the tale where Macaulay had left off.[165] He was following in his great ancestor's footsteps in other respects as well. J. W. Burrow has advanced the argument that Macaulay's *History of England from the Accession of James the Second* (1848–55)—originally intended to take the story all the way to the Reform Act of 1832—constituted its own conclusion in much the same fashion as did Hegel's *Philosophy of History*. Macaulay, engaged in describing the past, was simultaneously preparing a contemporary frame of reference for his work by constructing a modern national consciousness. In the process his book itself became a historical actor. If taken to completion at 1832, it, along with the Reform Act it finally described, would have helped to forge a seamless "common political culture."[166] If that historiographically generated cultural, political, and intellectual consensus had ever actually come to fruition—a doubtful proposition at best—by Trevelyan's day it was in decay. The Great War had clinched that unpleasant fact. Trevelyan's postwar efforts were directed to preserving and reasserting the salvageable modern remnants of the traditional nineteenth-century

Whig paradigms. Like those of Macaulay, his books, particularly his *History of England*, were historical participants, constituting the conclusion to their own narratives. The public internalization of their stories of centuries of principled disagreement, civilized debate, and liberal toleration would secure the durability of those selfsame attributes in the future, although perhaps under the rubrics of Labour and Conservatism.

With a World Going to Ruin

In large measure because of Trevelyan's exertions, Whig history evolved into a nonpartisan "National" history during the first half of the twentieth century. The vocabulary of morality, with its ritual appeals to constitutional liberty, remained but was now uttered sotto voce. Derivatives of Liberalism's distinctive mid-Victorian values and beliefs were assimilated as part of the received political culture of the national community of all Englishmen. The result was what has been described in another context as a "muffling inclusiveness."[167] Shorn away in the process were all the rough, partisan edges of traditional Whig history. In their place arose a comprehensive, nonsectarian national narrative to which no party could take exception or lay exclusive claim.[168]

As seen above, empirical academic historiography was well suited to the reduced domestic political temperature of the 1930s, spawning a quietism that manifested itself as a strict concern for the study of the mechanics of administration and governance. Likewise, Trevelyan's consensus history reproduced the interwar mood as well as the author's own state of mind. As early as 1922 the Hammonds thought they detected a rightward shift in Trevelyan's political sympathies which they ascribed to the effects of the war.[169] By 1935 Beatrice Webb dismissed him as a "convinced Conservative," an opinion later corroborated via his brother Charles, who reported that George, "though kindly and tolerant of other views, has become a hard-grained Tory; cynical towards all social reform, and intensely pessimistic."[170]

Trevelyan described himself in 1936 as "not any longer political." He would only allow that "insofar as every citizen has some politics, I am a supporter of the National Government."[171] In the third volume of *England under Queen Anne*, under the guise of a discussion of the splintering and emasculation of eighteenth-century Toryism by the feud between Bolingbroke and Harley, he vicariously mourned the Asquith–Lloyd George fracturing of the modern Liberal party. "Such quarrels of colleagues have often proved the most irremediable of all."[172] Left an orphan by postwar political realignments, Trevelyan sired a version of history that would preserve Liberalism by transforming it into a patriotic and latitudinarian "Englishness." His friendship with, and support for, Stanley Baldwin flowed from this same preoccupation. The prime minister's conciliatory and avuncular manner, his distaste for all forms of extremism, and his rustic invocation of the bipartisan rural myth all conveyed a sense of generic English toleration, decency, and character rather than Tory partisanship.[173]

In *England under Queen Anne* Trevelyan fastened upon these sorts of virtues. The coalition ministries who defeated Louis XIV merited praise for their moderation, good sense, and humanity. Godolphin, a man who like Baldwin performed the country's work "by patient and tactful plodding rather than by eloquence, genius and daring," won Trevelyan's approval as "much more a public servant than a party politician." Likewise, Harley was a "public servant and a moderator." Trevelyan disclosed to his daughter that he judged Marlborough "the most tolerant and reasonable of men . . . not passion's slave or party's." As early as 1926 Trevelyan had reappraised himself as "more of a Harleyite and a Marlburian than a true-blue Whig." It is little wonder that he assured Baldwin in 1935 that "Whiggism and Conservatism are not opposed as fundamentals."[174]

Perhaps because Trevelyan's prewar expectations for Liberalism were more modest and conventional, and also more muddled, than those of Belloc, the Webbs, or even the Hammonds, after 1918 he experienced less disillusionment at its failures. Although admitting in 1926, "I don't understand the age we live in, and what I do understand I don't like," Trevelyan managed to retain a strain of qualified optimism in his work that belied his own chronically morbid psychological state.[175] This is not to suggest that he was not profoundly depressed by the apparent cul-de-sac of postwar British politics and culture, yet his pessimism was creative and even personally therapeutic. His solution to his distressed state of mind was not, like that of Belloc or the Webbs, to attack Liberalism, or, like that of the Hammonds, to construct a subtle theoretical defense of Liberalism in a vain search for a nonexistent party of the center to which it could be attached. Ironically, Trevelyan the romantic was the most practical and resourceful of all. Hoping to rescue what little he could of the traditional Liberal ethos he loved so well, Trevelyan produced a version of the past that stretched Liberal paradigms to their logical limits and beyond to encompass the parallel myths of Labour and Conservatism.

But if this was a victory for Liberalism, it was an equivocal one. While the detached objectivity of scientific, university-based history marginalized its contribution to public discourse, the self-conscious impartiality of a consensus "National" history threatened to produce the same result. Self-consciously disinterested public historiography, whether of the academic or literary consensual variety, hovered above contemporary debate without directly participating in it. Indirect contributions to unspoken assumptions provided some solace, but the fact remained that the price exacted for the survival of Whig history engineered by Trevelyan was seepage of cultural authority. Manacled by qualification and shorn of partisan confidence that had once lent it power in the nineteenth-century public forum, modern Whig history would survive only as a shadowy reflection of its former self. Trevelyan could not have been entirely pleased with his own handiwork. But the spirit of his postwar writings was ultimately defensive in nature. His abandonment of the sureties of his Victorian predecessors and his return to the academic sanctuary both testified to a certain lack of conviction, a loss of faith in raw Liberalism's suitability for the modern era. As Trevelyan admitted guiltily in 1934, "I have not gone in for the rough and tumble of the world's debate. I think I was right, as my gifts were literary not administrative or political. But no one knows better than I do that I am no hero."[176]

5   WINSTON CHURCHILL
The Last Public Historian

G. M. Trevelyan engineered the survival of Whig history as
the essential core of a new national history of consensus.
But it was left to another public historian to perfect the
genre. With an ear for the sonorous phrase and a keen sense
of the dramatic, Winston Churchill completed the task Trevelyan originally set for himself, that is, to make English
history "known to a new generation," to exercise "a definite
and practical influence upon the future of our country"
by helping young readers "to realize they are heirs to a
great tradition."[1] While the timorous Trevelyan retreated to
Cambridge to ply his trade, Churchill presented the public
with an unapologetic defense of liberal and literary history
that clashed openly with the sneering irreverence of other

Winston Churchill at work on his History of the English-Speaking Peoples *in
his study in Chartwell in early 1939. (Hulton-Deutsch Collection)*

post—*Eminent Victorian* amateurs. Deferring to the dictates of his academic environment, Trevelyan offered his readers a rehabilitated version of English history surreptitiously via the back door, heaping qualification upon qualification. Churchill preferred the more direct—some might say foolhardy—approach. He possessed a confidence in the essential truth and eternal value of his message of ordered progress that eluded the dour and pessimistic Trevelyan after 1914, a confidence that allowed Churchill to return unashamedly to the rhetorical hubris of Macaulay.

Churchill's handling of British history contrasts subtly but significantly with Trevelyan's. Their different approach to the subject of the Magna Carta is a case in point. The latter could find nothing in the episode at Runnymede other than private vices turned to public good fortune over time by some benevolent invisible hand. "The barons were acting selfishly and class-consciously to just the same degree—no more and no less—as other English classes and parties who in successive centuries have taken part in developing 'our happy constitution' by self-assertion in a practical compromise."[2] In this version of the circumstances surrounding the Magna Carta, liberalism, defined as the ideological and philosophical counterpoint to the slow growth of constitutional practice, was devalued, for Trevelyan's analysis deposited in the mind of the reader a grating disjunction between intentions and results. The post-1918 Liberalism of principle could not handle this naked discrepancy. It demanded moral congruence between aims and consequences, in the past as well as in the present. The work of the Hammonds presented disturbing examples of good intentions conspiring to bring forth malignant results, while Trevelyan offered the opposite: a happy outcome originating in a long succession of suspect motives. It was left to Churchill to square the circle by bringing intentions and results, principle and practice, into some semblance of alignment and harmony.

This is not by way of arguing that Churchillian historiography remained comfortably blind to the paradox of good results issuing from the actions of the craven or selfish. There was enough irony scattered about in Churchill's version of the past to satisfy the tastes of all but the most cynical and jaded of the post-1918 reading public. Thus in *A History of the English-Speaking Peoples* he characterized the Magna Carta as "a redress of feudal grievances extorted from an unwilling king by a discontented ruling class insisting on its own privileges." But, as in this particular instance, Churchill often went on to disarm and then redeem his own ironic observations. Insisting that it would be a mistake to dismiss the Magna Carta lightly as "a monument of class selfishness," he proceeded to an evocative description of the barons of 1215 groping "in the dim light towards a fundamental principle." The idea, albeit only half understood, that government must henceforth mean something more than arbitrary rule of any man, that custom and law must stand even above the king, provided the charter with a higher and nobler character. "If the thirteenth-century magnates understood little and cared less for popular liberties or Parliamentary democracy, they had all the same laid hold of a principle which was to be of prime importance for the future development of English society and English institutions."[3] By exacting modern standards the barons of King John were found wanting, but Churchill refused to regard them as solely motivated by individual and class greed. In this rendering the grand legacy of the Magna Carta was not simply an unintended, fortuitous by-product of narrow and uncomprehending self-interest, but rather in some measure a function of the barons' spark of public virtue as defined according to medieval standards of community and obligation. Public virtue, even in this unfamiliar and rudimentary form, was laudable in any generation.

Through the use of this technique of exploded irony Churchillian prose overlapped the pre- and post–Great War mentalities of his readers and skillfully maximized its appeal. The ironic mode which after 1918 so mesmerized and eluded Trevelyan, received its due from Churchill, yet not at the expense of the author's faith in progress or in the general humanity, goodwill, and common sense that provided the pageant of English history with its uniquely noble aspect.

Like Trevelyan and the Hammonds, Churchill retained the use of a moral vocabulary in revisiting the traditional story of constitutional development. But his notion of England's political genius was tougher, broader, and more attuned to the harsh conditions of the twentieth century. The issue of the concentration and employment of power—political and military—bedeviled Trevelyan and the Hammonds, accounting, in part at least, for their reluctance to condone its periodic intrusions into the historical narrative. Churchill suffered from no such qualms, seeing power as neither intrinsically evil nor inevitably corrupting. Thus his chronicles stressed the links between the securing of parliamentary sovereignty, the acquisition and consolidation of empire, the waging of wars to combat foreign tyranny, and the growth of a centralized, efficient state to answer the requirements of war-making. Churchill oversaw the reconciliation of Trevelyan's ecumenical Liberal version of the past with the question of power and force, in the process creating a durable English national history which proved most serviceable in the 1930s and 1940s.

In many ways Churchill was ideal to superintend the maturation of history with a Liberal pedigree into a self-consciously nonsectarian national consensus. His itinerant political career anchored him firmly to no party in the mind of the public, particularly during his most productive years as a historian between 1920 and 1939. Beginning as a Tory by inheritance, switching to the Liberals in 1904, serving in Lloyd George's coalition, and then crossing the gangway a second time in 1924, Churchill never won the complete trust or acceptance of any formal political grouping. His ambition, egotism, and ideological idiosyncrasies ensured that he would always remain something of an outsider; even after becoming prime minister in May 1940 he hesitated to assume the leadership of the Conservative party until after Neville Chamberlain's resignation in October. Not only because he headed a National Government did Churchill, in his Commons acceptance speech, lay stress on the contributions to Britain's "modern progressive democracy" of "all living Parties—Conservative, Liberal, Labour and other Parties, like the Whigs who have passed away."[4] Serving as a Conservative M.P. in 1937, he had declared in a private confidence, "I believe in Liberalsm. I am still a Liberal," a sentiment later echoed by John Simon, who continued to view Tory prime minister Churchill as "a Liberal still" even in 1954.[5]

Whatever else such appraisals might signify, they point up the fact that one great difference separating Churchill and Trevelyan was the infinite and exasperating adaptability of the former. Trevelyan might create consensus historiography after 1918, but the demise of the Liberal party drained him of genuine political enthusiasm. Conversely, harboring an image of himself as above narrow party interests, Churchill generated a succession of avatars, each energetically accommodating itself to a fluid political landscape. Though his histories praised the accepted Whig engines of national progress—parliamentary institutions and the two-party system—Churchill had constantly to combat a tendency to sympathize with coalitionism, the idea of national parties above faction and parochial interest, and administrative efficiency as a substitute for ad hoc governance by an amateur debating society.

Churchill cultivated his supraparty image in all his histories, beginning with his first undertaking, a biography of his father. The timing of *Lord Randolph Churchill*, which appeared in 1906, exactly paralleled Winston's change of party over the issue of free trade. It is conceivable that his study of his father's political career spurred on the move, but more likely the son's slowly crystallizing decision to switch parties led him first to take up the biographical chore and then to pursue it so relentlessly. A vindication of the Victorian father became a complementary vindication of the Edwardian son.

Nearly a decade earlier, at the age of twenty-two, Winston had written to his mother from India, "I am a Liberal in all but name. . . . Were it not for Home Rule—to which I will never consent—I would enter Parliament as a Liberal. As it is—Tory Democracy will have to be the standard under which I shall range myself."[6] Tory Democracy, which he proceeded to define rather vaguely as "Peace & Power abroad—Prosperity & Progress at home," led him straight to his father's halfway house. By 1902 opposition to Chamberlain's campaign for tariff reform and an ambition natural to every politician had combined to overcome any lingering doubts about realignment with the Liberal party. In May 1904, after months of negotiation and vacillation, Churchill officially ranged himself with the followers of Campbell-Bannerman and Lloyd George.

All the while, work proceeded apace on *Lord Randolph Churchill*. The political figure who emerged from the pages of the biography bore all the marks of the son's recent inner struggle. Winston's Randolph Churchill was bound to the Conservative party by ties of family, friendship, and affection, yet he was to prove himself a man of uncommon principle and vision, above both party and tradition. The author traced these admirable qualities back to Randolph's father, Lord Blandford, who upon his election to Parliament in 1844 "immediately developed progressive tendencies in social and economic questions and became a steady supporter of Free Trade measures," this last well before the repeal of the Corn Laws.[7] Winston described Lord Randolph before the age of thirty as already "thoroughly out of sympathy" with his own party on Ireland and foreign policy.[8] His virulent attack in Commons debate upon a cabinet-sponsored County Government Bill in 1878 prompted the retort from another Tory M.P. that, if such were his opinions, he should "lose not a moment in going over to the other side of the house." In a self-referential aside, Winston noted that such "advice is often given and sometimes accepted."[9]

Winston argued that Randolph, stirred by "liberal and pacific sentiments" but restrained by "affection for the Conservative party," sought a way to reconcile these incompatible loyalties.[10] The manner chosen to relieve some of this tension was peculiarly unconstructive and posed great difficulty for his admiring biographer. Descriptions of the deflection and disruption of Commons debate through venomous attacks by the Churchill-led Fourth Party upon the hapless Sir Stafford Northcote rested uneasily in harness with Winston's editorial denunciations of parliamentary tactics of obstruction and its remedy cloture as "joint depredations" and with the cheery observation that "in modern times personal kindness and good feeling lie never far below the sullen surface of English politics."[11] But the Fourth Party of Randolph Churchill had to be presented in the best possible light, its public taunting of Northcote and Gladstone linked to principle rather than to naked ambition or mere caprice.

Winston chose to emphasize his father's unflagging devotion to "Tory Democracy" as the central idea unifying his Fourth Party ambuscades, his subsequent manipulation of the National Union of Conservative Associations, and his eventual resignation from the Salisbury cabinet in 1886. Tory Democracy the son equated with the proposition that "the Conservative party was willing and thoroughly competent to deal with the needs of democracy and the multiplying problems of modern life; and that the British Constitution, so far from being incompatible with the social progress of the great mass of the people, was in itself a flexible instrument by which that progress might be guided and secured."[12] According to an 1888 address at Birmingham by Lord Randolph, Tory Democracy was "animated by lofty and by Liberal ideas."[13] The book's emphasis made seem natural and inevitable the eventual rupture between Lord Salisbury, representative of old fashioned, backward-looking Toryism, and

Lord Randolph, "the responsible trustee and agent of Tory Democracy."[14] Between the two men the author found "a difference of belief, of character, of aspiration—and by nothing could it ever have been adjusted. . . . They represented conflicting schools of political philosophy. They stood for ideas mutually incompatible. Sooner or later the breach must have come."[15] In retrospect Winston consecrated his father's political suicide on the altar of high principle.

The importance of this flattering portrait of Lord Randolph to his son's own circumstances in 1902–6 are almost too obvious to warrant enumeration. Like his father, Winston's natural sympathies, formed by heredity and reinforced by habit, lay with the Tories, but he had now rejected that affiliation in the name of a higher loyalty and in the process risked calumny as a traitorous opportunist. It was necessary to demonstrate that by his actions he was only fulfilling the inevitable logic of Lord Randolph's position. Born and bred in the Tory party, Randolph Churchill had declared, "I could never join the ranks of their opponents."[16] But his blazing of a path to the frontier legitimized his son's later crossing over.[17]

The verification of ideological and intellectual consistency throughout Lord Randolph's career was the key to the book's entire argument, expiating the sins of both author and subject. Randolph Churchill's "harmony and unity of purpose and view" as delineated by the author provided the reader of the biography with an admirable fixed point against which to evaluate the ebb and flow of politics and party.[18] Winston expected his father to be judged above the narrow interests and parochial standards of party, and he asked no less for himself.

Clearly one of Winston's main objects with the book was to demonstrate to the British public the soundness and reliability of his own character, a theme that cropped up again and again in later years. In the 1920s with *The World Crisis*, Churchill attempted to overcome the taint of rashness and untrustworthiness that dogged his heels following the Dardanelles debacle; with *Marlborough* in the 1930s he continued his never-ending project of personal rehabilitation by clearing the reputation of his great ancestor, a reputation long tarnished by the implication of duplicity; and similarly, with his intensely personal *The Second World War* (6 vols., 1948–53) Churchill provided an eloquent rebuke to a country unwilling to trust in his leadership after the cessation of hostilities in 1945. Churchill's career in politics and history involved an individual struggle to establish his personal and political integrity, to underscore his loyalty to nation if not to party. One reader of *Lord Randolph Churchill* noted approvingly that "Lord Randolph had that feeling for England as a whole which so many Whigs, Liberals, and Conservatives often lack."[19] In the eyes of the author the stress laid on the national vision of its protagonist gave the biography an enduring value beyond just the satisfaction of historical curiosity. "Lord Randolph Churchill's name will not be recorded upon the bead-roll of either party. . . . A politician's character and position are measured in his day by party standards. When he is dead, all that he has achieved in the name of party, is at an end. . . . The years to come bring weights and measures of their own. . . . It was to England that Lord Randolph Churchill appealed; it was that England he so nearly won; it is by that England he will be justly judged."[20]

The notion of the primacy of duty to the nation over loyalty to party or class was one that always attracted Churchill. Like so many others during the Edwardian period he dreamed of the formation of a national coalition or of a party of the center that would subordinate narrow party advantage to the wider interests of the nation. His negotiations with Lord Rosebery in 1902 for a possible "Government of the Middle" presaged his later involvement in informal talks regarding the formation of a national government during the budget and Lords crisis of 1910, his support (despite his own exclusion from office) for the Lloyd George coalition of 1916 and the National Government of 1931, and his own leadership of an all-party administration between 1940 and 1945.[21]

In *Lord Randolph Churchill* Winston had very nearly provided a legitimate ancestry for such a party of the center, nearly but not quite. In a chapter entitled "The National Party" he had described the tremendous potential for an 1887 political alliance between his father and Joseph Chamberlain, two powerful men "adrift from the regular party organisations."[22] But the collaboration had come to nothing in the end, and Winston implied that the foundering of such joint plans, however nobly conceived, was ultimately inescapable.

> With this separation [of Chamberlain and Lord Randolph] the prospects of a National party fade again into that dreamland whence so many have wished to recall them. Few, indeed, are the politicians who have not cherished these visions at times

when ordinary party machinery is not at their disposal. To build from the rock a great new party—free alike from vested interests and from holy formulas, able to deal with national problems on their merits, patient to respect the precious bequests of the past, strong to drive forward the wheels of progress—is without a doubt a worthy ideal. Alas, that the degeneracy of man should exclude it for ever from this wicked world![23]

Particularly in the pre-1914 era Churchill partook in moderation of the heady wine of the National Efficiency movement with its advocacy of the subordination of politics as usual to sound disinterested administration. But in his recognition of the impossibility and even undesirability of any permanent submergence of party conflict and partisan public discourse, Churchill profoundly differed from the other professed advocates of National Efficiency. If democracy was the worst form of government except for all the others that had ever been tried, it was simply because the liberal parliamentary system, despite all its many frailties and blemishes, accepted human nature for what it was.[24] However desirable in theory, coalitions, because of their reliance upon a moratorium on human weaknesses and upon an artificial abeyance of legitimate political disagreement, could function without compromising liberty only during times of great national crisis, and then only for the briefest of intervals.

Churchill believed that strong and permanent partisan organizations organized around fundamental philosophical differences, however much they might appear to contribute to irrationality, untidiness, and inefficiency, lay at the heart of liberal governance. It was not for nothing that Edmund Burke, credited by Churchill with the invention of the modern party of principle and with having rescued party from its disreputable association with faction, was later extolled by a mature Churchill as "the greatest man that Ireland has produced."[25]

Churchill and the Experts:
To Exploit Rather Than Confront

It was Churchill's immersion in this rough-and-tumble world of partisan politics that most clearly set him apart from Trevelyan and Lawrence Hammond. He was one member of the traditional ruling class who had not lost the will to power or the assurance of his own fitness to govern the nation. Churchill refused to choose between a life in letters or a life in Parliament. R. B. Haldane and General Jan Smuts compared him to Julius Caesar, another "man of action and a great writer at the same time."[26] Rather than some ancillary appendage to his primary occupation of politics, Churchill's historical labors represented an essential cog in a well-integrated public life. The discipline of historiography abetted the practice of politics and vice versa, or as Henry Steele Commager put it, "Churchill wrote history in order to mould it,—so we sometimes suspect—he made history in order to write it."[27] Churchill was a true *public* historian in every sense of the term. His histories were a direct extension of his political utterances. The rhetoric of his Commons speeches merged effortlessly with the printed word of his historical prose. The vocabulary, style, cadence, and mode of composition were identical. This congruence provided Churchill with an approximation of the cultural influence of his Victorian counterparts. He wielded the sort of dual authority for which Trevelyan yearned. It is notable that with his first great historiographical undertaking, the life of his father, young Winston consciously patterned his method upon the Victorian example of John Morley, cabinet minister, journalist, editor, amateur historian, and biographer of Gladstone.[28]

The author of the Garibaldian trilogy deplored the modern segregation into separate spheres of politicians and intellectuals. Yet he felt personally ill-equipped to combat it. Contrasting with Churchill's overweening self-assurance, this shortage of confidence surfaced in Trevelyan's prose. He found it difficult to write about the post-1914 period. Pessimistic regarding the prospects of modern Liberalism, Trevelyan felt more comfortable revisiting past triumphs. Largely because of his own practical political experience, Churchill never hesitated to chronicle an optimistic version of the contemporary age and link it with the nation's heritage. (Egotism clearly played a part here, since Churchill usually wrote contemporary history with himself at the center of events. As one wit chortled over Churchill's history of the Great War, "Winston has written an enormous book about himself and called it *The World Crisis*."[29]) As a participant in the day-to-day workings of parliamentary government, Churchill retained a faith in the adaptability and resilience of the system in the face of any challenge. Conversely, Trevelyan, unable to overcome his fear of active political involvement, nourished the doubts of an outsider. Like J. L. Hammond—another reluctant Liberal politician turned historian—he underestimated liberal democracy's resources and overstated its fragility, often sounding more like its eulogist than its champion. Though possessed of an acute sense of the tragic and the ironic, Churchill as historian retained the demeanor of an optimist, for it took an optimist to write *A History of the English-Speaking Peoples* in the dark days of the late 1930s.

Churchill's pretensions to cultural authority were rooted in his absorption in parliamentary politics. This preoccupation did not mean, however, that he remained blind to the development of modern academic historiography with its monopolistic claims on interpretation. Churchill suspected—like Trevelyan, the Webbs, and the Hammonds—that weighty cultural influence was incompatible with, and inconsequential to, a professoriate in pursuit of narrowly focused academic authority. Yet, as an autodidact, he was quick to grasp the special power and prestige accorded the "cult of the expert." As a historian he was not so Victorian as to ignore the potential for exploitation of "scientific," university-based historiography in order to enhance the standing and influence of his own offerings.

A. L. Rowse once applauded Churchill the historian for having "beaten the professionals at their own game."[30] But of course, the key to Churchill's success was precisely that he eschewed playing the professional game at all, exhibiting instead a self-contained disregard—but never disdain—for the demands of the academic brand of the discipline that marks him off from the other figures in this study. Unlike the Webbs, Churchill refused to conform to the stylistic (always) and annotary (usually) requirements of modern scholasticism, and as an Oxbridge outsider he never craved formal acceptance into the academic community as did both J. L. Hammond and the spurned and grieving Hilaire Belloc. Prudently, he likewise refused to engage in a running polemical battle with the champions of the scientific school as did G. M. Trevelyan and, and to a lesser degree, Lytton Strachey.

Churchill never envisaged himself as a rival to the pundits of academia. Comfortable in his role as a popular historian, he had set for himself a different and complementary task, one he described as "essentially selective and generalising."[31] He accepted without demur the peaceful coexistence of the academic and literary genres.

The two were not mutually exclusive, nor could either ever hope to command the whole field. While he could agree that contemporary documents were "the only foundation upon which the judgment of history can be erected," Churchill asserted the equal or even superior importance of the aesthetic facade of the historiographical edifice.[32] The artful beauty and drama of literary history retained a passionate power forfeited by the dry logic of its scholarly cousin, a power latent in the stuff of history itself.

Initially, ignoring professional authorities involved few risks. In the composition of *Lord Randolph Churchill* Winston was dealing with events as contemporary as yesterday's headlines, and this fact simplified his task because it eliminated the need for the biographer to immerse himself in a historiographical canon. Churchill simply canvassed such august political acquaintances as Lord Salisbury, Lord Rosebery, Joseph Chamberlain, and Lord Lansdowne for old letters from his father and combined them with Lord Randolph's own personal papers. General counsel was all that was required, for the author, like the subject, was himself an experienced parliamentarian.

But with Churchill's more ambitious projects he did not hesitate to call upon authorities in any relevant specialized field for advice and corrections. This precaution began with the preparation of *The World Crisis* when Churchill picked the brains of, among others, Admirals Thomas Jackson, Roger Keyes, and Kenneth Dewar on naval affairs, General James Edmonds on military operations, and Sir James Headlam-Morley (historical adviser to the Foreign Office) on the intricacies of postwar diplomacy.[33] As might be expected, reliance upon experts increased as Churchill subsequently turned his pen to topics foreign to his own immediate experience. His easy relations with the academic community made consultation with professional historians a natural and mutually agreeable option.

During the nearly ten years of work on his biography of Marlborough, Churchill's academic connections and acquaintances multiplied apace. Supplementing expert commentary on seventeenth-century land and naval warfare by the usual active service officers—in this case Lieutenant Colonel R. P. Pakenham-Walsh, Captain Basil Liddell Hart, and Commander J. H. Owen—were Henry Spenser Wilkinson, Chichele Professor of Military History at Oxford, and Sir Charles Oman, occupant of Oxford's Chichele Chair in

Modern History.[34] Early on, when Churchill required a research assistant, he consulted the Oxford historian Keith Feiling, who recommended the promising young scholar Maurice Ashley for the job.[35] As the work on *Marlborough* proceeded, a number of university dons, including Feiling himself, G. M. Trevelyan, H. A. L. Fisher, and even L. B. Namier, provided general advice as well as detailed instruction on technical questions covering everything from the domestic politics of seventeenth-century Britain to European diplomacy in the age of Louis XIV.

Churchill's hardworking aides—first Ashley, then later Bill Deakin and Alan Bullock—performed the requisite primary research, provided annotated background reading lists, and sketched out the material for each chapter according to their master's broad guidelines. On occasion they were also expected to provide monographs on specialized topics which Churchill might cannibalize at his own discretion.[36] But usually he turned directly to university dons for these requisite doses of expertise. Possessing few insecurities about the significant gaps in his own knowledge, despite his lack of a university education, Churchill had little incentive to feign omniscience. Beyond that, he recognized the value of the academic community's official stamp of approval. The "accord and assistance" of Keith Feiling, whom Churchill praised as "the greatest of our modern Oxford historians," promised authoritative help in "setting back the tides of historical calumny that have flowed for centuries" against the first Duke of Marlborough.[37] Never averse to wooing a potential ally, Churchill frequently entertained Feiling overnight at Chartwell during the writing of *Marlborough*, using these occasions to discuss historiographical points of contention. After one such evening spent debating the authenticity of the Camaret Bay letter, Churchill wrote that "Feiling with all his vast knowledge was impressed by the argument I have marshalled."[38] An argument that survived intact such a trial by combat was deemed sound.

Churchill, bred in the debating atmosphere of the House of Commons, might employ dons as sounding boards to determine that an argument was both logical and euphonic, but as a veteran parliamentarian he was also ready to listen on occasion. In 1938 he petitioned Professor Mortimer Wheeler, lecturer on archaeology at University College London, to enlighten him (for a fifty-guinea "honorarium") on the mysteries of ancient Britain in preparation for the writing of the opening segments of the first volume of *A History of the English-Speaking Peoples*.

> I am most anxious . . . to be rightly guided and up-to-date in these early chapters where the spade is mightier than the pen. I wonder whether you would come here [to Chartwell] for the week-end of Saturday 16 to Monday 18, and also for the week-end Saturday 23 to Monday 25? Would you then be willing to give me three informal lectures or talks on (1) pre-Roman Britain, (2) Roman Britain and its downfall, and (3) the Saxon kingdoms to Alfred. Your audience would be attentive and select,—Mr. Deakin and me![39]

Unlike Belloc, Churchill had no desire to flout ostentatiously the conventional wisdom of modern scholarship. Rather, as with the issue of the Camaret Bay letter, he hoped to get his rendering of the tale "clear with all the authorities."[40] With that end in mind, he saw to it that his proofs of *Marlborough* and *A History of the English-Speaking Peoples*, already checked once by his young research assistants, were checked yet again by more seasoned academic heavyweights.[41]

Churchill pondered carefully all of their many suggestions, once telling his publisher, "You must not however suppose that I attach any finality to the proofs, because they are printed. I always knock them about a great deal and incorporate the criticisms of many authorities who read them."[42] Although on at least one occasion Churchill exploded in anger against the intellectual tyranny imposed upon historical explanation by "goddam dons," his general attitude was one of appreciation for "the mature wisdom of the dons, only to be obtained by devoting a lifetime to reading and reflection."[43] Respectful of the great erudition of professional historians without being slavishly deferential, Churchill measured the often impassioned rhetoric of his own arguments against their cooler judgments. A convenient by-product of this sort of caution was that he simultaneously tapped into academia's reservoir of accumulated prestige and influence. His flattering attention to the opinions and recommendations of university scholars likewise helped to preserve him from the worst excesses of academic criticism.

The style of research and composition employed by Churchill has been likened to historiography by committee, yet never since Carlyle has there been history in which the vision of a solitary mind and the force of a single personality so completely dominated the narrative.[44] Churchill milked the dons for all they were worth, consulting them without reservation and considering their dissenting views seriously, but he was never weighed down or deflected from his purpose by their opinions. Every word of every manuscript remained Churchill's own.[45] Although he might "incorporate the criticisms of many authorities," these additions invariably passed through the Churchillian prism and emerged with his characteristic personal signature.[46] Maurice Ashley has testified to the fact that "at every stage in his historical writing Churchill did the bulk of the work himself; it was his own mind, his own method of presenting the facts, his own rhetorical prose style that shaped all his books."[47]

Churchill wrote swiftly, dictating to his secretaries in the early hours of the morning at breakneck speed, the initial aim always to get something down on paper that embodied the general structure and embraced the principal themes of his historical vision. There would always be time later for the introduction of documentation as well as for corrections and qualifications. These sessions of concentrated activity were not without attendant hazards for the interim product. According to Ashley:

> Churchill might discuss a matter with them [his research assistants] before he committed himself to paper, but once he had decided how he was going to tell the story, he liked to go full steam ahead. Sometimes, inevitably, the argument might run completely off the rails not so often because he had the facts wrong . . . but because his imagination was so tumultuous that he would be carried away by the exuberance of his own rhetoric.[48]

To Churchill's consternation, even the facts sometimes conspired to disrupt the dramatic flow of the narrative. His military adviser's insistence about a disputed point involving the disposition of the allied army at the battle of Malplaquet posed a stylistic predicament for the author of *Marlborough*. "Winston is not keen as it spoils his story!" recorded Colonel Pakenham-Walsh in his diary.[49] Prudently Churchill capitulated with good grace before such minor inconveniences but always without doing violence to the integrity of his fundamental understanding of the meaning of events. His detente with academic history rested upon its provision of accurate data while he in turn monopolized the supply of organizational themes, of interpretation, and, most important, of style. Churchill never forgot that he wrote principally for the educated layman and that such a reader expected more than dull accuracy alone.

Marlborough was a partial exception to the rule. In this single instance Churchill specifically addressed himself to both the general public and a specialist audience. With the promise of a four-thousand-pound advance in hand, his original intention in 1930 was to produce a two-volume biography within three years' time, although presciently he informed his publisher, George S. Harrap, that "if necessary I shall not hesitate to take longer."[50] At the outset Maurice Ashley inquired about how scrupulous his employer wished to be in the examination of original documents, cautioning that to do it all thoroughly "would not take less than ten years." With that prediction in mind, he advised that if Churchill expected to write "a short and popular book" it would be expedient to "decide what original material it is most desirable to exploit and to take the rest for granted."[51] Churchill saw the wisdom in these recommendations, informing his young assistant that at present it would not be necessary to do more than "skim the surface of the authentic documents, as you suggest." As a self-confessed popular historian Churchill's initial ambition extended no further than "to see the old tale in a new light and in its true proportions and then," as Ashley put it, "exploit by research particular points."[52] But soon the project developed a momentum of its own. Skimming the surfaces of primary documents quickly turned into detailed examinations of the Sunderland, Portland, Godolphin, Spencer, Cadogan, Stowe, and Marlborough papers and the Reports of the Historical Manuscripts Commission, supplemented by lengthy foraging expeditions to the archives at Vienna, Paris, Turin, and the Hague.[53]

After reading through the proofs of the first volume of *Marlborough* H. A. L. Fisher declared to Churchill that "historical opinion"—by which he meant his academic peers—would be "greatly affected by what you have written."[54] Having taken up the task of biographer to rebut Macaulay's slanderous characterization of his ancestor, Churchill found himself addressing a body of historiographical precedents before a jury of experts in addition to sketching a story for his usual lay readership.[55] The manuscript bulged with scores of documents reproduced verbatim; an asterisk marked off those never before published, a detail that could have been of interest only to professional historians. Under these altered conditions the completion of the project in just the two originally planned volumes appeared doubtful.[56] From Cambridge a sympathetic G. M. Trevelyan urged Churchill to expand the scope of the work to three or more volumes. Rather than the "short and popular book" envisioned by Ashley in 1929, Trevelyan plumped for Churchill to write "the definitive life" of Marlborough.[57] Eventually, after more than nine years of work, Churchill published a fourth and final volume in September 1938. The 2,400-plus pages represented a consciously constructed compromise between copiously documented argumentation and a dramatic, sweeping narrative style.

With *Marlborough*, because he settled upon directly influencing the debate among the historiographical mandarinate, Churchill cautiously ventured onto potentially hostile ground following the directions of his advance scouts. But like the great commanders he so admired, Churchill was never one to fight on a field of his opponent's choosing, and with his very next project he returned to more familiar and congenial terrain. *A History of the English-Speaking Peoples*, despite its great length, represented a calculated reversion to a more popular format.[58] In an about-face after *Marlborough*, he advised Keith Feiling that there was to be "no question of research of any kind" for this new venture. Churchill hoped simply to produce "a vivid narrative picking up the dramatic and dominant episodes and by no means undertaking a complete account."[59] Once again he assembled a veritable army of experts to teach, proffer advice, and to criticize, but in this instance Churchill stuck exclusively to his self-appointed task of selection and generalization.[60] There was in evidence here no desire to influence "historical opinion" indoors. Churchill's expressed hope that *A History of the English-Speaking Peoples* might become "a standard work and possibly an advanced school book,"[61] testified both to his remunerative expectations and to his involvement with a campaign to influence opinion "out-of-doors."[62]

Churchill's quick return to a popular historiography of synthesis probably saved his free and easy relationship with the discipline's academic professionals. *Marlborough*, despite its dramatic style and flamboyant literary excesses, had clearly encroached upon the exclusive domain of the academic priesthood. In this one instance trespassing was tolerated and even rewarded with praise, but a second such endeavor would surely have come to grief at the hands of reviewers. The *English Historical Review*'s notice on the first volume of *Marlborough* was quite generous in many respects. Richard Lodge praised Churchill's prose as "equally fitted for impressive narration and for trenchant controversy," thanked the author for his inclusion of the complete texts of so many previously unpublished documents—"his main contribution to historical knowledge and criticism"—and noted with satisfaction Churchill's obvious historiographical competence: "An experienced reviewer may state with confidence that few academic historians, dealing with a period of fifty years, have made so few blunders in matters of fact." But the reviewer's reservations were just as numerous. Besides criticizing the bibliography as "not exhaustive," Lodge observed with regret Churchill's devotion of so many pages to "impassioned controversy." Clearly, by setting himself up as Marlborough's "unflinching champion," Churchill had courted controversy and invited failure. What remains most interesting about the *EHR* review as a whole, however, is the manner in which it downplayed these obvious reservations while emphasizing the author's many strengths instead. Exactly the opposite treatment of an amateur historian might have been expected. Lodge clearly wanted to like the book and closed on just that note. "It is comforting to think that in his next volume Mr. Churchill will stand upon more solid and less debatable ground."[63] As forecast, the *EHR* happily gave its sanction to the second volume, pronouncing it "a great service to historical students" despite "superficial and at times slipshod" digressions on general European affairs.[64] A. H. Bourne sustained this scholarly benevolence through the review of the final volume, ranking Churchill's *Marlborough* "among the greatest biographies in the English tongue."[65] Yet even amidst such enthusiastic outpourings, the impression conveyed by the great number of reservations and the conditional nature of much of the praise is that the academic verdict could just as easily have been an unfavorable one; there is the unmistakable sense of punches being pulled.

Churchill's academic reviewers never quite knew what to do with him. His work was unfailingly interesting but rarely if ever measured up to the rigorous dictates of the scholarly branch of the discipline. He paid court to professional historians but remained attentive to the voices of their bêtes noire as well. This generous (an academic historian might have said "uninformed") eclecticism even extended to academia's most outspoken critic, Hilaire Belloc. In imitation of other evenings spent by his host in learned discussion with Professor Feiling and other dons, Belloc spent a late August 1935 evening at Chartwell talking "at great length with Winston about his 'Marlborough.' "[66] By that time Churchill had already carefully studied Belloc's published analysis of Marlborough as a military commander, even citing it in his own book's bibliography.[67] While Oxbridge dons engaged in checking his proofs, Churchill simultaneously solicited the critiques of active politicians such as Alfred Duff Cooper (himself an amateur historian) who added a schizophrenic note to the proceedings by provocatively asserting that partisan history of any kind "knows more of the truth of the matter than the Dryasdust cold blooded historian can ever get at after sifting all the evidence and applying his microscope to the faded ink."[68]

In much the same way as the enigmatic Gladstone had been all things to all men, appealing to both the Whig and Radical wings of his party without ever sacrificing his own idiosyncratic predispositions, Churchill managed to satisfy both the practitioners of "Dryasdust" and its implacable enemies without compromising his own independent line. To one outspoken admirer Churchill the historian created "not dead academic research into the past but a living document breathing the authenticity of experience."[69] And paradoxically, it was precisely this experience of life and affairs that, in part at least, stayed the potentially harsh hand of Churchill's academic critics. Churchill's direct experience of politics and diplomacy put the professional historian at an unmistakable disadvantage.[70] During the composition of *Marlborough* it was a confident authority, born not from reading but from praxis, that provided Churchill with the ammunition to demolish as inconsistent with the true operation of politics a research assistant's carefully crafted, scholarly essay on the general election of 1710.[71] Professional historians sensed their inherent incapacity to gainsay Churchill's judgments on past politics.

Churchill's brief encounter with L. B. Namier best captured the ambiguous nature of the former's relationship with the academic community. In December 1933 the Manchester University professor acknowledged the receipt of a complimentary, inscribed copy of Volume 1 of *Marlborough* by informing his benefactor that "I have always been an admirer and follower of yours, and more now in view of the European situation than ever before."[72] Following this exchange of pleasantries, and at Churchill's behest, Namier provided him with a detailed critique of the book. He objected to the "polemic touch" of Churchill's preoccupation with Macaulay and also to the inclusion of imaginary passages concerning "what may have happened or what some people *must* have felt." (Namier admitted that his distaste for the latter might be "a professional 'malformation' with me.") He also offered suggestions for a more satisfactory gathering and use of primary sources. But his main criticism constituted in reality a lavish compliment; Namier asked that Churchill give even freer rein to his political instincts.

> There is no-one alive engaged on history work with your experience of politics, government, and war. Please do not try to write history as other historians do, but do it in your own way. Tell us more how various transactions strike you, and what associations they evoke in your mind. When studying the detail of government at that distant period of almost 250 years ago, many comparisons must have occurred to you, which you seem to have suppressed. Too much history is written by don-bred dons with no knowledge or understanding of the practical problems of statecraft.[73]

Namier is often held up as the antithesis of the popular literary historian, but his enthusiastic praise of Churchill's biography as "a work of art and at the same time a masterly analysis of the historical material" validated the alternative approach to the discipline. From the opposite end of the scholarly spectrum G. M. Trevelyan registered his own approval as well. "Professional historians most of them haven't the art of getting themselves read, and the unprofessional ones, like Wells and Belloc, usually have bees in their bonnet. So you fill a gap."[74] That Churchill had indeed carved out a special niche for his work was duly confirmed in David Douglas's 1957 observation in the *English Historical Review* that "a reviewer, especially if he can rest under the somewhat unhappy title of 'professional historian' must consider carefully by what standards of assessment its [Churchill's histories'] merits should be appraised."[75]

Churchill is sometimes portrayed as a failed politician before 1939. Whatever merit there may be in such claims, it was certainly not the case in his dealings with the academic community. His public relations success with professional historians and the unique immunity it provided bore all the earmarks of a consummate political campaign.[76] Trevelyan, the political manqué, realized along with Churchill the usefulness and even necessity of a modern alliance between literary history and academia. Yet he could envision no viable alternative other than his own return of the prodigal to Cambridge. Meanwhile, Churchill, driven by a self-assurance born of a life of activity, retained the unhindered freedom of an outsider with the connivance of the university priesthood. The proselytizing dons thought Churchill always near enough to conversion to call off the inquisitor. Besides, his hybrid doctrine was too flexible, unfamiliar, and elusive easily to accept the brand of heresy. With this semiofficial dispensation in hand, Churchill continued to create literary history that entertained and informed the layman while it flattered and often baffled the expert. Trevelyan's position inside the university as Liberalism's advocate allowed for only guarded assertions. By contrast, Churchill could give vent to his feelings and argue his case, for better or worse, with less reservation and fewer qualifications. It was Churchill, not Trevelyan, who met Strachey and Belloc on their own terms, brandishing the same panache and fortified by an equivalent dose of confidence.

In the six volumes of *The World Crisis* published between 1923 and 1931, Churchill employed traditional narrative form as a tacit rebuttal to the postwar ironic mode pioneered in Strachey's *Eminent Victorians*. Churchill's history of the Great War offered an implicit rebuke to the influential *Economic Consequences of the Peace* (1919), whose author, John Maynard Keynes, had clearly cribbed his style of portraiture from his Bloomsbury associate. Keynes's dabbling in character assassination with the depictions of Clemenceau, Lloyd George, and especially Wilson—characterizations that harmonized well with Strachey's own of Arnold, Manning, and Gordon—eroded trust in the good faith and intrinsic virtues of the democratic system represented by these leaders. With its relentless and desensitizing barrage of ironic burlesque unrelieved by any genuine enthusiasm, sincerity, civility, or even pity, the Stracheyesque technique of rendering the past represented precisely the sort of irresponsibly destructive historiography so deplored by Trevelyan and Churchill. *The World Crisis* served as an antidote to the mocking tone that struck a blow at the seriousness of the art and science of history, just as it trivialized the politics of restraint which distinguished the liberal state while subverting the culture that sustained such moderation.

Churchill's defense of traditional historiographic forms went one step further. In the late 1920s a rash of "war books" appeared chronicling individual experiences on the Western Front. Autobiographies and thinly disguised fiction by writers such as Graves, Blunden, Remarque, Sassoon, and Herbert Read created the impression that 1914–18 was an episode beyond the descriptive capacities of conventional historiographic techniques. Taken as a group, these war books implied that the story of the war was intensely subjective and personal, that as an event it was meaningless above the level of the individual victim. The only "authentic" record of the Western Front must come from the necessarily fragmentary impressions of the junior officers and other ranks.[77]

Churchill's treatment of the Great War challenged such antihistorical solipsisms. The narrative style and linear structure of *The World Crisis* harkened back to inherited literary traditions, refusing to acknowledge that 1914–18 constituted a break. Likewise, the work presented a panoramic view of the conflict in which events bore clear causal relationships one to another, in which the wider vision of the politician or general carried as much or more weight than the nominalism of the individual Tommy. There was no reluctance to use the Victorian moral vocabulary to provide signposts for the reader. Churchill portrayed the Great War as a conflict between armies, nations, cultures, and ideas, in the process banishing the appearance of incoherence and reasserting the claims of history to record and interpret on a grand scale.

As a public historian in the Victorian tradition, Churchill resisted all who would undermine historiography as a vital force in the life of the nation: academic specialists who would quarantine historical knowledge in the university cloister as well as literary nihilists who would deny even the possibility of historical meaning in the modern age of irony.

Liberalism versus Authoritarianism: From Personal to National Vindication

With a record of twenty years as a Liberal M.P., Churchill could plausibly present British history to his readers as the traditional Whig narrative of moral progress. But, as he never shared the squeamishness of Trevelyan or the Hammonds, this was Whig historiography with a difference. Personal combativeness, the conservative side of Churchill's political nature, and soldiering experience on four continents guaranteed his appreciation of the role of force in history. In analyzing the past he featured the mobilization of the power and resources of the state along with the judicious employment of military force as prime mechanisms in the advancement of English liberties. The end product was a harsher and perhaps more realistic Liberal version of history, one with a broadened ideological appeal, offering something for Conservatives concerned with national security and for Labour, which, however much it might condemn war in principle, applauded the growth and consolidation of centralized government that inevitably accompanied large-scale, state-sponsored violence.

As historian Churchill successfully fused the tale of constitutional gradualism basic to the Whig paradigm with his own conviction that "battles are the principal milestones of secular history," creating in the process an English national history that reconciled two apparently incompatible themes.[78] Moral progress via constitutional development did indeed provide the central focus of the ancient drama, but that story was not autonomous. Essential to provide forward thrust was the periodic application of force. The proper Churchillian object of power was the energetic defense of liberty against tyranny.[79] Thus, in his judgment, the wars fought by the British people, especially since the sixteenth century, constituted neither futile historical detours nor insignificant diversions from the primary movement of national history as the unfolding of liberty and democracy. Indeed, the two were inseparable.

The World Crisis was his first serious attempt to secure this connection in the public consciousness. In those pages he explicitly linked the conflict against Wilhelmine Germany to the Elizabethan struggle against imperial Spain, to the parliamentary rebellion against Charles I, and to the successive coalition wars against Louis XIV and Bonaparte. Despite the predominant postwar air of pacifism, Churchill displayed no reluctance in recording, even glorifying, what he saw as England's successful defense of liberty and parliamentary governance down through the centuries.

The original wartime consensus among British historians, led by Lewis Namier, A. F. Pollard, Arnold J. Toynbee, and G. W. Prothero, of the unique culpability of the Germany of Bismarck, Nietzsche, and Treitschke rapidly dissolved after 1919, replaced by a new orthodoxy that took its cue from Keynes's *Economic Consequences of the Peace*.[80] The latter's scathing critique of the reparation clauses undermined general belief in the justice of the peace and, by the extension of hindsight, in the justice of the cause of the victors. Critics of the war soon fleshed out the retroactive implications of the Keynesian analysis. In *The International Anarchy* (1926) G. Lowes Dickinson's substitution of the morally suspect system of international relations for German militarism as the war's chief cause found a receptive audience.[81] Dickinson hoped to convince these eager listeners that the Great War, "like previous ones, arose inevitably from the justifications of armed sovereign states bent upon extending by force their territory and markets and conducting their relations by the methods of secret diplomacy."[82] Here was an open-ended indictment that stretched backward in time to include Britain's protracted struggles against Philip II and Louis XIV.

Dickinson's revisionist combination of polemic and analysis received scholarly support from G. P. Gooch and Harold Temperley in their *British Documents on the Origins of the War*.[83] By diverting attention away from the broad trends of German *Machtpolitik* and instead focusing a microscope on the day-to-day machinations of the Foreign Office at Whitehall, Gooch and Temperley suggested a moral equivalency among all participants in the 1914–18 struggle. No European statesman had wanted war; war had simply broken out, and this adoption of the passive voice shifted the blame to the system of international relations. Of course, Britain's responsibility as one of the principal architects of the global system demanded that she shoulder a hefty portion of the burden of collective guilt. Already by 1925 the Liberal don Gilbert Murray could assure a German correspondent that "hardly any reasonable person in England continues to talk about Germany as solely responsible for the war."[84]

The World Crisis acted as a substantial counterweight to the new orthodoxy's provision of a fillip to this unprecedented and unseemly national urge to confession, mortification, and absolution. Churchill would not countenance the notion that four years of warfare and exertion were little more than a near fatal accident, devoid of either meaning or purpose. To the advertisers of its futility he replied that the titanic struggle between Germany and the Allies had been about real issues of legitimate national interest and of principle. The aggressive designs of German autocracy and militarism had threatened the survival of the liberal open society, not just in Europe but throughout the civilized world. "The victory of Germany and the concomitant disappearance of France and the British Empire as Great Powers must, after an uncertain interval, have left the peaceful and unarmed population of the United States nakedly exposed to the triumph of the doctrine of force without limit."[85] Recent examination of diplomatic documents by Gooch and others seemed to show that no European statesman had wanted war, rather that the state system by its very nature had produced a permanently unstable situation in which trifles and innocent miscalculations could spark a major conflagration. Yet according to the Churchillian calculus, this sort of blinkered analysis, however useful, misled the public through its focus upon surface phenomena alone. The immediate particulars of any diplomatic confrontation represented "only the symptoms of the dangerous disease, and are only important for that reason. Behind them lies the interests, the passions and the destiny of mighty races of men; and long antagonisms express themselves in trifles. 'Great commotions,' it was said of old, 'arise out of small things, but not concerning small things.'"[86] And incredibly, the "great thing" underlying all the sacrifice had been forgotten. The memory of the menace posed by Wilhelmine Germany to the continued existence of Britain as an independent, liberal, democratic society had been blurred by all of the postwar rhetoric over waste, futility, and collective guilt. Regrettably, a succession of blunders at the highest levels had plagued the war effort, particularly on the Western Front, but that did not detract from the essential justice of the Allied cause.

In 1934, as guest of a gathering of the Oxford University Conservative Association, Churchill was asked by a German Rhodes scholar whether he believed that "the German people, the men and women who live in Germany today, are responsible for the war?"[87] Churchill's unembellished reply of "yes" differed only in its brevity from his verdict of a decade earlier in *The World Crisis*. German valor, efficiency, and resolve, qualities for which he repeatedly expressed respect, did not mitigate Germany's overwhelming guilt. To those who preferred to blame the chaos of the international system, Churchill acknowledged that "one rises from the study of the causes of the Great War with a prevailing sense of the defective control of individuals upon world fortunes."[88]

Yet Churchill was never one to subordinate the significance of individual decisions to the tyranny of large, impersonal forces.[89] Europe had finally come upon the unmanageable predicament of the summer of 1914 because of a confused and misguided, but nonetheless deliberate, German foreign policy of intimidation and brinksmanship. A powerful and assertive German Empire, intoxicated by the unbridled ambitions of a novice, refused to accept its role as a mere equal among the other Great Powers. Her rulers would not contemplate the same self-restraint to which France, Russia, and Britain had long become accustomed.[90] Under these unpromising circumstances the "old diplomacy," so unfairly excoriated by Dickinson and E. D. Morel, had done its best to render harmless the minor irritations arising between sovereign nations.[91] But no amount of diplomatic skill and flexibility could have altered the consciously provocative movement of German policy with its built-in dissonance with the leitmotiv of European peace and stability and its ultimately self-destructive tendencies. "Ah! foolish-diligent Germans, working so hard, thinking so deeply, marching and counter-marching on the parade grounds of the Fatherland, poring over long calculations, fuming in new found prosperity, discontented amid the splendour of mundane success, how many bulwarks to your peace and glory did you not, with your own hands, successively tear down!"[92] Ultimately, the Allies, not without their own blemishes to be sure, found their range of options constrained by the need to respond to German aggression. Germany, ill-served by her intellectual and political elites, "clanked obstinately, recklessly, awkwardly towards the crater and dragged us all in with her."[93]

Churchill's characterization of Germany as inheritor of the hegemonic designs of Bonaparte legitimized Britain's use of force in the defense of freedom. Thus *The World Crisis*, though replete with examples of irony, paradox, disaster, pathos, and tragedy, remained essentially hopeful. It aimed to reaffirm in the mind of the bewildered, self-flagellating English reader the general health and stability of the nation's liberal institutions by emphasizing the war's successes, successes that had overcome a long catalog of failures, along with its essential justice which belied its apparent meaninglessness. The books all sold well throughout the 1920s, but it seems doubtful, in light of the conflicting critical reviews, that the public was prepared to accept or even fully comprehend the basis for Churchill's message of cautious optimism.[94] Casualties were too recent, mental and physical exhaustion too complete, and doubt too all-consuming for the average reader to be expected to view the war in some larger historical context that juxtaposed distant past, recent past, present, and future.

Churchill fretted over the shallow long-term memory of the modern Briton. "How strange it is that the past is so little understood and so quickly forgotten. We live in the most thoughtless of ages. Every day headlines and short views. [In *The World Crisis*] I have tried to drag history up a little nearer to our own times in case it should be helpful as a guide in present difficulties."[95] The 1930s created an entirely new and unexpectedly large audience for his once outmoded interpretation of the Great War.[96] The desperate times seemed to lend themselves to a revised understanding of the material. An illustrated, twenty-six-part fortnightly serialization of the entire work, published between September 1933 and October 1934 by Newnes, found 32,000 eager subscribers.[97] Not surprisingly, even greater popularity awaited following the declaration of war against Nazi Germany, with extensive excerpts appearing weekly in the *Sunday Chronicle* for the nine months between October 1939 and June 1940.[98] By 1930, however, Churchill had already discovered another historical vehicle—this one far enough removed from the present to discourage misinterpretation—for the presentation of the same lesson.

Squaring Democracy with Efficiency

In the wake of the 1929 publication of *The World Crisis* T. E. Lawrence suggested that Winston consider writing a life of his illustrious ancestor John Churchill, first Duke of Marlborough.[99] Churchill needed no urging. Preliminary research had already begun on the work he had contemplated for nearly three decades. With Churchill's interest in great men and high drama the match between author and subject seemed a faultless one—except perhaps to an exacting scholar concerned with the niceties of authorial detachment. The epic story of Marlborough's long struggle against Louis XIV provided Churchill with the ideal metaphorical medium for mounting a modern defense of liberal democracy.

Once again, as with all such Churchillian undertakings, personal motive merged with more universal aims. Filial piety played a role here just as it had in the biography of Lord Randolph. At the outset Winston informed his cousin, the present Duke of Marlborough, that his life of their common ancestor represented "a duty."[100] He claimed that it was not his "method . . . to attempt to 'defend' or 'vindicate' my subject"; rather, in the best inductive manner, he expected to "saturate" himself with the available material, then without prejudice form his views of Marlborough and his age.[101] But if anything, Churchill identified more strongly with Marlborough than with his own father. Unlike Lord Randolph, a man of unrealized potential, England's great eighteenth-century commander had been, in Churchill's eyes, a leader of remarkable achievement in the arts of war and politics who, in the end, found his unprecedented services to the nation repaid by contempt and, even worse, neglect. To the modern reader, fortified with the knowledge of the Second World War and the results of the 1945 election, the symmetry between author and subject is arresting, and the biography seems almost prophetic. But even in the early 1930s, to a Churchill out of office, at the height of his powers but facing the nadir of his political fortunes and influence, the parallel was clear enough. The Plutarchan echoes are unmistakable in Churchill's description of the 1711 parliamentary debate and, to his mind, wrongful censure of Marlborough's friend the Earl of Galway over the latter's unsuccessful conduct of the 1707 Spanish campaign and subsequent defeat at Almanza.[102] This was the Dardanelles investigation reexamined by proxy. With *Marlborough*, as before with *Lord Randolph Churchill* and *The World Crisis*, vindication of the protagonist—or of his confederates— signaled vicarious vindication for the biographer.

But Churchill's main focus lay elsewhere. In the Whig tradition, his narrative traced the origins of England's liberal institutions and values, perfected in the nineteenth century and assailed in the twentieth, back to the Glorious Revolution. A defense of the social and political system fashioned from the crucible of bloodless revolution, party strife, and continental warfare between 1688 and the Hanoverian succession amounted to a surrogate defense of its modern descendant. In addition to Marlborough, Churchill hoped to vindicate "the whole lot," that is, "all the statesmen who made the Revolution." Such a feat of advocacy was "in the interests not only of truth but of England."[103] It seemed necessary to draw attention to the very palpable threats to the foundations of liberty in the early twentieth century which replicated those of that earlier age. The "remarkable similarities" between 1914–18 and the wars of Marlborough were only one part of the equation, but it was this angle which Churchill stressed with the publication of Volume 1 in 1933.

> There was the same peril that the supremacy of one race and culture would be imposed by military force upon all others. . . . The wars of William and Anne were no mere effort of national ambition or territorial gain. They were in essentials a struggle for the life and liberty not only of England, but of Protestant Europe. . . . In no world conflict have the issues, according to modern standards, been more real and vital. In none has the duty to defend a righteous cause been more compulsive upon the British nation. In none have the results been more solid, more precious, more lasting. The triumph of the France of Louis XIV would have warped and restricted the development of the freedom we now enjoy, even more than the domination of Napoleon or of the German Kaiser.[104]

This circuitous justification through historical analogy of the Great War as a crusade of principle seemed more effective and, paradoxically, less ambiguous than the direct approach adopted in *The World Crisis*.

In a 1936 Commons speech during the height of the national debate on rearmament, Stanley Baldwin reminded his listeners that, regrettably but unavoidably, "a democracy is always two years behind the dictator."[105] A decade earlier Churchill's *World Crisis* had argued for the ultimate superiority in war of the parliamentary over the autocratic state. Victory in 1918 provided the definitive measuring rod of democratic competence. Clearly the intent in *Marlborough* was to restate this fundamental thesis of *The World Crisis*, that is, the innate superiority of liberal democracy in any confrontation with authoritarianism, whether of the seventeenth- or twentieth-century variety. But at times within the narrative it seemed as though Marlborough, beset by the carping of Whig and Tory alike, achieved what he did in spite of rather than because of the party system at the root of English parliamentary governance.[106] Churchill pictured himself as a man of strict principle, above narrow party constraints on the weightiest issues of national policy; his portrait of Lord Randolph had been taken from the same mold. Therefore it should come as no surprise that he laid stress on the fact that Marlborough stood outside of the violent intrigues and irresponsibilities of early eighteenth-century partisan politics. "Both parties looked to him with regard and recognized, however grudgingly, that he was above their warfare. This was not the result of calculation on his part. . . . Events had detached him from his party and left him, without partisan reproach, independent on the hub of affairs."[107] According to Churchill's empathetic reading, the Duke's ambitions and concerns had been overwhelmingly national rather than factional.

Before 1914 Churchill had hovered on the periphery of the National Efficiency movement.[108] One of a grab bag of ideas shared wholly or in part by most members of this diverse group was an antagonism to the traditional politics of party as unnecessarily divisive and therefore inherently wasteful of time and energy. As previously mentioned, Churchill had on several occasions voiced his preference for some sort of political truce or even coalition government at times of national crisis, crises that seemed to arise with dizzying regularity between 1900 and 1931. He had supported the Lloyd George coalition of 1916 and the Cabinet streamlining that followed in train. The vestiges of similar instincts regarding the correct approach to the possibility of war could still be heard in a Commons speech of March 1938 in which he vented his frustration with the Chamberlain administration's seeming inability to take decisive steps toward rearmament. "Is our system of government . . . adapted to the present fierce, swift movement of events? Twenty-two gentlemen of blameless party character sitting round an overcrowded table, each having a voice—is that a system which can reach decisions from week to week and cope . . . with the men at the head of the dictator States?"[109] In light of such contemporaneous Churchillian rhetoric (the final volume of *Marlborough* appeared six months later), it is tempting to see his characterization of the Duke as the quintessential National Efficiency ideal: a leader above faction with the broad national interest at heart, the focus of power concentrated at the center, the prototype of a modern "liberal" strongman to match the fascist dictators at their own game.

But the creation of such an impression does not appear to have been Churchill's intention at all. Clearly he was predisposed to admire the commanding personalities that populate history. His friends understood that Tolstoy's "absurd theory that 'Great Men' are flies on the wheel of History" was an anathema to Churchill.[110] Naturally he was far from advocating, even if feasible, the institutionalization in a bureaucratic elite of the Weberian charismatic power wielded by the world historical individual. But he also refused to endorse authority arbitrarily acquired and applied outside of standard legal avenues. Doubtless it was true that in the past "champions [had] reached the summit of England—Oliver Cromwell, William III, John, Duke of Marlborough who by their swords made this system of free government resound with ringing blows upon the pates of dictatorships of Europe."[111] Yet, while willing to concede that a towering figure like Cromwell, having "saved the cause of Parliament" with his military prowess, "cannot be wholly barred from his place in the forward march of liberal ideas," Churchill's distaste for the Lord Protector was undisguised. He explained the source of this antagonism to G. M. Young in 1939. "I remain hostile to him, and consider that he should be condemned as a representative of the dictatorships against which all the whole movement of English history has been continuous."[112]

Churchill did relent a little in this sweeping denunciation, portraying Cromwell as a dictator suffering from a bad conscience. "Cromwell, although crafty and ruthless as occasion claimed, was at all times a reluctant and apologetic dictator. He recognised and deplored the arbitrary character of his own rule." He also drew a clear distinction between the relatively benign Cromwellian despotism and the ruthless, twentieth-century totalitarian forms.

> Nevertheless the dictatorship of Cromwell differed in many ways from modern patterns. Although the Press was gagged and the Royalists ill used, although judges were intimidated and local privileges curtailed, there was always an effective vocal opposition, led by convinced Republicans. There was no attempt to make a party around the personality of the Dictator, still less to make a party state. Respect was shown for private property, and the process for fining the Cavaliers and allowing them to compound by surrendering part of their estates was conducted with technical formality. Few people were put to death for political crimes, and no one was cast into indefinite bondage without

trial. . . . There was in practice comparatively little persecution on purely religious grounds.[113]

This sort of qualification makes it no easier to fathom the rash judgment of a later critic who found that in Churchill's version of English history "men like Cromwell are presented, in the manner of Gardiner, as seventeenth-century anticipations of Gladstonian liberalism," for Churchill went on in the very next breath to reaffirm his hostility toward the Lord Protector.[114] "[Cromwell] must stand before history as a representative of dictatorship and military rule who, with all his qualities as a soldier and statesman, is in lasting discord with the genius of the English race."[115]

By comparison, Churchill's depiction of Marlborough represented something far different from the typical image of the man on the white horse. The leader of the grand alliance against Louis XIV did not hope to monopolize permanently the supreme military and political authority even for a good cause. His position above party infighting, once forced upon him by circumstances, was a consciously temporary one, maintained solely to deal with the immediate national crisis. His exercise of power was always necessarily, and with a minimum of complaint, tailored to the institutional and ideological confines of the liberal parliamentary system.[116] Thus when peace came and the crisis ended, he relinquished authority as effortlessly and disinterestedly as he had assumed it.

A version of Cincinnatus more acceptable to the liberal conscience than even the original, Marlborough had ruled by working through the mechanics of the system rather than by circumventing them. In a 1934 magazine article Churchill made the point that Britain should not long for a counterpart to Hitler, Mussolini, or Stalin.

> We hear the specious appeals and sometimes even clamour for the calm strong man, and for autocracy in all its neverending forms. But the lesson of the Great War was that the Parliamentary Governments, if boldly led, can beat the despots. . . . There is no need to alter our system of government. The flexible character of the English constitution enables the necessary adjustments to be made from one generation to another, in accordance with the needs and dangers of the times. . . . The task of the immediate future is to strengthen our institutions rather than to change them.[117]

Marlborough's character mirrored that of his biographer, who, in contrast to other advocates of National Efficiency, had no quarrel with the basic assumptions and institutions of liberal democracy, urging the adoption of temporary measures to increase governmental proficiency only during periods of great stress for the sole purpose of defending those selfsame assumptions and institutions. Though an advocate of a strong state, unlike the Webbs or Lord Milner, Churchill was never interested in the permanent installation of a highly centralized, apolitical bureaucratic administration as a substitute for the traditions of parliament and party, whose strengths were underestimated and whose attendant irrationalities, redundancies, and flagrant absurdities were more apparent than real.

Churchill expressed this all clearly enough in a January 1939 interview with Kingsley Martin, editor of the *New Statesman and Nation*, as part of the periodical's series "Conversations on Democracy and Efficiency." To Martin the relationship between the two was clearly problematic, and he inquired of Churchill whether he really thought it possible to combine the reality of democratic freedom with efficient military organization. Churchill, immersed in the writing of his *History of the English-Speaking Peoples*, replied that he saw no reason why democracies should not be able to defend themselves without sacrificing their "fundamental values." "I am convinced that with adequate leadership democracy can be a more efficient form of government than Fascism. . . . It may be that greater efficiency in military preparations can be achieved in a country with autocratic institutions than by the democratic system. But this advantage is not necessarily great, and it is far outweighed by the strength of a democratic country in a long war."[118] The successful prosecution of the wars of Marlborough represented historical confirmation, if any was still needed after 1914–18, of the compatibility of the vigorous exercise of power, even military power, with liberal institutions. In fact, Churchill felt that the 1930s were a particularly appropriate time for the public to acknowledge finally that the nation's liberal social and political heritage was anchored to a whole series of principled applications of force in the cause of freedom. "Marlborough's victorious sword established upon sure foundations the constitutional and Parliamentary structure of our country almost as it came down to us to-day."[119] In this fashion was ushered in a two-hundred-year supremacy of the party system with only brief and unnatural suspensions during the administration of Chatham and the "supreme emergencies" of the twentieth century. "It is astonishing," declared Churchill with feigned incredulity in the first volume of *Marlborough*, "that such a system should, on the whole, have proved so serviceable."[120]

The Victorian version of English history celebrated the slow, evolutionary accumulation of individual liberty, party machinery, and constitutional-parliamentary institutions. Churchill, although prone to emphasize the lubrication provided to this process by the use of legitimate force, clearly belonged to the same liberal tradition. However this fact was obscured to his contemporaries by his rough treatment of Macaulay in *Marlborough*.[121] One of the primary motivations for Churchill's undertaking the biography in the first place was to demolish Macaulay's bitterly antagonistic characterization of the Duke. Churchill's 1924 discovery in Lord Rosebery's library of John Paget's *Paradoxes and Puzzles*, a late nineteenth-century critique of Macaulay's sources and conclusions, clinched his decision to begin the task by clearing away any reservations about his ancestor's Camaret Bay betrayal.[122]

At the time many took Churchill's ruthlessly thorough attack upon Macaulay in the pages of *Marlborough* as evidence of the author's fundamental hostility toward the main thrust of traditional Whig historiography. His research assistant Maurice Ashley warned that to a professional historian "exposing" Macaulay was like "flogging a dead horse." But he also admitted that, because of the recent "whitewashing" of Whig historians combined with the fact that "the popular mind has never altogether shaken itself free from his [Macaulay's] and Swift's accusations [against Marlborough]," a rehashing of the whole argument might well be in order.[123] Undeterred by such reservations or halfhearted encouragement, Churchill devoted huge tracts of Volume 1 to an exposure of the errors in Macaulay's anti-Marlborough biases. Lewis Namier, no friend of Whig historians, judged Churchill's time and effort well spent, for the Whig mind was "not an open door," but rather a "rubber ball which speedily regains its previous shape."[124] Underscoring Namier's assessment was Alfred Duff Cooper, who in most circumstances was hardly one sympathetic to the opinions of an academic historian. He did not blame Churchill for exaggerating his hero's case, since it was only historiographical overstatement that survived. "If Macaulay had been fair we shouldn't read him. . . . You cannot be too harsh with him for my taste," Duff Cooper assured the biographer of Marlborough. "I am delighted to see the old boy shown up, and he deserves it for having imposed a perverted Whiggist theory of English history on three generations of Englishmen."[125] For many it was a natural assumption on reading the first volume of *Marlborough* to conflate Churchill's sustained disagreement with Macaulay as a theoretical break with the "perverted Whiggist" interpretation of English history.[126] Yet other readers saw no necessary connection between the two.

In a personal letter to Churchill, George Bernard Shaw protested against the mass of "Macaulayisms" dominating Volume 1 of *Marlborough*. He urged the biographer to bring his second volume more into "historical relation" with the contemporary situation as well as with the record of Churchill's own "personal struggle with the Party System," a system that had utterly destroyed the "Cause of Liberty" in England and prepared the way for fascism.[127] The pen of "Chesterbelloc" also saw through Churchill's masquerade. Although it was patently obvious that, in order to defend his hero, Churchill had to throw over the Whig historian Macaulay, G. K. Chesterton reminded his readers that in reality this still remained an intrafamilial "dispute among Whigs." Anglo-Catholicism had little patience with *Marlborough*, with its blind glorification of "party heroes," who, by forsaking "internationalism," were "hacking the old Christendom into narrow and jealous nations" and "preparing for the Great War."[128]

G. M. Trevelyan, because of the intimate family connection, was the historian with the greatest cause for angry reaction against Churchill's rough handling of Macaulay. Yet after a July 1933 installment of the *Sunday Times* serialization of *Marlborough* excerpts, an enthusiastic Trevelyan told the author, "That's the way to write about the Revolution and blow all this neo-Catholic nonsense about it to pieces."[129] Trevelyan did come to his great-uncle's defense in a long letter in the *Times Literary Supplement* of 19 October 1933, but the rebuttal was a heavily qualified one that conceded Macaulay's inaccurate reading of Marlborough's character as well as Churchill's familial obligation to vindicate his ancestor.[130] Trevelyan had already, in his own *England under Queen Anne*, painted an essentially flattering portrait of the Duke, which, in the estimation of Austen Chamberlain, atoned for Macaulay's earlier prejudices.[131]

Trevelyan was reluctant to attack Churchill's biography except insofar as family honor required it.[132] Like Shaw, Belloc, and Chesterton, the Cambridge don was not misled by extraneous arguments over the accuracy of Macaulay's characterization of Marlborough. Such petty surface disputes merely served to cloak deeper and more important congruences. "His [Macaulay's] insight into political movements was very keen," Trevelyan assured Churchill, "and his account of the Revolution is not substantially different from yours, barring Marlborough."[133] Churchill was due congratulations for vindicating the authors of 1688, and some sacrifice—even of family reputation—was acceptable toward furthering that greater end. In a Panglossian twist incompatible with his usual pessimistic outlook, Trevelyan took comfort in the fact that Churchill's separation of himself from the Macaulayan incubus would make the rest of *Marlborough*'s Whiggish arguments all the more credible and effective.[134]

Churchill's *Marlborough* (1933–38) and Trevelyan's *England under Queen Anne* (1930–34) appeared almost simultaneously, and Trevelyan saw them as in many ways complementary.[135] The arguments were clearly similar. Trevelyan found confirmation in England's great successes against Louis XIV "that a country of free institutions could defeat a State based upon autocratic rule. This was a new idea in the world, and caused men to think afresh on the maxims of State."[136] Like Churchill, he also linked these national successes with others against Philip II, Napoleon, and Kaiser Wilhelm.[137] The glorious record of England's achievement under Queen Anne was owing to interdependent systems of free and efficient economy and government "that the national genius had almost unconsciously evolved from the struggles of its sects and factions."[138] But there remained a subtle difference in tone between the works of Churchill and Trevelyan, perhaps accounted for by the latter's chronic inability to recoup his fragile confidence in a post-1914 world. In his eagerness to exhibit an impartiality that would accommodate all shades of modern sensibility within the aegis of Liberal historiography, Trevelyan refused to take sides or risk judgment on seventeenth- and eighteenth-century party disputes. Everything, from the Settlement of 1688–89 to the defeat of France, was homogenized into a compromise between Whig and Tory, church and Dissent, and honored accordingly.

Here Trevelyan parted company from the biographer of Marlborough, who found it impossible, indeed almost criminal, to withhold judgments of good and evil upon the events of history. Churchill expressed his astonishment in finding "serious writers" describing Bolingbroke's actions "as if they were deserving of impartial presentment."

> Whigs and Tories, Hanoverians and Jacobites—it was, they suggest, six of one and half a dozen of the other. Marlborough had won the war; Bolingbroke had made the peace. Great and respectable currents of opinion flowed in either cause, and history, we are enjoined, must with a cool detachment tolerate both points of view. But this weak mood cannot be indulged in a world where the consequences of men's actions produce such frightful calamities for millions of humble folk, and may rob great nations of their destiny.[139]

While Trevelyan was attempting to salvage the remnants of the Liberal version of history by invoking catholicity, impartiality, and accommodation, it was Churchill who instinctively understood that to avoid value judgments in the name of ecumenism involved the surrender of the essence of public history. Whatever Trevelyan might ransom through his timid tactics of reclamation would be emasculated, if not beyond recognition, at least beyond social, cultural, and political utility.

Both Trevelyan and Churchill were writing with one eye trained on the continental threats to the survival of liberalism posed by the twentieth-century totalitarian incarnations of authoritarianism: Soviet Russia, fascist Italy, and Nazi Germany. The two historians believed themselves to be working in harness for the same ends.[140] Unlike Churchill's *Marlborough*, however, Trevelyan's three volumes on the age of Queen Anne offered a shaky foundation for the erection of an intellectual defense against these newly arisen enemies of parliamentary democracy. Trevelyan legitimized the aggressive dissatisfaction of Germany in the 1930s through historical analogy by implicitly comparing the built-in inequities of the 1919 Treaty of Versailles with what he saw as the more reasonable and just 1713 Treaty of Utrecht. Unlike with the modern case of aggrieved Germany, the wisdom of the Utrecht negotiators had ensured that "ex-enemy France, though her power of aggression had been taken away, remained unembittered and unprovoked to revenge."[141] Contrast Trevelyan's generous assessment with Churchill's sterner judgments on the failure of Utrecht.

> Marlborough had always believed that unless France was reduced, not merely to temporary exhaustion, but to a definitely restricted power, the wars of his generation would be renewed in the future. This was looking far ahead, but the fact remains that in the century that followed Europe was racked with repeated conflicts and Great Britain fought four separate wars with France aggregating in all forty-three years of deadly strife.[142]

As testified to by Churchill in *The World Crisis*, the Versailles Treaty, by every liberal standard, had been fair, perhaps too fair. Thus were self-doubt and guilt assuaged and resistance sanctioned by one historian, while another provided only confused signals between the options of accommodation and confrontation.

The unsuitability and insufficiency of Trevelyan's prose as a rallying cry for liberalism, hidden among historiographical subtleties in most of his published work, were demonstrated more vividly in other written forms such as his letter to *The Times* of 12 August 1937:

> Dictatorship and democracy must live side by side in peace, or civilization is doomed. For this end I believe Englishmen would do well to remember that the Nazi form of government is in large measure the outcome of Allied and British injustice at Versailles in 1919.
>
> As to 1914 and the years before . . . Germans and English will seldom agree, the less so, I would add, because of the egregious folly of the "guilt" clause of the Treaty of Versailles, which has acted, as might have been foreseen, as a challenge to Germans to prove that their Government was not to blame at all.
>
> But the way to future goodwill does not lie in disputing about 1914. Rather . . . let us "recognize and appreciate what is good and what is great in the other nation."

Rather than attempting to arouse liberalism's combative instincts in opposition to its implacable enemy, Trevelyan proposed Western democracy's assumption of a substantial share of the guilt as extenuation of fascism's brutal excesses. This sort of culturopolitical insecurity could hardly have served as a rallying standard for liberal democracy or as a rival to Churchill's vigorous voice.[143]

To Influence the Destiny of the World

Long before completion of *Marlborough*, Churchill embarked upon the more broadly conceived four-volume *History of the English-Speaking Peoples*. A look at some of its chapter titles conveys Churchill's determination to harmonize the multifarious themes of Britain's national history into an integrated whole: "English Common Law," "The Round World," "The Spanish Armada," "The Indian Empire," "Reform and Free Trade," "Trafalgar," "The Mother of Parliaments," "The Migration of Peoples," and "The American Constitution." This grand survey of British and U.S. history repeated on a more epic scale the Whiggish arguments of *Marlborough* with the same end in mind, to defend what he saw as peculiarly English liberal values and institutions in the inhospitable atmosphere of the 1930s.[144] Immersed in the task of composition, he explained his purpose to Maurice Ashley in the spring of 1939: "In the main, the theme is emerging of the growth of freedom and law, of the rights of the individual, of the subordination of the State to the fundamental and moral conceptions of an ever-comprehending community. Of these ideas the English-speaking peoples were the authors, then the trustees, and must now become the armed champions. Thus I condemn tyranny in whatever guise and from whatever quarter it presents itself." He went on to remind his former research assistant, "All of this of course has a current application."[145]

Churchill approached this work with a certain frenetic desperation. As he was to write after the war, from the moment of taking up the task he had hoped his historical record of the language, law, and processes underlying English liberal culture "might well notably influence the destiny of the world."[146] He had confirmation that *Marlborough* had provided inspiration to its readers, and the broader canvas and mass appeal of his national history of English exceptionalism guaranteed an even greater effect.[147] Finishing up the section on the Seven Years' War on the evening before the German invasion of Poland, Churchill himself took courage from the example of the elder Pitt.[148] Every available minute between speeches, meetings, articles, correspondence, and international crises was devoted to completing the new history before the storm broke. Time constraints led Churchill to require even more input than usual from his research assistants.[149] Measuring progress by counting the number of words down on paper, always a favorite diversion of his, now became almost an obsession. Churchill prescribed for himself a minimum of 1,000 words daily, and under this strict regimen a total of 136,000 were produced by early December 1938, 221,000 by January, 450,000 by June, and 530,000 by the final day of August 1939.[150] By his own estimation it was "a formidable grind," and by midsummer he found himself "staggering along at the end of this job."[151] Yet, for all that, Churchill judged it "a comfort at times in this anxious year to retire into the past centuries."[152]

Belief in the future of the liberal ideal in 1939 required in the case of Churchill and many others an awakened historical sense, a re-recitation of the traditional Whiggish record of progress and continuity. That sort of public communion with England's past re-established in the national consciousness the legitimacy and transcendent value of liberal institutions and principles while it restored confidence—through the illustration of former tribulations overcome—in their resilience in the face of adversity. This was the "current application" to which Churchill referred. Political Liberalism as represented by the Liberal party and rooted in a particular historiography of England was incapable of capitalizing upon this resurgent interest in the old optimistic interpretation of the nation's history from which it had once drawn sustenance. The great national crisis of 1914–18 had marked the end of a century-long symbiosis between political Liberalism and Whig historiography. Now a second great crisis reawakened the latter from its brief semihibernation, but the Liberal party had been too long dormant to follow suit. Besides, by the 1930s Trevelyan and Churchill had transformed Liberalism's former historiographical preserve into national property retaining few, if any, partisan qualities.

Interwar political dynamics greatly simplified Churchill's adoption of an augmented Whig historiographical canon. The decline and then virtual disappearance of the Liberal party as a serious electoral force provided several advantages. Most notably, it allowed for the smooth incorporation of Whig historical paradigms and moral vocabulary into a national consensus; there were fewer partisan objections to a defense of liberalism as opposed to a defense of Liberalism. Churchill, much like Trevelyan, was quick to grasp the possibilities for a latitudinarian "English" history structured around a notion of liberalism shorn of direct party associations. After all, the early biography of Lord Randolph Churchill had pointed in that very direction. This ecumenical approach fed into Churchill's analysis of the Great War as a fundamental conflict between tyranny and freedom. It possessed even greater persuasive force by the mid-1930s with the rise of continental fascism, allowing Churchill in *Marlborough* and *A History of the English-Speaking Peoples* to fashion a liberal/national version of history which, ironically enough, he gainfully employed to criticize the conduct of a self-described National Government. With his personae as historian and politician merging into a single identity in the public mind, by the end of the decade Churchill could pose as spokesman for the nation, defender of liberalism against totalitarianism, and disinterested critic of the policies of Baldwin and Chamberlain.

Another winner in the sundering of partisan associations was Churchill's effort to broaden the sweep of Liberal history. As seen above, new conditions allowed for the acknowledgment of the timely contributions of the use of force in national development. Likewise, it provided Churchill with an opportunity to introduce the powerful, benevolent state as an important agent in the preservation of liberal forms of governance and in the moral maturation of the British people. His description in *Marlborough* of the triumphs of William and Anne over Louis XIV made it acceptable to speak of the English state, the organizer of victory, in the same hallowed terms once reserved for parliament and the constitution.

This surmounting of Whig historiographical insularity also involved an embrace of the imperial theme. In his *Expansion of England* (1883) J. R. Seeley had attempted a revision of the constitutionalist bias of the Whig canon, arguing for more attention to the central importance of the rise of the British Empire, for less emphasis on interparty squabbling at the expense of "national" history and Great Britain's role as a Great Power. Seeley's placement of power at the center of the narrative, his accent on the state and on events beyond the confines of the domestic parliamentary drama were all distinctly antagonistic to the Whig tradition. But in the interwar years Churchill was able to link the imperial saga directly with the prescriptive account of constitutional evolution. Churchillian prose fused together the idiom of power with the moral lexicon of Whiggism. As he said in 1940, "Alone among the nations of the world we have found the means to combine Empire and liberty."[153] Imperial expansion complemented the growth of liberty at home, much as

Seeley's writings complemented the works of Macaulay and Freeman. The British Empire stood as an example of the responsible use of power by a free nation.

With his cautious praise of the Treaties of Washington and Locarno, the Kellogg-Briand Pact, and the League of Nations in the final volume of *The World Crisis*, Churchill exhibited the general temptation of the 1920s to hitch the Whig story of the moral progress of an island people to the fashionable wagon of liberal internationalism. But the enthusiasm was short-lived. By the early 1930s he had decided to narrow his global perspective to the still considerable confines of the British Empire and its offspring. *Marlborough* and *A History of the English-Speaking Peoples* provided the perfect vehicles for his amalgamation of the themes of an Anglo-Saxon consensus: gradualism, the righteous use of force, imperial expansion, the growth of the peculiarly liberal state, and the compatibility of efficiency and democracy.

The context of the late 1930s and early 1940s created the ideal atmosphere for the public reception of Churchill's national history. For a time, at least, the Victorian message of exceptionalism reclaimed its cultural resonance. Though a member of Chamberlain's War Cabinet, Churchill found time to complete his manuscript of *A History of the English-Speaking Peoples* by the end of 1939. The subsequent paper shortage that held up the appearance of the books in Britain seemed "extremely unfortunate" in the opinion of the holder of the American rights, who judged July 1941 "to be the psychological moment to publish this work."[154] But those four volumes had to wait to see the light of day. When they finally appeared beginning in 1956, they sold in vast numbers, yet their moment had already passed. The world for which they had been created no longer existed. The chasm between professional and public history yawned wider than ever; the empire was gone or going; Britain survived as only a power of the second rank; and the post-1945 welfare state required a different usable past.

Like Trevelyan, Churchill, the man above party, had hoped to fashion a version of England's historical development acceptable to all shades of the ideological spectrum, a version that might endure outside of the partisan arena. But as the 1950s gave way to the 1960s, it appeared that a patriotic national history of consensus anchored to the old Whig shibboleths was no longer viable.

CONCLUSION
Putting Humpty Dumpty Together Again

Despite a series of obituaries over the years, there seems to be general agreement that the Whig historical tradition has survived into the present day. Herbert Butterfield attributed this resilience to its omnivorous nature, its undiscriminating talent for swallowing up interloping themes like monarchy, toryism, and imperialism and incorporating them into a wider synthesis.[1] Where Butterfield saw durability through fusion, J. W. Burrow distinguishes persistence via fission. He notes that it makes little sense to speak of the decline or extinction of the Whig tradition; rather, we should investigate its fragmentation and the forms of adaptation pursued by each shard, its breakup "into tributaries in which much remains recognisable."[2] Christopher Parker writes of "Liberalism without Liberals," a phrase that captures his contention that in the post-1945 era Marxist and Conservative historians are the *joint* heirs of the Whig tradition, both incorporating some aspects congenial to their own prejudices and rejecting others.[3] Rosemary Jann, rather perversely, cites the self-consciously anti-Whig administrative historians of the early twentieth century with unwittingly perpetuating a fundamentally Whiggish approach to the study of England's past.[4] David Cannadine writes of welfare state Whigs, a species that evolved when, in order to fashion a usable version of the past for the age of Attlee and Macmillan, Britain's academics replaced the dated works of gentlemen-scholars with more of the same, "the old Whig history of Britain's unique and privileged development dressed up in Butskellite guise."[5]

On behalf of the New Left, Gareth Stedman Jones has offered up a sweeping denunciation of the pervasive survivability of the Whig tradition, charging in 1967 that the simple fact that "the ingrained assumptions of British historical method have never been thoroughly shaken" accounted for the contemporary "pathology of English history." Jones allowed for few distinctions among British historians all trapped in an "extinct problematic" that was "tenacious and antique liberal individualism," lumping together Acton, Stubbs, Bury, Butterfield, Temperley, Wedgwood, Trevelyan, the Hammonds, and even Laski and Cole as members of the same rogues' gallery.[6] With this attitude in tow, it is hardly surprising that the New Left historians of the 1950s and 1960s returned time and again to the traditional nostrums of Whig historiography as the starting point for dissent. But in some respects at least, this sort of revisionism engaged in flogging a horse that was, if not actually dead, long since put out to pasture as past its racing prime. Faced with a succession of challenges, internal (the transformation of history as a discipline) as well as external (the recasting of British parliamentary politics that accompanied the slow-motion breakup of the Liberal party), challenges that were in large measure interdependent, Whig history had no choice but to adapt to altered circumstances. In the process of what appear to some as successful stages of assimilation and adaptation, however, Whig history transformed itself beyond recall.

Trevelyan and Churchill successfully ecumenized the Whig tradition and thereby preserved it. But their victory was largely a Pyrrhic one. The post-1918 insolvency of the Liberal party made the severing of Whig history from its partisan moorings to political Liberalism seem a logical and necessary step. Resurrection as a national history of consensus granted a new lease on life. But this makeover provided an existence increasingly drained of vitality. Detached from partisan political debate and diluted by the intentional incorporation of rival historiographical agendas, the Whig tradition relinquished its hold on the public consciousness. It still might contribute residues to some general unspoken assumptions, but it no longer constituted an essential medium for contemporary social and political discourse. Thus, when the fortunes of the Liberal party reached their nadir in the 1920s and 1930s it could expect little succor from Whig history. As a doctrine that had customarily drawn sustenance from a peculiarly sympathetic interpretation of English history, Liberalism could hardly find serviceable a consensual version of the past whose labored inclusiveness blurred all sectarian distinctions.[7]

And a continuation of the prominence accorded Victorian public history was essential to Liberalism's survival into the mid-twentieth century. The "new" historiography with its emphasis on primary research, objective detachment, abstruse presentation, exclusivity, and concentration of authority found sponsors among late Victorian Whig scholars, most prominently E. A. Freeman and S. R. Gardiner, so it was not readily apparent at the outset that there existed any inherent incompatibility between the old Whiggish product of the gentleman of letters and the modern "scientifically" engineered creation of the university mandarinate. But even when the historical interpretations of the two did not contradict each other, the simple fact of historiography's complete removal to the academic cloister represented a substantial blow struck at the very root of the Liberal ideal. One of the intellectual pillars of political Liberalism in Britain was a belief in the superiority of the amateur over the expert. Parliamentary supremacy as dogma was grounded on the notion that the man of general knowledge and wide interest was best qualified to control all formulation of state policy, relegating expert technicians and specialists in any field of knowledge to the auxiliary posts of adviser and administrator. Popular control and indeed the entire rationale of the Liberal state rested on this belief in the competency and preferability of ad hoc governance by the amateur.

National Efficiency advocates like the Webbs favored the replacement of the apparent chaos of parliamentary politics as usual by expert administration in the capable hands of the disinterested bureaucrat. A similar confiscation of authority in the intellectual realm would facilitate this revolutionary political transformation.

The exclusive claims for historiographical authority by a professional university community of specialists would hasten the embalming of Liberalism by removing the potentially divisive interpretation of the past from the arena of national debate. With a monopoly on such volatile knowledge confined to a mandarin preserve, occasional pronouncements not open to challenge or question could be released for public consumption and enlightenment.

The Webbs never understood Liberalism well enough to realize that it could not be easily suborned by their transparent political blandishments. But they did fathom that amateurism lay at its core and that unalloyed professionalism, whether of an administrative bureaucracy or of a university scholasticism, would poison its soul. The Webbs purposely adopted the detached and opaque modern academic forms of the university establishment for the writing of their histories as a secondary means of attack upon the Liberalism which they had already placed under direct indictment in their texts. These histories represented a perfect architectonic union of form and content. This adoption of "scientific" structure provided the Fabian couple with an indispensable veneer of objectivity. The Webbs looked upon modern professional historiography as their natural ally, as the inevitable antagonist of the Whig version of history and thus the enemy of their enemy. On the intellectual plane as well as on the political, the Webbs energetically wooed potential allies, unwitting and otherwise. The academic community's sympathetic reception of *English Local Government* demonstrated a greater return on the Webbs' investment of effort than that generated from their long and unhappy association with the Liberal party.

After 1900 many other amateur Liberal historians struggled with the same issue of the latent, and more often open, antagonism between literary public history and its reclusive scientific counterpart and the precariousness of the health of the former. The Hammonds seldom spoke directly to the issue. In part because of Lawrence's ambivalence regarding his 1895 rejection for an Oxford fellowship, the couple adopted many of the constraints of scientific scholarship but felt the unemotional reserve of the ideal academic style unsuitable to their historiographic purposes. The mere fact that they pursued culturopolitical ends through their writings at all— a fact the couple was seldom prepared to admit—jarred noticeably with the professed detachment of the dons and branded the Hammonds as unregenerate outsiders. During Lawrence's ultimately unsuccessful 1922 search for a tenured professorship Barbara's anxiety mounted at the thought of the restrictions of authorial possibilities within the "arid & cavilling atmosphere of Oxford" where "all the history people w[ou]ld love to get a knife" into the Hammonds. From an opposite perspective they understood at least as well as the Webbs the built-in academic obstacles to the modern practice of a utilitarian literary and Liberal history.

More directly, dramatically, and completely than the Hammonds, Trevelyan as historian defined himself in opposition to the suffocating "pseudoscientific" Buryite trends in the discipline. His 1903 "Latest View of History" analyzed in a public forum what the Hammonds discussed only in private asides. Trevelyan's rejoinder to Bury's inaugural address stressed in particular the threat to literary history of the university's new and pernicious absorption with modern historiographical techniques at the expense of the poetic. But of course he routinely spoke of "literary and liberal" history as one and the same, and Butterfield later accepted this intimate association as a given, his *Whig Interpretation of History* comprising as much an attack upon the genus *literary amateur* as upon the species *Macaulayesque*. In both form and content Trevelyan's Garibaldian epic was an open challenge to everything its author had left behind at Cambridge in 1902. But circumstances conspired to dampen the initial impudence and freedom that characterized his release from academic shackles. The sobering experiences of 1914–18 deepened Trevelyan's never negligible pessimism. Vulnerability stemming from postwar Liberalism's intellectual and political disarray presented a remarkable opening for the mischievous and opportunistic to oversee the disarticulation of the traditionally fruitful symbiosis between Liberalism and literary style in history. The success of Strachey's *Eminent Victorians* brought home to Trevelyan the danger of his exposed and seemingly isolated position outside the academy.

Trevelyan's response, nearly a decade in the making, was a return to the university as sanctuary. This was not the simple volte face which it appeared on the surface. Trevelyan's Liberalism, even before the war, was a barely peaceful coexistence of opposites. His Gladstonian proclivities, inherited from his father, were balanced by a New Liberal attraction to the Webbs' social and intellectual circle and by membership in the Fabian Society. Trevelyan had had his

Edwardian brush with the advocates of increased National Efficiency, and he understood well enough their substantial claims for the authority of the disinterested expert. His retreat back to Cambridge in 1927 represented an expedient compromise to a predicament with no ideal solution. Trevelyan still felt history undertaken in the academic setting and written in the academic style to be lethal to the spirit of Liberalism, yet Whig historiography and its partner political Liberalism appeared so vulnerable in the 1920s and 1930s as to be incapable of survival out in the open. Purely literary Whig history no longer possessed the strength or resilience to endure the wickedly pointed satire of Strachey and his mimics. Refuge in the university and co-optation of academic authority seemed to Trevelyan the best and last hope of the Whig interpretation of history. In these unnatural—although not unpleasant to Trevelyan personally—environs Whig historiography would successfully practice a Fabian form of permeation on a pliant academic elite, or it would slowly perish.

Amongst all of this defensiveness there was little evidence of the Millite confidence in the ultimate triumph within the intellectual marketplace of ideas of Liberal paradigms as expressed in Whig historiography. Similarly, Trevelyan doubted the ability of Liberalism to survive as a distinct political ideology in the inhospitable postwar climate. As witnessed above, his response to the threat of imminent extinction was to contribute to the creation of a transformed Liberalism that invited assimilation by both the Labour and Conservative parties. His belated return to the university conveyed his persistent doubts about the proselytizing power of this sort of latitudinarian message. At Trinity College he hoped to benefit from the professional aura of authority as compensation for his own nagging lack of conviction.

Churchill, like Trevelyan and the Hammonds, had a youthful dalliance with the Webbs and their doctrine of National Efficiency. He absorbed the lesson of the latent power of a specialist bureaucracy, but, perhaps because of his bitter experiences as a cabinet minister in the Great War, he understood the need to keep a safe distance from its suffocating embrace. Wisely refusing to take up an adversarial position against the professional historical community, a calculating Churchill instead tapped academia as a useful source of knowledge, prestige, and authority for his own exercises in history-writing. Meanwhile, having never attended Oxbridge himself, he felt no compulsion to ape the methodology of the don. Sustained, unlike Trevelyan or Hammond, by a personal historical vision corroborated by direct political experience, Churchill managed to turn academia into an ally without being absorbed by it.

Hilaire Belloc appears as the anomalous dissenting voice in this consensus of recognition that academic history threatened to asphyxiate the traditional Whig version of Britain's past. For Belloc, Whig history was indistinguishable from the "official history" of the don, and his own personal grievance against Oxford merely reinforced this intellectual prejudice. The apparent paradox of fervent anti-Liberal sentiments comingling with antiacademism in the person of Belloc is best explained by referring to Belloc's variant understanding of Liberalism. The propping up of a politically and economically spent Liberal system via the erection of the bureaucratic Servile State mirrored the flight of intellectually bankrupt amateur Whig history to an institutional refuge within the university. Unlike any of the other historians analyzed above—even those convinced enemies of Liberalism the Webbs—Belloc pictured modern Liberalism as fundamentally statist and bureaucratic rather than amateurish and laissez faire. Yet he could despise the Webbs and still agree with their attack on the intellectual, social, and constitutional alterations of the sixteenth and seventeenth centuries as the source of three hundred years of national failure.

Like the Hammonds, Trevelyan, the Webbs, and Churchill, Belloc recognized the great importance of contemporary academic history with its cultural authority and prestige born of the modern professional mystique. But while the others turned their hands with varying degrees of success to the task of co-opting academic history for their own purposes, Belloc attempted to undermine its credibility. The dismantling of the bastion of orthodoxy represented the first step in the struggle against pernicious Liberalism; later there would be time for conversion and reconstruction. Denied a point d'appui within the academic community, Belloc exploited the possibilities of literary history, once the sole property of Whig historians, as a popular and therefore rapid antidote to three centuries of unchallenged historical orthodoxy. Capitalizing on the heretofore unrealized anti-Liberal potential of popular historical forms, the postwar Stracheyesque "revolution" in biography merely followed Belloc's Edwardian lead.

Belloc attacked Liberalism at what he diagnosed as its most vulnerable point, its umbilical cord to the Whig historical tradition. Though alone his missiles proved insufficient to break this attachment, his analysis and aim were true, and he lived to see a crack in the edifice opened by other means. The closely related phenomena of the protracted breakup of the Liberal party, the rise of an anti-Whig reaction from within the historical profession itself, and long-term changes in British society that belied the inherited tale of moral progress through constitutional development all conspired to contribute to the severing of Whig historiography's connection to political Liberalism. The junction frayed at exactly the moment that the floundering Liberal party required the strongest possible reaffirmation of its intellectual/historical legitimacy. Ironically, the weakening of this vital connection was itself largely a consequence of the demoralization of political Liberalism, a stark reversal of Belloc's "vicious circle of mutual advantage." Whig historiography found it could endure only by jettisoning its partisan visage, but in doing so it risked forfeiting the immediacy and problematic nature that afforded public history cultural authority.

The Second World War furnished the props and scenery for a resurgent interest in, and enthusiasm for, the Whig interpretation of English history. Such manifestations of concern for preservation and restoration invariably arise after decay is well advanced. Even Butterfield, self-appointed arch-predator of Whig historiography, came to regret the severity of the wounds he had thoughtlessly inflicted on his prey in 1931. In the middle of the global crusade against fascism it seemed that the practical benefits of the standard nineteenth-century Liberal version of England's past outweighed its intellectual shortcomings. Butterfield now announced that "the whig interpretation came at exactly the crucial moment and, whatever it may have done to our history, it had a wonderful effect on English politics." In 1944 it seemed appropriate to declare "we are all of us exultant and unrepentant whigs." The Whig interpretation—"which was never more vivid than in the great speeches of 1940"—was in future to be further discredited only at the nation's peril.

Those who, amid the breeze and agitation of contemporary debate, affect to court a controversy with such diluted remnants of the whig interpretation as still keep their currency amongst us, must take heed when they sally forth in their carpet slippers against this entrenched tradition. They will find a more comfortable piece of coast for their commandos if they will carry their offensive, not against the whig tradition itself, but against surviving defects in historical method. It is not necessary or useful to deny that the theme of English political history is the story of our liberty.

Butterfield well understood that Whig history was long past its heyday. As he noted, new historical interpretations erupt upon the world as propaganda, making their way as "fighting creeds." Eventually they mellow, becoming "wise and urbane" and, in the end, "harmless."[8] Harmlessness was not much of an ambition for a public historian, yet nonsectarian Whiggism provided the means for little else.

After the Second World War the belletristic tradition of public history lived on outside the academy in the capable hands of C. V. Wedgwood, Maurice Ashley, Arthur Bryant, and Antonia Fraser, and even within the university through the work of Asa Briggs, J. H. Plumb, Hugh Trevor-Roper, Owen Chadwick, and others. But these names represented an ever-shrinking minority. In the post-1945 era for the first time, the vast majority of history written in Britain was the work of professional academics. By the early 1960s there were 1,300 full-time history teachers in British universities, climbing to 1,700 a decade later.[9] Amid all this expansion of the discipline professionals continued the process of self-marginalization launched before the turn of the century. The research ideal approximated reality as historians wrote more and more read by fewer and fewer. Generalists all but disappeared. Increasingly specialized research generated masses of scholarly books and monographs. Carried on in an ever more impenetrably arcane language and complicated by sophisticated methods of quantification, historical conversation completed its century-long migration from the public forum to the obscure journal. Paradoxically or not, the broadening of the fields of inquiry to encompass economic, urban, social, and family history paralleled a retraction in the scope of public interest. The devaluation of political history—particularly worrisome to a Whig tradition reliant upon the structure provided by a skeleton of constitutional development—testified to a fragmentation of thematic focus, underlined further by the replacement of the linear coherence of narrative with disembodied analysis.

That the lay reading public largely ignored this professionally generated, incomprehensible noise and confusion is hardly astonishing. More surprising is the equanimity with which the practitioners of historiography relinquished their listeners. R. G. Collingwood had postulated in 1939 that he might well be standing on the "threshold of an age in which history would be as important for the world as natural science had been between 1600 and 1900."[10] But the idea of "public history" was in rapid decline, and historians who took seriously their customary didactic role were sparse on the ground after the Second World War. From Oxford of the 1950s Hugh Trevor-Roper appealed to professionals to exert themselves toward reestablishing and maintaining the withering connection between historians and a lay readership, a link indispensable to the health of the discipline.[11] From Cambridge of the 1960s J. H. Plumb mourned the "death of the past," noting that though a few vestiges of its former strength and usability survived in politics, modern society had shed its visceral ties to memory, transforming the past into nothing more than a curiosity that evoked nostalgia and sentimentality. And professional historians had deliberately abetted this shift in public attitudes.[12]

This is not to imply that the postwar era did not generate its own usable versions of the past. The writings of two generations of administrative historians and offshoots from the works of the likes of G. D. H. Cole, R. H. Tawney, and the Webbs erected a legitimate historical ancestry for the welfare state. The radical departures of E. P. Thompson and Eric Hobsbawm provided a fillip to leftist critiques of the postwar consensus. But in both cases, the actual readership of published books remained small. In some fashion this represented a triumph of the Webbian ideal for a more exclusive form of "public" history, one in which experts settled the issues among themselves and passed along the results to a passive audience harboring only a modicum of interest. The problem was that that sort of indirect curiosity proved difficult to sustain over the long haul. Just as the loss of the unifying vision provided by political history alienated the lay readership, so this degree of separation from the source withered popular absorption in historical controversies, even ones with apparent contemporary relevance.

As we have seen, Whig history was not simply the presentation of a particular version of the past; it also encompassed a view of history's role in civic culture. History was to provide the forum for an ongoing public discussion about the present. Detachment, during the interwar years, from the politics of Liberalism introduced flexibility as nonsectarian Whig historiography revised, assimilated, and absorbed. Yet a national history of consensus, the outcome of all of this accommodation and appropriation, forfeited a considerable portion of its cultural resonance and therefore survived only as a dysfunctional form of public history. The final triumph of disciplinary professionalization after 1945 drained most of the remaining vitality from the Whig tradition.

Whig historiography's attempts to right itself during its long recessional generated an assortment of unintended consequences. With their gaze fixed upon the moral questions posed by the unacceptable social costs of the early rigidity of economic liberalism, the Hammonds laid the groundwork for the historiographical reaction of the 1960s. Although unrepentant Liberals, Barbara and Lawrence, because of the subtlety and ambiguity of their work and because of their deliberately chosen position midway between popular and academic history, found themselves adopted by historians of the far Left. Unwittingly they became godparents of the donnish, anti-Whig moralizing of Christopher Hill, E. P. Thompson, and Eric Hobsbawm.

The national history of consensus elaborated by Trevelyan and Churchill suffered a similar fate, providing the template for arguably the most widely read British historian of the postwar era, Arthur Bryant. Bryant's *English Saga, 1840–1940*, published in December 1940 after the Battle of Britain, pointed out at least one future evolutionary path for the national history of consensus, a form originally called into being as a means of preserving the Whig tradition. Bryant retained an emotive vocabulary, describing ordered progress and toleration as the core of modern democracy and England as a land uniquely blessed with reserves of justice, honesty, liberty, and prosperity. Credit was apportioned evenhandedly among all factions, sects, and parties. But coloring Bryant's interpretation was a pointed critique of classical liberal economics replete with denunciations of laissez-faire, private profit-making, and the glorification of the individual at the expense of the community. Bryant's history contained a healthy dose of Tory medieval sentimentalism, demonstrating a nostalgia for England's Catholic heritage that rivaled Belloc and Chesterton in their prime. There were even intimations of Belloc's Servile State. Bryant closed by writing of the period 1840 to 1940 as though it were a long mistake, in the process indirectly laying the blame for the Second World War at England's feet.

> Man, who had once tried to model his life on the divine, came to take his orders from the lender of money and the chartered accountant acting in their purely professional capacity. That has been the story of the last century of civilization. The age of enlightened selfishness begot plutocracy, and plutocracy begot the monstrous materialistic and pagan tyrannies we are now fighting to destroy. It was England that first unconsciously led the world into this morass. It is England—wisest and gentlest of the nations—that has now to discover the way out.[13]

Clearly Butterfield had been premature in his declaration that all were now exultant and unrepentant Whigs.

Trevelyan and Churchill were both great admirers of Bryant, in particular for his pronouncements in favor of narrative structure and literary style as essential elements of public history.[14] Yet neither man, not even Trevelyan at his most profoundly pessimistic, could have acceded to Bryant's analysis of Victorian and Edwardian Britain. In the case of Bryant, as with that of the Hammonds, Whig forms revealed themselves to be as vulnerable to, as they were adept at, assimilation.

Following on the heels of fourteen years of coalition government, the postwar sociopolitical consensus must share in the blame for the dearth of public interest in historical questions after 1945. In such a climate, debates about the meaning of the past were likely to arouse more patriotic curiosity than passion. But the coming of Thatcherism in the 1980s reintroduced the problematic into British national politics and culture. After a lag time, this sharpening of issues and public rhetoric may spawn a renewed appetite for historical prose aimed at the general reader, prose that trumpets its contemporary relevance and wears partisan insignia without blushing. It remains open to serious question whether such a development would be beneficial for the historical discipline as presently conceived. But it seems clear that any revival of the genre of civic history will be unlikely to herald a reincarnation of the Whig tradition. Future reports of sightings of the Whig interpretation should be viewed with a healthy skepticism born of the knowledge that there can be no contemporary duplication of the peculiar circumstances that once sustained it for so long.

NOTES

ABBREVIATIONS USED IN THE NOTES

AHR	*American Historical Review*
BLCh	Winston S. Churchill Papers, British Library, London
BP	Hilaire Belloc Papers, John R. Burns Library, Boston College
ChP	Sir Winston Churchill Archives Trust, Churchill Archives Centre, Churchill College, Cambridge
CKW	C. K. Webster Papers, British Library of Political and Economic Science
CPT	Charles P. Trevelyan Papers, Robinson Library, University of Newcastle-upon-Tyne
CV	Martin Gilbert and Randolph S. Churchill, *Winston S. Churchill: Companion Volumes* (with vol. no. and part no.)
DBW	*Diary of Beatrice Webb, 1873–1942* (holograph and typescript microfiche)
EconHR	*Economic History Review*
EconJ	*Economic Journal*
EHR	*English Historical Review*
ELG	Sidney and Beatrice Webb, *English Local Government from the Revolution to the Municipal Corporations Act*
FP	H. A. L. Fisher Papers, Bodleian Library, Oxford
GLD	G. Lowes Dickinson Papers, King's College Library, Cambridge
GM	Gilbert Murray Papers, Bodleian Library, Oxford
GMT	George Macaulay Trevelyan
GOT	George Otto Trevelyan Papers, Robinson Library, University of Newcastle-upon-Tyne
GW	Graham Wallas Papers, British Library of Political and Economic Science, London
HB	Hilaire Belloc
HJ	*Historical Journal*
HP	J. L. and Barbara Hammond Papers, Bodleian Library, Oxford
JCH	*Journal of Contemporary History*
JLH	J. L. Hammond
JModH	*Journal of Modern History*
LBH	L. Barbara Hammond
LWP	Leonard Woolf Papers, Sussex University Library, Brighton
OBP	Oscar Browning Papers, King's College, Cambridge
PP	Passfield Papers (Sidney and Beatrice Webb), British Library of Political and Economic Science, London
RCT	Robert C. Trevelyan Papers, Trinity College, Cambridge
RHT	R. H. Tawney Papers, British Library of Political and Economic Science, London

TLS   *Times Literary Supplement*
WSC   Winston S. Churchill

INTRODUCTION

1. Burrow, *Liberal Descent*.

2. Jann, *The Art and Science of Victorian History* and "From Amateur to Professional," pp. 122–47; Heyck, *Transformation of Intellectual Life*.

3. Blaas, *Continuity and Anachronism*.

4. Von Arx, *Progress and Pessimism*, esp. pp. 64–123.

5. Parker, *English Historical Tradition*, Cannadine, "British History," pp. 169–91.

6. Butterfield, *Whig Interpretation of History*.

7. For definitions of Whig historiography, Heyck refers readers to Blaas and Butterfield. See *Transformation of Intellectual Life*, p. 151 n. 9.

8. Bentley, *Liberal Mind*, p. 14.

9. Fisher, "Whig Historians," pp. 297–339.

10. See Collini, *Public Moralists*.

11. Ibid., pp. 54–56.

12. Kadish, "Scholarly Exclusiveness," pp. 183–98; Goldstein, "Origins and Early Years of the 'English Historical Review,'" pp. 6–19.

13. Seeley, "Liberal Education in Universities," in *Lectures and Essays* p. 216.

14. Trevelyan, "Autobiography of a Historian," in *An Autobiography and Other Essays*, pp. 16–17; Wormell, *Sir John Seeley*, p. 128.

15. See Soffer, "Development of Disciplines," pp. 933–46.

16. Cannadine, "British History," p. 171.

17. Osborne, "Endurance of 'Literary' History," pp. 7–17.

18. Hill, "Whig Historian," pp. 283–84.

19. "Prefatory Note," *EHR* 1, no. 1 (Jan. 1886): 5.

20. Ibid., p. 4.

21. *Proceedings of the British Academy* 1 (1903–4): 320.

22. Maitland to Henry Jackson, 14 Feb. 1903, in Fifoot, *Letters of Maitland*, p. 272.

23. For Maitland's unease at this development see Harvie, *Lights of Liberalism*, pp. 214–15.

24. Morley, *Diderot and the Encyclopedists*, 2:201–2.

25. Heyck, *Transformation of Intellectual Life*; Collini, *Public Moralists*, p. 55.

26. Presidential address of 1929 by T. F. Tout to the Royal Historical Society, quoted in Burrow, "Victorian Historians and the Royal Historical Society," p. 139.

27. Quoted in Blaas, *Continuity and Anachronism*, p. 333.

28. Blaas, *Continuity and Anachronism*, pp. 66, 196–239.

29. Toynbee, *Lectures on the Industrial Revolution*, p. 163.

30. See Coleman, *Myth, History and the Industrial Revolution*, pp. 1–42; and *History and the Economic Past*, pp. 37–92; Cannadine, "The Present and the Past in the English Industrial Revolution," esp. pp. 131–42, and *Trevelyan*, p. 130.

31. Pollard, *History of England*, pp. 163–64.

32. See Wormell, *Sir John Seeley*, pp. 154–80; and Burrow, *Liberal Descent*, pp. 231–85.

33. Cannadine, *Decline and Fall of the British Aristocracy*, p. 31.

34. Butterfield, *The Englishman and His History*. Burrow, *Liberal Descent*, pp. 286–301; Collini, *Public Moralists*, pp. 338, 346–51.

CHAPTER ONE

1. Quoted in Speaight, *Hilaire Belloc*, p. 392.

2. BP Box 330, HB to Maurice Baring, 28 Aug. 1933.

3. BP Box 58, HB to H. A. L. Fisher, 13 Aug. 1932, Box 377, HB to Lady Frances Phipps, 29 Nov. 1934. Although Belloc's *Richelieu* (1930) pleased his publisher and sold very well, the author himself labeled it a "bad book" and vowed, "I would not be seen dead in the field with it" (BP Box 7, HB to Duff Cooper, 17 Jan. 1930).

4. BP Box 94, HB to Lady Frances Phipps, 8 Jan. 1937.

5. BP Box 369, HB to Hoffman Nickerson, 15 Jan. 1931.

6. BP Box 369, HB to Lady Frances Phipps, 11 Mar. 1931. See also Box 330, E. S. P. Haynes to HB, 19 Oct. 1925, and Box 91, HB to A. D. Peters (his literary agent), 9 Oct. 1931.

7. BP Box 90, HB to Hoffman Nickerson, 20 Aug. 1923.

8. BP Box 42, HB to Maurice Baring, 31 Mar. 1939.

9. BP Box 38, HB to Katherine Asquith, 25 Apr. 1930.

10. Wilson, *Hilaire Belloc*, pp. 74–75.

11. *Parliamentary Debates* 4th scr., 156 (7 May 1906): 1072.

12. BP Box 61, HB to Charles Goodwin, 4 May 1933.

13. Oman, *Memories of Oxford*, p. 218. Decades later, Belloc's opinion of Oman was more equivocal. Like all "sheltered" Oxford dons, Oman was clearly "a gross charlatan in his pretence at knowledge . . . repeating the old routine history which is so lucrative" in complicity with "our routine official system." Yet Oman also possessed the cardinal virtue of writing with "verve: giving a good round 100, and the average Don zero" (BP Box 90, HB to Hoffman Nickerson, 3 May 1926).

14. BP Box 377, HB to Lady Frances Phipps, 16 Feb. 1934, Box 330, HB to Maurice Baring, 5 Dec. 1909, Box 42, HB to Maurice Baring, 22 May 1908.

15. BP Box 42, HB to Maurice Baring, 12 Nov. 1909.

16. Belloc, "On Footnotes," in Morton, *Selected Essays*, p. 175.

17. BP Box 38, HB to Mrs. Raymond Asquith, 31 May 1921.

18. HB to Mrs. Mervyn Herbert, 4 Nov. 1936, in Belloc, *Letters*, p. 260.

19. BP Box 61, HB to Charles Goodwin, 4 May 1933.

20. BP Box 40, HB to Bonnie Nickerson, 27 Nov. 1940.

21. BP Box 369, HB to Hoffman Nickerson, 15 Jan. 1931.

22. Quoted in Speaight, *Hilaire Belloc*, p. 31.

23. Belloc, *Crisis of Civilization*, p. 11. See also "On Historical Evidence" in Morton, *Selected Essays*, pp. 181–82.

24. Quoted in Speaight, *Hilaire Belloc*, p. 411.

25. HB to J. S. Phillimore, 9 Apr. 1912, quoted ibid., p. 323.

26. Belloc, *Case of Dr. Coulton*, and FP 53.129, HB to Fisher, 8 Sept. 1932. See also BP Box 58, HB to Fisher, 13 Aug. 1932.

27. Belloc, *Marie Antoinette*, p. 349; "On Method in History" and "On Historical Evidence" in Morton, *Selected Essays*, pp. 122 and 183.

28. See, e.g., Belloc, *Danton*, p. xviii; or *Robespierre* (1901), p. xvi; or FP 53.129, HB to Fisher, 8 Sept. 1932.

29. Belloc, *Danton*, p. xvii.

30. BP Box 99, HB to George Wyndham, 28 Nov. 1910.

31. Lunn, *And Yet So New*, p. 64.

32. BP Box 42, HB to Maurice Baring, 14 Apr. 1938.

33. FP 53.4–5, HB to Fisher, 8 June 1904.

34. FP 53.27–28, HB to Fisher, 4 July 1906.

35. FP 53.9, HB to Fisher, 1 Jan. 1905.

36. Belloc, *Danton*, p. xv.

37. Belloc, *Robespierre*, p. viii.

38. FP 53.5c, HB to Fisher, 29 Sept. 1904.

39. See BP Box 90, HB to Hoffman Nickerson, 15 Dec. 1923.

40. Belloc, *Crisis of Civilization*, p. 238. For example, Belloc believed it was his duty to rescue the reputation of James II "from the monstrous and deliberate lies told in the Whig histories, of which the most scandalous is Trevelyan's" (BP Box 94, HB to Lady Frances Phipps, 3 Feb. 1938).

41. Quoted in Wilson, *Hilaire Belloc*, p. 172. Belloc's animosity was personal as well as ideological and fully reciprocated. In 1939 he referred to Trevelyan as a "donkey" on the strength of the fact that "I knew him years ago and as he does not believe in miracles he cannot hope for a change" (BP Box 40, HB to Hester Balfour, 7 Nov. 1939). In a gossipy aside, A. L. Rowse records that Trevelyan "in conversation roundly called [Belloc] a liar" (*Portraits and Views*, p. 72).

42. Belloc, *Crisis of Civilization*, pp. 239–40.

43. BP Box 464A, clipping of Belloc's review of *England under Queen Anne* entitled "Prof. Trevelyan's History—II. More Samples from a Mass of Myth" in *Universe*, 2 Nov. 1934.

44. BP Box 99, HB to George Wyndham, 9 Apr. 1912.

45. BP Boxes 451 and 461 contain two folders filled with manuscript and typed carbon drafts for the anticipated article, and both folders are labeled "Article for *E.H.R.*"

46. *EHR* 25,99 (July 1910): 620–21.

47. BP Box 207, HB to George Wyndham, 27 Oct. 1911.

48. Belloc, "On Footnotes," in Morton, *Selected Essays*, p. 175.

49. HB to Maurice Baring, 10 Oct. 1916, in Belloc, *Letters*, p. 74.

50. BP Box 94, HB to Lady Frances Phipps, 5 July 1939.

51. BP Box 90, HB to Bonnie Nickerson, 17 Oct. 1940.

52. For Belloc's distinguished radical lineage see McCarthy, *Hilaire Belloc*, p. 16.

53. Chesterton, *Autobiography*, pp. 298–302.

54. See Greenleaf, *British Political Tradition*, 2:142–85, esp. 167–70. See also Clarke, *Liberals and Social Democrats*, pp. 29–30, 48–49, 75, 99, 133, 150, 191.

55. Belloc, "The Liberal Tradition," in Belloc, Hammond, Hirst, Macdonell, Phillimore, and Simon, *Essays in Liberalism*, pp. 1–30.

56. See Clarke, *Liberals and Social Democrats*, pp. 75–76; McCarthy, *Hilaire Belloc*, pp. 19–20; and Speaight, *Hilaire Belloc*, pp. 117–18.

57. BP Box 356, election address at South Salford, 28 Dec. 1905, Box 200, clipping from the *Manchester Evening News*, 14 May 1904.

58. Quoted in Speaight, *Hilaire Belloc*, p. 206.

59. Ibid., p. 202.

60. FP 53.20, HB to Fisher, 19 Jan. 1906.

61. BP Box 356, speech at South Salford, 8 Jan. 1910.

62. BP Box 207, HB to George Wyndham, 11 Aug. 1911.

63. BP Box 61, HB to Charles Goodwin, 5 Mar. and 6 Apr. 1910.

64. FP 53.56, HB to Fisher, 8 Dec. 1910.

65. Belloc, *Party System*, p. 76.

66. Ibid., p. 26.

67. Ibid., pp. 29–30. "The official Liberals and Conservatives are one very much like the other: what they really dread is the Radical" (BP Box 61, HB to Charles Goodwin, 19 Jan. 1910).

68. Belloc, *Party System*, p. 201.

69. For details see Martin, *"The New Age" under Orage*.

70. BP Box 207, HB to George Wyndham, 12 Aug. 1912.

71. Belloc, *Servile State*, pp. ix–xiv.

72. Ibid., pp. 15–16.

73. Ibid., pp. 156–63 and 183.

74. Ibid., pp. 155–78.

75. BP Box 42, HB to Maurice Baring, 23 Nov. 1911; FP 53.84, HB to Fisher, 4 Aug. 1911.

76. Belloc, *Servile State*, p. 28.

77. Ibid., p. 50.

78. Ibid., p. 69.

79. Ibid., pp. 124–30.

80. Quoted in McCarthy, *Hilaire Belloc*, p. 284.

81. Chesterton, *Autobiography*, p. 108.

82. Belloc, *Servile State*, pp. 127–28.

83. Michael Bentley says they dealt a "heavy blow" to progressivism and its enthusiasms (*Liberal Mind*, p. 164). See also Greenleaf, *British Political Tradition*, 2:88–95.

84. Reckitt, *As It Happened*, pp. 107–8.

85. FP 53.32, HB to Fisher, 6 May 1907.

86. HP 19.205, HB to JLH, 1 Nov. 1923.

87. Speaight, *Hilaire Belloc*, p. 412.

88. Belloc, *Crisis of Civilization*, p. 238.

89. Belloc, "On Method in History," in Morton, *Selected Essays*, p. 121; BP Box 90, HB to Hoffman Nickerson, 20 Aug. 1923. See also Box 58, HB to Fisher, 6 Dec. 1908, and Box 5, HB to Rev. Dr. H. Carr, 15 Mar. 1923.

90. BP Box 90, HB to Hoffman Nickerson, 13 Sept. 1923.

91. BP Box 369, HB to Lady Frances Phipps, n.d., ca. 1931.

92. BP Box 377, draft of an essay entitled "Getting Over the Footlights," [ca. 1933–34], p. 4, BP Box 464A, draft of an undated essay entitled "The Catholic Historian."

93. BP Box 272, HB to A. D. Peters, 31 Aug. 1935.

94. BP Box 99, HB to George Wyndham, 28 Nov. 1910.

95. Belloc, *Robespierre*, p. vii.

96. BP Box 369, HB to Hoffman Nickerson, 3 Nov. 1931.

97. Belloc, *Robespierre*, p. vii.

98. Belloc, *French Revolution*, p. 14.

99. Ibid., p. 19.

100. Belloc, *Danton*, pp. 3, xv, and 7.

101. Ibid., pp. xv and 12.

102. Ibid., p. 23.

103. McCarthy, *Hilaire Belloc*, p. 316. Belloc undoubtedly overemphasized the significance of the Catholic church in the Revolution but was prepared to defend this idiosyncratic preoccupation, as he did in the preface to his *French Revolution*, a 242-page book with 36 pages devoted solely to that topic.

104. Belloc, *Danton*, p. xii.

105. Belloc, *Robespierre*, pp. xvii and xx.

106. Belloc, *Danton*, p. 9.

107. Ibid., pp. 258–59. Presciently, Belloc foreshadowed here his subsequent attitude toward what he was to consider Asquith's Liberal government's inept and ineffectual direction of the war against Germany from 1914 to 1916.

108. HB to Maurice Baring, 31 Aug. 1916 in Belloc, *Letters*, p. 73.

109. Belloc, *History of England*, 3:viii.

110. Ibid., 4:vii.

111. Ibid., 3:ix.

112. Gooch, *History and Historians*, p. 284. See also Shea, *English Ranke*.

113. Lingard and Belloc, *History of England*, 11:xi.

114. Ibid., pp. xxiv–xxv.

115. Ibid., pp. xv–xvi.

116. Ibid., pp. 30–63. See also Belloc, *Shorter History of England*, p. 463.

117. Lingard and Belloc, *History of England*, 11:78. See also Belloc, *Shorter History of England*, pp. 443–46.

118. Belloc, *Shorter History of England*, pp. 490–91.

119. Lingard and Belloc, *History of England*, 11:233. See also McCarthy, *Hilaire Belloc*, p. 311.

120. Belloc, *Shorter History of England*, pp. 502–3.

121. Lingard and Belloc, *History of England*, 11:448–53.

122. Ibid., p. 454.

123. Ibid., p. 457.

124. HB to Maurice Baring, 10 Oct. 1916, in Belloc, *Letters*, p. 74.

125. Belloc was to repeat this same construction again and again over the years, most notably in *A Shorter History of England* (1934) and *The Crisis of Civilization* (1937).

126. Belloc, *Crisis of Civilization*, p. 67.

127. Belloc, *Shorter History of England*, pp. 185–86.

128. Belloc, *Crisis of Civilization*, p. 121.

129. Belloc, *History of England*, 4:vi–vii. See also *Crisis of Civilization*, p. 118.

130. Belloc, *Shorter History of England*, pp. 286–98.

131. See BP Box 91, HB to A. D. Peters, 25 Mar. 1931, C. W. Chamberlain (Methuen & Co.) to Peters, 12 Oct. 1931, Peters to HB, 18 Aug. 1932, and Box 161, J. A. White (Methuen & Co.) to HB, 1 and 3 Nov. 1938.

132. Belloc, *Shorter History of England*, p. 369.

133. Hilaire Belloc, "Reform: V. The Powers of the Crown," *Oxford and Cambridge Review* 26 (Dec. 1912): 85.

134. Belloc, *James the Second*, pp. 139–40.

135. Belloc, *Essays of a Catholic Layman*.

136. BP Box 94, HB to Lady Frances Phipps, 19 June 1939.

137. McCarthy, "Hilaire Belloc," pp. 165–73.

138. HP 19.214, HB to JLH, 5 Nov. 1923, 19.220, HB to JLH, 13 Nov. 1923.

139. HP 19.205, HB to JLH, 1 Nov. 1923.

140. Belloc, *Servile State* (new preface to the 1927 ed.), p. vii, *Crisis of Civilization*, p. 238.

141. Belloc, *Crisis of Civilization*, p. 238.

142. *Parliamentary Debates* 4th ser., 156 (7 May 1906): 1072. See also BP Box 91, HB to A. D. Peters, 9 Oct. 1931.

143. Belloc, *Shorter History of England*, p. 7. After sales of nearly 1,700 copies in the first fifteen months, its English publisher Harrap suggested an abridgment for use as a middle-form textbook. See BP Box 272, George Harrap & Co., royalty statement, 30 Apr. 1935, and G. O. Anderson (of Harrap) to A. D. Peters, 8 June 1936.

144. See Greenleaf, *British Political Tradition*, 2:89.

145. Ibid., pp. 30–102.

146. Bentley, *Liberal Mind*, p. 164.

147. BP Box 161, HB to F. Muller (of Methuen), 11 Mar. 1927.

148. BP Box 369, HB to Hoffman Nickerson, 26 Mar. 1931.

149. *TLS*, 23 July 1925, p. 490.

150. See Belloc's letter to the editor, *TLS*, July 1925, p. 509.

151. Belloc, *Crisis of Civilization*, p. 240.

152. HB to Maurice Baring, 31 Aug. 1916, in Belloc, *Letters*, p. 73.

153. BP Box 94, HB to Lady Frances Phipps, 3 Feb. 1938. See also Belloc, *Case of Dr. Coulton*; Coulton, *Mr. Hilaire Belloc as Historian*; Speaight, *Hilaire Belloc*, pp. 415–19; and Wilson, *Hilaire Belloc*, pp. 348–54.

154. Belloc began his attack in 1920 with an article in the *Dublin Review*. Wells answered this and the complaints of other Catholic apologists with a pamphlet, *The New Teaching of History* (1921). Belloc countered with twenty-four articles in the Catholic weekly the *Universe* (published together in 1926 as *A Companion to Mr. Wells' "Outline of History"*), which elicited from Wells *Mr. Hilaire Belloc Objects to 'The Outline of History* (1925). Belloc all but closed out the fracas with *Mr. Belloc Still Objects* in late 1926.

155. BP Box 90, HB to Hoffman Nickerson, 11 Nov. 1926. For a discussion

of the entire episode see Smith, *H. G. Wells*, pp. 255–59. See also Speaight, *Hilaire Belloc*, pp. 397–406, and Wilson, *Hilaire Belloc*, pp. 297–302.

156. BP Box 94, HB to Lady Frances Phipps, 19 June 1939.

157. HB to Mrs. Reginald Balfour, n.d., ca. 1939 in Belloc, *Letters*, p. 206.

158. BP Box 61, A. M. S. Methuen royalty statement, 30 June 1931 to 31 Dec. 1931, showed sales for the *History* totaled as follows: Vol. 1, 24; Vol. 2, 20; Vol. 3, 34; Vol. 4, 989.

159. BP Box 102, Cassell & Co. royalty statement of 30 Apr. 1940: *Cromwell*, total sales 16,139 copies; *The Last Rally*, 1,550 copies sold in less than six months; *Milton*, total sales 6,509 copies; *Napoleon* total U.K. and U.S.A. sales combined, 19,435 copies; republication of *Richelieu*, 1,024 copies; and *Wolsey*, total sales 19,022 copies.

160. *TLS*, 23 July 1925, p. 490. See also ChP 8.323, GMT to WSC, 16 July 1933, and 8.324, GMT to WSC, 20 Sept. 1933, for G. M. Trevelyan's fears over the need to counter the influence of "neo-Catholic propaganda against the essential truth of English history," a clear reference to Belloc and his work.

161. BP Box 90, HB to Bonnie Nickerson, 16 Oct. 1940.

162. BP Box 94, HB to Lady Frances Phipps, 10 Mar. 1936.

163. BP Box 38, HB to Katherine Asquith, 29 Jan. 1941.

164. BP Box 94, HB to Lady Frances Phipps, n.d., ca. 1938–39, and Box 90, HB to Bonnie Nickerson, 16 Oct. 1940.

165. See, e.g., Cannadine, "British History," p. 190.

166. Wells, *Mr. Belloc Objects*, p. vi.

167. BP Box 61, HB to Charles Goodwin, 6 Nov. 1908.

168. Rowse, *Portraits and Views*, pp. 79 and 85.

169. See Speaight, *Hilaire Belloc*, p. 483.

170. See Cole, *The Life of G. D. H. Cole*, pp. 52–53, 136–37; Glass, *Responsible Society*, pp. 21–22, 26–28; and Holton, *British Syndicalism*, pp. 28, 137–38, 182.

171. FP 53.27–28, HB to Fisher, 4 July 1906.

CHAPTER TWO

1. *DBW*, 7 July 1891. Sidney and Beatrice met in 1890 and were married in 1892.

2. *DBW*, 22 May 1900.

3. For the last two incarnations see respectively Hollander, *Political Pilgrims*, and Fremantle, *This Little Band of Prophets*.

4. McBriar, *Fabian Socialism*, p. 347.

5. Radice, *Beatrice and Sidney Webb*. One of the few recent works that carefully examines the crucial relationship between the Webbs as political activists and as historians is Kidd, "Historians or Polemicists?," pp. 400–417.

6. Gertrude Himmelfarb is a significant exception. See her short but trenchant interpretive essay "The Intellectual in Politics," pp. 3–11.

7. *DBW*, 21 May 1894.

8. PP VI.10, 11, 12. See also Beatrice to Sidney, (?)24 Oct. 1890, and Sidney to Beatrice, 29 Oct. 1890, in N. MacKenzie, *Letters of Sidney and Beatrice Webb*, 1:225, 228.

9. She also lectured at the Working Men's College on such topics as the "Economic History of Society in England." See PP VII.3.

10. For a discussion of Sidney Webb's early Comteanism see Wolfe, *From Radicalism to Socialism*, pp. 181–214; S. and B. Webb, *Methods of Social Study*, p. 105.

11. Besant, Bland, Clarke, Olivier, Shaw, Wallas, and S. Webb, *Fabian Essays in Socialism*, p. 29.

12. PP VI.10, "The Rise and Fall of Feudalism," p. 3.

13. S. and B. Webb, *Methods of Social Study*, p. 16.

14. *DBW*, 18 Oct. 1895.

15. *DBW*, 20 June 1894. See also 1 May 1897.

16. *DBW*, 31 Jan. 1900. See also 8 Oct. 1894.

17. *DBW*, 5 Mar. 1927.

18. *DBW*, 24 Apr. 1901.

19. *DBW*, 15 Nov. 1935.

20. Wolfe, *From Radicalism to Socialism*, pp. 211–14.

21. *DBW*, 10 Nov. 1902.

22. Besant et al., *Fabian Essays in Socialism*, pp. 46–47.

23. S. and B. Webb, *Methods of Social Study*, p. 251.

24. Himmelfarb, "The Intellectual in Politics," p. 3.

25. Quoted in Wolfe, *From Radicalism to Socialism*, p. 220; see S. and B. Webb, *Constitution for the Socialist Commonwealth*, pp. 97–356.

26. *DBW*, 14 Aug. 1896.

27. Sidney to Beatrice, 31 Jan. 1921, N. MacKenzie, *Letters of Sidney and Beatrice Webb*, 3:147.

28. *DBW*, 4 Jan. 1929.

29. B. Webb, *Our Partnership*, p. 15.

30. PP V.1, Box 1, Macmillan & Co. to S. Webb, 5 Oct. 1893.

31. PP V.1, Box 1, G. N. Putnam to S. Webb, 20 Oct. 1893.

32. See, e.g., *DBW*, 2 Dec. 1924.

33. *DBW*, 2 Jan. 1928.

34. *DBW*, 25 Dec. 1919.

35. *DBW*, 2 Oct. 1926.

36. GW 1/38.59, S. Webb to Wallas, 23 July 1908.

37. *DBW*, 14 Feb. 1927 and 28 Mar. 1929; Longman Archives, Part I.70.

38. See, e.g., Sidney to Beatrice, 25 Apr. 1928, and Beatrice to J. L. Hammond, 15 July 1927, N. MacKenzie, *Letters of Sidney and Beatrice Webb*, 3:298, 290, respectively. See also B. Webb, *Our Partnership*, p. 153.

39. OBP 1721, S. Webb to Browning, 19 Feb. 1897.

40. *DBW*, 20 Aug. 1900, 25 Dec. 1895, and 14 Oct. 1905.

41. See "The Art of Note-taking," Appendix C, in B. Webb, *My Apprenticeship*, pp. 412–19, esp. 418.

42. For the most extended example of this see S. and B. Webb, *Methods of Social Study*, pp. 1–17.

43. *DBW*, 10 Nov. 1902.

44. B. Webb, *Our Partnership*, p. 155. An almost identical quote can be found in "The Art of Note-taking," Appendix C, in B. Webb, *My Apprenticeship*, p. 413.

45. This essay on "The Art of Note-taking" was later reproduced with only a

handful of changes as Chapter 4 in S. and B. Webb, *Methods of Social Study*, pp. 83–97. See F. W. Galton, "Investigating with the Webbs," in Cole, *The Webbs and Their Work*, pp. 29–37, for a third-party corroboration of their preoccupation.

46. B. Webb, "The Art of Note-taking," in B. Webb, *My Apprenticeship*, pp. 412–19.

47. Himmelfarb, "The Intellectual in Politics," p. 6.

48. B. Webb, "The Art of Note-taking," in B. Webb, *My Apprenticeship*, p. 415.

49. See *DBW*, 10 Nov. 1902 and 24 Apr. 1901; B. Webb, *Our Partnership*, p. 155.

50. *EconHR* 3 no. 3 (Apr. 1932): 435–37.

51. J. H. Clapham's review of Volumes 8 and 9 of *English Local Government* in *EHR* 45 no. 180 (Oct. 1930): 660–62. For another laudatory review by Clapham see *EHR* 39 no. 154 (Apr. 1929): 288–92.

52. *EHR* 25 no. 98 (Apr. 1910): 353–64. The Webbs included a disclaimer in Volume 1 of *English Local Government* that let them off the hook. "We have forgone any attempt to produce a work of literature, by burdening our volume with footnotes and our text with actual quotations. We can only hope that the student, bent on further research of his own, will welcome that which the general reader may resent" (S. and B. Webb, *The Parish and the County*, p. xiii). Amazingly enough, some of the reviewers of *ELG* insisted on seeing something else there. The *Standard* found it "a sort of epic, not wanting in elements of adventure, and even tragedy." *Time and Tide* described the writing as "at once mellow and vivid," and the *Daily News* praised the authors' "literary skill." See press clippings in PP V.2.

53. By 1910 the *History*'s editors were A. W. Ward, G. W. Prothero, and Stanley Leathes.

54. *DBW*, 30 Mar. 1926. See also B. Webb, *Our Partnership*, p. 99.

55. *DBW*, 1 Mar. 1896.

56. *DBW*, 28 Apr. 1932, S. Webb, *Socialism in England*, p. 78.

57. Sidney to Beatrice, 11 Oct. 1890, N. MacKenzie, *Letters of Sidney and Beatrice Webb*, 1:208.

58. S. and B. Webb, *The Last Hundred Years*, 1:vii.

59. See B. Webb, *Our Partnership*, pp. 151 and 316.

60. *DBW*, 19 July 1907.

61. GW 2/3.35.40 from Wallas's review of the second and third volumes of *ELG* in *EconJ* (June 1908): 277.

62. For a provocative discussion of public science during this period see Turner, "Public Science in Britain," pp. 589–608.

63. *DBW*, 24 Sept. 1919.

64. *DBW*, 10 July 1894.

65. B. Webb, "What I Believe," *Nation* 132 (3 June 1931): 603–6.

66. At times the events of history seemed simply convenient forage for immutable, preconceived theories. Beatrice once wrote in her journal of a point she intended to make in an article, "It is absolutely necessary that I should get a proof from history" (quoted in Wrigley, "The Webbs," p. 55).

67. S. and B. Webb, *Methods of Social Study*, pp. 255–57.

68. B. Webb, "VI. Science, Religion and Politics," *St. Martin's Review* (Mar. 1929): 135–38.

69. Tout, *Chapters in the Administrative History of Medieval England*, 1:4–5.

70. Ibid., p. 27.

71. See Himmelfarb, *Poverty and Compassion*, pp. 358–63.

72. *DBW*, 1 Dec. 1892, quoted in J. MacKenzie, *Victorian Courtship*, p. 106.

73. Shaw to S. Webb, probably autumn 1900, quoted in Searle, *Quest for National Efficiency*, p. 126.

74. *DBW*, 10 Feb. 1908.

75. Sidney to Beatrice, 21 Feb. 1908, N. MacKenzie, *Letters of Sidney and Beatrice Webb*, 2:285.

76. PP II.4d, Churchill to S. Webb, 6 July 1908.

77. See Gilbert, "Churchill versus the Webbs," p. 856.

78. *DBW*, 20 Dec. 1909.

79. *DBW*, 18 June 1909.

80. *DBW*, 25 Dec. 1912.

81. PP VI.10, "Rise and Fall of Feudalism," pp. 27–31 and 36–37.

82. Ibid., p. 24; S. Webb, *Towards Social Democracy?*, p. 28.

83. PP.VI.10, "Rise and Fall of Feudalism," pp. 37 and 20.

84. PP VI.12, "The Reformation," pp. 42–48. This agrees in many respects with the modern analysis by Keith Thomas in his *Religion and the Decline of Magic*.

85. PP VI.12, "The Reformation," pp. 22, 60, and 62.

86. Besant et al., *Fabian Essays in Socialism*, p. xxi.

87. S. and B. Webb, *History of Trade Unionism* (1920), pp. viii–ix. The Webbs took the parallel so far as to claim that trade unionism's "universal aspiration" for the "enforcement of membership [i.e., the closed shop]—stands, in our opinion, on the same footing as the enforcement of citizenship [by the state]" (p. 296).

88. Ibid., pp. 66–71, 466–71.

89. Ibid., pp. 196–220.

90. S. and B. Webb, *History of Trade Unionism* (1894), p. 215. See Beatrice's discussion of the "Fabian Junta" in *Our Partnership*, pp. 37–40.

91. S. and B. Webb, *History of Trade Unionism* (1920), pp. 293 and 635.

92. Much of A. E. Musson's *British Trade Unions* is devoted to a critique of the Webbs' conclusions about the history of British trade unionism. Clegg, Fox, and Thompson, *History of British Trade Unions*, follow the Webb model closely. See also Musson, "The Webbs and Their Phasing of Trade-Union Development," and Allen, "Methodological Criticism of the Webbs as Trade Union Historians."

93. S. and B. Webb, *History of Trade Unionism* (1920), pp. 375 and 420.

94. *DBW*, 24 and 30 Dec. 1892 and 10 Mar. 1893.

95. *DBW*, 10 Mar. 1893.

96. The Fabian Society, "To Your Tents, Oh Israel!," *Fortnightly Review* 60 (Nov. 1893): 569–89.

97. DBW, 17 Sept. 1893. In the typescript of her diary the entry for this date reads, "The first fortnight alone with Rosie—we spent finishing the 5th chapter of our book." On page 36 in *Our Partnership*, however, Beatrice mistranscribes "5th" as "sixth."

98. S. and B. Webb, *History of Trade Unionism* (1894), p. 282; ibid. (1920), p. 297.

99. Ibid. (1920), pp. 338–39. In the 1894 edition (p. 276) the rendering was a little different.

100. Ibid. (1894), p. 360; ibid. (1920), p. 374.

101. *DBW*, 16 Sept. 1896.

102. S. and B. Webb, *History of Trade Unionism* (1920), pp. 706–7.

103. Besant et al., *Fabian Essays in Socialism*, pp. xxii–xxiii.

104. S. and B. Webb, *History of Trade Unionism* (1920), pp. 710–13.

105. B. Webb, *Our Partnership*, p. 149.

106. Ibid., pp. 149–50.

107. Ibid., p. 152.

108. Ibid., pp. 150–52.

109. Ibid., p. 151. Modern scholarship calls into question such sweeping conclusions about the eighteenth-century retreat of the central government. See, e.g., Brewer, *Sinews of Power*.

110. S. and B. Webb, *The Parish and the County*, pp. vi–vii.

111. *DBW*, [?] June 1902.

112. B. Webb, *Our Partnership*, p. 152.

113. S. and B. Webb, *The Parish and the County*, p. 40.

114. Ibid., p. 602.

115. Ibid., pp. 474–556.

116. Ibid., p. 573.

117. Ibid., pp. 360–72.

118. Ibid., p. 372.

119. Ibid., p. 378.

120. Ibid., pp. 553–56.

121. *DBW*, 3 Nov. 1903 (emphasis added).

122. S. and B. Webb, *The Manor and the Borough*, 1:5.

123. Ibid., pp. 125–26.

124. S. and B. Webb, *Statutory Authorities*, pp. 360–61.

125. Ibid., p. 397.

126. Ibid., pp. 397–413.

127. B. Webb, *Our Partnership*, p. 152.

128. S. and B. Webb, *Statutory Authorities*, p. 454.

129. Ibid., p. 457. In *The Last Hundred Years*, 1:218–23, the Webbs indulged in mild criticism of "Bureaucratic Formalism" but still concluded that it was in the community's best interest to have its "layman's government . . . gradually mitigated by professional advice."

130. See S. and B. Webb, *Constitution for the Socialist Commonwealth*, p. 204.

131. The Webbs' approving portrayal of the civil service functionary resembles nothing so much as Hegel's disinterested bureaucrat.

132. For a contrary view of the Webbs and liberalism see Crowley, *The Self, the Individual, and the Community*, esp. pp. 1–31. Crowley argues elegantly, though unpersuasively, that the Webbs were thorough liberals, placing them in "intimately related streams of liberal thought stretching back to the seventeenth century" (p. 13).

133. S. and B. Webb, *Industrial Democracy*, p. 843.

134. Alan J. Kidd in "Historians or Polemicists?" presents an excellent analysis of the circumstances, political and otherwise, that shaped the writing of the three volumes of *English Poor Law History*.

135. Sidney to Beatrice, 10 Dec. 1925, N. MacKenzie, *Letters of Sidney and Beatrice Webb*, 3:255.

136. That the two parts of *The Last Hundred Years*, both published in 1929, became Volumes 8 and 9 of *ELG*, while the Edwardian work *English Poor Law Policy*, published in 1910, became volume 10, demonstrates how the Webbs relied on old research for the new books and how little altered were their conclusions even after two decades.

137. Sidney to Beatrice, 25 Apr. 1928, N. MacKenzie, *Letters of Sidney and Beatrice Webb*, 3:298.

138. *DBW*, 2 Aug. 1927.

139. *DBW*, 4 Jan. 1929.

140. S. and B. Webb, *The Last Hundred Years*, 2:985.

141. Ibid., 1:viii.

142. See, e.g., reviews of *The History of Trade Unionism* in the *Manchester Guardian*, 1 May 1894, and the *Liverpool Daily Post*, 23 May 1894. See also reviews of *The Parish and the County* by R. S. Rait in *TLS*, 2 Nov. 1906, p. 366, and of the three volumes of *English Poor Law History* by E. Lipson in *EconHR* 3,3 (Apr. 1932): 435–37.

143. *DBW*, 12 May 1939.

144. Leonard Woolf, "Political Thought and the Webbs," in Cole, *The Webbs and Their Work*, p. 258.

145. PP V.2 (collection of *ELG* press notices).

146. D. Marshall, "Revisions in Economic History: The Poor Law," *EconHR* 1st ser., 7 (1937–38): 39. E. T. Devine wrote in 1930 that the Webbs' *English Poor Law History* was "not one history among others. It is *the* history" (quoted in Kidd, "Historians or Polemicists?," p. 400).

CHAPTER THREE

1. HP 13.75–76, LBH to JLH, 13 May 1924.

2. Gilbert Murray, "J. L. Hammond: An Appreciation," *Manchester Guardian*, 9 Apr. 1949.

3. For only one among scores of examples see Harold Cox, "The House of Longman," *Edinburgh Review* 240 (Oct. 1924): 239.

4. B. Webb to JLH, 21 Sept. 1926, in N. MacKenzie, *Letters of Sidney and Beatrice Webb*, 3:270.

5. Thompson, *Making of the English Working Class*, p. 592.

6. Quennell, *Marble Foot*, p. 95.

7. B. Webb to JLH, 21 Sept. 1926, in N. MacKenzie, *Letters of Sidney and Beatrice Webb*, 3:270; HP 19.9–11, S. Webb to LBH, 8 Feb. 1923.

8. HP 9.191, LBH to JLH, 11 June 1917.

9. *New Leader*, 4 Mar. 1927, review of the new cheap edition of *The Village Labourer*.

10. HP 20.99, W. Bucknall to JLH, 2 Oct. 1927.

11. HP 18.45, J. M. Cornford to JLH, 26 Jan. 1921.

12. *History* 9 (Oct. 1924): 256. Perhaps Lawrence's 1945 admission to R. H. Tawney of years of strong prejudice against the Webbs because of differences over the Boer War was simply the rationalization of a much more nebulous and fundamental divergence in values and temperament (RHT 24.2, JLH to Tawney, 24 Apr. 1945).

13. For a detailed biographical portrait of the Hammonds based on private papers see Clarke, *Liberals and Social Democrats*. For a brief sketch based on published sources see Winkler, "J. L. Hammond," pp. 95–119. For a personal recollection see Tawney, "J. L. Hammond," pp. 267–94.

14. By 1907 Lawrence was to refer to Murray as "the friend whose good opinion I value more than that of anybody else outside this house" (quoted in Wilson, *Gilbert Murray*, p. 179).

15. J. L. Hammond, "A Liberal View of Education," in Belloc, Hammond, Hirst, Macdonnell, Phillimore, and Simon, *Essays in Liberalism*, p. 176.

16. J. L. Hammond, Hirst, and Murray, *Liberalism and the Empire*, pp. 3, 161.

17. Arnold J. Toynbee provides a brief, sympathetic description of the Hammonds' spartan country existence in *Acquaintances*, pp. 95–107.

18. HP 9.93, LBH to JLH, 13 Mar. 1917.

19. HP 9.35, LBH to JLH, 24 Jan. 1917.

20. JLH to Gilbert Murray, 9 Nov. 1911, quoted in Clarke, *Liberals and Social Democrats*, p. 154.

21. Toynbee, *Acquaintances*, p. 99.

22. See HP 15.201–3, JLH to A. Montague Bradley (president of the Dover Liberal Association), 7 Nov. 1903. See also Buxton, Fairfax-Cholmeley, Hammond, Hirst, Hobhouse, Hobson, Masterman, Morgan, and Nash, *Towards a Social Policy*.

23. GM 140.65, JLH to Murray, 27 Aug. 1907.

24. J. L. Hammond (unsigned), "The Crisis in Liberal Policy," *Nation*, 6 Apr. 1907, pp. 213–14. Here I am relying on P. F. Clarke's careful evaluation of individual authorship of anonymous *Nation* articles for 1907–10. See the bibliographical notes in *Liberals and Social Democrats*, pp. 309–10. See also GM 140.105, JLH to Murray, 16 Nov. 1912 and GM 140.110–11, JLH to Murray, 7 Jan. 1913.

25. GM 140.128, JLH to Murray, 2 Nov. 1913 (emphasis added).

26. HP 30.33, Murray to JLH, 31 Jan. 1907.

27. *TLS*, 19 June 1903, p. 190.

28. Hammond, "A Liberal View of Education," in Belloc et al., *Essays in Liberalism*, p. 215.

29. GOT 100, GMT to GOT, 14 Dec. 1908.

30. J. L. Hammond, "History and Citizenship: Education for Citizenship—III," *Journal of Education*, Mar. 1939, p. 148.

31. HP 16.152–53, Murray to JLH, 7 Nov. 1911, and 16.121, A. M. D. Hughes to JLH, 25 Oct. 1911.

32. Hammond, "History and Citizenship," p. 148.

33. GM 140.36–37, JLH to Murray, 12 Oct. 1903.

34. J. L. Hammond, *Charles James Fox*, pp. v, 27, and 274.

35. Ibid., pp. 97 and 25.

36. Ibid., pp. 32–33 and 89.

37. Ibid., p. 33.

38. See, for example, *TLS*, 19 June 1903, p. 190.

39. GM 140.84–85, JLH to Murray, 24 Jan. 1911.

40. J. L. and B. Hammond, *Village Labourer*, p. vii.

41. Ibid., pp. 33–34.

42. Ibid., pp. 7, 16, 19 for direct references to the Webbs' work.

43. Ibid., pp. 35–36.

44. Ibid., pp. 328–30.

45. HP 16.172, Charles Trevelyan to JLH, 29 Nov. 1911.

46. Graham Wallas's review of *The Village Labourer* in the *Nation*, 11 Nov. 1911, pp. 248–50.

47. HP 16.198, Josiah Wedgwood to JLH, 27 Dec. 1911.

48. HP 16.278, A. F. Zimmern to JLH, 25 Sept. 1912.

49. HP 16.121, A. M. D. Hughes to JLH, 25 Oct. 1911.

50. J. L. and Barbara Hammond, " 'A Socialist Fantasy': A Reply," *Quarterly Review* 252 (Apr. 1929): 290. In an otherwise unflattering review of *The Village Labourer*, J. H. Clapham referred to the Hammonds' account of the 1830 laborers' revolt as their "main contribution to history" (*EconJ* 22 [1912]: 252).

51. The Hammonds' use of the archives was always painstakingly scrupulous, as Barbara demonstrated while going over proofs of *The Town Labourer* in 1917. See HP 9.75–76, LBH to JLH, 20 Feb. 1917.

52. Longmans was well pleased with 1,082 copies sold by April 1912. Sales of another 1,200 over the next year necessitated a second printing, followed by a new edition in 1913 (HP 16.230b, Longmans to JLH, 22 Apr. 1912; Longman Archives, Sales Ledger, Part I 68). There were eventually ten reprints of four editions with a total printing of 66,500. See Hartwell, *The Industrial Revolution and Economic Growth*, p. 377.

53. *EconJ* 22 (1912): 248–50.

54. Ibid., p. 248.

55. J. H. Clapham, "Economic History as a Discipline," in Stern, *Varieties of History*, p. 309. The essay originally appeared in the *Encyclopedia of the Social Sciences* (1932).

56. Barbara Hammond, "Urban Death-Rates in the Early Nineteenth Century," *Economic History* (supplement to *Economic Journal*) 1 no. 3 (Jan. 1926): 419.

57. Clapham, "Economic History as a Discipline," in Stern, *Varieties of History*, p. 312.

58. J. H. Clapham, *EconJ* 22 (1912): 250, 252–53, 251, and 255. For a modern version of this argument against the Hammonds see Coleman, *History and the Economic Past*, esp. pp. 73–77 and 81.

59. J. L. and B. Hammond, *The Village Labourer*, new preface to the 1913 edition, p. ix. This, of course, is a restatement of the quote from the text (pp. 26–27) used by Clapham in his 1912 *Economic Journal* article.

60. Ibid., p. x.

61. LBH to JLH, 7 Dec. 1916, quoted in Clarke, *Liberals and Social Democrats*, p. 185.

62. See J. L. Hammond, "A Lesson from the French War," *Nation*, 8 Aug. 1914, p. 698; "Workmen and the Army," *Nation*, 5 Sept. 1914, p. 809; and "Agricultural Labor [*sic*] and the Crisis," *Nation*, 24 Apr. 1915, p. 112. See also Hammond's memorandum "Reconstruction" (1917) in Johnson, *Land Fit for Heroes*, pp. 57–58.

63. GW 1/56.126v–127, LBH to Wallas, 29 Oct. 1915. Barbara wondered if "after the war will there be any publishers or any books?"

64. HP 17.58–61, G. Wallas to JLH, 4 Dec. 1915.

65. J. L. and B. Hammond, *Town Labourer*, p. vii.

66. GW 1/60.18–19, LBH to Wallas, 6 Mar. 1917.

67. HP 17.58–61, G. Wallas to JLH, 4 Dec. 1915. Graham Wallas suggested the division as well as the titles *The Town Workman* and *Trade Disputes, 1800–1825*, with Chapters 9–13 and 17–19 of the original text moved to the latter book (GW 1/56.143–144v, LBH to Wallas, 6 Dec. 1915).

68. Gilbert Murray predicted in July 1917 that *The Town Labourer* "ought to have a great influence. It is just the right moment for it" (HP 30.72, Murray to JLH, 2 July 1917, HP 17.100, Longmans to JLH, 1 June 1917). In an effort to broaden the volume's influence, Lawrence lobbied hard for a reduction in price from 12/6 to 10/6, and the W.E.A. requested an even cheaper edition (HP 17.124 and 17.127, A. C. Stewart to JLH, 24 and 30 July 1917).

69. J. L. and B. Hammond, *Town Labourer*, pp. vii–viii.

70. Ibid., pp. 210 and 114–15.

71. See Morgan, *John, Viscount Morley*, pp. 81–82, and A. E. Zimmern's review of *The Town Labourer* in *TLS*, 19 July 1917, p. 339. (In *Liberals and Social Democrats*, p. 190, P. F. Clarke attributes the unsigned review to R. H. Tawney, but records at *The Times* archives confirm that Zimmern was the author.) See HP 17.115, Hilaire Belloc to JLH, 5 July 1917. Discussing postwar reconstruction in 1918, Lawrence applauded the incisiveness of Belloc's analysis. "Mr. Belloc, when attacking the Insurance Act, with its frank discrimination between rich and poor, applied to a society that was governed on this general principle a phrase that has become classical. He called it 'the servile State.' The book he published with this title marks an important stage in the discrediting of the ideal of a beneficent State, controlling the lives of its citizens and securing them a return against unemployment and sickness" ("Jason" [J. L. Hammond], *Past and Future*, p. 108). A year later the Hammonds were to cite Belloc's *Servile State* in their own *Skilled Labourer*, recording their agreement with Belloc's conclusion that "the disastrous form that the new society took was determined by the moral atmosphere of the time" (J. L. and B. Hammond, *Skilled Labourer*, pp. 2–3 n. 3).

72. GM 140.105, JLH to Murray, 16 Nov. 1912. See also GM 140.127, JLH to Murray, 21 Nov. 1913.

73. See Clarke, *Liberals and Social Democrats*, p. 191. Hammond was to write in 1918 of "Mr. G. D. H. Cole, who has brought a mind of exceptional power to the discussion of the difficulties that beset any attempt to recast the Industrial State" ("Jason," *Past and Future*, p. 109).

74. LBH to JLH, 13 Nov. 1918, quoted in Clarke, *Liberals and Social Democrats*, p. 201.

75. HP 11.243, LBH to JLH, 10 Apr. 1919.

76. GM 140.217, JLH to Murray, 7 Nov. 1922.

77. HP 18.190, H. N. Brailsford to JLH, 18 July 1922.

78. Scott, *Political Diaries*, p. 481; GM 549.77–78, JLH to Lady Murray, 17 July 1924.

79. JLH to G. Murray, 16 May 1921, quoted in Clarke, *Liberals and Social Democrats*, p. 214.

80. LBH to Lady Murray, 10 June 1924, quoted ibid., p. 239.

81. See, for example, HP 14.92, LBH to JLH, 22 Aug. 1927, where Barbara refers to a certain Miss Fincke as "a rum un, Labour sympathies etc."

82. HP 21.185, Leonard Woolf to JLH, 19 Dec. 1928.

83. HP 17.85, Wallas to LBH, 4 Mar. 1917.

84. See, e.g., *EHR* 35 (Oct. 1920): 624–25.

85. HP 18.166, Ernest Barker to JLH, 2 May 1922.

86. HP 18.167–81, 3 May to 21 June 1922.

87. HP 12.145, Arnold J. Toynbee to JLH, 30 May 1922.

88. HP 12.173–76, LBH to JLH, 10 June 1922.

89. HP 12.177 and 176, LBH to JLH, 11 and 10 June 1922.

90. HP 12.183, LBH to JLH, 13 June 1922.

91. On this trend see Kadish, *Historians, Economists, and Economic History*.

92. HP 12.183, LBH to JLH, 13 June 1922.

93. J. L. and B. Hammond, *Lord Shaftesbury*, p. 261. Lawrence was invited to apply for a chair in history at Manchester University in 1930. Aged fifty-eight at the time, he politely refused. Both Lawrence and Barbara received honorary doctorates from Oxford in 1933.

94. HP 13.58, LBH to JLH, 2 Sept. 1923. D. L. Murray's review in the *TLS* (16 Aug. 1923) noted that Shaftesbury only just managed to avoid being "too glacial a hero."

95. See, e.g., HP 19.174, George Jackson to JLH, 13 Oct. 1923. See also Elie Halévy's review in *History* 9 (Oct. 1924): 255–57, where he admonishes the Hammonds for presenting, "from beginning to end, a caricature of Evangelicalism."

96. HP 13.68, LBH to JLH, 6 Sept. 1923.

97. HP 19.96, H. J. Laski to JLH, 20 Aug. 1923. "They obviously dislike him," said a respectful Laski, "and yet with perfect art they make you see his point of view" (Laski to Holmes, 29 Aug. 1923, in Howe, *Holmes-Laski Letters*, p. 532).

98. The year of *Lord Shaftesbury*'s appearance Lawrence wrote, "If we compare British politics with the politics of Continental countries in respect to tolerance, to the atmosphere of social conflict, to the readiness to give and take between class interest and opinion, to the willingness to face fiscal realities and painful duties, we shall conclude that the preservation of this system has advantages of which it is easy to lose sight in our impatience with its failures" (J. L. Hammond's review of A. G. Gardiner's *The Life of Sir William Harcourt* in the *New Republic*, 27 June 1923, p. 129).

99. J. L. and B. Hammond, *Lord Shaftesbury*, p. 268.

100. Ibid., p. 274.

101. J. L. Hammond, "New Light on the Industrial Revolution," *Contemporary Review* 131 (June 1927): 745.

102. J. L. and B. Hammond, *Lord Shaftesbury*, p. 276.

103. Still, by their account, the process was slow and painful. Thus the Hammonds were unwilling fully to accept G. M. Trevelyan's overly optimistic account of the Victorian Age as presented in his *British History in the Nineteenth Century*. See Lawrence's review, "The Bulwark of Parliament," *TLS*, 12 July 1923, pp. 461–62.

104. HP 19.13, JLH to Methuen & Co., 10 Feb. 1923. The book was modified to suit Sidney Webb's request for a popular account of the Industrial Revolution for the Fabian Society.

105. HP 20.173a and b, R. C. K. Ensor to JLH, 2 Dec. 1925.

106. J. L. and B. Hammond, *Rise of Modern Industry*, pp. 247 and 253.

107. Ibid., p. vii.

108. Clapham, *Economic History of Modern Britain*, 1:vii.

109. Griffith's conclusions were supplemented by Mabel Craven Buer's *Health, Wealth and Population in the Early Days of the Industrial Revolution* and Arthur Redford's *Labour Migration in England*. See also J. L. and B. Hammond, *Town Labourer*, p. 14.

110. W. H. Hutt, "The Factory System of the Early 19th Century," *Economica* 16 (Mar. 1926): 78–93.

111. A. A. W. Ramsay, "A Socialist Fantasy," *Quarterly Review* 252 (Jan. 1929). To follow the subsequent Hammond-Ramsay exchange see the Hammond correspondence of 5 Jan.–12 June 1929, HP 22.2–194 or Clarke, *Liberals and Social Democrats*, pp. 250–52.

112. J. L. and Barbara Hammond, "'A Socialist Fantasy': A Reply," *Quarterly Review* 252 (Apr. 1929): 291 (emphasis added).

113. Ibid.

114. HP 18.45, J. M. Cornford to JLH, 26 Jan. 1921.

115. HP 20.202, E. D. Bradley to JLH, 3 Feb. 1926. Wells's book is cited on page 12, note 1, of *Rise of Modern Industry*.

116. Thus by late 1929, he could be found insisting that his publisher advertise *The Rise of Modern Industry* in the new *Economic History Review* (HP 22.218, Methuen & Co. to JLH, 16 Nov. 1929). Eventually he was to become an occasional reviewer for the journal.

117. HP 22.2–3, G. M. Trevelyan to JLH, 5 Jan. 1929.

118. HP 5.21, JLH to LBH, 7 Aug. 1927.

119. HP 13.99, LBH to JLH, 8 Aug. 1924.

120. J. L. Hammond, "The Industrial Revolution and Discontent," *EconHR* 2 (Jan. 1930): 227.

121. *EHR* 46 (Oct. 1931): 657.

122. HP 22.225, T. S. Ashton to JLH, n.d. but probably July 1929.

123. Parker, *English Historical Tradition*, pp. 132–36.

124. HP 21.25, L. T. Hobhouse to LBH, 25 May 1927.

125. Clapham, *Economic History of Modern Britain*, 1:315–16.

126. The Hammonds used this term in reference to Ramsay's charges in their April 1929 retort "'A Socialist Fantasy': A Reply," p. 290.

127. HP 23.235, Arnold J. Toynbee to JLH, 29 Oct. 1931.

128. J. L. and B. Hammond, *Age of the Chartists*, p. 3.

129. HP 23.134, G. M. Trevelyan to JLH, 2 Nov. 1930.

130. J. L. and B. Hammond, *Age of the Chartists*, chaps. 8 and 9, pp. 106–43.

131. Ibid., pp. 359 and 349.

132. The Hammonds did not help to alter this critical tunnel vision when in 1934 they offered an abridged version of *The Age of the Chartists* called *The Bleak Age*, the suggestive new title clinching the reader's interpretation beforehand.

133. *EHR* 46 (Oct. 1931): 659.

134. A. H. Dodd's review of *The Age of the Chartists* in *History* 17 (Apr. 1932): 82; Proof of G. D. H. Cole's review, Cole Papers, A1/29/21.

135. J. L. Hammond, *Gladstone and the Irish Nation*, p. 710.

136. Ibid., pp. 532–54.

137. Laski to Holmes, 13 Oct. 1923, in Howe, *Holmes-Laski Letters*, p. 550.

138. See Thompson, *Making of the English Working Class*, esp. pp. 195–97, 207–8, 290, 332, 490, 575–76, 578, 582, and 591–94.

Chapter Four

1. Collini, *Public Moralists*, pp. 56–59, 208–9, 218–28.

2. Nicolson, *Diaries and Letters*, 2:199, diary entry of 16 Oct. 1941.

3. GOT 99, GMT to Parents, 18 June 1907.

4. GOT 103, GMT to Parents, 7 Oct. 1911.

5. Nicolson, *Diaries and Letters*, 2:329, diary entry of 10 Nov. 1943.

6. Longman Archives, Sales Ledger Part I.70.

7. Trevelyan's *English Social History* (1944) surpassed in popularity his *History of England*, selling nearly 400,000 by the end of 1949.

8. Quoted in Moorman, *Trevelyan*, p. 51. Sixteen years later, Trevelyan was still proclaiming, "I am *not* an academician" (RCT 14.80, GMT to RCT, 23 Jan. 1911).

9. *Independent Review* 1 no. 3 (Dec. 1903): 395–414. The original article made several specific references to Bury's views. It was greatly expanded and republished a decade later, with all mention of Bury expurgated, as "Clio, a Muse," in *Clio, a Muse and Other Essays Literary and Pedestrian*, pp. 1–55. The following quotations are from the 1913 redaction.

10. J. B. Bury, "The Science of History," in Stern, *Varieties of History*, p. 223; Wormell, *Sir John Seeley*, pp. 120–28. Goldstein, "J. B. Bury's Philosophy of History," pp. 896–919; Parker, *English Historical Tradition*, pp. 33–40, 83–101.

11. Trevelyan, "Autobiography of an Historian," in Trevelyan, *Autobiography*, p. 21.

12. Woolf, *Sowing*, p. 149 n, and 148–49.

13. Wells, *New Machiavelli*, pp. 236–37.

14. GMT to Russell, 23 May 1907, entire letter quoted in Russell, *Autobiography*, 1:301.

15. GW 1/29.110, GMT to Wallas, 13 Jan. 1903.

16. Quoted in Moorman, *Trevelyan*, pp. 116–17.

17. GMT to CPT, Aug. 1893, quoted ibid., p. 35.

18. GMT to CPT, 1893, quoted ibid., p. 30.

19. Moorman, *Trevelyan*, p. 40.

20. HP 16.152–53, Murray to JLH, 7 Nov. 1911; Buxton to JLH, 22 Sept. 1907, quoted in Clarke, *Liberals and Social Democrats*, p. 155.

21. GOT 93, GMT to Parents, n.d., ca. 1900.

22. GOT 94, GMT to GOT, 17 Nov. 1901.

23. Quoted in Holroyd, *Lytton Strachey*, 1:112.

24. GOT 94, GMT to Mother, 1 Dec. 1901. The letter continued, "He is worth leading, and I am getting very fond of him."

25. Quoted in Holroyd, *Lytton Strachey*, 2:262 n. 1.

26. See ibid., 2:301 n. 1, and p. 432 n. 1.

27. H. Trevelyan, *Public and Private*, p. 150.

28. Strachey, *Portraits in Miniature*, esp. p. 176.

29. Ibid., p. 203.

30. Holroyd, *Lytton Strachey*, 2:666. Virginia Woolf's amusement at his discomfiture would hardly have surprised Trevelyan, for he found her a "horrid woman" (Rowse, *Memories of Men and Women*, p. 129).

31. Trevelyan, "Clio, a Muse," p. 35.

32. Ibid., p. 19.

33. GMT to Strachey, 25 Nov. 1928, quoted in Holroyd, *Lytton Strachey*, 2:615.

34. GLD, L. Strachey to GLD, 26 May 1918.

35. GOT 104, GMT to Parents, 28 Oct. 1912.

36. Fitzsimons, "British Historiography of the Twentieth Century," p. 237.

37. Quoted in Rowse, *Memories of Men and Women*, p. 130.

38. GOT 101, GMT to Mother, 11 June 1909. One of the reasons he agreed to undertake the lectures was that he believed he recognized at the time the first stirrings of "a rebellion of the younger dons against what we know as 'Buryism' . . . it would be churlish and even wrong to refuse to help."

39. RCT 14.79, GMT to RCT, 24 May 1910.

40. See Moorman, *Trevelyan*, p. 115.

41. GOT 103, GMT to GOT, 24 June 1911.

42. Trevelyan wrote at the time that angering these people was what he had intended the essay to do (Moorman, *Trevelyan*, p. 118).

43. G. M. Trevelyan, "History and Literature," *History* n.s., 9 (July 1924): 86.

44. Ibid., pp. 86–87.

45. He stated that his purpose was to "help some unlearned people" to see his "vision of the evolution of English society and character and habit 'down the ages' " (quoted in Moorman, *Trevelyan*, p. 198).

46. Trevelyan, "History and Literature," p. 82.

47. For example, 94,479 copies of Strachey's *Queen Victoria* were sold between March 1921 and December 1939 (Chatto & Windus Archives, Sales Ledger 8.738, 8.741, 8.884, 9.62. 9.447 and 9.593).

48. GOT 111, GMT to Mother, 13 Dec. 1919.

49. FP 65.195, GMT to Fisher, 29 Jan. 1925.

50. GOT 116, GMT to Mother, 11 Jan. 1926.

51. Woolf, *Diary*, 5:333 (26 Oct. 1940) and 337 (5 Nov. 1940).

52. See Moorman, *Trevelyan*, p. 209.

53. GMT to Mary Trevelyan, (1924), quoted in Moorman, *Trevelyan*, p. 201, and in Plumb, *Making of an Historian*, 1:9. Counterbalancing this unflattering epigrammatic assessment is the well-known anecdote of Namier receiving his job offer at Manchester University in 1931 as a direct result of a favorable review of his *England in the Age of the American Revolution* by Trevelyan. To repay the debt, Namier claimed that in future he declined every opportunity to review Trevelyan's histories, books he was certain to have disliked. See Kenyon, *History Men*, pp. 257–58; Namier, *Lewis Namier*, p. 220; and Colley, *Lewis Namier*, pp. 12–13; Trevelyan, "Autobiography of an Historian," p. 40.

54. HP 21.89, GMT to LBH, 14 Feb. 1928.

55. His readiness to accept diverse types of historiography on their own terms was reiterated three years later in his review of Namier's *England in the Age of the American Revolution* (1930): "There are so many different ways in which things happen, or can be truly described as happening. Gibbon's is one, Carlyle's another, Macaulay's a third. Each is true, yet taken by itself each is false, for no one of them is the whole truth. In Mr. Namier's narrative things 'happen' in yet another new way—the Namier way. And it is one of the truths" (*Nation*, 15 Nov. 1930).

56. Trevelyan, "The Present Position of History," in *Clio, a Muse and Other Essays* (1930), p. 178. The Inaugural Lecture was delivered on 27 October 1927.

57. Ibid., pp. 195, 193 (emphasis added), 195.

58. A. F. Pollard, review of Trevelyan's new edition of *Clio, a Muse and Other Essays* in *TLS*, 26 June 1930, pp. 521–22 (emphasis added).

59. *TLS*, 25 Sept. 1930, p. 741–42.

60. See Cowling, *Religion and Public Doctrine*, 1:220–27.

61. Butterfield, *Whig Interpretation of History*, pp. 96–100, 30.

62. GOT 92, GMT to Parents, 1 Mar. 1899, GMT to Mother, 24 Oct. 1899; RCT 14.35, GMT to RCT, 2 Mar. 1899.

63. See RCT 13.96, GMT to Elizabeth Trevelyan, 23 Oct. 1901.

64. See Trevelyan, "Past and Future," in Masterman et al., *Heart of the Empire*, pp. 401–17.

65. *DBW*, 2 May 1904.

66. Trevelyan, "Autobiography of an Historian," p. 11; Coleman, *Myth, History and the Industrial Revolution*, pp. 24–26.

67. *DBW*, 14 Oct. 1905.

68. He was lecturing on "The Union and Freedom of Italy, 1796–1870" at the W.M.C. fully six months before his marriage. See Moorman, *Trevelyan*, p. 73.

69. GOT 98, GMT to Mother, 28 July 1906.

70. Trevelyan, "Autobiography of an Historian," pp. 31–32.

71. The Hammonds accompanied Trevelyan on some of the Italian walking tours during the preparation for Volume 3.

72. RCT, 14.68, GMT to RCT, 13 Apr. 1907; Trevelyan, *Garibaldi's Defence of the Roman Republic*, p. 23. *The Times* still found Trevelyan's style "unchaste in

places" (RCT 14.72, GMT to RCT, 1 Oct. 1909). Miss Sichel's review of *Garibaldi and the Thousand* in the *TLS*, 30 Sept. 1909, pp. 349–50, requested "a little chastening of his style. Garibaldi's story writes itself in purple patches, and needs no aid from without."

73. Trevelyan, *Garibaldi's Defence of the Roman Republic*, pp. 3–4.

74. RCT 14.68, GMT to RCT, 13 Apr. 1907.

75. Trevelyan, *Garibaldi's Defence of the Roman Republic*, p. 19.

76. GOT 98, GMT to GOT, 12 May 1906.

77. See Urban, *British Opinion and Policy*.

78. Trevelyan, *Garibaldi's Defence of the Roman Republic*, p. 6.

79. Ibid., pp. 101–5.

80. CPT Ex. 55, GMT to Mother, 25 May 1907.

81. Trevelyan, *Garibaldi's Defence of the Roman Republic*, p. 191.

82. Trevelyan, *Garibaldi and the Thousand*, p. 7.

83. GOT 100, GMT to GOT, n.d. [July 1908], 12 Dec. 1908, and 14 Dec. 1908.

84. Mack Smith, *Garibaldi*, pp. 182, 41, and 192–93.

85. Having just read Lord Cromer's history of modern Egypt, Trevelyan wrote, "His account of Gordon and Gordon's relation to the English people and government respectively might be quoted—whole sentences and paragraphs—about Garibaldi. The difference was that in Italy there was a job on the whole suitable for such a man, and not in Egypt" (GOT 100, GMT to Mother, 11 Nov. 1908). Such romantic notions about Gordon further help to account for his violent reaction to Strachey, whose cynical depiction of a mentally deranged Gordon in *Eminent Victorians* was the very antithesis of Trevelyan's noble Garibaldi. Strachey's reaction to the Garibaldi trilogy was none too flattering. By his reckoning, there was "much interest in it, but tiresomely told" (Strachey to Henry Lamb, 15 Feb. 1913, quoted in Holroyd, *Lytton Strachey*, 2:78).

86. Trevelyan, *Garibaldi and the Making of Italy*, p. 287.

87. GOT 98, GMT to GOT, 12 May 1906. At the same time G. O. Trevelyan was engaged in writing his multivolume history of the American Revolution so he readily understood the allusion.

88. Mack Smith, *Garibaldi*, pp. 123–35, 137, 151–70, and 178.

89. FP 59.87–90, GMT to Fisher, 18 Jan. 1909.

90. GOT 98, GMT to Mother, 28 July 1906.

91. GOT 98, GMT to Mother, 23 July 1906.

92. Trevelyan, *Garibaldi's Defence of the Roman Republic*, p. 82. Trevelyan also judged that although the ardor for the Mazzinian republic was less furious, forcible, and effective than that of France in 1793, "it was purer in its moral conception." This sounds much like his comparisons of the French with the English Revolution in *England under the Stuarts*, p. 196.

93. Mack Smith, *Garibaldi*, p. 89.

94. Churchill, *History of the English-Speaking Peoples*, 2:251.

95. W. Alison Phillips's review (unsigned), *TLS*, 26 Apr. 1907.

96. *TLS*, 26 Apr. 1907, p. 130. See also Miss Sichel's review (unsigned) of *Garibaldi and the Thousand*, *TLS*, 30 Sept. 1909, pp. 349–50, and Phillips's review (unsigned) of *Garibaldi and the Making of Italy*, *TLS*, 12 Oct. 1911, p. 380.

97. Gooch, *History and Historians*, p. 401.

98. Reviews of the Garibaldian trilogy in the *EHR*, all by William Miller: 22 (Oct. 1907): 816–17; 25 (Jan. 1910): 206; 27 (Jan. 1912): 173–75.

99. GOT 104, GMT to Parents, 28 Oct. 1912.

100. RCT 14.82, GMT to RCT, n.d. [1911], RCT 14.83, GMT to RCT, 4 Oct. 1911.

101. *EHR* 27 (Jan. 1912): 174.

102. GOT 109, GMT to Parents, 20 and 25 Mar. 1917, GMT to Mother, 8 Apr. 1917; Rowse, *Memories of Men and Women*, p. 108.

103. Trevelyan, *Garibaldi and the Thousand*, p. 27.

104. Letter to the editor, *History* n.s., 4 (Jan. 1920): 208.

105. GOT 112, GMT to Parents, 4 Feb. 1920. In 1920 668 copies distributed among the three books were sold (Longman Archives, Sales Ledger Part I.70).

106. Fussell, *The Great War and Modern Memory*.

107. Laski to Holmes, 14 Dec. 1920, in Howe, *Holmes-Laski Letters*, p. 299.

108. Longman Archives, Sales Ledger Part I.70. Only fifty-four, thirty-one, thirty-eight, nineteen, and three copies were sold in the second through the sixth years following publication.

109. See, e.g., the review of *Garibaldi and the Thousand* in the *Saturday Review* 109 (22 Jan. 1910): 114–15, or Bertrand Russell's otherwise mainly flattering critique of *Garibaldi's Defence of the Roman Republic* in the *Edinburgh Review* 205 (Apr. 1907): 489–507, where he judged that "some, who know only the Italy of to-day, may be inclined to question whether, after all, the achievement has been worth fighting for."

110. Trevelyan, *Historical Causes of the Present State of Affairs in Italy*, pp. 20, 18, 15.

111. HP 11, LBH to JLH, 10 Mar. 1919. In 1931, after years of outrages in fascist Italy, Trevelyan wrote, "I suppose the Romans were both more brutal and more artistic than the English. The combination has always disgusted me" (RCT 14.124, GMT to RCT, 30 May 1931).

112. For Trevelyan's opinion that "the times [were] just rife" for the appearance of Webster's interpretations, see CKW 1/5.61, GMT to Webster, 17 Aug. 1922.

113. See Cowling, *Religion and Public Doctrine*, 1:205–23; Parker, *English Historical Tradition*, pp. 104–17; and Wallace, *War and the Image of Germany*, pp. 58 - 73.

114. Trevelyan, *England in the Age of Wycliffe*, p. 352.

115. Review of *England in the Age of Wycliffe* in the *Edinburgh Review* 191 (Jan. 1900): 76–105. Trevelyan admitted his frequent tendency to lapse into "Macaulayese" (RCT 14.43, GMT to RCT, 9 July 1900).

116. GOT 93, GMT to Parents, 6 May 1900.

117. Lecky, "The Political Value of History," in *Historical and Political Essays*, p. 26.

118. Trevelyan, *England under the Stuarts*, pp. 400, 346, 516.

119. R. S. Rait in the *TLS*, 2 Dec. 1904, p. 378, noted the author's "impartial attitude."

120. Trevelyan, *England under the Stuarts*, pp. 103, 127, 196.

121. Actually Longmans had approached Trevelyan with the idea in 1908, but he postponed it to complete the Garibaldi series (GOT 100, GMT to GOT, n.d. [July 1908], 2, 12, 14 Dec. 1908).

122. Interestingly, Trevelyan, projecting his own insecurities, worried that after three books on a man of action like Garibaldi, an "orator's life" would fall flat. How could the new book exercise any real influence if people merely said, "see how much duller this is than Garibaldi" (GOT 100, GMT to GOT, 12 Dec. 1908).

123. *TLS*, 29 May 1913, p. 230.

124. GOT 105, GMT to Parents, 26 and 30 May 1913.

125. RCT 14.92, GMT to RCT, 25 July 1914.

126. His experiences in this capacity are covered in detail in Moorman, *Trevelyan*, pp. 138–90.

127. GOT 108, GMT to Parents, 9 Dec. 1916. After further consideration Trevelyan did not change his mind, saying virtually the same thing a week later in a letter to H. A. L. Fisher (FP 62.249–50, GMT to Fisher, 16 Dec. 1916).

128. GOT 94, GMT to GOT, 4 Dec. 1901.

129. Trevelyan, "Autobiography of an Historian," p. 38. In the preface to *Scenes from Italy's War*, p. xi, Trevelyan maintained that "as an historian" he was now "no longer under the delusions of youth."

130. GOT 111, GMT to Mother, 17 Feb. 1919.

131. GMT to Mother, July 1914, quoted in Moorman, *Trevelyan*, pp. 123–24.

132. Trevelyan, *Lord Grey of the Reform Bill*, p. 72.

133. Trevelyan, "Autobiography of an Historian," p. 34.

134. CPT Ex. 85, GMT to CPT, 17 Nov. 1922, CPT 96, GMT to CPT, 30 Oct. 1924.

135. Freeden, *Liberalism Divided*, p. 1.

136. Letter of 21 Jan. 1924, quoted in Moorman, *Trevelyan*, p. 206.

137. CPT 242, GMT to CPT, 2 Nov. 1935.

138. *Lord Grey* sold only 1,200 copies the first year, a disappointing showing by Trevelyan's standards. On the strength of Trevelyan's reputation, *Manin* sold over 2,400 copies the first year, but, unlike each volume of the Garibaldi trilogy, sales trickled away to nothing by the second (Longman Archives, Sales Ledger, Part I.70).

139. GOT 113, GMT to Parents, 28 Oct. 1921.

140. In his obituary of Clapham, Trevelyan awarded both the Hammonds and Clapham, despite their years of "courteous controversy," equal credit for putting economic history in "its true place in human history" and preventing the subdiscipline from becoming "an arid and theoretical study apart" ("Sir John Harold Clapham (1873–1946)," *EconJ* 56 no. 223 [Sept. 1946]: 499–507).

141. Trevelyan, *British History in the Nineteenth Century*, pp. xv, 15, 19–20, xvi, 146–47, 151–52.

142. Ibid., pp. 63, 56, 68, 269.

143. Ibid., pp. 344–47, 409, 401, 253, 403, xvi. The same spirit informed the speech Trevelyan composed for George V's Silver Jubilee address to Parliament in May 1935: "The complex forms and balanced spirit of our Constitution were not the discovery of a single era, still less of a single Party or of a single

person. They are the slow accretion of centuries, the outcome of patience, tradition and experience constantly finding channels old and new for the impulse towards liberty, justice and social improvement inherent in our people down through the ages" (*Parliamentary Debates*, House of Lords, 5th ser., 96 [1934–35]: 836–38).

144. Trevelyan, *British History in the Nineteenth Century*, pp. 405, 366.

145. J. L. Hammond (unsigned), "The Bulwark of Parliament," *TLS*, 12 July 1923, pp. 461–62.

146. Review by Gerald B. Hurst, *EHR* 38 (Jan. 1923): 116–18.

147. *New Statesman* 19 (5 Aug. 1922): 492.

148. Review by John C. Bailey (unsigned), *TLS*, 25 May 1922, pp. 329–30.

149. *Spectator* 129 (1 July 1922): 17–18; (8 July 1922): 48–49.

150. *Saturday Review* 134 (15 July 1922): 106–7.

151. *EHR* 38 (Jan. 1923): 118.

152. Quoted in Moorman, *Trevelyan*, p. 197.

153. Longman Archives, Sales Ledger Part I.70. Exact sales figures for the period were as follows: 1922, 1,269; 1923, 10,270; 1924, 2,394; 1925, 1,966; 1926, 1,824; 1927, 1,717; 1928, 2,500; 1929, 2,090; 1930, 2,325. Eventually, because of sustained demand, a second edition was published in 1937.

154. Trevelyan, *British History in the Nineteenth Century*, p. vii.

155. Moorman, *Trevelyan*, p. 165. A number of reviews of Trevelyan's book compared it favorably with Green's. For one example from the lay press see the *New Statesman* 27 (7 Aug. 1926): 471; for an example from academia see Godfrey Davies, "Recent Textbooks of English History," *JModH* 1 no. 1 (Mar. 1929): 105–12.

156. Trevelyan, *History of England*, pp. 153–54, 285–86, 365–70, 380, 505, 601, 528.

157. To be exact, 29,348. Longman Archives, Part I.70. Sales the next three years were respectively 11,725, 8,861, and 6,838.

158. *New Statesman* 27 (7 Aug. 1926): 471; *TLS*, 1 July 1926, pp. 437–38; *Spectator* 136 (26 June 1926): 1086.

159. See, e.g., the review by E. P. Cheyney in the *AHR* 31 (1926–27): 571–72.

160. Trevelyan, *History of England*, p. 178.

161. RCT 14.107, GMT to RCT, 27 Oct. 1926. Trevelyan's resistance to the addition of the epilogue did not prevent him from agreeing that Longman's was the "correct view."

162. *Edinburgh Review* 244 (Oct. 1926): 331–42.

163. Trevelyan, *English Revolution*, p. 247.

164. Trevelyan, *England under Queen Anne*, 3:206, 96.

165. Trevelyan, "Autobiography of an Historian," p. 46.

166. Burrow, *Liberal Descent*, pp. 79–80, 87–88.

167. Collini, *Public Moralists*, p. 346.

168. On this trend see Colls and Dodd, *Englishness*, esp. pp. 1–61 and 254–82.

169. Clarke, *Liberals and Social Democrats*, p. 207. See also J. L. Hammond's review of *British History in the Nineteenth Century* in the *TLS*, 12 July 1923, pp. 461–62.

170. *DBW*, 11 Apr. 1935 and 10 Oct. 1939.

171. GMT to W. M. Crook, 11 Feb. 1936, quoted in Cannadine, *Trevelyan*, pp. 132–33.

172. Trevelyan, *England under Queen Anne*, 3:292.

173. See Cannadine, *Trevelyan*, pp. 160–62, and Wiener, *English Culture and the Decline of the Industrial Spirit*, pp. 100–102.

174. Trevelyan, *England under Queen Anne*, 3:169, 184, 188; GMT to Mary Moorman, 28 Oct. and 29 Sept. 1926, GMT to Baldwin, 31 Mar. 1935, quoted in Cannadine, *Trevelyan*, pp. 117 and 161.

175. RCT 14.107, GMT to RCT, 27 Oct. 1926.

176. CPT 242, GMT to CPT, 17 Mar. 1934.

CHAPTER FIVE

1. Speech at luncheon given by publisher George G. Harrap & Co., 4 Oct 1933, reprinted in *CV*, Vol. 5, pt. 1, p. 660.

2. Trevelyan, *History of England*, p. 169.

3. Churchill, *History of the English-Speaking Peoples*, 1:199–201.

4. Gilbert, *Winston S. Churchill*, 6:836.

5. Recollection by Judge James Alexander Brown of a conversation with Churchill of 22 May 1937, *CV*, Vol. 5, pt. 3, p. 679; Viscount Simon, "Churchill as a Liberal," in Eade, *Churchill by His Contemporaries*, p. 77.

6. *CV*, Vol. 1, pt. 2, p. 751, WSC to Lady Randolph, 6 Apr. (1897).

7. Churchill, *Lord Randolph Churchill*, 1:19.

8. Ibid., p. 105.

9. Ibid., p. 108.

10. Ibid., p. 118.

11. Ibid., pp. 220–21 and 267.

12. Ibid., p. 293.

13. Ibid., p. 296.

14. Ibid., 2:248–49.

15. Ibid., p. 241.

16. Ibid., p. 442.

17. St. John Brodrick suggested that Winston write a chapter comparing the parliamentary careers of father and son, believing it would be "more read than any chapter in the book" (*CV*, Vol. 2, pt. 1, p. 455, W. St. John Brodrick to WSC, 22 Sept. 1904).

18. "The 'climate of opinion' in which he lived, the mood and intention with which he faced the swiftly changing problems of a stormy period, were never sensibly or erratically altered" (Churchill, *Lord Randolph Churchill*, 2:486).

19. ChP 8.23.40, T. W. Killick to WSC, 21 Jan. 1906.

20. Churchill, *Lord Randolph Churchill*, 2:488–89. This argument resurfaced in *Marlborough* and again in *A History of the English-Speaking Peoples*, 4:48, where Churchill said of Peel, "It is true that he split his party, but there are greater crimes than that."

21. *CV*, Vol. 2, pt. 1, p. 168, WSC to Lord Rosebery, 10 Oct. 1902.

22. Churchill, *Lord Randolph Churchill*, 2:344.

23. Ibid., pp. 348–49.

24. Churchill was to write in 1936: "Optimism has been the fatal defect of many Constitutions. . . . Anglo-Saxon political genius, on the other hand, has been distinguished by its pessimism. Distrust has been the secret of its success. Where power has been established by law or usage, checks have been placed upon its exercise" (ChP 8.545.3, draft of article titled "Constitution—Bulwark or Fetter?").

25. Churchill, *History of the English-Speaking Peoples*, 3:143–44.

26. ChP 8.46.76, Smuts to WSC, 13 Aug. 1923, 8.46.23, Haldane to WSC, 16 Apr. 1923.

27. Commager, "Introduction" to Churchill, *Marlborough*, p. xix.

28. See BLCh 60391AA.173, WSC to Morley, 12 Oct. 1903, 187–88, WSC to Morley, 12 Aug. 1904, 189, WSC to Morley, 9 Sept. 1904.

29. Cowles, *Winston Churchill*, p. 246.

30. Rowse, *Memories of Men and Women*, p. 6.

31. ChP 8.597, WSC to Mortimer Wheeler, 4 July 1938.

32. Churchill, *World Crisis*, 2:ix.

33. Prior, *Churchill's "World Crisis" as History* is most useful on Churchill's use of military experts as historical advisers during the composition of his multi-volume history of the Great War.

34. ChP 8.271, M. Ashley to WSC, 18 July 1930, 8.325, Sir Charles Oman to WSC, 22 Dec. 1933.

35. ChP 8.223, M. Ashley to WSC, 22 July 1929. See Ashley, *Churchill as Historian*, pp. 1–4, for a description of the origins of the collaboration.

36. The initiative for these essays was expected to come from Churchill himself. The intrepid Maurice Ashley recalled Churchill's polite but unenthusiastic response to unsolicited drafts (*Churchill as Historian*, p. 33).

37. ChP 8.289, WSC to the Duke of Marlborough, 10 Jan. 1931.

38. Ibid. Macaulay, among others, had charged Marlborough with having warned the French in advance of a 1694 British expedition against Brest. Churchill went to great lengths in Volume 1 of his biography to demonstrate conclusively that the letter upon which the charge was based, the so-called Camaret Bay letter, was a forgery.

39. ChP 8.597, WSC to Mortimer Wheeler, 4 July 1938.

40. ChP 8.289, WSC to M. Ashley, 3 Jan. 1931.

41. H. A. L. Fisher proofed for Volume 1 of *Marlborough* (ChP 8.323, Fisher to WSC, 2 Aug. 1933); Feiling and G. M. Trevelyan proofed Volume 2 (*CV*, Vol. 5, pt. 2, p. 836, WSC to C. C. Wood, 4 Aug. 1934); and G. M. Young (not a member of the university community but a well-respected scholar) proofed *A History of the English-Speaking Peoples* (ChP 8.626, WSC to Young, 17 Feb. 1939).

42. ChP 8.315, WSC to George S. Harrap, 18 July 1932.

43. See Ashley, *Churchill as Historian*, p. 27; Harrod, *The Prof*, p. 8.

44. The expression was used by Malcolm Muggeridge in "Churchill the Biographer and Historian," in Eade, *Churchill by His Contemporaries*, p. 295.

45. In April 1955 Churchill told his physician about the mechanics of the composition of *A History of the English-Speaking Peoples* before the Second World

War: "Of course I had a team to help, but I wrote every word myself" (Moran, *Winston Churchill*, p. 651).

46. An August 1932 visit to Chartwell by Keith Feiling—seven conversations of two hours each described by the host as "a great success"—resulted in the dictation of a number of short summaries by Churchill. These " 'Feiling' notes" provided the basic material for 20,000 words of *Marlborough* text on English domestic politics and the European scene up to the death of William III. But by the time they had reached their final form these pages had acquired a decidedly Churchillian flavor (ChP 8.307, WSC to M. Ashley, 20 Aug. 1932).

47. Ashley, *Churchill as Historian*, p. 25.

48. Ibid., p. 27.

49. *CV*, Vol. 5, pt. 3, p. 860, Pakenham-Walsh diary entry of 15 Dec. 1937.

50. ChP 8.271, WSC to George S. Harrap, 14 Jan. 1930.

51. ChP 8.223, M. Ashley to WSC, 5 Aug. 1929.

52. ChP 8.223, WSC to M. Ashley, 30 Aug. 1929.

53. J. H. Plumb has complained, with some justice, that a number of important caches of documents were ignored by Churchill and his assistants (particularly the Harley papers at Welbeck and Longleat) and that much of the archival research was "superficial" (Plumb, *Making of an Historian*, 1:238–39). But these oversights, however important, do not alter the fact that the project quickly outgrew its initially modest aims.

54. ChP 8.323, Fisher to WSC, 11 Aug. 1933.

55. Regarding Volume 1, Churchill informed Harrap that "we have taken a great deal of trouble in verifying all the original sources, and as you see we have upset the long-accepted statements of the historians on numerous points of fact" (ChP 8.315, WSC to George S. Harrap, 6 June 1932).

56. ChP 8.325, WSC to GMT, 28 Dec. 1933.

57. ChP 8.325, GMT to WSC, 30 Dec. 1933.

58. ChP 8.308, WSC to Newman Flower (of Cassell & Co.), 30 Oct. 1932. Churchill's expectations were "for a work of wider character. I saw this work in a two volume book of about a quarter of a million words, popularly written." In the end four volumes were written rather than the originally envisioned two.

59. ChP 8.486, WSC to Keith Feiling, 22 Sept. 1934.

60. Bill Deakin, G. M. Young, and Keith Feiling provided assistance before 1940. When the project was taken up again after the war there was a new list of distinguished names: Alan Hodge, A. R. Myers, Joel Hurstfield, D. H. Pennington, A. L. Rowse, J. H. Plumb, Steven Watson, Asa Briggs, Maurice Shock, Frank Freidel, and M. A. Jones. See Ashley, *Churchill as Historian*, p. 212; ChP 8.597, WSC to Prof. Mortimer Wheeler, 4 July 1938.

61. ChP 8.308, WSC to Newman Flower, 30 Oct. 1932.

62. Before its publication after the Second World War Churchill said, "I have my book, *A History of the English-speaking Peoples*. It is an important book. People will lap it up" (Moran, *Winston Churchill*, p. 581, diary entry of 20 July 1954).

63. *EHR* 49 (Oct. 1934): 715–20. An American review by William T. Morgan of the same volume of *Marlborough* came to most of the same conclusions: praising the book's factual accuracy and documentation while criticizing the

inadequate bibliography and the author's "special pleading" on behalf of his protagonist. Morgan ended by describing Churchill's volume as "scholarly," presumably his highest accolade (*JModH* 6 [1934]: 462–64).

64. *EHR* 50 (Apr. 1935): 338–41. Once again Richard Lodge was the reviewer.

65. *EHR* 54 (Jan. 1939): 130–32.

66. BP Box 71, HB to Mary Herbert, 1 Sept. 1935.

67. ChP 8.321, WSC to Pakenham-Walsh, 9 Feb. 1933, 8.323, WSC to Pakenham-Walsh, 13 July 1933, 8.323, Pakenham-Walsh to WSC, 16, 19, and 23 July 1933.

68. ChP 8.322, Alfred Duff Cooper to WSC, [9] July 1933.

69. ChP 8.323, Lord Ivor Spencer-Churchill to WSC, 23 Aug. 1933.

70. See, e.g., University College London don H. C. Allen's review of Volume 4 of *A History of the English-Speaking Peoples* in *EHR* 74 (Apr. 1959): 305–11.

71. Ashley, *Churchill as Historian*, p. 33. The unlucky assistant in this case was Bill Deakin.

72. ChP 8.326, Namier to WSC, 15 Dec. 1933.

73. ChP 8.484, Namier to WSC, 14 Feb. 1934. Namier's opinions echoed those expressed a decade earlier by the don A. F. Pollard. See his unsigned review of Volume 2 of *The World Crisis* in *TLS*, 8 Nov. 1923, p. 139. Julia Namier recorded an account of the upshot of the Churchill-Namier correspondence. "The sequel was an interview in the Churchills' London house. By this time a tentative offer of a possible future collaboration had been delicately hinted at and L[ewis] had been preparing a carefully worded, politely evasive little piece. But this he never had the opportunity to recite. Preliminaries over, Churchill turned out of position a fire-screen, rested his arms on its top and proceeded to deliver a fascinating oration on the writing of history. When he had finished, it was time for L[ewis] to leave. On the way to his club for lunch, he clearly saw why the collaboration could never have worked. Had the parts been reversed, L[ewis] would have acted almost exactly as Churchill had. Neither was a great listener. Both needed additional hands to do their work. In any joint venture Churchill would be the head. But in history-writing L[ewis] could only follow his own lead. Thoughtlessly to build up a collision with a national leader whom he revered would have been silly" (Namier, *Lewis Namier*, p. 231). Here we see distilled in an anecdote Churchill's consistently cautious attitude toward academic historians, always respectful of the don's expert knowledge and advice but refusing to become his willing captive.

74. ChP 8.549, GMT to WSC, 10 Oct. 1937.

75. *EHR* 72 (Jan. 1957): 88–91.

76. In the preface to Volume 1 of *A History of the English-Speaking Peoples* Churchill publicly denied any ambition "to rival the works of professional historians" (p. viii). But privately he hoped to tap into the jealously guarded vein of academic prestige. Regarding the young scholars responsible for the new postwar lay monthly *History Today* Churchill observed: "These young historians will be very useful to me. Before the war I wrote *A History of the English-speaking Peoples*, in four volumes—a million words. I will get them to check its accuracy" (Moran, *Winston Churchill*, p. 457, diary entry of 19 Aug. 1953). Alan

Hodge, editor of *History Today*, directed the revision of the old manuscript of Churchill's *English-Speaking Peoples* in the 1950s.

77. See Hynes, *A War Imagined*.

78. *CV*, Vol. 1, pt. 2, p. 922, WSC to Lady Randolph, 25 Apr. 1898.

79. Cowling, *Religion and Public Doctrine*, 1:306.

80. On this topic see Cline, "British Historians and the Treaty of Versailles," pp. 43–58.

81. *The International Anarchy* was simply an expanded version of Dickinson's *The European Anarchy* (1916), which echoed the wartime arguments of E. D. Morel's Union of Democratic Control.

82. Allen & Unwin Archives, Correspondence Files 1925–26, GLD to A & U, 10 June 1925.

83. Dickinson sent his manuscript of *The International Anarchy* to Gooch for "his criticism and correction" before publication (Allen & Unwin Archives, Correspondence Files 1925–26, GLD to A & U, 22 Apr. 1925).

84. Gilbert Murray to the Secretary of the Fichte-Bund, 18 Aug. 1925, quoted in Gilbert, *Roots of Appeasement*, p. 25.

85. Churchill, *World Crisis*, 3:235.

86. Ibid., 1:52.

87. Gilbert, *Winston S. Churchill*, 5:504–5.

88. Churchill, *World Crisis*, 1:5–6.

89. See, for example, ibid., p. 19.

90. Ibid., p. 16.

91. Ibid., pp. 52–53.

92. Ibid., p. 37.

93. Ibid., p. 6.

94. In Britain Volumes 1 and 2 sold 14,669 and 12,603 copies respectively in the first ten years after publication. In the first nine *months* after publication 12,894 sets of Volumes 3 and 4 were sold. Sales in the first nine months after publication of Volume 5 equaled 9,713. See Woods, *Bibliography of the Works of Sir Winston Churchill*, pp. 50–54. According to Churchill's own calculations, approximate domestic sales figures for the entire series by the end of 1933 were respectively, Volume 1, 15,600; Volume 2, 13,600; Volumes 3 and 4, 13,900; Volume 5, 10,000. See ChP 8.325, WSC to George S. Harrap, 26 Dec. 1933.

95. ChP 8.224, WSC to Lady Frances Horner, 5 Apr. 1929.

96. An 831-page, single-volume abridged edition of *The World Crisis*, published in February 1931 at twenty-one shillings, sold nearly 7,000 copies by the end of the year, necessitating a reprint of 3,000 more in January 1932 (Woods, *Bibliography of the Works of Sir Winston Churchill*, pp. 56–57).

97. ChP 8.496, WSC to Thornton Butterworth, 18 Sept. 1934.

98. Woods, *Bibliography of the Works of Sir Winston Churchill*, p. 50. *The World Crisis* had been serialized originally in *The Times*: Volume 1 daily 8 to 26 Feb. 1923; Volume 2 daily 8 to 27 Oct. 1923; Volumes 3 and 4 daily 7 Feb. to 1 Mar. 1927; Volume 5 daily 11 Feb. to 6 Mar. 1929. See Woods, pp. 213–14, 218, and 220.

99. ChP 8.224, T. E. Shaw [Lawrence] to WSC, 18 Mar. 1929. Churchill had been seriously considering such a task since the summer of 1924. See *CV*, Vol. 5, pt. 1, pp. 149–50, WSC to Clementine Churchill, 22 Aug. 1924.

100. ChP 8.224, WSC to the Duke of Marlborough, 9 June 1926.

101. ChP 8.223, WSC to M. Ashley, 13 July 1929, and 8.271, WSC to George S. Harrap, 14 Jan. 1930.

102. See Churchill, *Marlborough*, 4:358–62. See also 2:298–300, where Churchill argues for the similarity of strategic conception that underlay both the 1704 Blenheim campaign and the 1915 Gallipoli campaign.

103. ChP 8.271, WSC to Keith Feiling, 9 Dec. 1930; 8.325, WSC to GMT, 14 Dec. 1933.

104. Churchill, *Marlborough*, 1:4–5.

105. *Parliamentary Debates*, 5th ser., 317 (12 Nov. 1936): 1144.

106. See, e.g., Churchill, *Marlborough*, 3:6 and 332.

107. Ibid., 1:551.

108. See Searle, *Quest for National Efficiency*, esp. pp. 173–204 and 248–56.

109. *Parliamentary Debates* 5th ser., 333 (24 Mar. 1938): 1452–53.

110. ChP 4.2, Sir Edward Marsh to WSC, 12 Mar. 1937.

111. Winston S. Churchill, "Are Parliaments Obsolete?" *Pearson's Magazine*, June 1934, p. 556.

112. ChP 8.626, WSC to G. M. Young, 18 July 1939.

113. Churchill, *History of the English-Speaking Peoples*, 2:241 and 250.

114. Lewis, "Mr. Churchill as Historian," p. 391.

115. Churchill, *History of the English-Speaking Peoples*, 2:251.

116. ChP 8.321, WSC to Mrs. F. E. Roberts, 3 Feb. 1933: "Mar[l]borough was never at any time false to his constitutional government or to the Protestant cause. I hope to make this plain to all unprejudiced minds."

117. Churchill, "Are Parliaments Obsolete?," p. 557.

118. Kingsley Martin, "Mr. Churchill on Democracy," *New Statesman and Nation* 17 (7 Jan. 1939): 5.

119. Churchill, *Marlborough*, 1:4.

120. Ibid., p. 510.

121. The confusion sometimes carries over to the present. Maurice Ashley wrote in 1968 that "Churchill is reluctant to accept the Whig interpretation of history, having acquired a strong dislike for Macaulay as a historian when he himself was writing about the first Duke of Marlborough" (*Churchill as Historian*, pp. 217–18). For the alternative modern view of Churchill as a prototypical Whig historian see Plumb, *Making of an Historian*, 1:225–52, and Lewis, "Mr. Churchill as Historian."

122. Churchill, *Marlborough*, 1:7. "Lord Rosebery said, 'Surely you must write *Duke John* [as he always called him]: he was a tremendous fellow.' I said that I had from my childhood read everything I came across about him, but that Macaulay's story of the betrayal of the expedition against Brest was an obstacle I could not face. The aged and crippled statesman arose from the luncheon table, and, with great difficulty but sure knowledge, made his way along the passages of The Durdans to the exact nook in his capacious working library where 'Paget's Examen' reposed. 'There,' he said, taking down this unknown, out-of-print masterpiece, 'is the answer to Macaulay.' "

123. ChP 8.223, M. Ashley to WSC, 10 July 1929. The recent "whitewashing" to which Ashley referred was the 1928 Raleigh Lecture by H. A. L. Fisher, *The Whig Historians*, in which Fisher strenuously defended Macaulay.

124. ChP 8.484, Lewis Namier to WSC, 14 Feb. 1934. Namier praised Churchill's exposure of Macaulay but criticized its artistic merit. He advised that the entire argument should be excised from the main text and condensed into a single appendix of approximately fifty pages. With this organizational method Namier believed Churchill would avoid giving the book "the polemic touch, which is disturbing in a great work of art."

125. ChP 8.322, Alfred Duff Cooper to WSC, [9] July 1933. Duff Cooper, however, thought that Churchill's anger had gotten the better of him. Labeling Macaulay a "Liar" outright and comparing him to a Hollywood film producer reduced rather than enhanced the effectiveness of Churchill's devastating analysis.

126. See also ChP 8.322, J. L. Garvin to WSC, 20 May 1933, where Garvin rejoices that the "truth" had at last "overcome the pictorial captivation of Macaulay's partisan method."

127. ChP 8.484, Shaw to WSC, 8 May 1934.

128. Review of the second volume of *Marlborough* by G. K. Chesterton in the *Listener* 12 (31 Oct. 1934): 751–52. Belloc was asked to review Volume 1 of *Marlborough* by the *Listener* but refused because the journal offered too little money (HB Box 91, HB to A. D. Peters, 4 Nov. 1931). A more detailed Roman Catholic attack on Churchill's biography came in the form of Malcolm V. Hay's *Winston Churchill and James II*.

129. ChP 8.323, GMT to WSC, 16 July 1933. Trevelyan underscored the point two months later when he wrote, "You put the Revolution in its true light, and it will do a world of good in these days of neo-Catholic propaganda against the essential truth of English history" (ChP 8.324, GMT to WSC, 20 Sept. 1933).

130. G. M. Trevelyan, "Mr. Churchill's Marlborough," *TLS*, 19 Oct. 1933, p. 711. Although he disputed anyone's right to call Macaulay a "liar," Trevelyan found Churchill's reasoning on the issue of the Camaret Bay letter "so cogent that I intend to alter a passage of my own 'Blenheim', p. 181, in any later edition." This *TLS* letter was later reprinted in *England under Queen Anne*, 3:xi–xiii. Trevelyan's rejoinder on Macaulay's behalf was written with the full knowledge and good-natured approval of Churchill. See ChP 8.323, WSC to GMT, 19 July 1933, and 8.325, GMT to WSC, 12 Dec. 1933. Before the appearance of Trevelyan's *TLS* piece Churchill had apologized to him privately for all the attacks on his great-uncle (ChP 8.324, WSC to GMT, 13 Sept. 1933). In fact, Churchill later wrote to inform Trevelyan that he was "indeed pleased by what you wrote in the Times Literary Supplement" (ChP 8.325, WSC to GMT, 14 Dec. 1933).

131. ChP 8.326, Sir Austen Chamberlain to WSC, 7 Oct. 1933.

132. He excused the aforementioned *TLS* letter as a "duty."

133. ChP 8.324, GMT to WSC, 9 Oct. 1933.

134. ChP 8.324, GMT to WSC, 20 Sept. 1933.

135. There was much cross-discussion between the two men to ensure, for remunerative and publicity purposes, that the earlier Churchill volumes and final Trevelyan volumes did not appear at the same time. See ChP 8.307, GMT to WSC, 6 and 12 May 1932, and WSC to GMT, 5 May 1932; CPT 242, GMT to

CPT, 25 Feb. 1935. Trevelyan was reading Churchill's proofs, and as a reciprocal gesture Churchill requested that his kinsman, the present Duke of Marlborough, open the Blenheim archives—originally reserved for Churchill alone—to Trevelyan for use in the research for the final volume of *England under Queen Anne* (ChP 8.484, WSC to M. Ashley, 1 Feb. 1934).

136. Trevelyan, *England under Queen Anne*, 3:vii.

137. Ibid., 1:107.

138. Ibid., 2:162.

139. Churchill, *Marlborough*, 4:619.

140. Political relations had not always been so cordial and compatible between the two men. In 1922 Trevelyan had described Churchill's election defeat at Dundee as "splendid" (CPT Ex. 85, GMT to CPT, 17 Nov. 1922).

141. Trevelyan, *England under Queen Anne*, 3:viii.

142. Churchill, *Marlborough*, 4:599.

143. In *England under Queen Anne*, 1:127, Trevelyan had expressed irritation at the unwillingness of the Spain of 1700 to consent to any diminution of the worldwide territories she was admittedly incapable of defending. "How the safety and interests of the rest of Europe were affected, whether peace was preserved or not, was of no account to Castilian pride. But no province, no fortress must be given away, even to avert Armageddon." Although this passage was written in 1930, it voiced the sentiments of one who might one day cheer Neville Chamberlain's agreement to the dismemberment of Czechoslovakia in the name of European peace. After the Munich Agreement in the fall of 1938, Trevelyan described both himself and his wife as "Chamberlainites" (RCT 14.141, GMT to RCT, 18 Oct. 1938).

144. In fact, Churchill, with Harrap's consent, freely plagiarized *Marlborough* to write the section on the age of Queen Anne in *A History of the English-Speaking Peoples* (ChP 8.626, WSC to George Harrap, 28 Mar. 1939).

145. ChP 8.626, WSC to M. Ashley, 12 Apr. 1939. See also ChP 8.308, WSC to Sir Newman Flower, 30 Oct. 1932, where Churchill envisioned the work as "telling the whole story of the origin, quarrels and the re-assertion of the English-speaking peoples" with special stress "on the birth of those traditions, institutions and ideas which have become characteristic to our common civilisation in all parts of the globe."

146. Churchill, *History of the English-Speaking Peoples*, 1:vii. Of course, the accelerated pace of Churchill's work was also always partly a function of the need to generate income and of his own fanaticism for honoring contracts. On finishing the *History* by the end of 1939 Churchill would receive £7,000, which constituted half his income for the year and made the books' completion a financial necessity. See Gilbert, *Winston S. Churchill*, 5:1089, n. 1.

147. See, e.g., ChP 2.304, Wing-Commander Charles Torr Anderson to WSC, 5 Aug. 1937.

148. ChP 8.626, WSC to G. M. Young, 31 Aug. 1939.

149. See, e.g., ChP 8.626, WSC to Bullock, 15 Apr. 1939.

150. Gilbert, *Winston S. Churchill*, 5:1024; *CV*, Vol. 5, pt. 3, p. 1340, WSC to Clementine Churchill, 8 Jan. 1939; ChP 8.626, WSC to Edward Marsh, 6 June 1939; ChP 8.624, WSC to Sir Newman Flower, 31 Aug. 1939.

151. *CV*, Vol. 5, pt. 3, p. 1340: WSC to Clementine Churchill, 8 Jan. 1939; ChP 8.626, WSC to Edward Marsh, 20 July 1939.

152. ChP 8.626, WSC to Sir Newman Flower, 9 July 1939. For similar sentiments see also ChP 8.597, WSC to Mortimer Wheeler, 19 Sept. 1938, and 8.626, WSC to G. M. Young, 31 Aug. 1939.

153. Quoted in Gilbert, *Winston S. Churchill*, 6:836.

154. ChP 8.681, Dodd, Mead & Co. to Sir Gerald Campbell, 9 July 1941.

CONCLUSION

1. Butterfield, *The Englishman and His History*, pp. 81–82.

2. Burrow, *Liberal Descent*, pp. 293–94.

3. Parker, *English Historical Tradition*, pp. 177–242.

4. For Jann's disagreement with Blaas on this point see *Art and Science of Victorian History*, p. 228, n. 57.

5. Cannadine, "British History," pp. 173–75.

6. Jones, "Pathology of English History," pp. 29–38.

7. Of course, cause and effect are impossible to disentangle here. Trevelyan's consensus history was as much a response to the crisis of Liberalism as a contributor to it.

8. Butterfield, *The Englishman and His History* pp. 7, vi, 3–4.

9. Cannadine, "British History," p. 171.

10. Collingwood, *Autobiography*, p. 88.

11. Trevor-Roper, *History, Professional and Lay*.

12. Plumb, *Death of the Past*.

13. Bryant, *English Saga*, pp. 323–24.

14. See Bryant, *Art of Writing History*.

BIBLIOGRAPHY

MANUSCRIPT COLLECTIONS

Boston, Massachusetts
John J. Burns Library, Boston College
    Hilaire Belloc Papers

Brighton, England
Sussex University Library
    Leonard Woolf Papers

Cambridge, England
Churchill College
    Winston S. Churchill Papers (Chartwell Trust)
King's College
    Oscar Browning Papers
    G. Lowes Dickinson Papers
Trinity College
    Robert C. Trevelyan Papers
    Trinity College Add. Ms. (G. M. Trevelyan Papers)

London, England
British Library
    Winston S. Churchill Papers
    Mary Gladstone Papers
    John Morley Papers
    C. P. Scott Papers
British Library of Political and Economic Science
    Passfield Papers (Sidney and Beatrice Webb)
    R. H. Tawney Papers
    Graham Wallas Papers
    Charles K. Webster Papers

Newcastle-upon-Tyne, England
Robinson Library, University of Newcastle-upon-Tyne
    Charles P. Trevelyan Papers
    George O. Trevelyan Papers

New Haven, Connecticut
Sterling Memorial Library, Yale University
    Fabian Society Archives (microfilm)

Oxford, England
Bodleian Library
    H. A. L. Fisher Papers
    J. L. and Barbara Hammond Papers
    Gilbert Murray Papers
Nuffield College
    G. D. H. Cole Papers

Reading, England
Reading University Library
    Allen & Unwin Archives
    Chatto & Windus Archives
    Longman Archives
    Macmillan Archives

NEWSPAPERS, JOURNALS, AND PERIODICALS

American Historical Review
Contemporary Review
Daily News
Daily Telegraph
Economic History
Economic History Review
Economic Journal
Economica
Edinburgh Review
English Historical Review
Fortnightly Review
History
Independent Review
Journal of Education
Journal of Modern History
Listener
Liverpool Daily Post
Manchester Evening News
Manchester Guardian
Nation (London)
Nation (New York)
New Leader
New Republic
New Statesman (and Nation)
Nineteenth Century
Oxford and Cambridge Review
Pearson's Quarterly
Political Quarterly
Quarterly Review
St. Martin's Review
Saturday Review
Speaker
Spectator
Standard
Sunday Chronicle
Sunday Times
Time and Tide
The Times
Times Literary Supplement
Truth
Universe
Yorkshire Observer
Yorkshire Post

PUBLISHED DOCUMENTS

Belloc, Hilaire. *Letters from Hilaire Belloc*. Edited by Robert Speaight. London: Hollis & Carter, 1958.
Diary of Beatrice Webb, 1873–1942 (holograph and typescript microfiche). Somerset, N.J.: Chadwick-Healey, 1978.

Gilbert, Martin, and Randolph S. Churchill, eds. *Winston S. Churchill: Companion Volumes*. Boston: Houghton Mifflin, 1966–88.

Gooch, G. P., and Harold Temperley, eds. *British Documents on the Origins of the War*. 11 vols. London: H.M.S.O., 1926–38.

Howe, Mark DeWolfe, ed. *Holmes-Laski Letters: The Correspondence of Mr. Justice Holmes and Harold J. Laski*. 2 vols., continuous pagination. Cambridge, Mass.: Harvard University Press, 1953.

MacKenzie, Norman, ed. *The Letters of Sidney and Beatrice Webb*. 3 vols. Cambridge: Cambridge University Press, 1978.

MacKenzie, Norman, and Jeanne, eds. *The Diary of Beatrice Webb*. 4 vols. Cambridge, Mass.: Belknap Press of Harvard University Press, 1982–85.

Nicolson, Harold. *Diaries and Letters*. Edited by Nigel Nicolson. 3 vols. London: Collins, 1966–68.

Parliamentary Debates, House of Commons. London: H.M.S.O.

Parliamentary Debates, House of Lords. London: H.M.S.O.

Riddell, Lord. *More Pages from My Diary, 1908–1914*. London: Country Life, 1934.

Scott, C. P. *The Political Diaries of C. P. Scott, 1911–1928*. Edited by Trevor Wilson. Ithaca, N.Y.: Cornell University Press, 1970.

Woolf, Leonard. *Letters of Leonard Woolf*. Edited by Frederic Spotts. London: Weidenfeld & Nicolson, 1990.

Woolf, Virginia. *The Diary of Virginia Woolf*. Vol. 5: *1936–1941*. Edited by Anne Olivier Bell. London: Hogarth, 1984.

BOOKS AND ARTICLES

Allen, V. L. "A Methodological Criticism of the Webbs as Trade Union Historians." *Bulletin—Society for the Study of Labour History* 4 (Spring 1962): 4–6.

Arnstein, Walter L. "G. M. Trevelyan and the Art of History: A Centenary Reappraisal." *Midwest Quarterly* 18 (Oct. 1978): 78–97.

Ashley, Maurice. *Churchill as Historian*. London: Secker & Warburg, 1968.

Ball, Oona Howard. *Sidney Ball: Memories and Impressions of "an Ideal Don."* Oxford: Blackwell, 1923.

Bann, Stephen. *The Clothing of Clio: A Study of the Representation of History in Nineteenth-Century Britain and France*. Cambridge: Cambridge University Press, 1984.

Beer, Max. *A History of British Socialism*. 2 vols. 1919. Rev. ed. London: G. Bell, 1929.

Belloc, Hilaire. *Anti-Catholic History*. London: Catholic Truth Society, 1914.

——. *The Battle of Blenheim*. London: S. Swift, 1911.

——. *The Campaign of 1812 and the Retreat from Moscow*. London: Nelson, 1924.

——. *The Case of Dr. Coulton*. London: Sheed & Ward, 1938.

——. *Characters of the Reformation*. London: Sheed & Ward, 1936.

——. *Charles the First, King of England*. London: Cassell, 1933.

——. *A Companion to Mr. Wells' "Outline of History."* London: Sheed & Ward, 1926.

——. *A Conversation with a Cat and Others*. London: Cassell, 1931.

——. *A Conversation with an Angel: And Other Essays*. London: Jonathan Cape, 1928.

——. *Cranmer*. London: Cassell, 1931.

——. *The Crisis of Civilization*. New York: Fordham University Press, 1937.

——. *Cromwell*. London: Cassell, 1934.

——. *Danton*. London: J. Nisbet, 1899.

——. *Essays of a Catholic Layman in England*. London: Sheed & Ward, 1931.

——. *Europe and the Faith*. London: Constable, 1920.

——. *The French Revolution*. London: Williams & Norgate, 1911.

——. *A History of England*. 4 vols. London: Methuen, 1925–31.

——. *How the Reformation Happened*. London: Jonathan Cape, 1928.

——. *James the Second*. London: Faber & Gwyer, 1928.

——. *Malplaquet*. London: S. Swift, 1911.

——. *Marie Antoinette*. New York: Doubleday Page, 1909.

——. *Milton*. London: Cassell, 1935.

——. *Mr. Belloc Still Objects*. London: Sheed & Ward, 1926.

——. *Monarchy: A Study of Louis XIV*. New York: Harper, 1938.

——. *Napoleon*. Philadelphia, Lippincott, 1932.

——. *On Anything*. London: Constable, 1910.

——. *On Everything*. London: Methuen, 1909.

——. *On Something*. London: Methuen, 1910.

——. *The Party System*. London: S. Swift, 1911.

——. *The Path to Rome*. London: G. Allen, 1902.

——. *Pongo and the Bull*. London: Constable, 1910.

——. *Robespierre: A Study*. 1901. Reprint. New York: G. P. Putnam's, 1928.

——. *The Servile State*. 1912. Reprint. London: Constable, 1927.

——. *A Shorter History of England*. London: Harrap, 1934.

——. *The Tactics and Strategy of the Great Duke of Marlborough*. London: Arrowsmith, 1933.

——. *Wolsey*. London: Cassell, 1930.

Belloc, Hilaire, J. L. Hammond, F. W. Hirst, P. J. Macdonnell, J. S. Phillimore, and J. A. Simon ("Six Oxford Men"). *Essays in Liberalism*. London: Cassell, 1897.

Beloff, Max. *Imperial Sunset: Britain's Liberal Empire, 1897–1921*. London: Methuen, 1969.

Bentley, Michael. *The Climax of Liberal Politics: British Liberalism in Theory and Practice, 1868–1918*. London: Edward Arnold, 1987.

——. *The Liberal Mind, 1914–1929*. Cambridge: Cambridge University Press, 1977.

Besant, Annie, Hubert Bland, William Clarke, Sydney Olivier, G. Bernard Shaw, Graham Wallas, and Sidney Webb. *Fabian Essays in Socialism*. 1889. Reprint. London: Allen & Unwin, 1920.

Blaas, P. B. M. *Continuity and Anachronism: Parliamentary and Constitutional Development in Whig Historiography and in the Anti-Whig Reaction between 1890 and 1930*. The Hague: M. Nijhoff, 1978.

Bowler, Peter. *Evolution: The History of an Idea*. Berkeley: University of California Press, 1984.

Brewer, John. *The Sinews of Power: War, Money and the English State, 1688–1783*. New York: Knopf, 1989.

Briggs, Asa. *The Collected Essays of Asa Briggs*. Vol. 2: *Images, Problems, Standpoints, Forecasts*. Brighton, Sussex: Harvester, 1985.

Bryant, Arthur. *The Art of Writing History*. London: Oxford University Press, 1946.

——. *English Saga, 1840–1940*. London: Collins, 1940.

——. *The Lion and the Unicorn*. New York: Doubleday, 1970.

——. *Macaulay*. New York: D. Appleton, 1933.

Buer, Mabel Craven. *Health, Wealth and Population in the Early Days of the Industrial Revolution*. London: G. Routledge, 1926.

Buitenhuis, Peter. *The Great War of Words: British, American, and Canadian Propaganda and Fiction, 1914–1933*. Vancouver: University of British Columbia Press, 1987.

Burroughs, Peter. "J. R. Seeley and British Imperial History." *Journal of Imperial and Commonwealth History* 1 (Jan. 1973): 191–211.

Burrow, J. W. *A Liberal Descent: Victorian Historians and the English Past*. Cambridge: Cambridge University Press, 1981.

——. "Victorian Historians and the Royal Historical Society." *Transactions of the Royal Historical Society* 5th ser., 39 (1989): 125–40.

Butterfield, Herbert. *The Englishman and His History*. Cambridge: Cambridge University Press, 1944.

——. *The Whig Interpretation of History*. London: G. Bell, 1931.

Buxton, C. R., H. C. Fairfax-Chomeley, J. L. Hammond, F. W. Hirst, L. T. Hobhouse, J. A. Hobson, C. F. G. Masterman, J. H. Morgan, and Vaughan Nash. *Towards a Social Policy: Or, Suggestions for Constructive Reform*. London: The Speaker, 1905.

Cannadine, David. "British History: Past, Present—and Future?" *Past and Present* 116 (Aug. 1987): 169–91.

——. *The Decline and Fall of the British Aristocracy*. New Haven: Yale University Press, 1990.

——. *G. M. Trevelyan: A Life in History*. London: Harper Collins, 1992.

——. "The Present and the Past in the English Industrial Revolution, 1880–1980." *Past and Present* 103 (May 1984): 131–72.

Canovan, Margaret. *G. K. Chesterton: Radical Populist*. New York: Harcourt Brace Jovanovich, 1977.

Chadwick, Owen. *Freedom and the Historian*. London: Cambridge University Press, 1969.

Chancellor, Valerie E. *History for Their Masters: Opinion in the English History Textbook, 1800–1914*. Bath: Adams & Dart, 1970.

Chesterton, G. K. *Autobiography*. London: Hutchinson, 1936.

——. *A Short History of England*. London: Chatto & Windus, 1917.

Churchill, Winston S. *Great Contemporaries*. London: T. Butterworth, 1937.

——. *A History of the English-Speaking Peoples*. 4 vols. London: Cassell, 1956–58.

——. *Ian Hamilton's March*. London: Longmans, Green, 1900.

——. *Liberalism and the Social Problem*. London: Hodder & Stoughton, 1909.

———. *London to Ladysmith: Via Pretoria*. London: Longmans, Green, 1900.

———. *Lord Randolph Churchill*. 2 vols. London: Macmillan, 1906.

———. *Marlborough: His Life and Times*. 4 vols. London: Harrap, 1933–38.

———. *The River War: An Historical Account of the Reconquest of the Soudan*. 2 vols. London: Longmans, Green, 1899.

———. *A Roving Commission: My Early Life*. New York: Charles Scribner's, 1930.

———. *The Second World War*. 6 vols. Boston: Houghton Mifflin, 1948–53.

———. *The Story of the Malakand Field Force: An Episode of Frontier War*. London: Longmans, Green, 1898.

———. *The World Crisis*. 5 vols. London: T. Butterworth, 1923–31.

Clapham, J. H. *Economic History of Modern Britain*. Vol. 1: *The Early Railway Age, 1820–1850*. 1926. Reprint. Cambridge: Cambridge University Press, 1930.

Clark, G. Kitson. "G. M. Trevelyan as an Historian." *Durham University Journal* 55 (1962): 1–4.

———. "A Hundred Years of the Teaching of History at Cambridge." *Historical Journal* 16,3 (1973): 535–53.

Clark, G. N. "George Macaulay Trevelyan, 1876–1962." *Proceedings of the British Academy* 49 (1963): 375–86.

———. "The Origin of the Cambridge Modern History." *Cambridge Historical Journal* 8 (1945): 57–64.

Clark, J. C. D. *English Society, 1688–1832*. Cambridge, Cambridge University Press, 1985.

Clarke, Peter F. *Lancashire and the New Liberalism*. Cambridge: Cambridge University Press, 1971.

———. *Liberals and Social Democrats*. Cambridge: Cambridge University Press, 1978.

Clegg, H. A. "The Webbs as Historians of Trade Unionism, 1874–1894." *Bulletin—Society for the Study of Labour History* 4 (Spring 1962): 8–9.

Clegg, H. A., Alan Fox, and A. F. Thompson. *A History of British Trade Unions since 1889*. Vol. 1: *1889–1910*. Oxford: Clarendon, 1964.

Cline, Catherine Ann. "British Historians and the Treaty of Versailles." *Albion* 20 no. 1 (Spring 1988): 43–58.

———. "E. D. Morel and the Crusade against the Foreign Office." *Journal of Modern History* 39 no. 2 (1967): 126–37.

———. *Recruits to Labour: The British Labour Party, 1914–1931*. Syracuse, N.Y.: Syracuse University Press, 1963.

Cole, Margaret. *The Life of G. D. H. Cole*. London: Macmillan, 1971.

———, ed. *The Webbs and Their Work*. London: Frederick Muller, 1949.

Coleman, D. C. *History and the Economic Past: An Account of the Rise and Decline of Economic History in Britain*. Oxford: Clarendon, 1987.

———. *Myth, History and the Industrial Revolution*. London: Hambledon, 1992.

Colley, Linda. *Lewis Namier*. London: Weidenfeld & Nicolson, 1989.

Collingwood, R. G. *An Autobiography*. London: Oxford University Press, 1939.

Collini, Stefan. *Liberalism and Sociology: L. T. Hobhouse and Political Argument in England, 1880–1914*. Cambridge: Cambridge University Press, 1979.

———. *Public Moralists: Political Thought and Intellectual Life in Britain, 1850–1930*. Oxford: Clarendon, 1991.

Collini, Stefan, Donald Winch, and John Burrow. *That Noble Science of Politics: A Study in Nineteenth-Century Intellectual History*. Cambridge: Cambridge University Press, 1983.

Colls, Robert, and Philip Dodd, eds. *Englishness: Politics and Culture, 1880–1920*. London: Croom Helm, 1986.

Commager, Henry Steele. Introduction to Winston S. Churchill, *Marlborough: His Life and Times*. Abridged single-volume ed., pp. xix–xxxiii. New York: Scribner, 1968.

Cookson, Christopher, ed. *Essays on Secondary Education*. Oxford: Clarendon, 1898.

Corrin, Jay P. *G. K. Chesterton and Hilaire Belloc: The Battle against Modernity*. Athens: Ohio University Press, 1980.

Coulton, G. G. *Mr. Hilaire Belloc as Historian*. London: Simpkin, Marshall, Hamilton, Kent, 1930.

Cowles, Virginia. *Winston Churchill: The Man and the Era*. New York: Harper, 1953.

Cowling, Maurice. *Religion and Public Doctrine in Modern England*. 2 vols. Cambridge: Cambridge University Press, 1980–85.

Crowley, Brian L. *The Self, the Individual, and the Community: Liberalism in the Political Thought of F. A. Hayek and Sidney and Beatrice Webb*. Oxford: Clarendon, 1987.

Deakin, F. W. "Churchill the Historian." *Schweizer Monatschefte* 49, 4 Sonderbeilage (July 1969): 1–19.

Dickinson, G. Lowes. *The European Anarchy*. London: Macmillan, 1916.

——. *The International Anarchy, 1904–1914*. London: Allen & Unwin, 1926.

Eade, Charles, ed. *Churchill by His Contemporaries*. London: Hutchinson, 1954.

Egerton, George W. "The Lloyd George 'War Memoirs': A Study in the Politics of Memory." *Journal of Modern History* 60 no. 1 (Mar. 1988): 55–94.

Eksteins, Modris. *Rites of Spring: The Great War and the Birth of the Modern Age*. Boston: Houghton Mifflin, 1989.

Elton, G. R. *F. W. Maitland*. London: Weidenfeld & Nicolson, 1985.

——. "Herbert Butterfield and the Study of History." *Historical Journal* 27 no. 3 (1984): 729–43.

——. "The Historian's Social Function." *Royal Historical Society Transactions* 27 (1977): 197–211.

Emy, H. V. *Liberals, Radicals and Social Politics, 1892–1914*. Cambridge: Cambridge University Press, 1973.

Engel, Arthur J. *From Clergyman to Don: The Rise of the Academic Profession in Nineteenth-Century Oxford*. New York: Oxford University Press, 1983.

Eyck, Frank. *G. P. Gooch: A Study in History and Politics*. London: Macmillan, 1982.

Ffinch, Michael. *G. K. Chesterton*. San Francisco: Harper & Row, 1986.

Fifoot, C. H. S., ed. *The Letters of Frederic William Maitland*. Cambridge: Cambridge University Press, 1965.

Firth, C. H. *A Plea for the Historical Teaching of History*. Oxford: Clarendon, 1909.

Fisher, H. A. L. *An Unfinished Autobiography*. London: Oxford University Press, 1941.

——. "The Whig Historians." *Proceedings of the British Academy* 14 (1928): 297–339.

Fitzsimons, Matthew A. "British Historiography of the Twentieth Century." In *The Development of Historiography*, edited by M. A. Fitzsimons, Charles E. Nowell, and Alfred G. Pundt, pp. 225–39. Harrisburg, Pa.: Stackpole, 1954.

Forbes, Duncan. *The Liberal Anglican Idea of History*. Cambridge: Cambridge University Press, 1952.

Freeden, Michael. *Liberalism Divided: A Study in British Political Thought, 1914–1939*. Oxford: Clarendon, 1986.

——. *The New Liberalism: An Ideology of Social Reform*. Oxford: Clarendon, 1978.

Fremantle, Anne Marie. *This Little Band of Prophets: The British Fabians*. London: Allen & Unwin, 1960.

Fussell, Paul. *The Great War and Modern Memory*. New York: Oxford University Press, 1975.

Gairdner, James. *History of the Life and Reign of Richard the Third*. 1878. Reprint. Cambridge: Cambridge University Press, 1898.

Gilbert, Bentley. *The Evolution of National Insurance in Great Britain: The Origins of the Welfare State*. London: Joseph, 1966.

——. "Winston Churchill versus the Webbs: The Origins of British Unemployment Insurance." *American Historical Review* 71 no. 3 (Apr. 1966): 346–62.

Gilbert, Martin. *The Roots of Appeasement*. New York: New American Library, 1966.

Gilbert, Martin (vols. 3–8), and Randolph S. Churchill (vols. 1–2). *Winston S. Churchill*. 8 vols. London: Heinemann, 1966–88.

Glaser, John F. "English Nonconformity and the Decline of Liberalism." *American Historical Review* 63 (1958): 352–63.

Glass, S. T. *The Responsible Society: The Ideas of Guild Socialism*. London: Longmans, 1966.

Goldstein, Doris S. "J. B. Bury's Philosophy of History: A Reappraisal." *American Historical Review* 82 no. 4 (Oct. 1977): 896–919.

——. "The Organizational Development of the British Historical Profession, 1884–1921." *Historical Research* 60 no. 132 (Nov. 1982): 180–93.

——. "The Origins and Early Years of the 'English Historical Review'." *English Historical Review* 101 no. 398 (Jan. 1986): 6–19.

——. "The Professionalization of History in Britain in the Late Nineteenth and Early Twentieth Centuries." *Storia della Storiografia* 3 (1983): 3–27.

Goldstein, Erik. "Historians Outside the Academy: G. W. Prothero and the Experience of the Foreign Office Historical Section, 1917–20." *Historical Research* 63 no. 151 (June 1990): 195–211.

Gooch, G. P. *Historical Surveys and Portraits*. New York: Barnes & Noble, 1966.

——. *History and Historians in the Nineteenth Century*. London: Longmans, Green, 1913.

——. *Under Six Reigns*. London: Longmans, Green, 1958.

Green, J. R. *A Short History of the English People*. 1874. Reprint. New York: Harper, 1883.

Greenleaf, W. H. *The British Political Tradition*. Vol. 2: *The Ideological Heritage*. London: Routledge, 1983.

Griffith, G. Talbot. *Population Problems in the Age of Malthus*. Cambridge: Cambridge University Press, 1926.

Hall, J. A. "The Roles and Influence of Political Intellectuals: Tawney vs. Sidney Webb." *British Journal of Sociology* 28 no. 3 (Sept. 1977): 351–62.

Hamburger, Joseph. *Macaulay and the Whig Tradition*. Chicago: University of Chicago Press, 1976.

Hamer, D. A. *Liberal Politics in the Age of Gladstone and Rosebery: A Study in Leadership and Policy*. Oxford: Clarendon, 1972.

Hamilton, Keith A. "The Pursuit of 'Enlightened Patriotism': The British Foreign Office and Historical Researchers during the Great War and Its Aftermath." *Historical Research* 61 no. 146 (Oct. 1988): 316–44.

Hamilton, Mary Agnes. *Remembering My Good Friends*. London: Jonathan Cape, 1944.

——. *Sidney and Beatrice Webb: A Study in Contemporary Biography*. London: S. Low, Marston, 1933.

Hammond, J. L. *Charles James Fox: A Political Study*. London: Methuen, 1903.

——. *C. P. Scott of the Manchester Guardian*. London: G. Bell, 1934.

——. *Gladstone and the Irish Nation*. London: Longmans, Green, 1938.

——. "Gladstone and the League of Nations Mind." In *Essays in Honour of Gilbert Murray*, edited by J. A. K. Thomson and Arnold J. Toynbee, pp. 95–118. London: Allen & Unwin, 1936.

Hammond, J. L., and Barbara Hammond. *The Age of the Chartists, 1832–1854: A Study in Discontent*. London: Longmans, Green, 1930.

——. *The Bleak Age*. London: Longmans, Green, 1934.

——. *Lord Shaftesbury*. London: Constable, 1923.

——. *The Rise of Modern Industry*. London: Methuen, 1925.

——. *The Skilled Labourer*. London: Longmans, Green, 1919.

——. *The Town Labourer, 1760–1832: The New Civilisation*. London: Longmans, Green, 1917.

——. *The Village Labourer, 1760–1832: A Study in the Government of England before the Reform Bill*. 1911. Reprint. London: Longmans, Green, 1913.

Hammond, J. L., and M. R. D. Foot. *Gladstone and Liberalism*. London: English Universities Press, 1952.

Hammond, J. L., F. W. Hirst, and Gilbert Murray. *Liberalism and the Empire*. London: R. B. Johnson, 1900.

Harris, José. "The Webbs." In *Founders of the Welfare State*, edited by Paul Barker, pp. 52–60. London: Heinemann, 1984.

Harrod, R. F. *The Prof: A Personal Memoir of Lord Cherwell*. London: Macmillan, 1959.

Hartwell, R. M. *The Industrial Revolution and Economic Growth*. London: Methuen, 1971.

Harvie, Christopher. *The Lights of Liberalism: University Liberals and the Challenge of Democracy, 1860–86*. London: Allen Lane, 1976.

Hay, Malcolm V. *Winston Churchill and James II*. London: Harding & More, 1934.

Hernon, Joseph M. "The Last Whig Historian and Consensus History: George Macaulay Trevelyan, 1876–1962." *American Historical Review* 81 no. 1 (Feb. 1976): 66–97.

Heyck, T. W. *The Transformation of Intellectual Life in Victorian England*. London: Croom Helm, 1982.

Hill, Christopher. "A Whig Historian." *Modern Quarterly* 3 no. 1 (July 1938): 275–84.

Himmelfarb, Gertrude. "The Intellectual in Politics: The Case of the Webbs." *Journal of Contemporary History* 6 no. 3 (1971): 3–11.

———. *Poverty and Compassion: The Moral Imagination of the Late Victorians*. New York: Knopf, 1991.

———. *Victorian Minds*. Gloucester, Mass.: Peter Smith, 1975.

Hobsbawm, E. J. "The Fabians Reconsidered." In Hobsbawm, *Labouring Men: Studies in the History of Labour*, pp. 250–71. New York: Basic Books, 1964.

Hollander, Paul. *Political Pilgrims: Travels of Western Intellectuals to the Soviet Union, China, and Cuba, 1920–1978*. New York: Oxford University Press, 1981.

Holroyd, Michael. *Bernard Shaw*. Vol. 2: *1898–1918. The Pursuit of Power*. New York: Random House, 1989.

———. *Lytton Strachey: A Critical Biography*. 2 vols. London: Heinemann, 1967–68.

Holton, Robert. *British Syndicalism, 1900–1914: Myths and Realities*. London: Pluto, 1976.

Hurwitz, Samuel J. "Winston S. Churchill." In *Some Modern Historians of Britain*, edited by Herman Ausubel, J. Bartlet Brebner, and Erling M. Hunt, pp. 306–24. New York: Dryden, 1951.

Hutchins, B. L., and A. Harrison (Mrs. F. H. Spencer). *A History of Factory Legislation*. London: P. S. King, 1903.

Hynes, Samuel. *A War Imagined: The First World War and English Culture*. New York: Atheneum, 1991.

James, Robert Rhodes. *Lord Randolph Churchill*. London: Weidenfeld & Nicolson, 1959.

Jann, Rosemary. *The Art and Science of Victorian History*. Columbus: Ohio State University Press, 1985.

———. "From Amateur to Professional: The Case of the Oxbridge Historians." *Journal of British Studies* 22 (Spring 1983): 122–47.

"Jason" [J. L. Hammond]. *Past and Future*. London: Chatto & Windus, 1918.

Johnson, Paul Barton. *Land Fit for Heroes: The Planning of British Reconstruction, 1916–1919*. Chicago: University of Chicago Press, 1968.

Jones, Gareth Stedman. "The Pathology of English History." *New Left Review* 46 (Nov.–Dec. 1967): 29–43.

Jones, Greta. *Social Darwinism and English Thought: The Interaction between Biological and Social Theory*. Brighton, Sussex: Harvester, 1980.

Kadish, Alon. *Apostle Arnold: The Life and Death of Arnold Toynbee, 1852–1883*. Durham, N.C.: Duke University Press, 1986.

———. *Historians, Economists, and Economic History*. London: Routledge, 1989.

———. "Scholarly Exclusiveness and the Foundation of the 'English Historical Review'." *Historical Research* 61 no. 145 (June 1988): 183–98.

Kenyon, John. *The History Men: The Historical Profession in England since the Renaissance*. London: Weidenfeld & Nicolson, 1983.

Keynes, J. M. *The Economic Consequences of the Peace*. London: Macmillan, 1919.

——. *Essays in Biography*. 1933. New edition with three additional essays edited by Geoffrey Keynes. New York: Horizon, 1951.

Kidd, Alan J. "Historians or Polemicists? How the Webbs Wrote Their History of the English Poor Law." *Economic History Review* 2d ser., 40 no. 3 (1987): 400–417.

Knights, Ben. *The Idea of the Clerisy in the Nineteenth Century*. Cambridge: Cambridge University Press, 1978.

Laquer, Walter, and George L. Mosse, eds. *Historians and Politics*. London: Sage, 1974.

Leathes, Stanley, G. W. Prothero, and A. W. Ward, eds. *The Cambridge Modern History*. Vol. 12: *The Latest Age*. London: Cambridge University Press, 1910.

Lecky, W. E. H. *Historical and Political Essays*. London: Longmans, Green, 1908.

Lee, Alan J. "The Radical Press." In *Edwardian Radicalism, 1900–1914*, edited by A. J. A. Morris, pp. 47–61. London: Routledge & Kegan Paul, 1974.

Letwin, Shirley. *The Pursuit of Certainty*. Cambridge: Cambridge University Press, 1965.

——. "Representation without Democracy: The Webbs' Constitution." *Review of Politics* 16 (1954): 352–75.

Lewis, Gordon K. "Mr. Churchill as Historian." *Historian* 20 no. 4 (Aug. 1958): 387–414.

Lewis, John. *The Left Book Club: A Historical Record*. London: Gollancz, 1970.

Lingard, John (vols. 1–10), and Hilaire Belloc (vol. 11). *The History of England, from the First Invasion by the Romans to the Accession of William and Mary in 1688*. Vols. 1–10: 6th ed., London: C. Dolman, 1855, orig. pub. in 8 vols., 1819–30; and vol. 11: *To the Accession of King George the Fifth*. New York: Catholic Publication Society, 1915.

Lowndes, Marie Belloc. *The Young Hilaire Belloc*. New York: P. J. Kenedy, 1956.

Lunn, Arnold. *And Yet So New*. London: Sheed & Ward, 1958.

McAleer, Joseph. *Popular Reading and Publishing in Britain, 1914–1950*. Oxford: Clarendon, 1992.

McBriar, A. M. *An Edwardian Mixed Doubles*. Oxford: Clarendon, 1987.

——. *Fabian Socialism and English Politics, 1884–1918*. Cambridge: Cambridge University Press, 1962.

McCarthy, John P. *Hilaire Belloc: Edwardian Radical*. Indianapolis: Liberty, 1978.

——. "Hilaire Belloc: Jacobite and Jacobin." *Chesterton Review* 12 no. 2 (May 1986): 165–73.

Mack Smith, Denis. *Cavour and Garibaldi, 1860: A Study in Political Conflict*. Cambridge: Cambridge University Press, 1954.

——. *Garibaldi*. 1956. Reprint. Westport, Conn.: Greenwood, 1982.

MacKenzie, Jeanne. *A Victorian Courtship*. London: Oxford University Press, 1979.

MacKenzie, Norman, and Jeanne MacKenzie. *The Fabians*. New York: Simon & Schuster, 1976.

——. *The Time Traveler: The Life of H. G. Wells*. London: Weidenfeld & Nicolson, 1973.

McKibbin, Ross. *The Evolution of the Labour Party, 1910–1924*. London: Oxford University Press, 1974.

Magnus, Sir Philip. *Gladstone: A Biography*. London: Murray, 1954.

Maloney, John. *Marshall, Orthodoxy and the Professionalization of Economics*. Cambridge: Cambridge University Press, 1985.

Markel, Michael H. *Hilaire Belloc*. Boston: Twayne, 1982.

Martin, Wallace. *"The New Age" under Orage*. Manchester: Manchester University Press, 1967.

Marwick, Arthur. *The Nature of History*. London: Macmillan, 1970.

Masterman, C. F. G., R. A. Bray, Noel Buxton, G. P. Gooch, F. W. Head, Walter Hoare, F. W. Lawrence, A. C. Pigou, G. M. Trevelyan, and P. W. Wilson. *The Heart of the Empire: Discussions of Problems of Modern City Life in England, with an Essay on Imperialism*. 1901. Reprint. London: Unwin, 1907.

Masterman, Lucy. *C. F. G. Masterman: A Biography*. London: Cass, 1939.

Matthew, H. C. G. *The Liberal Imperialists: The Ideas and Politics of a Post-Gladstonian Elite*. Oxford: Oxford University Press, 1973.

Mendelssohn, Peter de. *The Age of Churchill: Heritage and Adventure, 1874–1911*. London: Thames & Hudson, 1961.

Mill, John Stuart. "Considerations on Representative Government." In *Three Essays*, pp. 143–423. Oxford: Oxford University Press, 1975.

Moore, James R. *The Post-Darwinian Controversies: A Study of the Protestant Struggle to Come to Terms with Darwin in Great Britain and America, 1870–1900*. Cambridge: Cambridge University Press, 1979.

Moorman, Mary. *George Macaulay Trevelyan: A Memoir*. London: H. Hamilton, 1980.

——. *Poets and Historians*. Lincoln, Eng.: Tennyson Society, 1974.

Moran, Lord. *Winston Churchill: The Struggle for Survival, 1940–1965*. London: Constable, 1966.

Morgan, John H. *John, Viscount Morley: An Appreciation and Some Remembrances*. London: J. Murray, 1929.

Morley, John. *Diderot and the Encyclopedists*. 1878. Reprint. London: Macmillan, 1921.

Morris, A. J. A. *C. P. Trevelyan, 1870–1958: Portrait of a Radical*. Belfast: Blackstaff, 1977.

——. *Radicalism against War, 1906–1914*. London: Longman, 1972.

Morton, J. B., ed. *Selected Essays of Hilaire Belloc*. London: Methuen, 1948.

Muggeridge, Kitty, and Ruth Adam. *Beatrice Webb: A Life, 1858–1943*. London: Secker & Warburg, 1967.

Muir, Ramsay. *An Autobiography and Some Essays*. London: Lund, Humphries, 1943.

Murray, Gilbert. *The Foreign Policy of Sir Edward Grey*. Oxford: Clarendon, 1915.

——. *An Unfinished Autobiography*. Edited by Jean Smith and Arnold J. Toynbee. London: Allen & Unwin, 1960.

Musson, A. E. *British Trade Unions, 1800–1875*. London: Macmillan, 1972.

——. "The Webbs and Their Phasing of Trade-Union Development between the 1830s and the 1860s." *Bulletin—Society for the Study of Labour History* 4 (Spring 1962): 6–8.

Namier, Julia. *Lewis Namier: A Biography*. London: Oxford University Press, 1971.

Novick, Peter. *That Noble Dream: The "Objectivity Question" and the American Historical Profession*. Cambridge: Cambridge University Press, 1988.

Ogg, David. *Herbert Fisher, 1865–1940: A Short Biography*. London: E. Arnold, 1947.

Oman, Sir Charles. *Memories of Oxford*. 2d ed. London: Methuen, 1941.

Osborne, John. "The Endurance of 'Literary' History in Great Britain: Charles Oman, G. M. Trevelyan, and the Genteel Tradition." *Clio* 2 no. 1 (Oct. 1972): 7–17.

Paget, John. *The New "Examen," with a Critical Introduction by Winston S. Churchill*. 1861. Reprint. Halifax: Haworth, 1939.

Parker, Christopher. "English Historians and the Opposition to Positivism." *History and Theory* 22 no. 2 (1983): 120–45.

——. *The English Historical Tradition since 1850*. Edinburgh: John Donald, 1990.

Perkin, Harold. *The Rise of Professional Society: England since 1880*. London: Routledge, 1989.

Plumb, J. H. *The Death of the Past*. London: Macmillan, 1969.

——. *The Making of an Historian: The Collected Essays of J. H. Plumb*. 2 vols. Athens: University of Georgia Press, 1988–89.

Pollard, A. F. *The History of England: A Study in Political Evolution*. 1912. Reprint. London: Oxford University Press, 1947.

Poynter, J. R. *Society and Pauperism: English Ideas on Poor Relief, 1795–1834*. London: Routledge & Kegan Paul, 1969.

Prior, Robin. *Churchill's "World Crisis" as History*. London: Croom Helm, 1983.

Quennell, Peter. *The Marble Foot: An Autobiography, 1905–1938*. London: Collins, 1976.

Radice, Lisanne. *Beatrice and Sidney Webb: Fabian Socialists*. London: Macmillan, 1984.

Reckitt, Maurice. *As It Happened: An Autobiography*. London: J. M. Dent, 1941.

Redford, Arthur. *Labour Migration in England, 1800–1850*. London: Longmans, Green, 1926.

Robbins, Keith. *The Abolition of War: The "Peace Movement" in Britain, 1914–1919*. Cardiff: University of Wales Press, 1976.

Robson, William. "The Founding of the *Political Quarterly*." *Political Quarterly* 41 no. 1 (Jan.–Mar. 1970): 1–17.

Rose, M. E. "The Crusade: The Webbs and the Campaign to Break-Up the Poor Law." *Manchester Literary and Philosophical Proceedings* 120 (1977–80): 72–89.

Rothblatt, Sheldon. *The Revolution of the Dons: Cambridge and Society in Victorian England*. New York: Cambridge University Press, 1968.

Rowse, A. L. *The English Spirit: Essays in Literature and History*. London: Macmillan, 1966.

———. *Memories of Men and Women*. London: Eyre Methuen, 1980.

———. *Portraits and Views: Literary and Historical*. London: Macmillan, 1979.

Russell, Bertrand. *The Autobiography of Bertrand Russell*. Vol. 1: *1872–1914*. Boston: Little, Brown, 1967.

Scally, Robert J. *The Origins of the Lloyd George Coalition: The Politics of Social Imperialism, 1900–1918*. Princeton: Princeton University Press, 1975.

Searle, G. R. *The Quest for National Efficiency: A Study in British Politics and Political Thought, 1899–1914*. London: Basil Blackwell, 1971.

Seeley, J. R. *Lectures and Essays*. London: Macmillan, 1870.

Shea, Donald F. *The English Ranke: John Lingard*. New York: Humanities, 1969.

Simey, T. S. "The Contribution of Sidney and Beatrice Webb to Sociology." *British Journal of Sociology* 12 no. 2 (June 1961): 106–23.

Slee, Peter. *Learning and a Liberal Education: The Study of Modern History in the Universities of Oxford, Cambridge and Manchester, 1800–1914*. Manchester: Manchester University Press, 1986.

———. "Professor Soffer's 'History at Oxford'." *Historical Journal* 30 no. 4 (1987): 933–42.

Smith, David C. *H. G. Wells: Desperately Mortal*. New Haven: Yale University Press, 1986.

Soffer, Reba. "The Development of Disciplines in the Modern English University." *Historical Journal* 31 no. 4 (1988): 933–46.

———. *Ethics and Society in England: The Revolution in the Social Sciences, 1870–1914*. Berkeley: University of California Press, 1978.

———. "Nation, Duty, Character and Confidence: History at Oxford, 1850–1914." *Historical Journal* 30 no. 1 (1987): 77–104.

Speaight, Robert. *The Life of Hilaire Belloc*. London: Hollis & Carter, 1957.

Stephens, W. R. W. *The Life and Letters of Edward A. Freeman*. 2 vols. London: Macmillan, 1895.

Stern, Fritz, ed. *The Varieties of History*. 2d ed. London: Macmillan, 1970.

Strachey, Lytton. *Elizabeth and Essex, a Tragic History*. London: Chatto & Windus, 1928.

———. *Eminent Victorians*. London: Chatto & Windus, 1918.

———. *Portraits in Miniature*. London: Chatto & Windus, 1931.

———. *Queen Victoria*. London: Chatto & Windus, 1921.

Street, Pamela. *Arthur Bryant: Portrait of a Historian*. London: Collins, 1979.

Swartz, Marvin. *The Union of Democratic Control in British Politics during the First World War*. Oxford: Clarendon, 1971.

Sydenham, George Sydenham Clarke, baron, et al. *"The World Crisis" by Winston Churchill: A Criticism*. London: Hutchinson, 1927.

Tawney, R. H. *The Acquisitive Society*. London: G. Bell, 1920.

———. *The Agrarian Problem in the Sixteenth Century*. London: Longmans, Green, 1912.

———. *The Attack and Other Papers*. New York: Harcourt, Brace, 1953.

———. "J. L. Hammond, 1872–1949." *Proceedings of the British Academy* 46 (1960): 267–97.

———. *Religion and the Rise of Capitalism*. New York: Harcourt, Brace, 1926.

Taylor, A. J. P. *The Trouble Makers: Dissent over Foreign Policy, 1792–1939*. London: H. Hamilton, 1957.

Taylor, Arthur J., ed. *The Standard of Living in Britain in the Industrial Revolution*. London: Methuen, 1975.

Terrill, Ross. *R. H. Tawney and His Times: Socialism as Fellowship*. Cambridge, Mass.: Harvard University Press, 1973.

Thomas, Keith. *Religion and the Decline of Magic*. New York: Scribner, 1971.

Thomis, Malcolm I. *The Town Labourer and the Industrial Revolution*. London: Batsford, 1974.

Thompson, E. P. *The Making of the English Working Class*. 1963. Reprint. New York: Vintage, 1966.

Tout, T. F. *Chapters in the Administrative History of Medieval England*. 6 vols. Manchester: Manchester University Press, 1920–33.

Toynbee, Arnold. *Lectures on the Industrial Revolution of the Eighteenth Century in England*. 1884. Reprint. London: Longmans, Green, 1919.

Toynbee, Arnold J. *Acquaintances*. London: Oxford University Press, 1967.

Trevelyan, C. P. *From Liberalism to Labour*. London: Allen & Unwin, 1922.

Trevelyan, G. M. *An Autobiography and Other Essays*. London: Longmans, Green, 1949.

——. *British History in the Nineteenth Century (1782–1901)*. London: Longmans, Green, 1922.

——. *Clio, a Muse and Other Essays*. London: Longmans, Green, 1930.

——. *Clio, a Muse and Other Essays Literary and Pedestrian*. London: Longmans, Green, 1913.

——. *England in the Age of Wycliffe*. London: Longmans, Green, 1899.

——. *England under Queen Anne*. 3 vols. Vol. 1: *Blenheim*. Vol. 2: *Ramillies and the Union with Scotland*. Vol. 3: *The Peace and the Protestant Succession*. London: Longmans, Green, 1930–34.

——. *England under the Stuarts*. 1904. Reprint. London: Methuen, 1928.

——. *English Literature and Its Readers*. London: Oxford University Press, 1951.

——. *The English Revolution, 1688–1689*. London: Oxford University Press, 1938.

——. *English Social History*. London: Longmans, Green, 1944.

——. *Garibaldi and the Making of Italy*. London: Longmans, Green, 1911.

——. *Garibaldi and the Thousand (May, 1860)*. London: Longmans, Green, 1909.

——. *Garibaldi's Defence of the Roman Republic, 1848–9*. 1907. Reprint. London: Longmans, Green, 1919.

——. *Grey of Fallodon*. London: Longmans, Green, 1937.

——. *The Historical Causes of the Present State of Affairs in Italy*. London: Oxford University Press, 1923.

——. *History and the Reader*. London: Cambridge University Press, 1945.

——. *History of England*. London: Longmans, Green, 1926.

——. *A Layman's Love of Letters, Being the Clark Lectures*. London: Longmans, Green, 1954.

——. *The Life of John Bright*. London: Constable, 1913.

——. *Lord Grey of the Reform Bill*. 1920. Reprint. London: Longmans, Green, 1929.

——. *Manin and the Venetian Revolution of 1848*. London: Longmans, Green, 1923.

——. *Scenes from Italy's War*. London: T. C. & E. C. Jack, 1919.

——. *Sir Otto Trevelyan: A Memoir*. London: Longmans, Green, 1932.

——. *The Two-Party System in English Political History*. Oxford: Clarendon, 1926.

Trevelyan, Humphrey. *Public and Private*. London: H. Hamilton, 1980.

Trevor-Roper, H. R. *Historical Essays*. London: Macmillan, 1957.

——. *History, Professional and Lay*. Oxford: Clarendon, 1957.

Turner, Frank M. *Between Science and Religion: The Reaction to Scientific Naturalism in Late Victorian England*. New Haven: Yale University Press, 1974.

——. *The Greek Heritage in Victorian Britain*. New Haven: Yale University Press, 1981.

——. "Public Science in Britain, 1880–1919." *Isis* 71 no. 259 (1980): 589–608.

Urban, Miriam B. *British Opinion and Policy on the Unification of Italy, 1856–1861*. Scottsdale, Pa.: Mennonite Press, 1938.

Vincent, John. *The Formation of the Liberal Party, 1857–68*. London: Constable, 1966.

Von Arx, Jeffrey Paul. *Progress and Pessimism: Religion, Politics and History in Late-Nineteenth Century Britain*. Cambridge, Mass.: Harvard University Press, 1985.

Wallace, Stuart. *War and the Image of Germany: British Academics, 1914–1918*. Edinburgh: J. Donald, 1988.

Wallas, Graham. *Human Nature and Politics*. London: Constable, 1908.

Ward, Maisie. *Gilbert Keith Chesterton*. New York: Sheed & Ward, 1944.

Warwick, Frances, Countess of. *Discretions*. New York: Scribner 1931.

Watson, George. "The War against the Whigs: Butterfield's Victory . . . and Defeat." *Encounter* 66 (Jan. 1986): 19–25.

Webb, Beatrice. *My Apprenticeship*. London: Longmans, Green, 1926.

——. *The New Crusade against Destitution*. Manchester: National Labour Press, 1909.

——. *Our Partnership*. London: Longmans, Green, 1948.

Webb, Sidney. *Socialism in England*. London: S. Sonnenschein, 1890.

——. *Towards Social Democracy? A Study of Social Evolution during the Past Three-Quarters of a Century*. London: Fabian Society, 1916.

Webb, Sidney, and Beatrice Webb. *A Constitution for the Socialist Commonwealth of Great Britain*. London: Longmans, Green, 1920.

——. *The Decay of Capitalist Civilization*. London: Allen & Unwin, 1923.

——. *English Local Government from the Revolution to the Municipal Corporations Act*. 11 vols. London: Longmans, Green, 1904–29. Vol. 1, *The Parish and the County* (1906); vol. 2, *The Manor and the Borough. Part One* (1908); vol. 3, *The Manor and the Borough. Part Two* (1908); vol. 4, *Statutory Authorities for Special Purposes* (1922); vol. 5, *The Story of the King's Highway* (1913); vol. 6, *English Prisons under Local Government* (1922); vol. 7, *English Poor Law History. Part One. The Old Poor Law* (1927); vol. 8, *English Poor Law History. Part Two. The Last Hundred Years. Volume One* (1929); vol. 9, *English Poor Law History. Part Two. The Last Hundred Years. Volume Two* (1929); vol. 10, *English Poor Law Policy* (1910); vol. 11, *The History of Liquor Licensing in England* (1904).

——. *The History of Trade Unionism*. London: Longmans, Green, 1894 and 1920.

——. *Industrial Democracy*. 2 vols. 1897. Reprint. London: Longmans, Green, 1902.

——. *Methods of Social Study*. London: Longmans, Green, 1932.

——. *The Prevention of Destitution*. London: Longmans, Green, 1911.

——. *The State and the Doctor*. London: Longmans, Green, 1910.

Wedgwood, C. V. *The Last of the Radicals: Josiah Wedgwood, M.P.*. London: Jonathan Cape, 1951.

Weidhorn, Manfred. *Sir Winston Churchill*. Boston: Twayne, 1979.

——. *Sword and Pen: A Survey of the Writings of Sir Winston Churchill*. Albuquerque: University of New Mexico Press, 1974.

Weiler, Peter. *The New Liberalism: Liberal Social Theory in Great Britain, 1889–1914*. New York: Garland, 1982.

Wells, H. G. *Experiment in Autobiography: Discoveries and Conclusions of a Very Ordinary Brain (since 1866)*. New York: Macmillan, 1934.

——. *Mr. Belloc Objects to "The Outline of History."* London: Watts, 1925.

——. *The New Machiavelli*. London: J. Lane, 1910.

——. *The New Teaching of History*. London: Cassell, 1921.

——. *The Outline of History*. New York: Macmillan, 1920.

Wiener, Martin J. *Between Two Worlds: The Political Thought of Graham Wallas*. Oxford: Clarendon, 1971.

——. *English Culture and the Decline of the Industrial Spirit, 1850–1980*. Cambridge: Cambridge University Press, 1981.

Williams, Raymond. *Culture and Society, 1780–1950*. 1958. Reprint. New York: Columbia University Press, 1983.

Willis, Kirk. "In Defence of the True Whiggism: Bertrand Russell and the Whig Interpretation of History." *Storia della Storiografia* 12 (1987): 17–43.

Wilson, Adrian, and T. G. Ashplant. "Whig History and Present-Centered History." *Historical Journal* 31 no. 1 (1988): 1–16.

Wilson, A. N. *Hilaire Belloc*. London: Hamish Hamilton, 1984.

Wilson, Duncan. *Gilbert Murray O.M., 1866–1957*. Oxford: Clarendon, 1987.

——. *Leonard Woolf: A Political Biography*. London: Hogarth, 1978.

Winkler, Henry. "George Macaulay Trevelyan, 1876–." In *Some Twentieth-Century Historians*, edited by S. William Halperin, pp. 31–55. Chicago: University of Chicago Press, 1961.

——. "J. L. Hammond." In *Historians of Modern Europe*, edited by Hans A. Schmitt, pp. 95–119. Baton Rouge: LSU Press, 1971.

Wolfe, Willard. *From Radicalism to Socialism: Men and Ideas in the Formation of Fabian Socialist Doctrines, 1881–89*. New Haven: Yale University Press, 1975.

Woodruff, Douglas, ed. *For Hilaire Belloc*. New York: Sheed & Ward, 1942.

Woods, Frederick. *A Bibliography of the Works of Sir Winston Churchill KG, OM, CH*. 1963. Reprint. London: Kaye & Ward, 1969.

Woodward, Llewellyn. "The Rise of the Professional Historian in England." In *Studies in International History*, edited by Kenneth Bourne and Donald Cameron Watt, pp. 16–34. London: Longmans, 1967.

Woolf, Leonard. *Beginning Again: An Autobiography of the Years 1911 to 1918*. London: Hogarth, 1964.

——. *Downhill All the Way: An Autobiography of the Years 1919 to 1939*. London: Hogarth, 1967.

——. *Sowing: An Autobiography of the Years 1880–1904*. London: Hogarth, 1960.

Wormell, Deborah. *Sir John Seeley and the Uses of History*. Cambridge: Cambridge University Press, 1980.

Wright, Anthony. *R. H. Tawney*. Manchester: Manchester University Press, 1987.

Wrigley, Chris. "The Webbs: Working on Trade Union History." *History Today* 37 no. 5 (May 1987): 51–55.

Index

Page numbers in italics indicate the main discussion of the subject.

Acton, Lord, 3, 154, 229
Almanza, battle of, 213
Anne, Queen, 221, 222, 226
Arnold, Thomas, 145, 147, 206
Ashley, Maurice, 198, 200–1, 224,
    236; on Macaulay, 219; on unso-
    licited draft essays for Churchill,
    267 (n. 36)
Ashton, T. S., 129
Asquith, H. H., 17, 29, 43–45, 105,
    117, 120–21, 184, 246 (n. 107)
Attlee, Clement, 229
Austria, 48, 161, 174

Baldwin, Stanley, 153, 184, 214
Balfour, Arthur, 94
Balkan Committee, 143
Balliol College, Oxford, 18–19,
    21, 27, 57, 70, 121, 152. *See also*
    Oxford University
Baring, Maurice, 16, 27
Barker, Ernest, 122
Belloc, Hilaire, 11–14, *15–60*, 62, 80,
    97, 171, 184, 196, 221; "Chester-
    belloc," 15, 28, 54; importance of
    history to, 15–17, 53–54, 56–57,
    234–35; self-appraisal as his-
    torian, 16, 26, 243 (n. 3); view
    of the Middle Ages, 17, 35, 41,
    49–50, 58; Catholicism and,
    17–18, 39–42, 46, 49, 56; versus
    "official" history, 18–19, 37–40,
    46, 52, 54–58, 170, 199, 234,
    235; at Oxford, 18–21, 27,
    70–71; rejection for academic
    post, 19–21, 25; hatred of dons,
    20–22, 24–27; methods of
    research and writing, 22–27, 52;
    admiration for Macaulay's style,
    24, 52; and Trevelyan, 24–25, 38,

149, 151, 155–56, 172, 205, 244
(n. 40); and the *English Historical
Review*, 25, 55, 244 (n. 45); and
the House of Lords' crisis,
27–30, 43, 45; and Liberalism/
Liberal party, 27–31, 32, 34, 37,
43–45, 53, 59, 76, 105, 235;
on Britain's ruling elite, 31, 38,
47–49, 52; dismisses party system as sham, 31–33, 48; on
the Servile State, 31–37, 48–50,
53–54, 76; on capitalism, 33–34,
36; on Catholic civilization,
34–35, 41–42, 49, 51; on the
Reformation, 34–37, 45–52; on
socialism, 36–37; influence of,
37, 59–60; on "Catholic history,"
38–39, 45, 51–52, 56; on English
culture's anti-Catholic bias,
38–40, 51–56, on the French
Revolution, 40–45, 51; and
Tout, 55, 57; interest in publicity,
55–57; and H. G. Wells, 56–57,
59, 247 (n. 154); fears efforts
wasted, 58–60; and Hammonds,
102–5, 112, 120–21, 256 (n. 71);
and Churchill, 204, 206, 272
(n. 128); and Arthur Bryant, 239;
opinion of Sir Charles Oman on,
243 (n. 13)
—Works: *Cautionary Tales for Children*, 15; *Charles the First*, 16, 50;
Charles II, 16, 51; *Cromwell*, 16;
Danton, 16, 40; *Europe and the
Faith*, 15; *The French Revolution*,
40; *A History of England*, 16–17,
46, 49–50, 55, 57–58; *James the
Second*, 16, 51; *The Last Rally*,
50–51; *Marie Antoinette*, 16,
24–25, 40; *Monarchy: A Study of*

Edmonds, General James, 197
Elizabeth I, 50
English Historical Review: as organ
    of professional history, 5; origi-
    nal intent to address educated
    layman, 7; Belloc and, 25, 55;
    Webbs and, 70; Hammonds and,
    114, 127, 133; Trevelyan and,
    153, 164–65, 278; Churchill and,
    203, 205
Essays in Liberalism, 28, 103, 106
Eye Witness, 31

Fabian Research Department, 101
Fabian Society/Fabianism, 61;
    affinity for scientific expert, 12;
    Belloc's hostility to, 37; historiog-
    raphy of, 62; interest in gradual
    change, 64, 81–82; preoccupa-
    tion with bureaucratic state,
    73; and Liberalism, 82; and the
    Hammonds, 101, 121; and Tre-
    velyan, 156–57, 177, 232. *See also*
    Webb, Sidney and Beatrice
Fascism, 168, 181, 182, 217–18,
    220, 223
Feiling, Keith, 198, 202, 204, 268
    (nn. 46, 60)
Fielding, Henry, 110
First World War, 51, 117, 119–20,
    145, 172, 173, 182, 188, 192, 214,
    217, 226, 232, 233, 246 (n. 107);
    literature of, 206–7, 208–12
Firth, Sir Charles, 182
Fisher, H. A. L., 152; gives exam-
    ples of archetypal Whig histori-
    ans, 4; accused of writing old-
    fashioned history, 7; as friend of
    Belloc, 22, 27; on Belloc, 23–24;
    and Churchill, 198, 201; defends
    Macaulay, 271 (n. 123)
Fourth Party, 191
Fox, Charles James, 28, 105–9, 174,
    176
France, 40–45, 48, 163, 211, 214,
    223, 246 (n. 103)

Fraser, Antonia, 236
Freeman, E. A.: as Whig historian,
    1–2, 38, 227; as populist and
    Romantic nationalist, 2; as parlia-
    mentary candidate, 4; as transi-
    tional figure, 6, 230; Strachey on,
    147
French Revolution, 40–45, 48, 163,
    246 (n. 103)
Froissart, Jean, 25
Froude, J. A.: as Whig historian, 1;
    as Tory Radical, 2; as transitional
    figure, 6; interest in power as the
    fulcrum of national history, 11

Galway, Earl of, 213
Gardiner, S. R., 217, 230
Garibaldi, Giuseppe, 157–69, 172,
    264 (n. 122)
General Strike (1926), 129, 180
George III, 4, 48
George V, 264 (n. 143)
Germany, 52, 137, 164, 182,
    208–11, 222, 223, 224
Gibbon, Edward, 38, 52, 261
    (n. 55)
Girondins, 43–45, 172–73
Gladstone, William Ewart, 17, 105,
    109, 133–34, 139, 157, 162, 177,
    191, 195, 204
Glorious Revolution (1688–1689):
    central event of Whig version
    of history, 9, 44, 163, 213; Belloc
    and, 32, 46; Webbs and, 86–87,
    176; Hammonds and, 108–10;
    Trevelyan and, 163, 176, 182,
    221; Churchill and, 213, 214, 221
Godolphin, Lord, 184, 201
Gooch, G. P., 46, 164, 169, 209, 210,
    270 (n. 83)
Gordon, General Charles George,
    145, 161, 206, 262 (n. 85)
Graves, Robert, 207
Green, J. R., 179
Grey, Lord, 174, 175, 176–77
Grey, Sir Edward, 182

Griffith, G. Talbot, 127
Grote, George, 4
Guedella, Philip, 149
Guild Socialism, 37, 59

Haldane, R. B., 70, 195
Halévy, Elie, 102
Hammond, John Lawrence, 194,
196, 234; and Belloc, 19, 27–28,
103; at Oxford, 19, 103; on imperialism, 102–4; marriage, 104;
unsuitability for life in politics,
105–7, 143; and England's Whig
heritage, 107–9; on Reconstruction Committee, 117–18; attempt
to obtain university position,
121–23
—Works: *Charles James Fox*, 106–9,
112, 133; *Gladstone and the Irish
Nation*, 133–34
Hammond, Lucy Barbara: satisfaction at Lawrence's rejection for
academic post, 13, 122–23, 232;
marriage, 104; intellectual talents,
104–5; research expeditions, 105
Hammond, J. L., and Barbara, 14,
98-136, 141, 176, 184, 188, 208,
229, 233–34; influence of Arnold
Toynbee on, 10, 113; as qualified
defenders of Whig tradition,
12–13, 99, 102, 116, 123; and
scientific/academic history,
99, 114–16, 126–30, 135, 196,
231–32; and academic history,
99–100, 114–16, 126–30, 135,
196, 231–32; and Webbs, 99–
102, 110, 132–33, 254 (n. 12);
histories seen as inflammatory,
101–2, 120; Elie Halévy on, 102;
and Trevelyan, 102, 106, 128,
131, 156, 178, 261 (n. 71); and
Liberalism, 102–3, 105–6, 109,
112–13, 117, 120–21, 123–25,
130–35; ascetic lifestyle, 104–
105; history as sublimated politics, 105–9; on the Industrial

Revolution, 110, 113–14, 118–
19, 124–26, 131–33; on enclosure, 110–11; defense of traditional ruling elite, 111–12,
124–25, 132; forge new type
of economic history, 113–16,
127–30, 135, 231; use of moral
vocabulary, 115, 123, 135–36,
188; affinity with literary Whig
history, 115–16, 123, 136; and
the Great War, 117–20; relations
with political Left, 120, 130,
135–36, 238–39; and Labour
party, 120–21, 129, 135; unsuitability of works as basis for
revival of Liberal political fortunes, 134–35; and Belloc, 256
(n. 71)
—Works: *The Age of the Chartists*,
131–33; *Lord Shaftesbury*, 102,
123–25; *The Rise of Modern Industry*, 125–26, 131; *The Skilled
Labourer*, 122, 124, 126; *The
Town Labourer*, 101, 109–10,
117–19, 122, 126–27; *The Village
Labourer*, 101–2, 106, 109–17,
119, 124, 134
Harley, Robert, 184
Harrap, George S., 201
Headlam-Morley, Sir James, 197
Heart of the Empire, 156
Hegel, G. W. F., 182
Henry VIII, 36, 50, 169
Herbert, Auberon, 57
Heyck, T. W., 1, 8
Hill, Christopher, 7, 238
Himmelfarb, Gertrude, 65
Hirst, F. W., 27
History, academic: versus amateur
history, 6–8, 13, 57–58, 230, 237;
sacrifice of cultural authority,
7–9, 99, 142; identified as Whig
orthodoxy by Belloc, 11, 20,
25–27, 37–39, 45, 53, 57–58, 156,
234–35; the Webbs and, 67–70,
73; the Hammonds and, 99,

Industrial Revolution, 35, 80, 91,
137; Whig history's need to
accommodate, 10; Hammonds
and, 12, 110–20, 124–33; Trevelyan and, 176, 178, 180
Inge, W. R., 180
Irish Home Rule, 28, 29, 156, 190
Italy, 157–69, 172, 182, 222

Jackson, Admiral Thomas, 197
Jacobins, 41, 45, 51, 172–73
Jacobites, 222
James II, 51
James, William, 72
Jann, Rosemary, 1, 229
Jones, Gareth Stedman, 229
Jowett, Benjamin, 21, 152

Kellogg-Briand Pact (1928), 227
Keyes, Admiral Roger, 197
Keynes, John Maynard, 206, 209
Kossuth, Louis, 167

Labour party, 60, 129, 149; Webbs
and, 76–77, 93; Advisory
Committee on International
Relations, 120; Romney Street
Group, 120; Hammonds and,
120–21, 129, 135; consensus
history's appeal to, 171, 177–
78, 183, 208, 233; Trevelyan's
approval of, 174–75; Churchill
and, 189, 208
Lansdowne, Lord, 197
Laski, Harold, 121, 125, 167, 229
Lassalle, Ferdinand, 161
Lawrence, T. E., 212
League of Nations, 227
Lecky, W. E. H., 4, 170
Liberal Imperialism: the Webbs
and, 75–76, 93; Trevelyan and,
156
Liberal internationalism, 168–69
Liberal party. *See* Liberalism
Liberalism: link with Whig version
of history, 4, 14, 59, 225, 229,

230–31, 235; pressures upon,
9–10; electoral collapse of, 11,
174–75, 225, 231, 235; Belloc
and, 17, 29–31, 42, 60, 234–35;
loss of nerve, 30–31; Webbs
and, 75–77, 81–83, 97; image of
politics, 88–92, 130; and efficiency, 88–92, 217–19; and amateurism, 91–93, 231; and civic
virtue, 92–93, 124–27, 132–33;
and imperialism, 103; ambivalence of Hammonds toward,
104–6, 117, 120–21; belief in
latent public support for, 134;
Trevelyan and, 139, 140–41,
143–44, 155–57, 173, 175, 178,
195, 232, 233; swaps parochial
for international canvas, 168–69;
advantages of its electoral weakness for Whig history, 174–75,
225, 231; Churchill and, 189, 190,
233. *See also* New Liberalism/
New Liberals
Liberalism and Empire, 103
Liddell Hart, B. H., 197
Lingard, John, 46
Lloyd George, David, 7, 17, 29, 34,
43, 45, 111, 117, 120–21, 165,
172, 184, 189–90, 193, 206, 215
Local Government Act (1888), 74
Local Government Act (1929), 67,
93
Locarno Pact (1925), 227
Locke, John, 108–9
Lodge, Richard, 203
London School of Economics, 72,
122, 144
London Working Men's College,
141
Longmans Publishers, 109, 139
Louis XIV, 51, 208–9, 212, 214,
217, 221, 226

Macaulay, Thomas Babington, 1,
227, 261 (n. 55); as Whig centrist,
2; as archetypal Whig historian,

4; dismissed by Seeley as a charlatan, 6; familial link to Trevelyan, 25, 139, 220–21; in opposition to Belloc, 38; artistry
admired by Belloc, 52; Trevelyan
as his disciple, 140, 180–83;
ridiculed by Strachey, 147; target
of Butterfield, 155–56; attempt
to create common political culture, 182; rebutted by Churchill,
219–21, 271 (nn. 121, 122), 272
(n. 130); defended by H. A. L.
Fisher, 271 (n. 123)
McBriar, A. M., 62
MacDonald, James Ramsay, 175
Macmillan, Harold, 229
Magna Carta, 4, 9, 187–88
Maitland, F. W.: academic conde-
scension toward amateur, 8; as
pioneer of administrative history,
11, 73; refuses Cambridge Regius
professorship, 154
Malplaquet, battle of, 200
Manchester Guardian, 123
Manchester School, 132
Manchester University, 204, 257
(n. 93), 261 (n. 31)
Manning, Cardinal, 145, 206
Marlborough, first Duke of. *See*
Churchill, John
Marriott, J. A. R., 6
Marshall, T. H., 129, 133
Martin, Kingsley, 218
Marx, Karl, 177
Maximilian of Hapsburg, 161
Mazzini, Giuseppe, 158–60,
166–68
Michelet, Jules, 23
Michels, Robert, 31
Miller, William, 165
Milner, Lord, 218
Milton, John, 16, 113
Mommsen, Theodor, 38
Moore, George, 143
Morel, E. D., 211, 270 (n. 81)
Morley, John, 4, 8, 195

Morris, William, 12, 28
Motley, John L., 38
Munich Agreement (1938), 272
(n. 143)
Municipal Corporations Act
(1835), 74, 86
Murray, Gilbert, 103, 105, 106, 121,
209
Murray, Mary, 121
Mussolini, Benito, 168, 217

Namier, Lewis, 47, 108, 208; Trevelyan and, 153, 261 (nn. 53, 55);
Churchill and, 198, 204–5, 219,
269 (n. 73), 272 (n. 124)
Napoleon Bonaparte, 208, 211,
214, 221
National Efficiency Movement:
opposition to parliamentary politics, 30, 45, 230; bureaucratic
affinities, 45, 77, 107, 230; the
Webbs and, 74, 75, 230–31, 233;
Lord Rosebery and, 75; Edwardian Liberalism and, 75–77; the
Hammonds and, 107, 233; Trevelyan and, 156, 233; Churchill
and, 194, 215, 218, 233
National Liberal Federation, 9
National Union of Conservative
Associations, 191
New Age, 33
Newcastle Programme, 81
New Liberalism\New Liberals, 12;
as ginger group, 9; Belloc and,
17, 28, 45, 55, 59, 60, 76, 156; and
the Servile State, 37; Churchill
and, 75–76; courted by the
Webbs, 75–76, 93; tension at its
core, 102; the Hammonds and,
102–3, 105, 107, 108, 112–13,
125, 130, 156; Trevelyan and,
156–57, 158, 159, 232
Newman, John Henry, 18, 22
New Statesman, 178, 218
Nickerson, Hoffman, 16
Nietzsche, Friedrich, 209

and Liberalism, 139–44, 155–59, 173, 175, 178, 195, 232, 233; creation of consensus history, 140, 159, 170–72, 175–85, 221–22, 225, 229, 233; defense of literary history, 141–42, 145–49, 151, 154, 158–59, 233; on Balkan and Russian Committees, 143, 162; reluctance to pursue active politics, 143–44, 150, 164–65; and Lytton Strachey, 145–49, 232; and Lewis Namier, 153, 261 (nn. 53, 55); return to Cambridge, 153–55; and National Efficiency movement, 156, 233; and Garibaldi, 157–69, 264 (n. 122); Liberal bias in his works, 158, 170–73; and Russian revolutions, 162, 165–66, 173; and the Great War, 172–73; and Churchill, 186–90, 194–98, 202, 205–6, 215, 220–24, 227, 272 (nn. 129, 130, 135), 273 (nn. 140, 143); as "Chamberlainite," 223, 272 (n. 143); compares Gordon and Garibaldi, 262 (n. 85); contra "neo-Catholic propaganda," 272 (n. 130)

—Works: *British History in the Nineteenth Century,* 140, 175–81; "Clio, a Muse," 150, 154; *England in the Age of Wycliffe,* 140, 169–70; *England under Queen Anne,* 25, 140, 181–84, 220–21, 272 (n. 130); *England under the Stuarts,* 140, 170–71; *The English Revolution, 1688–1689,* 181; *English Songs of Italian Freedom,* 165; *Garibaldi and the Making of Italy,* 139, 158; *Garibaldi and the Thousand,* 158; *Garibaldi's Defence of the Roman Republic,* 158, 162; *Grey of Fallodon,* 181; *The Historical Causes of the Present State of Affairs in Italy,* 168; *History of England,* 151–53, 179–80; "The Latest View of

History," 6, 141, 150, 152, 232; *The Life of John Bright,* 172–73; *Lord Grey of the Reform Bill,* 173–75; *Manin and the Venetian Revolution,* 167, 175; "The Present Position of History," 153–54

Trevelyan, George Otto, 4, 139, 140, 150, 157, 161
Trevelyan, Robert C., 158
Trevor-Roper, Hugh, 236, 237

Uncle Tom's Cabin, 113
University College, London, 198
Utrecht, Treaty of, 222–23

Vaihinger, Hans, 72
Versailles, Treaty of, 120, 222–23
Vinogradoff, Paul, 153
Violence: Belloc on, 40–45; Trevelyan on, 150–67, 172–73, 208; Churchill on, 206–19, 226
Von Arx, Jeffrey Paul, 2

Wallas, Graham, 28, 62, 71; work not seen as influential by Webbs, 66; and Hammonds, 113, 117, 122; and Trevelyan, 143
Ward, A. W., 169
Warner, G. Townsend, 10, 157
Washington, George, 161
Washington Naval Treaty (1922), 227
Waterloo, battle of, 23, 26
Webb, Beatrice: marriage, 61; fear of work being undervalued, 61–62; work with Charles Booth, 63
—Works: *The Minority Report on the Royal Commission on the Poor Law,* 62, 94; *My Apprenticeship,* 69
Webb, Sidney, 121; marriage, 61; Comtean influences on, 63; as Labour M.P., 64; on the Middle Ages, 78–80
—Works: *Fabian Essays in Socialism,* 63, 71, 80, 84; "The Rise and Fall

of Feudalism," 78, 79; "Social
Movements," 70
Webb, Sidney and Beatrice, 13, 36,
59–60, *61–97*, 130, 171, 176, 184,
196, 237; influenced by Arnold
Toynbee, 10; fashion new form
of public history, 12, 14, 67, 69,
93–94, 237; and Whig history,
12, 72–73, 86–87, 231; as Victorian figures, 14, 63–64, 71; Belloc's opinion of, 36; on state
as vehicle of progress, 60, 73;
on history as political tool, 62,
64–66; and Poor Law reform,
62, 93–105; on relation between
history and sociology, 63, 71;
their books as a substitute for
offspring, 64; and Labour party,
64, 77, 93; Whiggish vestiges in
their histories, 64–66, 97; as
intellectuals in politics, 65–66;
and literary history, 66–70, 73,
142, 250 (n. 52); target audience,
67, 69, 93–94, 237; and scientific
history, 67, 71–73, 94–97, 141,
231; and academia, 67–74, 97,
135, 231, 234; obsession with
facts, 68, 95; and Trevelyan, 68,
156–57, 183, 232; use of scientific analogies, 68–69; opinion of
dons, 70–71; history as instrumental, 71, 96; views on truth,
72; and Churchill, 75–76, 233;
and Liberalism/Liberal party,
75–77, 81–83, 93, 97, 231; and
the bureaucratic state, 77–78,
91–93, 97, 230–31; phasing of
trade union history, 81–83, 251
(nn. 87, 92); on evolution of local
government, 83–93; on failure of
liberalism, 86–93; and the Hammonds, 98–105, 110–12, 132–33,
254 (n. 12)
—Works: *A Constitution for the*
Socialist Commonwealth of Great
Britain, 63; *The Decay of Capitalist*
Civilization, 63; *English Local Gov-*
ernment from the Revolution to the
Municipal Corporations Act, 62–63,
66–67, 70, 72, 85–94, 96, 100,
116, 132, 250 (n. 52); *The History*
of Trade Unionism, 62, 66, 81–83,
86, 101–2, 135; *Industrial Democ-*
racy, 62, 92; "To Your Tents, Oh
Israel!," 82–83. *See also* Fabian
Society/Fabianism
Weber, Max, 34, 35
Webster, Charles K., 169
Wedgwood, C. V., 229, 236
Wedgwood, Josiah, 9, 113
Wells, H. G.: versus Belloc, 15,
56–57, 247 (n. 154); on Belloc's
influence, 59; Hammonds criti-
cized for citing, 128; on Trevel-
yan, 143; criticized by Trevelyan,
151, 205
—Works: *The New Machiavelli*, 143;
The Outline of History, 56, 151
Wheeler, Mortimer, 198
Wilhelm II, Kaiser, 214, 221
Wilkinson, Henry Spenser, 197
William III, 3, 216, 226
Wilson, Woodrow, 120, 206
Wolsey, Thomas, Cardinal, 50
Woolf, Leonard: criticism of
Webbs' methodology, 96; woos
J. L. Hammond for editorship,
121; on Trevelyan, 143, 146
Woolf, Virginia, 147, 152, 153
World War I. *See* First World War
World War II. *See* Second World
War
Wyndham, George, 25

Young, G. M., 216, 268 (n. 60)

Zetetical Society, 63
Zimmern, A. E., 113

DATE DUE

GAYLORD

PRINTED IN U.S.A.